Institutional Innovation and Change in Value Chain Development

George Bernard Shaw once said that reasonable people adapt themselves to the world but unreasonable people adapt the world to themselves. In a sense, this book explores how these so-called 'unreasonable people' may interact to re-fashion the world around them in fragile economic development. Drawing on empirical research in the volatile and traditional context of Afghanistan, the study investigates the challenge of poor women's participation in business and diverse outcomes for local development.

Institutional Innovation and Change in Value Chain Development takes a unique look at nuanced institutional phenomena through the lens of social institutions, with a subtle appreciation of the interaction of structure and agency. Drawing on in-depth qualitative research in Afghanistan, the case studies specifically investigate the transformation of the women's norm of *purdah*, and the subsequent development of new market institutions in three women's enterprises.

Shedding new light on the opaque process of *institutional change*, the research shows that external actors (such as NGOs) can both initiate and guide institutional development in fragile environments. Yet there may be limitations to their endeavours, with strong resistance from local power holders. Meanwhile, dominant entrepreneurs are shown to play a major role in fostering institutional development pathways. This influences the scope of inclusion and exclusion in enterprise and value chains, and broader streams of socio-economic development.

Holly A. Ritchie is currently a research fellow at the Institute of Social Studies (ISS), Erasmus University, the Netherlands, and part-time lecturer with a strong interest in gender, institutions and economic development in fragile environments.

Routledge Studies in Development Economics

For a complete list of titles in this series, please visit www.routledge.com.

66 The Chronically Poor in Rural Bangladesh
Livelihood constraints and capabilities
Pk. Md. Motiur Rahman, Noriatsu Matsui and Yukio Ikemoto

67 Public-Private Partnerships in Health Care in India
Lessons for developing countries
A. Venkat Raman and James Warner Björkman

68 Rural Poverty and Income Dynamics in Asia and Africa
Edited by Keijiro Otsuka, Jonna P. Estudillo and Yasuyuki Sawada

69 Microfinance: A Reader
David Hulme and Thankom Arun

70 Aid and International NGOs
Dirk-Jan Koch

71 Development Macroeconomics
Essays in memory of Anita Ghatak
Edited by Subrata Ghatak and Paul Levine

72 Taxation in a Low Income Economy
The case of Mozambique
Channing Arndt and Finn Tarp

73 Labour Markets and Economic Development
Edited by Ravi Kanbur and Jan Svejnar

74 Economic Transitions to Neo-liberalism in Middle-Income Countries
Policy dilemmas, crises, mass resistance
Edited by Alfedo Saad-Filho and Galip L. Yalman

75 Latecomer Development
Innovation and knowledge for economic growth
Banji Oyelaran-Oyeyinka and Padmashree Gehl Sampath

76 Trade Relations between the EU and Africa
Development, challenges and options beyond the Cotonou Agreement
Edited by Yenkong Ngangjoh-Hodu and Francis A.S.T. Matambalya

77 The Comparative Political Economy of Development
Africa and South Asia
Edited by Barbara Harriss-White and Judith Heyer

78 Credit Cooperatives in India
Past, present and future
Biswa Swarup Misra

79 Development Economics in Action (2nd edition)
A study of economic policies in Ghana
Tony Killick

80 The Multinational Enterprise in Developing Countries
Local versus global logic
Edited by Rick Molz, Cătălin Ratiu and Ali Taleb

81 Monetary and Financial Integration in West Africa
Edited by Temitope W. Oshikoya

82 Reform and Development in China
What can China offer the developing world?
Edited by Ho-Mou Wu and Yang Yao

83 Towards New Developmentalism
Market as means rather than master
Edited by Shahrukh Rafi Khan and Jens Christiansen

84 Culture, Institutions, and Development
New insights into an old debate
Edited by Jean-Philippe Platteau and Robert Peccoud

85 Assessing Prospective Trade Policy
Methods applied to EU-ACP Economic Partnership Agreements
Edited by Oliver Morrissey

86 Social Protection for Africa's Children
Edited by Sudhanshu Handa, Stephen Devereux and Douglas Webb

87 Energy, Bio Fuels and Development
Comparing Brazil and the United States
Edited by Edmund Amann, Werner Baer and Don Coes

88 Value Chains, Social Inclusion and Economic Development
Contrasting theories and realities
Edited by A.H.J. (Bert) Helmsing and Sietze Vellema

89 Market Liberalism, Growth, and Economic Development in Latin America
Edited by Gerardo Angeles Castro, Ignacio Perrotini-Hernández and Humberto Ríos-Bolivar

90 South-South Globalization
Challenges and opportunities for development
Edited by S. Mansoob Murshed, Pedro Goulart and Leandro A. Serino

91 Trade Infrastructure and Economic Development
Edited by Olu Ajakaiye and T. Ademola Oyejide

92 Microcredit and International Development
Contexts, achievements and challenges
Edited by Farhad Hossain, Christopher Rees and Tonya Knight-Millar

93 Business Regulation and Non-State Actors
Whose standards? Whose development?
Edited by Darryl Reed, Peter Utting and Ananya Mukherjee Reed

94 Public Expenditures for Agricultural and Rural Development in Africa
Edited by Tewodaj Mogues and Samuel Benin

95 The Global Economic Crisis and the Developing World
Implications and prospects for recovery and growth
Edited by Ashwini Deshpande and Keith Nurse

96 The Microfinance Impact
Ranjula Bali Swain

97 Gendered Insecurities, Health and Development in Africa
Edited by Howard Stein and Amal Hassan Fadlalla

98 Financial Cooperatives and Local Development
Edited by Silvio Goglio and Yiorgos Alexopoulos

99 State-Business Relations and Economic Development in Africa and India
Edited by Kunal Sen

100 Digital Interactions in Developing Countries
An economic perspective
Jeffrey James

101 Migration and Inequality
Edited by Tanja Bastia

102 Financing Regional Growth and the Inter-American Development Bank
The case of Argentina
Ernesto Vivares

103 Globalization and Development
Rethinking interventions and governance
Edited by Arne Bigsten

104 Disasters and the Networked Economy
J.M. Albala-Bertrand

105 Microfinance, Debt and Over-Indebtedness
Juggling with money
Edited by Isabelle Guérin, Solène Morvant-Roux and Magdalena Villarreal

106 The Universal Social Safety-Net and the Attack on World Poverty
Pressing need, manageable cost, practical possibilities, favourable spillovers
Anthony Clunies-Ross and Mozammel Huq

107 Youth and Employment in Sub-Saharan Africa
Working but poor
Edited by Hiroyuki Hino and Gustav Ranis

108 Financial Stability and Growth
Perspectives on financial regulation and new developmentalism
Edited by Luiz Carlos Bresser-Pereira, Jan Kregel and Leonardo Burlamaqui

109 A History of Development Economics Thought
Challenges and counter-challenges
Shahrukh Rafi Khan

110 Economic Complexity and Human Development
How economic diversification and social networks affect human agency and welfare
Dominik Hartmann

111 Building Businesses in Emerging and Developing Countries
Challenges and opportunities
Edited by Elie Chrysostome and Rick Molz

112 The Informal Economy in Developing Countries
Edited by Jean-Pierre Cling, Stéphane Lagrée, Mireille Razafindrakoto and François Roubaud

113 African Industrial Development and European Union Cooperation
Prospects for a reengineered partnership
Francis A.S.T. Matambalya

114 Developmental Macroeconomics
New developmentalism as a growth strategy
Luiz Carlos Bresser-Pereira, José Luis Oreiro and Nelson Marconi

115 Industrial Innovation, Networks and Economic Development
Informal information sharing in low-technology clusters in India
Anant Kamath

116 Employment and Inclusive Development
Rizwanul Islam and Iyanatul Islam

117 Growth and Institutions in African Development
Edited by Augustin K. Fosu

118 Public Finance and Economic Growth in Developing Countries
Lessons from Ethiopia's reforms
Stephen B. Peterson

119 Peripheral Visions of Economic Development
New frontiers in development economics and the history of economic thought
Edited by Mario Garcia-Molina and Hans-Michael Trautwein

120 The Political Economy of Natural Resources and Development
From neoliberalism to resource nationalism
Edited by Paul A. Haslam and Pablo Heidrich

121 Institutional Innovation and Change in Value Chain Development
Negotiating tradition, power and fragility in Afghanistan
Holly A. Ritchie

122 China's War against the Many Faces of Poverty
Towards a New Long March
Jing Yang and Pundarik Mukhopadhaya

Institutional Innovation and Change in Value Chain Development

Negotiating tradition, power and fragility in Afghanistan

Holly A. Ritchie

Routledge
Taylor & Francis Group

LONDON AND NEW YORK

First published 2016 by Routledge

2 Park Square, Milton Park, Abingdon, Oxfordshire OX14 4RN
52 Vanderbilt Avenue, New York, NY 10017

Routledge is an imprint of the Taylor & Francis Group, an informa business

First issued in paperback 2019

British Library Cataloguing in Publication Data
A catalogue record for this book is available from the British Library

Library of Congress Cataloging in Publication Data
Ritchie, Holly A.
Institutional innovation and change in value chain development :
negotiating tradition, power and fragility in Afghanistan / Holly A. Ritchie.
pages cm
ISBN 978-1-138-92734-6 (hardback) – ISBN 978-1-315-68273-0 (ebook)
1. Organizational change. 2. Economic development. 3. Entrepreneurship.
4. Social exchange. I. Title.
HD58.8.R58 2016
658.4'063-dc23
2015036591

ISBN: 978-1-138-92734-6 (hbk)
ISBN: 978-0-367-87394-3 (pbk)

Typeset in Times New Roman
by Florence Production Ltd, Stoodleigh, Devon, UK

Contents

List of figures   xii
List of tables   xiii
Preface   xiv
Acknowledgements   xvi
List of abbreviations   xx
Map of Afghanistan and location of case studies   xxi

1   Exploring institutional complexity in a less formal context   1
  1.1   Institutions and institutional processes   1
    1.1.1   What do we mean by institutions?   1
    1.1.2   Exploring institutional complexity in a fragile context   3
  1.2   A critical realist lens with tools from development studies   4
    1.2.1   Building knowledge through making sense of reality   4
    1.2.2   Guiding research themes   6
    1.2.3   Reflections on research approach and methods   8
  1.3   Introduction to cases   9
    1.3.1   Case 1: women's rural food processing association   10
    1.3.2   Case 2: women's rural vegetable production business   12
    1.3.3   Case 3: women's urban electronics business   15
  1.4   Concluding remarks and book structure   17

2   The ubiquity of institutions: shaping economic development   23
  2.1   Towards a paradigm shift in theories of institutional change   23
    2.1.1   Beyond rationality: the influence of history, culture
    and power   24
    2.1.2   An evolutionary approach to institutional development   29
    2.1.3   Incorporating social structure and embeddedness   31
    2.1.4   Towards an appreciation of the interaction of structure
    and agency   34
  2.2   Exploring actors and networks   35
    2.2.1   Catalysing change? Entrepreneurs and innovation   36

    2.2.2 'Institutional entrepreneurs', power and strategic agency 37

    2.2.3 Institutional activity in networks 39

  2.3 'Bundles of institutions' in informal developing economies 40

    2.3.1 Dominance of informal institutions and power asymmetries 41

    2.3.2 Trust: an outcome and an antecedent of economic activity 43

  2.4 Concluding remarks 44

3 Afghanistan: persisting instability, informality and tradition   **52**

  3.1 A weak state and complex people 52

    3.1.1 Resilience and adaptability in the face of uncertainty 53

    3.1.2 Diverse tribes and elaborate social organisation 56

    3.1.3 Migration and transnational links shaping livelihoods and trade 57

  3.2 Society, religion and politics 59

    3.2.1 Sociocultural dynamics shaping power and agency 59

    3.2.2 Local power structures and collective action 61

    3.2.3 Traditional decision-making and conflict resolution 62

  3.3 'Zan, zar and zamin': honour and women 63

    3.3.1 'Makr-i-zan' Afghan women's tricks . . . 'Seven steps ahead of the Devil' 64

    3.3.2 Nuanced and heterogeneous realities 65

    3.3.3 Resistance and change 66

  3.4 Dynamic but distorted Afghan markets 68

    3.4.1 Markets shaped by informality and uncertainty 69

    3.4.2 Trading elite, regionalism and evolving politics 71

    3.4.3 Traditional market regulation: sociocultural institutions and gender 72

    3.4.4 Markets and risk: the Faustian bargain? 73

  3.5 Concluding remarks 75

4 Transforming norms towards unlocking societal barriers   **82**

  4.1 Social norms, values and their persistence 82

    4.1.1 Unwrapping dynamics and dimensions of social norms 83

    4.1.2 Cultural influences on social norms: honour codes and religion 85

    4.1.3 Economic development: cultural systems as barriers and resources 86

    4.1.4 Transforming norms: actors and strategies 87

4.2 Afghan norm of *purdah*: entrenched in religion and culture 88

4.3 Transformation of 'layered' *purdah* 90

    4.3.1 Case 1: changing attitudes through strategic religious education 91

    4.3.2 Case 2: changing attitudes through designated champions and skills 97

    4.3.3 Case 3: changing attitudes through designated champions and charisma 103

    4.3.4 Examining new dynamics of language and power in norm change 107

4.4 Discussion 109

    4.4.1 Complex institutional change processes: from concept to dissemination 109

    4.4.2 Examining nature of evolving purdah rules across cases 113

    4.4.3 Outcomes of evolving purdah: new relations, values and preferences 114

4.5 Concluding remarks 117

5 Constructing institutions in enterprise 124

5.1 Socially embedded institutions in economic activity 124

    5.1.1 Building blocks: routines shaping organisations and firms 125

    5.1.2 Economic coordination through multiple institutional arrangements 127

    5.1.3 Institutions for collective action: diverse outcomes in different settings 131

    5.1.4 Creating institutions: actors, collaboration and strategies 132

5.2 Constructing 'nested' institutions in enterprise 133

    5.2.1 Case 1: simple institutions with organic innovation and guided evolution 134

    5.2.2 Case 2: innovative elaborate institutions with guided/own evolution 141

    5.2.3 Case 3: underdeveloped institutions with little innovation/ evolution 147

    5.2.4 Evolving dynamics of language and power in rule development 151

5.3 Discussion 153

    5.3.1 Complex institutional construction: nested institutions in enterprise 153

5.3.2 *Examining evolving routines across cases as a 'window'
on enterprise 159*

5.3.3 *Outcomes of bundles of enterprise institutions: new
evolving sociopolitical norms, and economic institutions 161*

5.4 Concluding remarks 165

6 Unwrapping agency: interests, power and networks   171

6.1 Entrepreneurs, networks and agency 171

6.1.1 *Towards a broader perspective of institutional
'entrepreneurs' 172*

6.1.2 *Networks and entrepreneurial outcomes 172*

6.1.3 *Collective agency in learning, adoption and diffusion 174*

6.2 A closer look at case study actors and context 176

6.2.1 *NGOs driven by women's socio-economic development 176*

6.2.2 *Entrepreneurs driven by economic and sociopolitical
interests 180*

6.2.3 *Power holders driven by control (and community
development) 184*

6.2.4 *Appreciating local conditions within greater Afghan
context 186*

6.3 Examining actor strategies in institutional processes 188

6.3.1 *NGOs as designers and advisors 189*

6.3.2 *Entrepreneurs as shapers and diffusers 190*

6.3.3 *Power holders as authorisers and boundary makers 191*

6.4 Dominant entrepreneurs and collective power 195

6.4.1 *Emerging entrepreneur types and institutional
characteristics 195*

6.4.2 *Drawing on collective power for group or self-interest 198*

6.4.3 *Entrepreneurial networks in institutional diffusion and
adoption 201*

6.5 Concluding remarks 202

**7 Towards a dynamic and interdisciplinary theory of institutional
change**   209

7.1 Multilevel drivers in institutional emergence 210

7.1.1 *Nested institutions in enterprise 210*

7.1.2 *Dual motivations in emergence of new embedded
market institutions 213*

7.1.3 *Nuanced group cooperation and coordination 215*

7.1.4 *Role of trust and authority in institutional development/
formalisation 218*

7.2 Muddling through or strategic design: multiple-actor negotiation in institutional development 219

    7.2.1 Institutional design process: devils in the detail 220

    7.2.2 Interaction of dynamic and diverse actors 222

    7.2.3 Agents of uncertain change: diverse interests and power 223

7.3 Innovation, learning, adoption and diffusion in networks 226

    7.3.1 Harnessing power of allies in creating support and critical mass 227

    7.3.2 How institutions affect networks, and how networks affect institutions 228

    7.3.3 Towards re-conceptualising a multi-actor institutional construction scheme 229

7.4 Institutional outcomes: robust or fragile? Evolving or stagnated? 230

    7.4.1 Social stratification: heterogeneous purdah norms towards a new order? 230

    7.4.2 Enterprise institutions: healthy hierarchies or arrested development? 231

    7.4.3 Critical junctures and emerging pathways 233

    7.4.4 New attitudes and preferences with broad institutional spin-off effects 236

    7.4.5 What makes rule-making more or less successful? 237

7.5 Concluding remarks and reflections on inclusive development 239

Appendix 1: Reflections on research methods and process   247

Appendix 2: Case study business backgrounds   253

Appendix 3: Case study business dynamics at end of research   262

Appendix 4: Evolving routines in cases and nature of enterprise   268

Appendix 5: Indicators of socio-economic change for enterprise women   271

Glossary of local terms   273

Index   275

Figures

1.1	Interaction of structure and agency	8
3.1	The evolving Afghan state and economy 1970s–2001	55
3.2	Afghanistan's sub-economies	70
4.1	Unwrapping values, norms and habits	83
4.2	Layered reality of *purdah* on Afghan women	90
5.1	A general taxonomy of institutional arrangements	128
5.2	Institutional environments, organisations and innovativeness	129
5.3	Nested institutional development led by NGO and shaped by the entrepreneur	156
5.4	Phases in institutional construction: shaped by actors and context	158
6.1	Emerging networks and their interrelations	200
7.1	Nested institutional development rooted in social and cognitive institutions	212
7.2	Interaction of multi-actors in institutional-action-information double loop	229
7.3	Shades of diverse *purdah* observed through economic empowerment	232
A1.1	Visual technique with cards and beans exploring local actor strategies	250
A1.2	Visual techniques with (a) cards exploring scope of change in attitudes/practices at the village level and (b) cards, string and beans exploring type/importance of links between the enterprise and other actors	251
A2.1	Women's food processing business management and operations	255
A2.2	Upgrading food processing technology in the village	256
A2.3	Women's vegetable business management and operations	258
A2.4	Women's electronics business management and operations	260

Tables

1.1	Overview of research cases	17
4.1	*Purdah* transformation influenced by environment and actors	112
4.2	Evolving *purdah* rules: scope, shaping boundaries, enforcement and change	115
4.3	*Purdah* practices shaping new community values and preferences	116
5.1	Evolving institutions influenced by dynamic actor strategies and shifting conditions	160
5.2	Embedded enterprise institutions shaping new women's institutions	164
6.1	Summary of context variations across cases	189
6.2	Exploring key actor strategies and their typical usage	192
6.3	Looking across cases: emerging entrepreneurs and institutions	196
6.4	Dominant entrepreneurs and motivations/interests	198
6.5	Character of emerging networks across cases, and nature of diffusion/adoption	202
7.1	Motivation and triggers of layers of nested institutional arrangements	214
7.2	Emerging institutional pathways and influence on value chain development	235
A4.1	Layered evolving routines (in production): scope, flexibility and change	269
A5.1	Typical indicators for community women before and after the businesses were initiated	271

Preface

As a passionate community development practitioner, the research for this book began its original journey at the intersection of the value chain and livelihoods debates, in endeavouring to unwrap market processes for poorer groups in developing countries. Yet in traversing the broader literature, the research finally found its rightful (and exciting) intellectual home in the heart of the institutional discourse. This is where the *essence* of core debates on actors and context reside, with wide-ranging discussions spanning across several disciplines, including economics, sociology, anthropology, psychology, development studies and organisation studies. While these discussions are indeed lively, it was clear that there were stark gaps in this institutional discourse, particularly since academic fields remained dislocated and compartmentalised.

At the forefront of the institutional debate, a key challenge for the theory has been in deconstructing the influence of existing institutions in institutional creation. In recent years, social, cultural and political institutions have been given more weight in the institutional discourse, towards a greater appreciation of non-economic forces in institutional change, going beyond narrow notions of efficiency and rationality. This has included the influence of culture and power in institutional emergence and design, the evolutionary nature of informal institutions (incorporating agents' habits) and the socially embedded nature of economic action (the role of networks and relations). In these discussions, the interaction between structure and agency has been clearly emphasised, drawing attention to the influence of existing institutions, interests and preferences, and individual and collective power. The specific role of entrepreneurs has been highlighted in the process of innovation. And the value chain approach has been useful in exploring actors and institutions within broader market systems, drawing attention to power relations between firms. Yet it has stumbled on 'market complexities' arising in more fragmented contexts with the dominant and less understood role of informal institutions and power.

Contributing to this gap in the institutional theory, this book has endeavoured to empirically unravel the complexity of institutional processes in the uncertain context of Afghanistan, and varied outcomes in fragile economic development. Building on several years of field experience, the research adopted an exploratory and in-depth case study approach to generate a nuanced understanding of institutional construction in women's emerging enterprise, at the cusp of value chain development. Looking through the lens of a particular boundary social institution (women's norm of *purdah*), the study investigated how entrepreneurs and their networks negotiated with power holders and navigated local conditions to transform *purdah*, and subsequently develop institutions in enterprise, enabling women to participate in economic development. The research shows that external actors (such as NGOs) can both initiate and guide institutional development. Yet there may be limitations to their endeavours, with strong resistance from local power holders, unpredictable entrepreneurs and disruptive events. Towards overcoming local opposition, the use of sociocultural strategies has proved particularly notable. For example, progressive aspects of local culture (e.g. proverbs) and more favourable interpretations of religious texts have enabled the introduction of new ideas on women's roles. This has crucially opened up attitudes regarding women's mobility, permitting their culturally acceptable engagement in enterprise, and influencing their broader roles in society.

Lessons for successful rule development within fragile environments include the critical role that NGOs can play as institutional innovators and guides, the need for reshaping (and legitimacy) in ongoing institutional development led by dominant entrepreneurs and the importance of gaining the support of local authorities. And ultimately, for more sustainable institutional development, the research emphasises the value of attaining 'cognitive synergies' between these major players in a receptive and stable (local) context. With significant implications for local economic development, the research has particularly indicated the emergence of ideal types of entrepreneurs in enterprise. Thriving under stable and conducive conditions, *trailblazer entrepreneurs* were shown to draw on their allies to facilitate open, democratic and inclusive institutions with equitable participation. Meanwhile, flourishing under less stable conditions, *gatekeeper entrepreneurs* may foster more destructive pathways, in the generation of closed and exclusive institutions. Going beyond Afghanistan, the research provides pertinent insights into complex institutional processes in less certain contexts, as well as into the role of local actors and conditions. For the field of *development studies*, it has also generated deeper and more nuanced understandings of fundamental processes of change in human societies.

Acknowledgements

This book stems from my doctoral thesis,[1] and is the result of a life-changing, and often all-consuming, academic journey that was extraordinary in ways that I could not have imagined. Yet this journey would not have been possible without an exceptional array of people that were there for me along the way, in Holland, Afghanistan, Kenya and the UK. These advisors, mentors, colleagues and friends opened my eyes up to new perspectives, inspired me, allowed me to develop and grow my ideas, and were truly magnificent all-round supporters.

First and foremost, I must thank my two fantastic supervisors, Prof. Bert Helmsing and Prof. Peter Knorringa, the best supervisory team I could have wished for in this challenging study. On a fateful day, 18 months before the start of my PhD, I arranged a meeting with Prof. Peter Knorringa, having found his profile almost by chance on the Internet. Amazingly, he gave me two hours of his valuable time, and believed in me enough to encourage me through the initial application process. With much nervousness and excitement, I then started my self-funded PhD in 2009, with the ambitious idea to juggle this research with consulting assignments in Afghanistan. My supervisors were instrumental in not only creating a strong structure for our interactions, but also in allowing me to slowly develop my own ideas while subtly pushing me further and further, often to the point where I would feel that I could not climb any higher or be stretched any further! And when difficult choices were tantalisingly presented to me (usually between an 'easier' and a more 'difficult' (yet exciting!) route), the typical comment was: 'well it is up to you, Holly'! Yet I knew that with their strong support, the latter choice would indeed be possible, if tough! At the beginning, the uncertain thesis trajectory was often intimidating, but as the study became clearer, the thesis formulation and development proved to be profoundly rewarding. While deliberately building on several years of practical work in community and market development, the choice of my precise research area was a tricky one. Yet, after writing around the topic over the course of the first year, I eventually stumbled upon the rightful home of my research in a moment of epiphany, having been given the challenging, but eye-opening, task to simply write about 'institutions in economic development'! And I remember exclaiming to my supervisors that I could not have possibly proceeded with my PhD without this crucial foundation! I am more than grateful for this directional nudge, as it has allowed this study to be centrally rooted in an exciting debate at the very heart of the social sciences.

Second, besides my supervisors, there were also several people at both ISS and beyond that provided critical guidance in my PhD and enabled me to grow as an academic. In particular, Dr Georgina Gomez was, and continues to be both an incredible colleague and friend, and provided honest and insightful advice during the study, greatly influencing the rigour of the research process and thesis development. Meanwhile, the ever-supportive and enthusiastic Prof. John Cameron, with his exceptional ISS course on *Development Research: Comparative Epistemologies and Methodologies*, illuminated the importance of scientific research. He inspired me to contribute to the incredible 'body of knowledge' that exists in a meaningful way and to ensure a coherent and consistent research approach. He was also extremely helpful in providing useful comments both during the practical research process and in the thesis draft, allowing me to sharpen up both my methods and my final research conclusions. I must also give special thanks to Prof. Thea Hilhorst, and those participating in the IS Academy on Fragile States at the University of Wageningen, which permitted the broader exchange of ideas and international experience during the course of my research, strengthening crucial field reflections and enhancing the overall development of the thesis. I am also very appreciative of those at the University of Amsterdam – both friends and academics – that nurtured my initial seeds of passion in development during my Masters in 2002, and remained wonderful supporters during this later PhD process.

Third, I am wholly indebted to both the accommodating NGO teams and some of the amazing women that participated in this study. In particular, the women in my cases allowed me, a foreign stranger, to enter into their lives: to ask often peculiar and difficult questions (and often several times over!) and to spend extended amounts of time in their company. And eventually, many of them then opened up to me in such a wonderful way, going well beyond the research boundaries. They shared the emotional journeys that they had endured and were still enduring. They talked candidly about their lives, their ambitions, and their struggles and hopes for the future. They permitted me to explore their fragile worlds, and to meet their families, communities, business connections and friends. Not only did I learn about their complex lives, but I also began to better understand the layered Afghan reality, and to appreciate the ways that the women had negotiated their (own) changing dynamics. While conservative, I learnt about the extraordinary strength of their society, and experienced the true extent of wonderful Afghan hospitality and friendship. They taught me the value of patience, attention to detail, commitment and determination in fruitful social science research. More broadly, almost a decade in Afghanistan has brought me in contact with countless inspiring people – Afghans and foreigners alike – dedicated to development and to understanding Afghanistan and its challenges. These practitioners and experts have provided me with valuable insights, and forced me to re-evaluate assumptions and to consider diverse perspectives. Special mention must go in particular to the original organisation that first brought me to Afghanistan in 2004, Afghanaid (despite being 'the least experienced practitioner' in the interview process in London, although 'the most determined'!). They have remained close supporters of my work, and have always offered constructive advice and constant encouragement.

Fourth, I would like to thank all of the amazing ISS support staff for their excellent assistance, and who make ISS what it is today: a true community of dedicated and committed people that make the ISS such a pleasurable and welcoming place to study. I must mention in particular Maureen Koster, who was so encouraging in those early stages as I signed up to the PhD with much trepidation, truly terrified of the intimidating journey ahead, and Dita Dirks for her constant enthusiasm and smiling face over the PhD trajectory.

Fifth, I would like to thank my fantastic cluster of PhD friends at ISS, especially Ariane Corradi, Angelica Maria Ocampo Talero, Djalita Fialho, Deena Class and Kai Tevapitak, that made the journey so worthwhile, being there at core moments during the process, sharing stimulating conversations, suffering my worries along the way, and ensuring that together we maintained a sense of humour and laughed at life's absurdities. I am so thrilled that they shared this adventure with me, and I thank them for being so inspiring! I could not have completed the PhD without them.

Finally, I must thank my incredible broader circle of friends and family for bearing with me throughout this extensive process, believing in me and supporting me at key stages! I am extremely grateful to Cyrus Hendry, as well as Duncan Jepson and Tony Loda, for providing financial assistance (and moral encouragement) during the first part of the research. I am also so indebted to amazing friends in Afghanistan and beyond that have been so long-suffering over the course of this study, have kept up my spirits when times were tough, and equally celebrated with me when key milestones were crossed, including Sophie Ball, Leslie Knott, Amandine Roche, Michele Bradford, Gemma Stevenson, Thalia Kennedy, Matt Waldman, Eric Davin, Summer Coish and Tina Blohm. And as always in my career, my family has been especially supportive of this study, and enthusiastic, even if the research topic was not always clear for them! My parents, in particular – from my early childhood onwards – have constantly championed the fundamental values of pursuing one's ambitions, embracing life's challenges, taking initiative and daring to be different! These have been imperative in realising this thesis in all of its twists and turns, navigating unexpected events, and keeping strong in my convictions. Meanwhile, my grandmother – just tragically passing away before the end of my PhD – was so wonderfully interested in all of the details of this research (and my work in general), and through her string of open questions forced me to often reflect against prevailing Afghan narratives and to articulate my emerging ideas more succinctly. And then ultimately, in the latter part of this study – the final critical writing phase – I was fortunate to be living in my cosy log cabin, close to my immediate family and to my sister, Amber, in the beautiful Rift Valley of Kenya, with my loyal, much-loved dog. This retreat allowed me the space to think, to be removed from the usual distracting whirls of life and to be fully immersed in my thesis development. For this, I will be eternally grateful: thank you little Nimrod, and thank you to my family for all their patience and support (and help with supplies!) over those long, intensive months! I dedicate this book to you all.

Holly A. Ritchie
Naivasha, Kenya

Note

1 *Negotiating Tradition, Power and Fragility in Afghanistan: Institutional Innovation and Change in Value Chain Development*, PhD thesis, defended at ISS Erasmus University, The Hague, Sept 2013 (*cum laude*).

Abbreviations

CDC   Community Development Council (NGO facilitated under the National Solidarity Programme)

INGO   International NGO

ISAF   International Security Assistance Force (Afghanistan)

NGO   Non-governmental organisation

SHG   Self-help group – group of people (approximately 15–20 per group) with similar economic backgrounds that are typically organised by NGOs to learn basic accounting, and participate in joint savings and lending activities

Map of Afghanistan and location of case studies

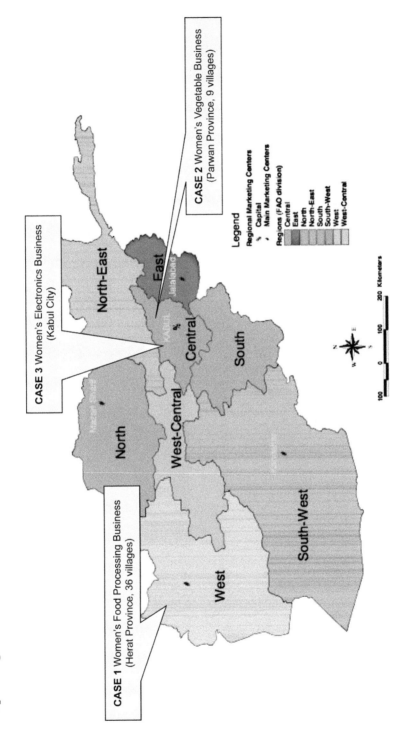

CASE 3 Women's Electronics Business
(Kabul City)

CASE 2 Women's Vegetable Business
(Parwan Province, 9 villages)

CASE 1 Women's Food Processing Business
(Herat Province, 36 villages)

North-East

East

Central

South

North

West-Central

South-West

West

Legend

Regional Marketing Centers
Capital
Main Marketing Centers

Regions (FAO division)
Central
East
North
North-East
South
South-West
West
West-Central

100 0 100 200 Kilometers

1 Exploring institutional complexity in a less formal context

George Bernard Shaw once said that reasonable people adapt themselves to the world but unreasonable people adapt the world to themselves. Thus all progress must depend on unreasonable people. In a sense, this book explores how these 'unreasonable people' may interact to remould and refashion the world around them through the lens of institutional change. In this opening chapter, I consider evolving discussions on 'institutions', towards investigating in-depth institutional processes in women's enterprise in the context of Afghanistan. I present the overall framework for the study, emphasising the epistemological departure, and guiding research themes. I reflect on the methodological techniques and fieldwork in the fragile and war-stricken Afghan setting. Introducing the research cases, I finally give a brief overview of the specific businesses featured in this book, describing their background, situation and reasons for selection. Looking ahead, I discuss the emerging book structure and arguments.

1.1 Institutions and institutional processes

Institutions shape human behaviour and provide structure in society, including critical mechanisms for decision-making. Across the social sciences, broad debates have spurred various theories of institutions and process of change, ranging from the narrow economist perspectives to more progressive evolutionary-oriented understandings of institutional change. Significantly, the institutional discourse has also broached more complex theoretical discussions, including the various effects of 'structure and agency'. In exploring micro-institutional processes in this book, particularly in a less formal context, I highlight the influence of social and cultural and political institutions in the development of new (economic) institutions, and the need to integrate a careful and more subtle examination of structure and agency.

1.1.1 What do we mean by institutions?

While central to human societies, there is still little consensus on a common definition of institutions or how we may do institutional analysis (Hollingsworth, 2002). Academic disciplines have tended to develop their own approaches to discussing and examining institutions and there is little collaborative learning. These include several approaches by economists (e.g. Williamson, 1985; Hodgson, 1988, 1998, 1999, 2003, 2007; North, 1990); political scientists, sociologists and historians (e.g. Ostrom, 1990; Campbell *et al.*, 1991; Powell and DiMaggio, 1991; Hall and Taylor, 1996; Chang, 2002); and anthropologists (e.g. Geertz, 1995). More recently, the field of organisation studies has also been drawn to institutional theories (e.g. Greenwood and Hinings, 1996, 2006; Stern and Barley, 1996; Greenwood *et al.*, 2002; Battilana *et al.*, 2009, 2012).

From the dominant institutional economics, Douglass North famously defined formal and informal institutions as the 'rules of the game' (North, 1990: 4). Viewing institutions as 'constraints', he described these as the framework structuring human interaction, and the incentives and disincentives to behave in certain ways. This includes the rules themselves, enforcement mechanisms, and norms of behaviour. Formal rules are described to include laws, constitutions and regulations; and these are specific and codified. Informal rules incorporate unwritten norms, conventions and moral codes of conduct (e.g. taboos, standards of behaviour), and may include gender-based norms, land inheritance customs and local trust-based credit systems. The enforcement of rules refers to the costs in measuring the performance of agents or the characteristics of goods and services in addition to the terms of exchange. These are considered non-existent in a neoclassical perfect world (North, 1989: 1321). Meanwhile, with an emphasis on coordination, Ostrom (2005: 3) defined institutions as 'prescriptions' that are used to organise 'all forms of repetitive and structured interactions' within families, communities, organisations and markets, across social, cultural, political and economic realms. In the economic arena, Hollingsworth and Boyer (1997) described the notion of 'institutional arrangements' to capture the (multi) coordination of various economic actors ('governance' mechanisms) by markets, hierarchies and networks, associations, the state, communities and clans.

Taking a more sociological approach, Fligstein (2001: 108) described institutions as both rules and 'shared meanings' that 'define social relationships, help define who occupies what position in those relationships, and guide interactions by giving actors cognitive frames or sets of meanings to interpret the behaviour of others'. Drawing off these broader views, from an evolutionary perspective, Hodgson suggests that institutions are structures that are both external to individuals, as well as 'ideas' inside the mind (Hodgson, 2004b: 424). Hodgson criticised North's theory of institutions for definitional ambiguities, particularly related to informal and formal rules. Going beyond institutions as just rules or constraints, Hodgson redefines institutions as 'durable systems of established and embedded social rules that structure social interactions . . . [that] both constrain and enable behaviour' (ibid.). The rule refers to 'an injunction or disposition', including norms of behaviour and conventions as well as formal rules: 'in circumstances X do Y'. Hodgson contends that rule durability comes through the capacity of institutions to 'create stable expectations of the behaviour of others' and thus permit (but not be reducible to) 'ordered thought, expectation and action' (ibid.).

1.1.2 Exploring institutional complexity in a fragile context

In turning to the challenging topic of *institutional change*, social scientists have indicated the existence of complex dynamics involving the interplay of structure and agency (e.g. Ostrom, 1990; Chang and Evans, 2000; Hodgson, 2004b). Crossing into fields such as management, Koene (2006) highlights the varied influence of the context – affected by local pressures, societal confidence and agent power – and the potential behaviour of agents affecting institutional change and outcomes. In recent years, social, cultural and political institutions have been given more weight across the institutional debate towards a greater appreciation of non-economic forces in institutional processes, going beyond the narrow notions of efficiency and rationality. This has included the influence of culture and power in institutional emergence and design, the evolutionary nature of informal institutions (incorporating agents' habits), and the socially embedded nature of economic action (the role of networks and relations). The various effects of structure and agency has been highlighted, drawing attention to social relations and power, and agent interests and preferences. Yet the process of institutional construction and development is still poorly understood, in part due to disciplinary compartmentalisation.

Contributing to a gap in the institutional theory, this book specifically endeavours to explore how existing institutions influence the construction of new market institutions, and how this affects evolving value chains in a less formal context. The theoretical framework draws from the broad institutional discourse with relevant insights from enterprise and value chain development. In particular, the enterprise literature has highlighted the role of entrepreneurs in the process of innovation, and their varied motivations and objectives. Meanwhile, with a strong focus on the participation of poor producers, the value chain[1] approach has been useful in studying links between market actors within market systems, drawing attention to power relations in the governance of value chains. But it has often stumbled on the 'market complexities' arising in more fragmented and informal contexts where markets remain exclusive (particularly for the poor and women), with strong power distortions. In such situations, it is the prior existence of dominant non-economic institutions that may influence the necessary development of market institutions.

In this study, the empirical research takes a practical look at institutional processes in emerging women's businesses in the context of Afghanistan. Advancing theoretical understandings, the study elaborates on how actors navigate existing institutions to reshape the 'rules of the game' (institutions) through institutional construction in enterprise, at the cusp of value chain development. In particular, the research explores the uncertain role of women entrepreneurs and other actors in fostering new institutions to engage in new forms of enterprise, and 'shades of initiative' by different groups along a continuum to evolving institutions. These themes resonate as both relevant and significant in the informal and volatile research context of Afghanistan. A traditional and conservative society, gender-prescribed behaviour remains strong. Meanwhile, instability and conflict appear to be (almost) 'institutionalised' in society, and research indicates that conflict has had a limited impact on the prevalence of enterprise activity (Ciarli *et al.*, 2009: 2). A great deal of effort has been channelled into 'pro-poor enterprise and value chain' development by the government and aid agencies with varying degrees of success and failure. Baumol (1990) suggests entrepreneurship may have varied outcomes for economic development, and distinguished between productive, unproductive and destructive activities. This study looks at the underlying nature of enterprise through a 'nuanced' institutional lens to better understand economic development 'pathways', particularly in a traditional and fragile environment.

1.2 A critical realist lens with tools from development studies

To investigate the unusual phenomenon of poorer women's businesses in Afghanistan and institutional change, the research took a strong focus on understanding the interaction of structure and agency. This aimed to generate new insights into the influence of existing sociocultural institutions, prevailing politics and the dynamic role of actors in the emergence of new market institutions. In appreciating these deeper yet unknown institutional processes, the research strived to initially find an epistemological departure that allowed for both a suitable research approach and interpretation that could provide pertinent theoretical insights into institutional processes – in vein with key thinkers such as Geoff Hodgson – yet also aligned to the emerging field of development with useful insights for practice.

Development studies is a recent distinctive branch of the social sciences concerned with understanding the poor in developing countries. Challenged by the need to incorporate both natural and social phenomena within its domain of inquiry, studies have traversed different ontologies exploring research objectivity, methodologies and approaches (Sumner and Tribe, 2004). Adopting an episte-mological approach that best suits the key themes and type of investigation is viewed as critical in rigorous development research, as well as ensuring an appro-priate mix of quantitative and qualitative methods/techniques in conjunction with a 'reflective practitioner approach'. To this end, with the focus on examining less known social phenomena and the interplay between structure and agency, the research herein sought an 'exploratory' in-depth approach, and finally identified the useful lens of *critical realism*.

1.2.1 Building knowledge through making sense of reality

As a reaction to postmodernism, and with the demise of the dominance of logical positivism, the critical realist perspective emerged in the 1970s with roots in Marxism and social economy (Polanyi, 1944). Advocated by Bhaskar (1975), critical realism endeavoured to present a normative model for the social sciences, describing the interface between the natural and social worlds. The approach emphasises layered 'open' realities, which may be understood through transi-tive objects of knowledge (facts, methods, theories) and intransitive objects of knowledge ('real' events, structures and mechanisms in the world) (Baert, 2005: 91). Knowledge production is conceived through retroduction, with reality assessed through a broad range of methods and sources. Going beyond the surface of action and events, the critical realist perspective underscores the 'interplay between structural factors and individual agency' and emphasises an interdisciplinary approach. The critical realist lens is argued to generate ontological depth in incorporating structure, causal mechanisms, and events within geohistorical contexts (Sayer, 2000: 15). Yet Baert (2005: 102) criticises this realist epistemology as still being trapped in a scientific (logical positivist) perspective that tries to fully explain and holistically map reality, in vein with a 'spectator theory of knowledge' (Dewey, 1938). However, a cluster of less orthodox economists such as Tony Lawson and Geoffrey Hodgson advocate the use of critical realism in institutional discourse. They have embraced this position as going beyond 'closed' positivist models that fail to incorporate dimensions of reality not immediately observable. Lawson (1997) suggests that the phenomena of the world can be better explained through reference to powers, mechanisms and related tendencies. He highlighted different levels of reality, including empirical ('experience and impression'), actual ('actual events and states of affairs') and real ('structures, powers, mechanisms, and tendencies'), towards generating a more holistic and penetrating picture of the world.

Drawing from social constructivism: language and power

Adopting this standpoint and responding to shortfalls of critical realism (Baert, 2005), the research for this study sought to integrate more nuanced processes and dynamics of power in an expanded critical realist approach. To this end, the research drew on tools from social construction, which builds on the philosophy of Berger and Luckmann (1966), and later Foucault, Knorr-Cetina and Latour. Departing from an empiricist/logical positivist confidence in a self-evident and objective truth where generalisations are sought, social construction emphasises the subtleties of the human condition, with a greater subjective/interpretative emphasis towards 'quality', not 'quantity', in research data. Social constructivism is concerned with the ways that reality is socially constructed in a dynamic process by both individuals and groups through the reproduction and negotiation of their interpretations of reality and knowledge of it: 'we do not find or discover knowledge so much as we construct or makeit' (Schwandt, 2000: 197). Such understandings are drawn from a set of shared values, practices and language. Also called 'perspectivism' (Fay, 1996), social constructivism holds that knowledge claims take place within a conceptual framework. Claiming closure is regarded with suspicion. The approach highlights the researcher as present in the research, and 'values' as part of the reality with subjectivity 'celebrated'.

In appreciating some aspects of speech, discourse and context, the research specifically drew from the 'moderate' social constructivist approach, putting emphasis on both *language* and *power* in assessing claims to 'know a reality' (e.g. Bernstein, Bourdieu, Derrida, Gramsci, Foucault). For some, Foucault's less tangible concept of power in particular – which is neither attributed to agency nor structure – appears problematic: both structures and agents are constituted by and through power (Gaventa, 2003). Yet Foucault's theory has indicated, for example, how the embeddedness of norms in society (shaped by power dynamics) can lead actors to adhere to these unconsciously without coercion (ibid.). More recently, in development studies, Gaventa (2006) has elaborated on nuances of power entrenched within local social structures, and the role of dominant actors. He describes three dimensions of power, including 'visible power', pertaining to political power, and the mechanisms and institutions of decision-making; 'hidden power', pertaining to powerful people that dominate and control decision-making; and 'invisible power', described as the most 'insidious', relating to the internalisation of power that influences psychological and ideological boundaries of participation embedded in social norms and local power dynamics.

1.2.2 Guiding research themes

With this critical realist lens, and emphasis on language and power, the research intended to generate subtle insights into actors and conditions in the process of institutional change in women's enterprise in Afghanistan. The investigation focused in particular on the role of entrepreneurs and their allies in institutional development, and how they navigated and negotiated existing institutions and powerful actors in the community. The research looked at the types of institutions constructed and their effects, and the dynamic forces influencing both entrepreneurs and their broader networks in construction, learning, enforcement and diffusion towards 'thick institutionalism' (Portes, 2006: 236). These various themes provided a broad framework to explore complex institutional processes.

In the initial stages of institutional change, it was important to identify specific events and actors (and decisions) that tended to characterise the process. This was vital to appreciate the various circumstances under which change took place, and triggers both from within the environment, or by particular catalytic agents. In the subsequent emergence of new or revised institutions, it was then significant to look at the nature of evolving 'dominant' institutions. Closely associated with this, the research also sought to examine the conditions under which related 'dominant entrepreneurs' might emerge. Two types of women entrepreneurs were hypothesised.[2] These included 'trailblazer entrepreneurs' that may nurture more open institutions, and 'gatekeeper entrepreneurs' that may foster more exclusive institutions. Local *power holders* in the research referred to existing members of authority, including religious leaders, local community leaders and other influential (community) actors.

Institutional focus in the research

In the research, *institutions* were specifically investigated at both a societal and enterprise/market level. With a strong focus on women's participation and interaction, the research looked at the initial transformation of the specific boundary social institution of *purdah*, permitting women's entry into collective enterprise, and the construction of 'enterprise' institutions in business. Sociocultural *purdah* norms determine the scope of individual women's mobility and public interaction, and shape all potential aspects of women's life beyond the household. Meanwhile, the associated development of market-orientated institutions permit participation in firms and markets. At a primary level, these included enterprise 'routines' within the group (as described by Hodgson, 2007). Rules here pertained to group production and management. At a secondary level, these included 'chain rules' between the group and other market actors (in vein with 'institutional arrangements' described by Hollingsworth and Boyer, 1997). These external rules pertained to business linkages, and related to physical marketing and procurement. Finally, at a tertiary level, rules included 'collective action institutions' across firms (in vein with Ostrom, 1990). Collective action rules described agreements between similar firms for joint marketing and exchange. Overall, as described by Ostrom, these enterprise rules may generally be understood as 'working rules'. At the group level, these were largely uncodified but were considered 'common knowledge' to enterprise agents, and monitored and enforced (Ostrom, 1990: 51). Meanwhile, at the market level, working rules were often also accompanied by the subsequent development of formal rules such as contracts. For the purpose of this study (and in line with Ostrom, 1990), the research differentiates between lower level 'deeper' rules, applying to social and cognitive institutions, and the development of higher-level rules in enterprise, including routines, chain rules and collective action institutions, and broader economic institutions.[3]

Clarifying entrepreneurs in the research

Drawing off entrepreneurial discourse by Schumpeter (1934), Baumol (1968) and others, Binks and Vale (1990: 18) defined *entrepreneurs* as those that respond to market signals, are involved with the innovation of ideas and facilitate market processes in economic development. In the research, while the women entrepreneurs did not theoretically initiate the business, they were involved with leading a business group, and championing the development of enterprise rules (organisational innovations). Entrepreneurs were either selected by the local elite, or by the group themselves. Two dichotomous dominant categories were highlighted for investigation: 'gatekeeper' and 'trailblazer' entrepreneurs. 'Gatekeeper' entrepreneurs were hypothesised to stem from the traditional business elite, and to act as 'rule-makers' in the creation of new 'discriminatory' rules that tended to perpetuate existing norms. 'Trailblazer' entrepreneurs were hypothesised to stem from the less powerful non-business class (the middle sections of society) and to act as creative pioneers in 'rule breaking', towards establishing new 'non-discriminatory' rules. Entrepreneur networks included their direct allies within the business (co-workers), as well as broader relations with power holders, relations in the market place and collaborative relations across similar firms. According to Kristiansen (2004), networks enable entrepreneurs to reduce risks and transaction costs, and to improve access to business ideas, knowledge and capital. Yet Klyver and Schott (2011) indicated that entrepreneurial intentions could influence the emerging network scope and usage. Building off Davern (1997), (nascent) social networks were explored in terms of the scope of individual social relations, and the overall network value/use (collective action, resources (and power) achieved and outcomes).

Interplay between structure and agency

Hodgson (2004b) described a 'non-conflationary' and 'casually interactive' approach to appreciate the interplay between structure and agency, and to capture how individual intentions or preferences change. Drawing off this, in a loose depiction for this research (see Figure 1.1), actors are influenced by their own dynamic motivations and interest, and skills, capacity and networks. These are in turn continually influenced by structure (existing institutions, endogenous politics).

1.2.3 Reflections on research approach and methods

Capturing different realities and situations, the practical field research for this study straddled three different geographical areas of Afghanistan: the western province of Herat (rural business case), the central province of Parwan (rural business case) and the capital city of Kabul (urban business case).[4] Each of the respective women's businesses had been initially supported by an NGO that had been

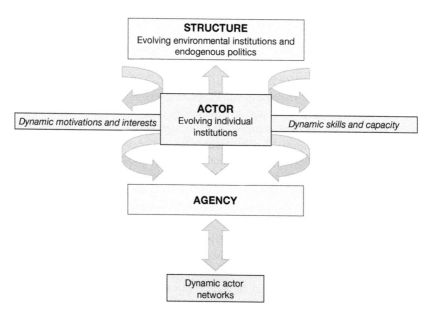

Figure 1.1 Interaction of structure and agency

Source: Author's own illustration

instrumental in mobilising the women and establishing the business organisation. While employing multiple techniques to investigate the three cases,[5] the research also placed a strong emphasis on flexibility, reflection and openness to studying the complex and little understood phenomena of interest (in line with grounded theory). Building on previous interactions with the businesses, the early research phase drew on updated documents, observation and semi-structured interviews with key informants from the supporting NGOs, community and business leaders, and value chain actors.

In the second and third intensive research phases, more exploratory and innovative ethnographic techniques were employed to take a deeper look at business and societal dynamics, with a view to investigating more sensitive issues, and tensions and processes beneath the surface.[6] These included extensive village-level participatory sessions with local women in particular. In the final research stages, business leaders and NGO supporters participated in workshops to discuss observations, reflect on enterprise institutions, and elaborate on emerging networks and future strategies. It is important to note that over the entire course of the research, concerted effort was made to engage more broadly with other NGOs, local business associations, government offices and civil society actors to better understand contextual conditions, institutional transformation and development, and the role of different actors in the process. While slower than expected, the research process generated both expected and less expected 'layered' findings, going beyond predicted results and early conceptualised research directions.

Appendix 1 reflects further on the ethnographic techniques used, and research biases.

1.3 Introduction to cases

Due to the rarity of (poorer) women's enterprise in Afghanistan, the women's businesses that were selected for this research had been initiated by external NGOs. The first case study was a *rural women's food processing association*, and comprised a formal network of 36 village food processing centres. The second case study was a *rural women's vegetable production business*, and was straddled across nine villages with a total of 90 women's groups. While not formalised, villages were loosely linked for technical exchange and (higher-level) marketing. Meanwhile, the third case study was a small *urban women's electronics business* from a deprived area of Kabul, and comprised just a single group of women. To explore local dynamics (i.e. core attributes of the environment, key personalities involved and significant events), two specific villages were preselected for this investigation in Cases 1 and 2 that appeared interesting (with each having faced different challenges), and were accessible.[7] In Case 3, the point of situational focus was the local neighbourhood from where the business had originated. This section further introduces these three research cases, giving a brief overview of the respective enterprises, and expanding on the local contexts and backgrounds of the facilitating NGOs and entrepreneurs.

1.3.1 Case 1: women's rural food processing association

Located across a network of villages close to Herat City in West Afghanistan, the first case study was an outwardly flourishing women's food processing business association. Facilitated by a largely inexperienced (but determined) local NGO, the first batch of food processing groups were established six years prior to the research. By the end of the research, the business comprised 36 food processing groups or centres (15–20 women per centre) across 36 villages (with a total of approximately 700 workers), and had growing levels of production and sales.[8] Food processing production was organised at the village level by individual food processing centres. Depending on the season and availability, products included tomato paste, jams, chutney and dried produce. Seventy per cent of the produce was sold by weight (unpackaged) locally by individual groups, with the rest being co-marketed as premium packaged produce in the city under a common label. The main city marketing channels included the direct shops of some of the groups, local grocery stores and exhibitions.

Local context: traditional but progressive amongst city elites

Taking a look at the research context, the western province of Herat remains traditional and strictly Islamic, although it is culturally more progressive among the urban elites. Ethnically mixed, the province comprises populations of Pashtun, Tajik and Hazara tribes. The provincial capital of the same name was a thriving ancient cultural and trading centre. At the time of the study, the city of Herat was described to be a hub for growing business activities, mainly due to its accessibility to bordering Iran and Turkmenistan. While conflict continued in neighbouring regions in the south (Helmand), the province itself remained largely calm, and local people described normalising instability into their livelihoods. In the rural areas, the main source of income tended to be from agriculture, predominantly from cereal crops such as wheat, barley and rice. Herat was also well known for horticultural production such as grapes and raisins. In the rural non-farm sector, handicrafts, carpets and rug production were the major traditional (women's) activities.

For the investigation, I selected two mature village-based groups – that had just formalised as their own village-based associations, in addition to being part of the network association (Cases 1a and 1b). Villages were selected that had been involved with the network since its inception, were accessible, and where both challenges and successes had been faced with a range of actors. Located just outside of the city, each of the villages had only basic access to services, and after decades of war had been initially closed, fearful of new ideas and change. While situated in different districts, the villages were fairly similar in terms of wealth, ethnicity, access to resources (water and power) and proximity to the city. They also displayed an equal persistence of traditional livelihoods, although there appeared to be more openness to change in the second village (Case 1b). Elaborating on specific characteristics, Case 1a was a well-established ethnically Tajik village (300 years old) and comprised approximately 1,200 families (notably, in the past, there had been significant numbers of Pashtun families residing there). During the war years, the village had been particularly affected by the Russian occupation and had strong memories of local massacres. Similarly, Case 1b was also predominantly Tajik, but a third of the size, with a total of 360 families. Typical (male) income generation activities in both of the villages included cereal farming and horticulture (mostly vegetables). Meanwhile, women had traditionally been involved in carpet weaving, yoghurt production and fruit harvesting (on their own land).

Facilitating NGO: a small, locally oriented organisation

With experience in Pakistan (Peshawar), the local facilitating NGO comprised a dedicated group of Afghan community development practitioners that had returned to the western region of Herat in 2004. In 2005, the NGO managed to forge a long-term partnership with a well-established international NGO in the region that specialised in rural livelihoods (with a strong interest in enterprise development). While the local NGO had been recognised as inexperienced, they were perceived as honest and hard-working, with rare skills in food processing as well as community development. The NGO was specifically contracted by the INGO to mobilise local women from rural communities into self-help groups (SHGs),[9] and to train the women in food processing skills to sell foodstuffs in the local market. To support this work, the NGO staff received initial training in SHG methodology and community enterprise development from the INGO, in addition to further skills development in food processing and post-production technologies. Meanwhile, the organisation itself also benefited from intensive support to develop their internal systems, including finance, project management, and monitoring and evaluation. This background and mentoring shaped the foundation of the NGO's core work with the women in food processing and enterprise development.

At the time of research, the NGO comprised a strong team of 20 staff, with only light support from the international NGO to strengthen financial administration (periodic auditing), as well as ongoing mentoring in monitoring and evaluation. The NGO was involved with both the women's food processing enterprise (now situated across 36 villages), as well as other smaller projects related to women's vocational training and rights development (with independently obtained funding). They had also opened a second office in the north part of the country and planned to initiate further food processing (and poultry) enterprises with women. In both locations, they had close connections with regional officials and the local Department of Agriculture. In terms of the Herat women's food processing programme, they were still involved with intensive support but they concentrated most of their efforts on the newer food processing centres. And they had tended to withdraw support from mature centres. Yet they continued to facilitate (crucial) networking and coordination across the groups.

From being highly dependent on the international NGO at the start of their community development work, the NGO had achieved both regional and national recognition for their successful projects with women in food processing enterprise. They were known for the commendable quality of their work, strong commitment and maintaining excellent community/regional relations. Yet with the growth of the business, they faced new challenges in supporting the formalisation and upgrading of the enterprise.

Entrepreneurs: leading village food processing groups

For this research, 'the entrepreneurs' related to the group heads of the village food processing groups (networked into one business). In Case 1a, the food processing group was managed by a quiet but determined woman from a humble, religious family. Married with children in her early thirties, she was elected by the group (and approved by the village leaders) for her intelligence, strong Islamic faith, sense of responsibility and reliability. As the village business developed, she has demonstrated remarkable skills and perseverance in garnering the cooperation of the group of women, negotiating with difficult local leaders, and subtly pushing the business forward through expanding levels of production (beyond the village centre) and diversifying marketing options. Meanwhile, in Case 1b, the food processing group was led by an outwardly tough but soft-spoken widow in her fifties. Replacing an earlier choice that proved less capable (and voluntarily self-retired from the group), the entrepreneur was initially an uncertain alternative as a poor widow, and not well known in the community. Yet as an active group member, she persuaded the women that she could lead the group, and was then subsequently approved by the community leaders (and as an older widow, she was considered a good choice). With time and experience, she demonstrated strong skills in leadership and business management, and unusual courage and risk-taking in the face of adversity. Through this she has gained deep respect from the group and within the community. She has emerged to be both dedicated and committed to the business, and later, even took strides to invest her own resources (land) in the business (for vegetable/fruit production).

1.3.2 Case 2: women's rural vegetable production business

Turning to the second case study, this women's enterprise included a series of highly structured and innovatively organised women's village vegetable production groups, situated in the central province of Parwan. The business was established by an international NGO (INGO) with the collaboration of a local NGO in 2007. At the time of the study, a total of 90 women's farmer groups straddled nine villages, with approxi-mately 20 women per group and 10 groups per village (a total of approximately 2,250 members). With high demand in local and regional markets, the village groups were thriving and collaborating across villages for city sales. Vegetable production was boosted by new techniques and technologies with emerging diversification into food processing. As production levels increased,[10] their village reputations were growing fast. And large traders were even travelling directly to the villages to source fresh, high-quality vegetables! Towards the end of the research, the INGO withdrew support, although ties remained with the local NGO. While the 'business' remained largely informal (with no common business name),[11] loose links had been established between the villages for joint marketing in exhibitions, and technical troubleshooting.

Local context: traditional rural trading zone near to Kabul

The villages in this business case were located in the province of Parwan, a central trading zone of Afghanistan (close to the capital city), and on a major crossroads with Pakistan to the east, and the thriving border city of Mazar to the north. Charikar, Parwan's provincial capital, was a bustling market town situated approximately two hours drive from Kabul. In addition to its prime geographical position, the province was known to have good-quality irrigated farmland, and diverse agricultural production (with significant horticulture and livestock). A historically turbulent area, the people tended to describe themselves as both strong and fiercely resilient. Before relative peace returned in 2001, the region had been on the front line of the conflict for more than two decades, with many families seeking temporary refuge across the border in Pakistan. At the time of the research, the population of Parwan province had largely returned and resettled. Ethnically, the majority of the population was Tajik, with a small minority of more conservative Pashtuns. Besides agriculture and local business, employment wise, the province was a known traditional feeder for Kabul-based ministries (for the educated elite) and for wage labour.

The two villages selected for the research were located relatively close to the market town of Charikar. While these communities were not far from the town and the capital city, Kabul, after many years of war, there were still high levels of illiteracy and infant/maternal mortality. There was also persisting fear and distrust of both outsiders and their own neighbours, affecting levels of trust and cooperation. The two villages were fairly similar in terms of size and ethnicity, but were notably different in terms of wealth, location, livelihoods and access to resources. Case 2a was located on the fringes of Charikar (less than one hour walking distance), and was described as a secure, open and active village (where 'change was happening fast'), although notably poor. It was predominantly Tajik in ethnicity, and comprised around 300 families. With little agricultural land, men worked as sharecroppers in nearby areas, and many ran small businesses in Charikar. Meanwhile, in contrast, Case 2b was a highly traditional, conservative and wealthy village located slightly further away from Charikar town centre. This community comprised a mix of Tajik (mainly) and Pashtun ethnicities, and, similar to Case 2a, approximately 300 families. In this village, the majority of households owned their own land, with almost half of these also owning livestock. Notably, at the start of the project, there was a very high degree of illiteracy among women (93 per cent).

Facilitating NGOs: partnership between international and local organisations

Taking a collaborative approach, a joint international and local NGO team were the 'facilitating NGOs' in this case. A well-known champion of the value chain approach, the international NGO was initially motivated to start value chain projects for women in Afghanistan after experience in neighbouring Pakistan and South East Asia. In Pakistan in particular, the NGO had worked in the conservative tribal area, and had gained key insights into working in societies where the segregation of the sexes was common, and where women faced similar constraints in terms of their mobility to Afghanistan. Securing a significant donor contract in Afghanistan, they began work in rural villages in the central province of Parwan in 2007 with a focus on integrating rural women into targeted 'priority' horticultural value chains (including carrots, cucumbers, onions, potatoes and tomatoes). The international NGO gathered a team of approximately 20 staff with strong expertise in horticulture and business management (including two international staff). With little Afghan experience and relations on the ground, however, the international NGO identified a local (urban) partner (a new local women's business council) to assist with community mobilisation and support.

At the time of the research, the INGO project was in its mid to final phases. Nine villages had been successfully mobilised and over 2,000 women organised into village farmers' groups. Intensive and impressive training in horticulture had been delivered, Farmer Field Schools set up, and training given in post-harvest technologies and marketing to selected participating women. Other 'complementary' training courses offered to the farmers groups included literacy and numeracy. Group leaders were further supported with special 'leadership skills' and (notably) 'consultation' training (emphasising the importance of 'shared decision-making' with relevant family/leaders). Meanwhile, to assist with high-level joint marketing and access to resources, designated saleswomen were connected to city markets and exhibitions, as well as to input suppliers, microfinance institutions (MFIs) and packaging agents. In general, the joint NGO partnership and project approach was considered to be successful in facilitating rural women into horticultural enterprise, with the business persisting after the project closed. As in Case 1, the international NGO regularly shared their work with key government/non-government offices in Kabul. They were particularly known for introducing impressive new technologies and creating scale in their work. Yet it appeared that local dynamics were (sometimes) overlooked in their approach, and there was significant variation in the level and quality of participation of the farmers at the village level.

Entrepreneurs: leading village horticultural production groups

Similar to Case 1, for this research 'the entrepreneurs' related to the village heads of the farmers' groups, selected by the community leaders (loosely networked into one business). In Case 2a, the village entrepreneur was from a large landowning family and the only female teacher in the community. She was well known and respected as practical and forthright. Married with children in her late thirties, she was strong but both warm and community-spirited. As the most educated woman in the village (and with the most mobility), she was the natural choice of the community leaders. Yet as the business developed, she proved herself to be not only a good educator, but also a strong businesswoman and respected leader. With gentle but firm authority, she has overseen the women's farmers groups, facilitated exchange and supported marketing. Meanwhile, in Case 2b, the semi-literate village entrepreneur was an unusual unmarried woman in her early thirties from an elite family, with rare degrees of mobility (due to an unconventional upbringing in being raised as a boy – this is further discussed in Chapter 6). She was head of the village women's committee but distanced herself from other women, and tended to intimidate them. As the business has evolved, she has further relished the power that this has given her. With little interest in the other women's welfare, she has focused on gaining networks and prestige through marketing and representation.

1.3.3 Case 3: women's urban electronics business

Supported and trained by an international agency, the third case study was a small struggling urban women's electronics business based in the capital city, Kabul. The company was predominantly involved with assembling basic electrical appliances such as solar lanterns and circuit boards. During the research, the women in the business were also trained to repair common domestic appliances. Established four years prior to the research, the business originally included 13 women workers. By the end of the study, however, only four women remained due to limited work contracts. Business linkages for local supply and contract development have included both international organisations and local companies.

Local context: deprived urban neighbourhood of capital, Kabul

The electronics business was situated in the midst of the populous, fast-moving and rapidly expanding capital city of Kabul. After years of war, the city was gradually being rebuilt, although development remained uneven, with many parts of the city still cut off from basic services. As the main seat of power of a weak government, the city was politically volatile, and continued to suffer from periodic instability from insurgents. The city was ethnically diverse, and pockets of population groups resided in different parts of the city (and these often comprised displaced groups from across the country). The business participants originated from a poor war-scarred Pashtun neighbourhood located on the fringes of the city. According to the NGO, more than 80 per cent of the area was destroyed by the war in the previous decades. During the early phases of the business, a total of 5,000 families were estimated to be resident in the area, and public services (water, electricity, schools and clinics) were extremely limited. At the time of the research, the physical neighbourhood had improved significantly, although social attitudes still remained largely conservative, and the area deemed insecure. While the business had relocated to different parts of the city in later phases, strict family members from their own home neighbourhood still influenced the level of participation of worker women.

Facilitating NGO: international organisation

In this final case, the facilitating NGO was an international organisation. The organisation focused on urban community development, enterprise and gender.

In particular, projects sought to empower poor women with new productive skills, and then link them to the market. Embedded in a foreign ministry, but with an NGO-like status, the organisation began their 'integrated skills development' project in Kabul with one marginalised city community in 2005. With family approval, a total of 60 women from needy families were selected, and initially organised into several enterprise groups. Training was then delivered in key thematic areas, including solar lantern assembly and electronics (the focus of this research), as well as restaurant and catering, gem cutting and design, and mobile phone repair. Staff were predominantly local Afghans, led by a charismatic and determined male coordinator in his mid forties (with one short-term international staff member as an advisor). From the outset, there appeared to be both a tension with their international headquarters and a significant lack of relevant expertise (particularly community development and enterprise facilitation) within the country-based team, leading to a disjointed programme approach and strategy.

In the research phase, the project had been running for over five years. All four of the businesses had been mobilised by the NGO, and the target women had been trained in the relevant technical skills as planned (despite extensive social challenges). Additional training included literacy courses, English, and basic health and hygiene. In so doing, the NGO had endeavoured to go beyond skills development to help the women overcome social barriers and to promote broader community development. Yet the organisation wrestled with a mixture of ongoing cultural battles, and identifying sustainable and workable business strategies. City consultants were brought in to assist with the development of commercial business plans but these remained aspirational without internal expertise and guidance. While the NGO had succeeded in enabling women's enterprise development, they ultimately struggled to establish viable businesses (including the women's electronics business) that were fully integrated into the market and sustainable. They had fostered links between the businesses to international organisations, yet these contracts were invariably based on 'charity', as opposed to being commercially competitive.

Entrepreneur: leading the group enterprise

More straightforward than the previous cases, the entrepreneur in this case was simply the overall business head that was selected by the group members to lead the group (and approved by the local neighbourhood leaders). Married with children in her early thirties, she was perceived to have a quiet strength and to be more educated than the other group members. Notably from an open tribe, the Tajiks, this has enabled her to negotiate higher degrees of mobility than the other women that were from more conservative Pashtun families. As the business has developed, she has visibly enjoyed leading and representing the group, and has emerged to be a charismatic and proud business head, adopting new 'professional' styles of dress and behaviour. Yet she has struggled with the actual business management with only basic literacy and numeracy skills. This has led her to bring in her family members (husband and son) for support. She was highly respected by the members

Table 1.1 Overview of research cases

Research case	Type	Description	Reasons for selection
CASE 1	Women's food processing business	36 village groups led by village entrepreneurs, networked into one business (approx. 700 women).	Large network of villages and entrepreneurs with collaboration in city marketing
Case 1a		Two villages selected for the research.	Significant progress over several years
Case 1b			Long-term evolving strategy
CASE 2	Women's vegetable production business	Nine villages with 10 farmers' groups per village, led by village entrepreneurs. Villages loosely networked together (approx. 2,000 women).	Innovative institutional design with large numbers of participating rural women
Case 2a		Two villages selected for the research.	Collaborative marketing at the city level
Case 2b			New technology introduced at village level
CASE 3	Women's electronics business	Single group of women from poor urban neighbourhood (13 women at start of research).	Urban-based business Non-women economic sector Struggling enterprise with diminishing worker numbers Long-term support with unclear strategy

of the group, although as the business has matured she has visibly distanced herself from them, possibly to consolidate her position and new-found power.

Table 1.1 summarises the research cases and the main reasons for their selection.

Appendix 2 provides brief business overviews of the research cases (with supplementary technical and market data).

1.4 Concluding remarks and book structure

This introductory chapter has opened up progressive discussions on the central themes of this book, institutional change and economic development. The study centres specifically on empirical research from selected women's businesses in the challenging context of Afghanistan. In exploring institutional processes, a particular emphasis was placed on evolutionary perspectives championed by Hodgson (2004b). In this vein, the chapter highlighted the pertinence of the *critical realist* epistemology in examining subtle dynamics and the interplay between structure and agency, and incorporating additional tools from 'social construction' to explore nuances of language and power. As a guiding frame for the study, key themes of interest were highlighted to carefully unravel institutional change and development in women's emerging enterprise in Afghanistan, including the role of entrepreneurs and local power holders, and influences from within the local environment. The discussion briefly reflected upon the research approach and fieldwork, drawing attention to ethnographic techniques used to investigate less known institutional phenomena. Finally, the chapter presented an overview of the three research cases featured in this study: a women's rural food processing association, a women's rural vegetable business and an urban women's electronics business; and introduced the respective facilitating NGOs and entrepreneurs.

In summary, this chapter has placed the essence of this book as strongly and firmly embedded in the ongoing and challenging institutional discourse, with a strong focus on the interaction of structure and agency. Appreciating these subtle themes, the chapter highlighted the 'critical realist' research framework as both appropriate and progressive in examining nuanced phenomena in institutional change and development. Looking ahead, the book is structured as follows: Chapter 2 provides an overarching framework of institutional theory and critical arguments, introducing core emerging themes and broad debates on institutional change. It emphasises key actors in institutional processes such as entrepreneurs and their engagement in networks. Finally, the chapter discusses the informal nature of markets in fragile environments, emphasising social exclusion, power distortions and the role of trust. Chapter 3 turns to the specific research setting of Afghanistan, describing the particular sociocultural, political and economic context, exploring pertinent issues related to actors, power and structure. In Chapter 4, the discussion carefully examines the transformation of norms in the research cases, precipitating later engagement in enterprise. The chapter initially expands upon relevant discourse related to social norms and change. It then presents crucial findings related to the transformation of the boundary social institution of *purdah* in the course of enterprise development. Building on this, Chapter 5 discusses the emergence and development of subsequent institutions in enterprise, including internal routines, chain rules and collective action institutions across firms. Once again, the chapter elaborates on the relevant literature including discussions on routines, economic coordination in the form of institutional arrangements, and collective action institutions. The chapter then critically analyses findings from the research. Advancing an analysis of actors, Chapter 6 further unwraps notions of agency, first expanding on the literature insights on institutional entrepreneurs, networks and collective agency in institutional development. It then looks closer at research findings to discuss actor motivations, the influence of local micro-conditions and actor strategies in institutional processes. It discusses dominant entrepreneurs and collective power, and the role of networks in institutional diffusion and adoption. Finally, Chapter 7 draws together the key arguments of this book on institutional change, further reflecting on the cases and specific theories, and advancing new empirical insights both supporting and challenging existing propositions. The chapter also reflects more generally on the research for the field of development studies, and the importance of inter-disciplinary approaches, straddling anthropology, political science to economics, in generating new insights into equitable and inclusive development.

Notes

1 A value chain describes the various activities required for a product or service to pass from production to the final delivery to the consumer (Kaplinsky and Morris, 2000: 4).

2 The hypothesis was shaped by pre-research observation and interaction with two of the case businesses for two years prior to the formal research.

3 It is important to note that there are several different approaches and conventions to examining institutional 'levels' within the institutional discourse. Others for example, focus on institutional strength, in the duration of institutional change and scale of applicability (e.g. Williamson, 2000; Brousseau and Raynaud, 2007).

4 The fieldwork took place over a period of 14 months (2010–2011), in three research phases.

5 The research process drew on a mix of different methods and tools, including innovative ethnographic techniques (at a group level), semi-structured interviews, focus groups, workshops and observation. This included over 30–40 formal research sessions conducted per case. These sessions incorporated a range of actors, including the entrepreneurs, workers and their families (major focus); local councils and religious clerics; the facilitating NGOs; local value chain actors (e.g. buyers, packaging agents, suppliers); as well as broader businesses, other NGOs and local governing authorities. (In addition to this, relevant documents were analyzed, e.g. NGO reports, local research, etc.) The research also included many informal research sessions during which the author simply observed the groups, engaged in day-to-day discussions, shared refreshments and exchanged life stories.

6 In exploring actor behaviour and relations, the research deliberately adopted two particular approaches to exploring institutional change dynamics (with both entre-preneurs and broader stakeholders). First, I endeavoured to understand historical change through my own observations over time, and respondent accounts. Second, I took a dialectical approach to exploring existing tensions and pressures within the present, which may be precursors or forces for potential change. Indicators of social (and cultural) change could thus be viewed through the lens of historical pathways, existing tensions and emerging trends. Complementing other techniques, ethnographic tools proved particularly critical in further unravelling the intricacies of the transformation and construction processes and the role of key actors with the women's groups themselves, and delving into sensitive topics around culture, religion and local power. In the research analysis, I drew partly on techniques derived from critical realism, such as those articulated by Bygstad and Munkvold (2011). This included: (i) initially, drafting a rich description of situations, events and roles of different actors in the course of institutional transformation and development; (ii) second, identifying key components of these descriptions; (iii) third, reflecting upon the theory and emerging research findings; (iv) fourth, identifying key mechanisms in institutional processes, and examining the subtle influence of structure and agency; (v) fifth, analysing those mechanisms; and (vi) finally, consolidating research material with cross-case analysis.

7 In Cases 1 and 2, it is worth noting that the experiences of other participating villages (in the respective women's enterprise) were appreciated in the course of the research, including some 'near project failures'. These (less secure) villages required extensive efforts in social mobilisation due to pervasive levels of mistrust, and limited (male and female) leadership. Due to their instability, however, these villages were deemed off limits for either simple visits, or intensive research.

8 Urban-based sales had increased by 75 per cent in the 12 months prior to the research.
9 A highly successful concept developed initially in India, self-help groups (SHGs) or savings and credit groups (SCGs) organise people (approximately 15–20 in one group) with similar economic backgrounds to learn basic accounting, and initiate and expand economic activities. Group cohesiveness, financial discipline and business skills are developed through regular group meetings with savings, internal lending/repayments and capacity building. When groups mature, the NGO may facilitate access to external financing for new or existing family-based enterprises. When groups mature further, the whole group or parts of them may evolve into producer groups. Loyalty to the group is viewed as important, as this is considered to increase the strength of the group and enable joint action, increasing the bargaining power of group members. In Afghanistan, self-help groups are usually formed in coordination with the local village councils, and participants are selected from common wealth backgrounds and those with an interest in joint collaboration for savings and potentially productive activities (Ritchie, 2009).
10 At the time of the research, the village women farmers were producing, on average, over 150,000 kg of produce annually per community.
11 It is important to note that during the INGO support period, the villages had begun marketing using a common label (with the INGO name).

References

Baert, P. (2005) 'Critical realism', in P. Baert (ed.), *Philosophy of the Social Sciences: Towards Pragmatism*, Cambridge: Polity Press.

Battilana, J. (2012) 'Change agents, networks, and institutions: a contingency theory of organizational change', *Academy of Management Journal*, 55(2): 381–98.

Battilana, J., Leca, B. and Boxenbaum, E. (2009) 'How actors change institutions: towards a theory of institutional entrepreneurship', *The Academy of Management Annals: A Journal of the Academy of Management*, 3(1): 65–107.

Baumol, W. (1968) 'Entrepreneurship in economic theory', *The American Economic Review*, 58(2): 64–71.

Baumol, W. (1990) 'Entrepreneurship: productive, unproductive and destructive', *The Journal of Political Economy*, 98(5): 893–921.

Berger, P. and Luckmann, T. (1966) *The Social Construction of Reality*, New York: Doubleday.

Bhaskar, R.A. (1975/1997) *A Realist Theory of Science* (2nd edn), London: Verso.

Binks, M. and Vale, P. (1990) *Entrepreneurship and Economic Change*, Maidenhead, UK: McGraw-Hill.

Brousseau, E. and Raynaud, E. (2007) 'The economics of multilevel governance', unpublished working paper.

Bygstad, B. and Munkvold, B.E. (2011) 'In search of mechanisms: conducting a critical realist data analysis', presented at *The Thirty Second International Conference on Information Systems*, Shanghai, China.

Campbell, J.L., Hollingsworth, J.R. and Lindberg, L. (eds) (1991) *The Governance of the American Economy*, Cambridge and New York: Cambridge University Press.

Chang, H.-J. (2002) 'Breaking the mould: an institutionalist political economy alternative to the neo-liberal theory of the market and the state', *Cambridge Journal of Economics*, 26(5): 539–59.

Chang, H.-J. and Evans, P. (2000) 'The role of institutions in economic change', *Proceedings of the 'Other Canon' Group*, Venice, Italy, 13–14 January.

Ciarli, T., Parto, S. and Savona, M. (2009) 'Conflict and entrepreneurial activity in Afghanistan: findings from the national risk vulnerability assessment data', *UNU WIDER Discussion Paper for Workshop on Entrepreneurship and Conflict INCORE*, University of Ulster, Northern Ireland, 20–21 March.

Davern, M. (1997) 'Social networks and economic sociology: a proposed research agenda for a more complete social science', *American Journal of Economics and Sociology*, 56(3): 287–302.

Dewey, J. (1938) *Logic: The Theory of Enquiry*, New York: Holt.

Fay, B. (1996) *Contemporary Philosophy of Social Science*, Oxford: Blackwell.

Fligstein, N. (2001) 'Social skill and the theory of fields', *Sociological Theory*, 19(2): 105–25.

Gaventa, J. (2003) *Power after Lukes: A Review of the Literature*, Brighton, UK: Institute of Development Studies.

Gaventa, J. (2006) 'Finding the spaces for change: a power analysis', *IDS Bulletin*, 37(6): 23–33.

Geertz, C. (1995) *After the Fact*, Cambridge, MA: Harvard University Press.

Greenwood, R. and Hinings, C.R. (1996) 'Understanding radical organizational change: bringing together the old and the new institutionalism', *Academy of Management Review*, 21(4): 1022–54.

Greenwood, R., and Hinings, C.R. (2006) 'Radical organizational change', in S.R. Clegg, C. Hardy, T.B. Lawrence and W.R. Nord (eds), *Sage Handbook of Organisation Studies*, London: Sage.

Greenwood, R., Suddaby, R. and Hinings, C.R. (2002) 'Theorizing change: the role of professional associations in the transformation of institutionalized fields', *Academy of Management Journal*, 45(1): 58–80.

Hall, P. and Taylor, R. (1996) 'Political science and the three new institutionalisms', *Political Studies*, 44(4): 936–57.

Hodgson, G. (1988) *Economics and Institutions: A Manifesto for a Modern Institutional Economics*, Cambridge: Polity.

Hodgson, G. (1998) 'The approach of institutional economics', *Journal of Economic Literature*, 36: 166–92.

Hodgson, G. (1999) *Evolution and Institutions: An Evolutionary Economics and the Evolution of Economics*, Cheltenham, UK: Edward Elgar.

Hodgson, G. (2003) 'The hidden persuaders, institutions and individuals in economic theory', *Cambridge Journal of Economics*, 27: 159–75.

Hodgson, G. (2004a) 'Reclaiming habit for institutional economics', *Journal of Economic Psychology*, 25: 651–60.

Hodgson, G. (2004b) *The Evolution of Institutional Economics: Agency, Structure and Darwinism in American Institutionalism*, London: Routledge.

Hodgson, G. (2007) 'Institutions and individuals: interaction and evolution', *Organisation Studies*, 28(1): 95–111.

Hollingsworth, J.R. (2002) 'Some reflections on how institutions influence styles of innovation', Paper for *Swedish Collegium for Advanced Study of the Social Sciences*, 26 September, available at: http://history.wisc.edu/hollingsworth/documents/Some_ Reflections_on_How_Institutions_Influence_Styles_of_Innovation.htm, accessed 1 December 2012.

Hollingsworth, J.R. and Boyer, R. (1997) 'Coordination of economic actors and social systems of production', in J.R. Hollingsworth and R. Boyer (eds), *Contemporary Capitalism*, Cambridge: Cambridge University Press.

Kaplinsky, R. and Morris, M. (2000) *A Handbook for Value Chain Research*, London: IDRC.

Klyver, K. and Schott, T. (2011) 'How social network structure shapes entrepreneurial intentions?', *Journal of Global Entrepreneurship Research*, 1(1): 3–19.

Koene, B.A.S. (2006) 'Situated human agency, institutional entrepreneurship and institutional change', *Journal of Organizational Change Management*, 19(3): 365–82.

Kristiansen, S. (2004) 'Social networks and business success: the role of subcultures in an African context', *The American Journal of Economics and Sociology*, 63(5): 1149–71.

Lawson, T. (1997) 'Realism, explanation and science', in T. Lawson (ed.), *Economics and Reality*, London: Routledge.

North, D. (1989) 'Institutions and economic growth: a historical introduction', *World Development*, 17(9): 1319–32.

North, D. (1990) *Institutions, Institutional Change and Economic Performance*, Cambridge: Cambridge University Press.

Ostrom, E. (1990) *Governing the Commons: The Evolution of Institutions for Collective Action*, Cambridge: Cambridge University Press.

Ostrom, E. (2005) *Understanding Institutional Diversity*, Princeton, NJ and Oxford: Princeton University Press.

Polanyi, K. (1944/2001) *The Great Transformation: The Political and Economic Origins of Our Time*, Boston, MA: Beacon Press.

Portes, A. (2006) 'Institutions and development: a conceptual reanalysis', *Population and Development Review*, 2(2): 233–62.

Powell, W.W. and DiMaggio, P.J. (1991) *The New Institutionalism in Organizational Analysis*, Chicago, IL: University of Chicago Press.

Ritchie, H. (2009) 'Hand in Hand Afghanistan organisation external progress review and lessons learnt report, mass mobilisation into entrepreneurship project (through SHGs)', Balkh, Afghanistan, unpublished.

Sayer, A. (2000) *Key Features of Critical Realism: Realism and Social Science*, London: Sage.

Schumpeter, J.A. (1934) *The Theory of Economic Development*, Cambridge, MA: Harvard University Press.

Schwandt, T. (2000) 'Three epistemological stances for qualitative inquiry', in N. Denzin and Y. Lincoln (eds), *Handbook of Qualitative Research*, Thousand Oaks, CA: Sage Publications.

Stern, R.N., and Barley, S.R. (1996) 'Organizations and social systems: the neglected mandate', *Administrative Science Quarterly*, 41(1): 146–62.

Sumner, A. and Tribe, M. (2004) 'The nature of epistemology and methodology in development studies: what do we mean by rigour?', Paper prepared for The Nature of Development Studies DSA Annual Conference, 'Bridging Research and Policy', Church House, London, 6 November.

Williamson, O.E. (1985) *The Economic Institutions of Capitalism*, New York: The Free Press.

Williamson, O.E. (2000) 'The new institutional economics: taking stock, looking ahead', *Journal of Economic Literature*, 38: 595–613.

2 The ubiquity of institutions

Shaping economic development

> To understand institutions, one needs to know what they are, how and why they are crafted and sustained, and what consequences they generate in diverse settings.
>
> (Ostrom, 2005: 3)

In this second chapter, the prevailing discourse on institutional change is examined as an overarching framework for this book, and key themes are introduced for subsequent exploration. Challenging the dominant institutional standpoint entrenched in neoclassical principles, I specifically review more heterodox economics discussions, incorporating social, cultural and political dimensions. I draw attention to power and interests, evolutionary perspectives, and economic sociology towards appreciating the interaction of structure and agency in institutional development. In unwrapping actor roles in institutional processes, I highlight 'institutional entrepreneurs' and emphasise institutional activity as embedded in social networks. Finally, I turn to the particular situation of developing country environments, and the dominance of informal institutions affecting agency, power dynamics and trust, influencing institutional processes and broader outcomes in economic development.

2.1 Towards a paradigm shift in theories of institutional change

In 1776, Adam Smith famously postulated that gains made from trade are the key to the wealth of nations, and that the size of the market was a function of specialisation and the division of labour. Indeed, the Industrial Revolution precipitated the process of specialisation and trade towards the evolution of modern market societies with monetarised exchange of goods and services. However, it is only recently that economists have recognised that this exchange process is not without costs to economic agents, and that these 'transaction costs', and importantly the *institutions* influencing them, are central to the performance and development of economies.

Spurred in the early 1900s, and revitalised recently, institutional discussions have embraced wide-ranging topics in an attempt to understand the role of institutions in economic development. Institutions are now recognised as playing a central function in economies, and these insights have received considerable attention with several scholars honoured as Nobel laureates (including Douglass North, 1993; Eleanor Ostrom, 2009 and Oliver Williamson, 2009). Yet there is still much debate over the nature and emergence of institutions, the relations between them, and their impact on economic development. Three main approaches have been posited that attempt to explain the influence of institutions in the economy, and the process of institutional change and development. An early perspective emerged at the turn of the twentieth century, known as *(Old) institutional economics*, and this has seen a recent revival in light of broader discussions in the social sciences (e.g. Hodgson, 2000, 2004). Meanwhile, in the last three decades, the neoclassical-based approach *New institutional economics* has been introduced and tended to dominate economic thinking (e.g. North, 1989). Finally, drawing attention to theories of 'embeddedness', *Economic sociology* has also been conceived (e.g. Granovetter, 1992), chiefly in reaction to new institutional economics. Institutional discussions now straddle diverse and wide-ranging fields from anthropology and sociology to history, political science and economics, challenging notions of functionalism and individualism. Debates tend to diverge on perspectives related to core neoclassical principles, in particular actor-centric explanations and the influence of social structure. Yet while the general theory has seen significant progress (although empirical evidence is still thin), a 'shared' reflection remains constrained by the 'existing compartmentalization of the social sciences' (Hodgson, 2004: 447). Maseland (2011) elaborates on three major structural biases in the dominant discourse on institutional economics, namely in under-examining differences in kind (often studies focus on one particular institution yet several institutions may be co-exerting an influence on specific issues), in neglect of interaction (between societies and other institutions) and in representing societies from a partial perspective (i.e. not appreciating the local context). He argues for a greater appreciation of institutions within their institutional context, and ensuring a dynamic perspective of societal evolution and interaction through the lens of the country concerned.

2.1.1 Beyond rationality: the influence of history, culture and power

> ... past, present and future economic growth is not a mere function of development, technology and preferences. It is a complex process in which the organisation of society plays a significant role. The organisation of society itself, however, reflects historical, cultural, social, political and economic processes ...
>
> (Greif, cited in Woolcock, 1998: 187)

The original approach to institutional economics grew out of a failure of neoclassical economics to explain the broad institutional framework within which economic transactions take place, and how such institutions shape and are shaped by human behaviour. Emerging in the early twentieth century and precipitated particularly by Darwinism, the debate was spearheaded by US economists such as

Thorstein Veblen, John Commons, Wesley Clair Mitchell and John Dunlop, and famously drew on broad disciplines, such as psychology, sociology, law, biology and politics, with minimal economic theory. Veblen (1898) explored evolutionary ideas such as natural selection, and emphasised institutions as 'repositories of knowledge', and highlighted the influence of 'habits' on institutional processes (Hodgson, 2004: 9). Other classical thinkers inspiring this movement included Karl Marx, Joseph Schumpeter and Karl Polanyi. Recently, old institutional economics debates have been reactivated, and generated a spin-off championed by Chang (2002), known as *Institutionalist Political Economy* (IPE) due to its emphasis on power structures (and history) shaping actor behaviour. This perspective contrasts with NIE, which narrowly views actors as rational and independent, maximising their utility, with preferences set as exogenous and steady. In maintaining this position, NIE has been criticised for applying 'classroom economics' to 'real-world' situations where individuals and organisations are involved with economic transactions and production (Dorward *et al.*, 2005).

Today's OIE approach rechallenges mainstream views in arguing that economics cannot be separated from the social, political and cultural systems in which they are embedded. According to Hodgson (2000), the most important characteristic of institutionalism is the notion that individuals are indeed both 'socially and institutionally constituted'. And going beyond just 'efficiency' outcomes, Chang and Evans (2005) highlights three critical functions of institutions in fostering economic development: learning and innovation, income redistribution and social cohesion. Further, while in neoclassical economics the market is perceived as the 'ideal' mechanism for coordinating economic activity, Hollingsworth and Boyer (1997: 3) elaborate on the existence of diverse 'institutional arrangements' with different degrees of agent interest and power, influencing actor 'needs, preferences and choices'. And they emphasise that a single optimum institutional arrangement does not exist. Taking a broad perspective, heterodox economics discussions have highlighted the significance of sociocultural institutions, power struggles and agency in institutional change and development.

Sociocultural institutions shaped by history, beliefs and practices, driven by cognition

In particular, the evolving OIE debate has looked at the significance of historical legacies and culture in institutional development and change. Arguing against the logic of the neoclassical paradigm, there is recognition that existing social and cultural institutions influence both economic and non-economic behaviour. In this view, the complex interplay between social norms, values, belief systems and their cultural heritage shape how agents interact with and develop institutions. Weber's (1904) classic *Protestant Ethic* earlier postulated a religious foundation to capitalist behaviour. But such a cultural determinant approach subsequently came under attack in the 1960s and 1980s from neo-Marxists and postmodernists (Fukuyama, 2003: 4). In recent decades, culturalist explanations of economic behaviour have been revisited. Platteau (1994, 2000) has expanded ideas on non-economic influences in the economy in studies of social norms and economic development. Platteau drew attention to African societies and the origins of highly egalitarian norms with restraints on individual wealth, which he argues has led to 'cultural' obstacles to accumulation and subsequent economic growth (Platteau, 2000). Fukuyama (2003) elaborates on a wide range of areas of human behaviour that are in fact non-rational in origin (i.e. non-optimising behaviour) such as actions based on religious belief, inherited social habits and other deeply embedded cultural values. Meanwhile, Chang and Evans (2005: 11) highlights dominant cultural influences generating broader sets of social institutions. He describes the example of Japan and their rice-growing culture within a heavily populated, disaster-prone environment, which promoted institutions of social cooperation. And emphasising the influence of historical experience on subsequent institutional development, Greif (2006) pointed to the example of the 'community responsibility system' as an existing institution that functioned in Europe from medieval to modern times, which fostered gradual institutional development through 'self-governed communes'.

Further to this, and disputing the notion of institutions as merely restrictive (North, 1989, 1990), Streeck (1997) draws on a 'Durkheimian' sociological perspective, describing certain social institutions that can act as 'beneficial constraints' ensuring actors behave within certain boundaries, thus limiting individual volition and the pursuit of self-interest. Yet the solution is not to simply transplant institutions from one context to another. Hollingsworth (2002: 14) warns of 'serious limitations' in the potential imitation of institutions (e.g. rules and norms) of other societies (or 'institutional monocropping'; Evans, 2004), since each institution is 'interdependent' with other institutions. Citing Roland (1990), Hollingsworth described how existing institutional arrangements might inhibit certain institutional innovations while enabling others. Meanwhile, Roland (2004) described the 'slow moving' pace of change of cultural institutions in contrast to the 'fast moving' institutions such as legal rules and organisational systems. Exploring the varying levels of sociocultural institutions, Portes (2006: 237) differentiates between the influence of culture in the 'realm of values, cognitive frameworks and accumulated knowledge' (with values underlying norms), and social structure in the 'realm of interests, individual and collective', reinforced by varying degrees of power, and draws links between them at the individual and collective level. Douglas (1986: 91) brilliantly draws attention to human cognition in particular, and its dependence on institutions, with institutions built by 'squeezing each other's ideas into a common shape' to gain legitimacy by 'sheer numbers'. Douglas describes the stabilisation of institutions and the gaining of legitimacy through 'distinctive grounding in nature and reason', and the development of cognitive conventions, or 'analogies' (masking their human origin). Related to this, Powell and DiMaggio (1991: 26) highlight Bourdieu's innovative (cognitive) concept of *habitus*, related to people's common histories and backgrounds, as leading to shared thoughts, dispositions and strategies of action. This may explain why actors behave in certain ways and reproduce social structures, influencing institutional development.

Recognising the significance of societal and actor influences in later work, North (2003: 4) has now emphasised the cultural heritage of individuals (i.e. the deeply embedded institutions and aggregated beliefs 'carried forward' over generations – path-dependent patterns), in addition to new positive and negative experiences. These beliefs and experiences are argued to fundamentally shape the way that we perceive the world and comprehend what is happening around us, and influence our response. Such awareness of the world is considered to lower 'information costs' and increase our ability to understand what makes economies work, but it also may constrain behaviour and perpetuate inefficiency (North, 2003: 5). Clearly, it is critical to appreciate the background of a society and cultural heritage (and the dynamic shifts as societies evolve) to understand the emergence of dynamic institutions with 'complex chains of causality', and particularly the 'interplay' between the formal rules and the informal norms (North, 2003). And drawing off psychology in vein with sociological debates, North *et al.* (2004) further contend that an examination of underlying *cognitive processes*, and individual/collective learning, is crucial to analysing institutional emergence, and their economic and political outcomes. This notably moves NIE away from its original standpoint. While these theories resonate with the broader debate, it is difficult to see how such ideas can still be integrated into the neoclassical framework underpinning NIE.

Incorporating power and interests into institutional development

Bringing in the role of actors, traditional game theorists (e.g. Schotter, 1981) view institutions as the 'equilibrium solutions' from 'repeated games' between competing actors. Taking a more nuanced approach, other scholars argue for a greater appreciation of the role of power across actors in institutional development with design influenced not just by efficiency (e.g. Perrow, 1986; Bardhan, 1989; Bowles *et al.*, 1993). IPE critics suggest that the NIE approach suffers from the inherent 'flaws of neoclassical economics' as human behaviour is reduced to 'rational' and economic processes deemed as 'efficient', with little recognition of social and political dimensions (e.g. Chang and Evans, 2000). From an institutional political economy perspective, the notion of power is elaborated in institutional development. Challenging the NIE's view that interests are 'exogenously' assigned at an individual level (Chang and Evans, 2000: 17), proponents of institutional political economy view interests as being framed by existing institutions, and institutional change involving changing power balances between existing interests with changes to prevailing institutional structures. The construction of new institutions may also involve 'power struggles' between different interest groups as they wrestle for political power to gain some control over the 'rules of the game', and build 'asymmetries' within the economy (Marghlin, 1991). In this regard, economic institutions may be described as 'political and social constructions' (Hollingsworth and Boyer, 1997: 450). Eggertsson draws attention to states where there is a lack of information and endogenous politics, which can affect institutional design and may bring increased transaction costs (Eggertsson, 1997: 1193).

Hollingsworth and Boyer (1997) describe the process of institutionalisation as further embedded in the potential intentions and interests of the different groups involved. Contesting both rationalism and functionalism, Streeck (2002) suggests that preliminary institutional design by actors may indeed be random and unintended, but these institutions may later be fitted with existing institutions or made 'complementary' through entrepreneurial creativity in the given conditions but remain dynamic. Meanwhile, drawing particular attention to the effects of power of different actors, Knight (1992) describes institutional development and change as by-products of 'distributional conflict', shaped by 'asymmetries of power in a society'. Advancing theory further, Campbell (1997) suggests that most change in existing institutions may take place through a process of delimited selection, as permitted by the existing arrangements, in addition to prevailing power relations. Differentiating between incremental and radical institutional change, he holds that radical institutional change particularly occurs when social actors with diverse norms/interests clash with one another generating changes in the interpretation of problems and interests. Yet individual action may also be shaped by the influence of institutions on decision-making. Friedland and Alford (1991: 251) describe existing institutions as affecting both institutional processes, as well as their outcomes. Returning to Douglas (1986), they highlight institutions influencing conceptions of needs, preferences and choices. Ostrom (1990) looked at the development of institutions as further shaped by the local context, in addition to actor capacities and interests. Similarly, Maseland (2011) underscored a need to examine specific circumstances to assess relevant institutions within the context, the interaction between institutions, and (multiple) institutional effects.

These broader OIE/IPE perspectives have generated useful insights into institutional change mechanisms. In institutional development, existing institutions, actors and the wider context can affect both the scope of the institutional process and institutional outcomes. These factors may act as both barriers and resources. Chang emphasises institutions not just as 'constraints' on economic behaviour, but also as 'enabling' and 'constitutive' (Chang and Evans, 2000: 8). And while existing institutions are crucial in institutional change, Lawson suggests that related human agency should be considered as equally significant (Lawson, 1997).

Institutional outcomes: shaped by powerful actors and existing institutions

Looking closer towards institutional outcomes, this may reflect a 'hierarchy involving a constitutional order' and 'the way constituent members play the game' (Hollingsworth and Boyer, 1997: 453). Further, Hollingsworth (2002) suggests that different 'institutional arrangements' and different 'social systems of production' (i.e. the integration of society's institutions, its institutional arrangements and its institutional sectors) may generate different types of economic performance. Yet while there may be institutional stability at the macro level providing an overall 'cognitive framework' guiding how individuals navigate reality, at the micro level individuals may be more autonomous; and there may be significant institutional diversity, emphasising the importance of micro-level analysis (ibid.). Hollingsworth draws on Hodgson (1988), who argues that 'most institutions exist in a temporal sense, prior to the individuals in any given society'. And in terms of institutional outcomes, these may ultimately reflect a balance of the pursuit of self-interest, social obligation, social relations and prevailing power asymmetries (Hollingsworth and Boyer, 1997: 53). Chang (2002) argues that competing cultures and traditions may exist within one society, and that political choices may ultimately determine the institutional development path. Chang describes the hierarchy of rules resulting from power struggles between affected groups (ibid.). Adding to these insights, Hollingsworth (2002: 6) points to Legro (1997), who highlights the differing strengths of actual norms and rules themselves, as indicated by their 'simplicity' (in how well they are interpreted and ease of application), their 'durability' (in terms of how long they were in existence and their legitimacy), and their 'concordance' (in terms of the breadth of application). Those norms and rules that are more durable tend to play a greater role in shaping societies and contributing to path dependence. Meanwhile, Brousseau and Raynard (2007) describe the influence of 'time and space' on institutional flexibility and strength, with earlier stage institutions more adaptable but (still) threatened by alternative rules. In their theoretical paper, they discuss institutional options that are available from different localities. They describe the launching of a competitive process, as institutions created locally by self-interested actors participate in a 'race for generalisation'. They suggest that local lower-level institutional arrangements tend to seek to become part of 'higher order institutions' in the overall institutional framework, in a concept they describe as 'climbing the ladder'. Yet actor interests may be more nuanced than this, and actors may be further influenced by environmental effects, or even other actors. And as much as institutions influence economic development, Chang (2011) describes economic development itself as influencing the nature of institutions. He describes economic development as triggering agents to demand new and better quality institutions, and permitting the 'affordability' of these new institutions.

2.1.2 An evolutionary approach to institutional development

> Although economics is not reducible to biology, propositions in economics must be consistent with those in biology.
>
> (Hodgson, 2003: 163)

Taking a step closer to the original institutional discourse, several prominent economists explore an evolutionary approach to institutional development. Old institutional economics introduced the idea of evolutionary processes in the development of institutions (Veblen, 1898), following the influential publication of Darwin's *Origin of Species*. This was later revived by Hamilton (1953). Both emphasised the importance of Darwinism, and processes of natural change. Outside the realm of just biology, they contended that evolutionary thinking had important relevance for social science, although a systematic theoretical approach to this was not conceived (Hodgson, 2003). Nelson and Winter (1982) were two prominent modern evolutionists who revisited this topic under the theme of 'evolutionary economics', and examined key economic concepts and topics through evolutionary language. In their influential book *An Evolutionary Theory of Economic Change*, Nelson and Winter (1982) view institutional development in evolutionary terms with institutions resulting from random variation, selection and retention. In this way, they draw on an evolutionary orientated approach which essentially attempts to use principles derived from biology to look at variable change over time and the dynamic processes behind the observed change (Nelson, 1995: 54). Yet Nelson theorises that while institutions are evolutionary, they do not pursue unidirectional evolutionary pathways (ibid.). Indeed, a full adoption of biological theories or terminology may not in fact be helpful. But arguably, a general evolutionary approach has facilitated deeper understandings of the interaction between agents and institutions. It has also stimulated an appreciation of more subtle dynamics precipitating institutional processes. Nelson (2002) still views technology development as the main driving force behind institutional change, however, but evolutionary thinking begs a broader incorporation of both agent and structural influences.

Role of habit in institutional change

Advancing evolutionary ideas put forward by the old institutional economists, a major contribution to economic thinking has been in the insights generated into the role of 'habit' (Hodgson, 1997, 2003, 2004, 2007). Habit is described as the 'constitutive material of institutions, providing them with enhanced durability, power and normative authority' (Hodgson, 2004: 425). Chang (2002) sees this as the 'hallmark' of a truly institutionalist approach. The role of human habits has been identified as particularly significant by OIE in the development of institutions. Originally postulated by Veblen (1909), habitual behaviour is considered to dominate rationality. In vein with Veblen and Commons, Hodgson describes individuals creating and shaping institutions, as much as institutions themselves moulding individuals, influencing individual motivations and broader preferences (Hodgson, 2000: 326). These principles have been used to further understand broader patterns of behaviour such as habits, and their relation to rules (Hodgson, 1997, 2003, 2004). In general, rules are considered patterns of conscious or deliberate behaviour adopted by agents (Murphy 1994, cited in Hodgson, 1997: 664) (i.e. 'in circumstances X, do Y'). Meanwhile, habit is described as the acquired propensities to do things, and defined as a largely 'unconscious tendency' by agents to 'engage in a previously adopted or acquired form of action' (Hodgson, 1997: 664) (i.e. 'in circumstances X, action Y follows'). With this logic, a rule can become a more engrained 'habit', and as Hodgson points out, it is therefore easier to break a rule than to change a habit.

Towards understanding the emergence and modification of habits, Hodgson (2003) examines the way that institutions subtly influence individual habits and dispositions in an innovative concept called '*reconstitutive downward causation*'. This challenges Packard (1957) and Galbraith's (1969) simplistic view that information is purely manipulative, or informative (Becker and Stigler, 1977). Taking a more nuanced perspective, Hodgson suggests that institutions have a 'hidden and pervasive' ability to shape individual aspirations. A concept originating from psychology (Sperry, 1964, 1969), *reconstitutive downward causation* refers to a psychological process where both individuals and populations are constrained, but also influenced by causal powers at higher ontological levels (individual preferences and dispositions). From the evolutionary viewpoint, lower ontological processes (i.e. agents) can thus both generate changes within, and be influenced by, higher ontological processes (i.e. institutions). Institutions are conceived to be social structures with this 'capacity' for reconstitutive downward causation, influencing deep-seated habits of thought and action. Institutions are thus deemed to not only inhibit and enable behaviour, and be dependant on the activities of individuals, but also influence and shape individual habitual dispositions, which in turn can modify individual understandings, purposes and preferences. Hodgson (2003) suggests reconstitutive downward causation goes beyond Becker's narrow view that individual purposes/choices are simply moulded by institutions (Becker, 1996). And *upward causation* (individuals to institutions) may also be possible towards a potential 'positive feedback' loop and a 'self-reinforcing institutional structure'.

Recently, Hodgson (2007) applied this theory to look at social structures, and organisations as a special type of 'bounded' institution. He rejects the positions of methodological individualism, methodological collectivism and reductionism. Taking a more balanced stance between structure and agency, and building off Giddens' *'structuration theory'* (1984), he suggests that individuals should be considered alongside 'structure' (relations between individuals) for a 'fuller two way explanation' (Hodgson, 2007: 106). He describes organisations as dependent on the existence of complex habits, and labels these as 'routines'. Both habits and routines are considered to be institutions evolved out of practice and regularity. He contends that congruent habits may also lead to congruent purposes and beliefs. Individual habits can thus become socio-economic institutions if shared and reinforced by society or groups, in the same vein, that cultural values and norms can be linked to institutions. Such evolutionary ideas have taken institutional discourse into new realms of understanding, highlighting the link between institutions, and human beliefs and behaviour. Yet Hodgson (2003) calls for more empirical research to understand the way that 'institutions mould human agents', and an examination of different cultures, circumstances and cases.

2.1.3 Incorporating social structure and embeddedness

In further debating the ideals of self-interest and rational behaviour in NIE, the introduction of *economic sociology* has drawn crucial attention to classical sociological theories, particularly the theory of 'embeddedness' in institutional development. Polanyi (1944) famously described the 'socially embedded' nature of exchange in pre-capitalist or traditional societies, contrasting with exchange systems in modern capitalist societies. Economic sociologists argue that economic activity is often nested within social relations and networks spanning family, religion, and ethnicity (Hamilton, 1991; Whitley, 1992), particularly in less formal contexts where 'word-of-mouth' systems operate and formal institutions are lacking. Granovetter (1985: 49) highlighted the role of such relations in generating trust and minimising 'malfeasance'. Rejecting the 'oversocialized view' where agents pursue customs, habits or norms automatically/unconditionally, and the 'undersocialized view' where agent behaviour is unaffected by existing social institutions, Granovetter posed a more balanced perspective, arguing that agent behaviour is entrenched in ongoing systems of social relations (Granovetter, 1985).

Social networks: enabling and constraining

Davern (1997) defined a social network as a series of formal and informal ties, or relations, between a central actor (or group) and broader actors. Further to this, Lin (1999) highlights two core observations: first, that social networks influence the outcomes of actions; and second, that the nature of resources obtained from social networks are influenced by people's positions and by the strength of ties. Bringing in culture and class, Nordstrom (2000) emphasises the entrenchment of such social networks in prevailing social rules of exchange and codes of conduct (i.e. social institutions), and societal hierarchies of deference and power. Davern (1997: 299) suggests that social networks can be used to understand the scope of labour markets, organisations, exchange processes and transaction costs. The economics literature has demonstrated pathways through which social networks and relations – or 'social capital' – have positively facilitated productivity growth, technology adoption and access to informal finance (e.g. Durlauf and Fafchamps, 2004). Meanwhile, van Staveren and Knorringa (2007) highlight the importance of social relationships and networks in influencing access to, and productivity over economic resources. In particular, Kristiansen (2004) showed that networks enable entrepreneurs to reduce risks and transaction costs, and can improve access to business ideas, knowledge, and capital. Yet social networks can also be exclusionary, and this may be socially or self-regulated (Chantarat and Barrett, 2007). For example, people may be barred from networks, or choose not to engage, due to association with a particular social group (e.g. age, gender, ethnicity, religion, caste, disability), circumstance (e.g. geography, migration, illness, disaster), a lack of assets, or trading activities (Harriss-White, 2003a, 2003b; Johnson, 2006; Turner, 2007). Such exclusionary elements have been highlighted as significant in polarised economies (Mogues and Carter, 2005). Embedded in institutions and power, Field (2003) summarised four ways that social capital or networks may influence institutions, equality and inclusion: first, access to types of social networks may not be equally distributed; second, social capital in networks may be used negatively to disadvantage others; third, social capital may benefit members, but reproduce inequality or have unintended consequences; and fourth, social capital may dampen incentives of those in a group to participate in individually beneficial activities.

Social relations matter in institutional development

Looking through the lens of dense social relations and their effects, Hollingsworth and Boyer (1997: 451) describe the value of social embeddedness, with tradition and trust used to construct 'useful and efficient economic institutions'. Yet while such embeddedness is perceived to be strongly the case for less formal economies, social scientists disagree with the 'traditional' versus 'capitalist' dichotomy and contend that market exchange even in modern capitalist economies is in fact often still strongly linked to social relationships. Taking a hybrid position, Grabowski (1999: 799) suggests that impersonal exchange may eventually arise out of the 'vigorous development of socially embedded exchange'. Building off the view that economic goals are socially embedded, Granovetter (1992) later incorporates an efficiency objective in the notion of socially embedded 'collective action' and 'group coordination'. Inspired by Granovetter's 'embedded' approach and emerging out of political economy, the *regulation school* of thinking underlines the 'social embedded and socially regulated' nature of economies (Jessop, 1997, 1998). With a focus on social relations, this economics approach has particularly explored ways in which economies are exposed to dynamic market and non-market forces, causing economic agents to act in certain ways. This has included reflections on the formulation of government policy, and environmental, economic and social regulations, all of which have transformed economies.

Beyond relations in markets and the economy, Portes (2006: 239) draws attention to the deep-seated nature of social relations and power within social life itself influencing the scope of institutional development in local economies, building off Marx and Weber. He emphasises Bourdieu (1985) and the command of resources by dominant classes, including wealth, influence of others and knowledge/culture, generating status hierarchies. He describes the transformation of existing institutions as meeting significant resistance from power holders in the social structure. Pre-existing bonds and social relations may also influence agent behaviour and efficiency seeking, and subsequent institutional design (Gomez, 2008: 255). Highlighting the limitations of exogenous interventions, Boettke *et al.* (2008) describe the innovative concept of 'institutional stickiness', or the likely success of institutional change, as related to how well new institutions are linked to 'indigenous agents in the previous time period'. Meanwhile, pushing the theory further, Hollingsworth and Boyer (1997: 470) describe the innovative concept of institutional 'nestedness' with higher-level global institutions nested in (and vulnerable to) lower-level local institutions in a complex institutional system. Overall, the broad debates of economic sociology, and related discourses, have emphasised the embedded nature of social relations, and more diverse forms of power by agents and within the environment, influencing both agent behaviour and institutional interaction, adding another crucial dimension to the institutional discourse. However, the discussions between old institutional economics (and evolutionary insights) and these more sociological debates still remain largely disconnected.

2.1.4 Towards an appreciation of the interaction of structure and agency

Drawing the discourse closer together, institutional theories are embedded in ongoing critical debates on the influence of 'structure and agency'. Following the elaboration of concepts of 'social structure' by Marx and Durkheim, Parsons (1937) developed an initial theory of social action in sociology, prompting and stimulating the subsequent debate on structure and agency. Expanding ideas, Bourdieu (1977) emphasised three major interconnected concepts to explain human action that are still much theorised in sociology: 'field', referring to a social domain comprising sets of relations in a configuration or network and embedded power dynamics; 'capital', referring to the resources of actors; and the much less explored notion of 'habitus' (as discussed earlier), described as the 'relatively durable principles of judgment and practice generated by an actor's early life experiences and modified (to a greater or a lesser degree) later in life' (Emirbayer and Johnson, 2008: 4). The concept of 'field' has been adopted in organisational analysis ('organisational field') and described as 'a recognized area of institutional life' (DiMaggio and Powell, 1991: 64), comprising sets of relations between actors in a similar (social/economic/political) sphere. The concept of 'capital' has been used in various forms to describe an actor's level of resources, particularly the popular notion of 'social capital', relating to the scope of actor's social relations. More recent debates have endeavoured to explore notions of agency. Long (2001) emphasised the central role of human agency with actors playing an active role in shaping their own and others' lives. In standing between structure and agency, Lawson (1997) contended that actions of actors are informed and shaped by social structures such as norms and institutions prevalent in society. And simultaneously, the actions of actors may – individually or collectively – alter and shape the nature of social structure such as norms and institutions. Meanwhile, Emirbayer and Mische (1998) argued that the concept of agency requires an incorporation of temporality to integrate the influence of the past, orientation towards the future and dynamics of the present. Adding to these insights, discussions from organisational studies put forward a multidimensional view of agency, highlighting various actor behavioural characteristics, including 'iteration (habit), projection (imagination) and practical evaluation (judgment)' (Battilana and D'Aunno, 2009).

Advancing theoretical arguments of structure and agency, Hodgson (2004) elaborated a cognitive conception of agency, describing agency as the capacity of agents to 'reflect and deliberate upon the context, options, purpose and possible outcomes of action'. And structure is referred to as a 'set of significant relations between individuals that can lead to causal interactions' (Hodgson, 2004: 13). Related to agents, structure is emphasised to involve rules, norms, meanings and relations. According to Hodgson (2004), the critical agency-structure relationship has been somewhat evaded by modern theorists in social theory. Touched upon earlier, he highlights four common problematic approaches to understanding this relationship that result either in reductionism or conflation. Promoted by scholars such as Hayek (1948), the first approach, 'methodological individualism', tends to view explanations as residing with individuals. Hodgson describes this view as ambiguous and unclear as to whether this also includes individual interactions or social structures, leading to the problem of potentially 'infinite regress'. The second approach is the reverse explanation, and is known as 'methodological collectivism'. This perspective describes structure as the main explanatory unit typical in classical theorists such as Marx, Durkheim, Levi-Strauss and Parsons. In this approach, Hodgson describes limited acknowledgement of individual purpose or dispositions, and the tendency for structural determinism, cultural determinism or economic determinism. Meanwhile, the third all-embracing approach is described to result in 'central conflation' (Archer, 1995). This view is based on a theory of 'structuration' that incorporates both structures and agents (Giddens, 1979, 1984). It highlights the notion of the 'duality of structure', with structure and agency as 'mutually and symmetrically constitutive of each other' and 'routinization' as explaining the persistence of social structures (Hodgson, 2004: 33). In this interpretation, 'human agents create and reproduce social structures, while a socially structured environment shapes human agents' (Jackson, 2003: 731).

Towards resolving reductive or conflation issues, and moving closer to evolutionary thinking, a fourth approach to this structure-agency problem is similar to the third, but makes a conceptual advance in suggesting that agents and structure remain different, rather than 'sinking into each other', in a 'critical realist' perspective (Hodgson, 2004: 435). A key proponent, Bhaskar (1979, 1983) queries Giddens' duality and suggests that agents perceive social structure as externally situated but may reproduce it passively, forcibly or through action (Jackson, 2003: 732). Yet Hodgson (2004) suggests that this critical realist position remains incomplete, and re-proposes this fourth approach with a greater evolutionary dimension in a 'non-conflationary and casually interactive' approach that tries to capture how individual intentions or preferences change. He describes this as anti-reductionist, and incorporating a causal process of time in the relationship between structure and agents. This view encompasses the interactions between individuals, and interactions between individuals and their environment; and causal explanations for 'individual intentions' and the 'human capacity of intentionality' (Hodgson, 2004: 452). With an emphasis on habit, he describes actor and structure as distinct but 'connected in a circle of mutual interaction and interdependence' (Hodgson, 2004: 446).

2.2 Exploring actors and networks

To better understand the influence of particular actors in institutional change, it is evident that a careful analysis of the interaction of structure and agency is required. While path dependence is pervasive, it is clear that actors play a significant role in more disruptive institutional processes. As discussed in the previous section, mainstream economists tend to assume that actors are rational and make optimising decisions. North (1989) contends that prevailing interest groups pressurise or lobby for institutional change, with those with the most bargaining power driving 'efficient' solutions. Institutional political economists draw attention to more nuanced power struggles between actors in the development of institutions with interests structured by existing political, cultural and social institutions (e.g. Chang and Evans, 2000). Others, such as March and Olsen (1989), describe limitations in the capacity of actors for example, to foresee the future or absorb all of the necessary information to make rational decisions. Meanwhile, Hollingsworth (2002) emphasises the myriad strategies that actors may use to navigate an 'uncertain world' (Lanzara, 1998), which may be contradictory in nature in part due to contradictions in existing institutional arrangements. Weakening the concept of the utilitarian individual (or 'power-oriented' organisation), existing diverse – and potentially contradictory – institutions may also shape both individual preferences and organisational interests and behaviours, and these present 'multiple logics' in the transforming of societal relations and institutional development (Friedland and Alford, 1991: 232).

2.2.1 Catalysing change? Entrepreneurs and innovation

While technological development is often viewed as a major driver of institutional change, Joseph Schumpeter (1934) highlighted the inadequacy of the rational actor model in understanding the process of innovation, and emphasised the role of entrepreneurs (Beckert, 2003: 780). Going beyond Weber and the *Protestant Ethic*, and individualistic rationality, Schumpeter spearheaded discourse on entrepreneurship to understand actors and dynamics of change in the economy (Brouwer, 2002: 85). Schumpeter described the entrepreneur as both the 'founder of a new firm and an innovator who breaks up established routines and opposes the old way of doing things' (Brouwer, 2002: 89). The entrepreneur thus disrupts the (stationary) 'circular flow', and actively diverts the economy away from old paths towards new possibilities (ibid.), thus breaking 'path dependence' (Dosi, 1995). In the process, the entrepreneur overcomes the opposition of the environment in 'integrating resources in production for the marketplace' (Li, 2006: 358). Disputing the Marshallian perspective, Schumpeter distinguished between the managers in a firm, responding 'adaptively' to the environments; and the entrepreneurs as leaders, responding 'creatively' (Beckert, 1999: 786). Schumpter famously used the term 'creative destruction', referring to the simultaneous destruction of traditional practices and the generation of innovations in providing new models for fulfilling a task (ibid.). Knight (1921) built on this work and drew attention to notions of uncertainty and perceptiveness (Brouwer, 2002).

As agents of change and innovation, various theorists have endeavoured to explore key characteristics of 'entrepreneurs' (Schumpter, 1934; Baumol, 1968; Leibenstein, 1968; Casson, 1982; Drucker, 1986). Binks and Vale (1990: 18) summarise three different entrepreneurial categories with an understanding of dynamic flux between the groups, and impermanence. First, entrepreneurs may be those that are reactive and respond to market signals, and facilitate the market processes as 'agents of adjustment'. Alternatively, second, entrepreneurs may be those involved with facilitating economic development by the introduction and innovation of ideas, which cause the rearrangement of the 'allocation of factors of production'. Or, third, entrepreneurs may be those that generate gradual improvements to existing products and processes through gradually changing market processes. Baumol (1968) further championed the discourse on entrepreneurs, building on Schumpeter to integrate entrepreneurial insights (and the rewards generated) into discussions on the theory of the firm. More recently, Baumol (1990: 984) takes a more nuanced approach, highlighting productive, unproductive and destructive entrepreneurship, going beyond the purely constructive and innovative entrepreneur to underscore potentially negative and 'parasitical' activities such as organised crime and rent-seeking that can damage the economy.

Unwrapping entrepreneur motivations and strategies

In current discussions, there have been further attempts at differentiation between types of entrepreneurs, integrating their motivations and capacity. In developing contexts, Lazonick (2007) described entrepreneurs as innovating to survive rather than innovating within 'stable parameters'. More expansively, Berner *et al.* (2009) differentiated between 'survivalist' and 'growth' oriented entrepreneurs with different objectives and outcomes. They described the influence of high-risk environments, which can impact upon the nature of entrepreneurial strategies constraining longer-term perspectives. Moving away from this dichotomy, Battilana *et al.* (2009) highlights several studies that indicate a more flexible position, where entrepreneurs may move from one strategy to the other (e.g. Lozano, 1989; Edgcomb and Thetford, 2004). Meanwhile, Baron (2004) emphasises a cognitive perspective which draws attention to the varying behaviour of entrepreneurs as strongly influenced by subjective and possibly biased perceptions. Others consider differing levels of knowledge, experience and skills influencing the scope of entrepreneurial activities (e.g. Wagner and Sternberg, 2004). As evidence of this, Lazear (2005) cites a study by Landier (2002) that demonstrates differences across countries in which part of the 'ability distribution' of entrepreneurs emerge.

2.2.2 *'Institutional entrepreneurs', power and strategic agency*

Closely associated to concepts of institutional change, 'organisational innovation' has been described by sociologists as the 'adoption of an idea or behaviour that is new to an organization' (Hage, 1991: 599). According to Hage (1991: 598), research on organisational innovation has raised issues related to both societal and institutional change, and highlighted the significance of micro and macro levels of analysis. In organisational innovation, the complexity of the division of labour emerges as particularly interesting, since it draws attention to the organisational learning, problem-solving and creativity capacities of organisations (Hage, 1991). Broad theories of organisational change – including structural contingency theory, political theory, organisational ecology and meso-institutional theory – have endeavoured to shed light on the consequences of organisational innovation. From the field of organisational studies, there has been particular discussion on 'institutional entrepreneurs' in institutional development within organisations. Coined by DiMaggio (1988), 'institutional entrepreneurs' are actors that are involved with transforming existing institutions, or creating new institutions. Using a resource-mobilisation argument, these agents may draw on resources to influence institutionalised rules to support prevailing institutions, or to formulate new institutions. They can support both the socialisation of actors and the mobilisation of actors. Towards a more elaborate definition, Battilana *et al.* (2009: 72) describes 'institutional entrepreneurs' as organisations or individuals who 'initiate, and actively participate in the implementation of, changes that diverge from existing institutions, independent of whether the initial intent was to change the institutional environment and whether the changes were successfully implemented'. Such changes may be within organisations, or within their existing environment. Gomez (2008) highlights the characteristics of such entrepreneurs or 'market makers' engaged in institutional construction, as 'skilful and resourceful' and noted their capacity to engage in 'collective action'. Yet 'change agents' may have diverse capacities and influences (Ford *et al.*, 2008). Meanwhile, beyond the role of such 'institutional entrepreneurs', Battilana *et al.* (2009) cites Eisenstadt (1980), who argued that these agents may be just one 'variable' among a 'constellation' of others, in the change process.

Agents of uncertain change: influence of existing institutions and power

Furthering sociological discussions (e.g. DiMaggio, 1988; DiMaggio and Powell, 1991; Scott, 1991; Fligstein, 1997), Beckert (1999) explores integrating 'interest-driven behaviour in institutional change' into institutional organisation theory. Beckert critically advances an understanding of the role of entrepreneurs, 'strategic agency', and institutionalised practices in proposing a dynamic and more comprehensive model of institutional change. In strategic agency, he refers to the 'systematic attempt to reach conceived ends through the planned and purposeful application of means' (Beckert, 1999: 783). While the role of the environment has been much discussed in organisational change (e.g. Oliver, 1992), the role of strategic choice and the interest-driven behaviour of agents have been under-theorised. He suggests that institutional rules and agency act as 'antagonistic mechanisms that contradict each other', and destabilise each other but remain interconnected. He puts the variable of uncertainty at the core of his thesis, referring to situations in which rational actors cannot respond within their existing frames of reference (Knight, 1921; Beckert, 1996). From organisational studies, he draws on notions of complexity and conflict (e.g. Greenwood and Hinings, 1996). He describes institutionalisation as a 'process of social interaction through which actors realize that their expectations in the behaviour of others will not be disappointed' (ibid.).

Adding to these propositions, Beckert (1999) conceives of three factors that may contribute to the subsequent stabilisation of institutions: habits, legitimacy and power. The latter may be based on resources such as finance, knowledge or position within social networks (embedded in organisations or in the environment). In the example of the market, he distinguishes between two levels of institutionalisation: meta-institutions and lower-ranking institutional rules. In more recent work, drawing from action theory, Beckert (2003) attempted to further deconstruct the basic notion of 'embeddedness' to understand how embeddedness of economic action in social contexts influences the creativity of the action process itself, and applies this to situations of cooperation and innovation (new routines). Strategies of action are formulated from an actor's own interpretation of their social context, and rationality is centred on their perception of social group expectations. For example, innovation may be spurred by a falling demand of the market, and the new proposed solutions may be based on the agents' own interpretation of the situation (i.e. influenced by entrenched social institutions). Exploring the effects of such innovations, studies have looked at the role of actors and the influence of existing institutions, in broader institutional diffusion and adoption (Redmond, 2003). Redmond draws attention to 'loss' as well as 'gain' in creative destruction (with new practices replacing or transforming the old), and the different types of innovation adopters and non-adopters (e.g. conservative groups). Broadening the theory, this paper sheds new light on various factors in institutional diffusion and adoption including cognition (initially), levels of self-interest and risk-taking, and numbers of previous adopters (and social pressures). Yet the impact of both individual and collective agency of actors (and their interrelations), and power dynamics, as highlighted by Beckert (1999), in addition to more structural influences (such as degrees of trust), remain less clear.

2.2.3 Institutional activity in networks

In moving away from individualism and towards exploring collective agency, it is necessary to return to our discussion on networks. Granovetter (1992) posits that 'stable' economic institutions emerge as growing 'clusters of activity' around existing personal networks. Granovetter theorises that the level of network fragmentation and cohesion, or 'coupling and decoupling', is a significant indicator of potential outcomes, and that actors whose networks straddle the largest number of institutional spheres will have the most advantage. Fligstein (1996) theorised that new paths of action could be opened up and institutionalised by 'skillful actors' by repeated learning within networks. Meanwhile, Hollingsworth and Boyer (1997: 451) describe collective action as required to overcome the 'hysteresis of inefficient institutions'.

Bottom-up institutional design facilitated in networks

Recent empirical institutional insights have integrated evolutionary and network discussions. Looking at the creation of rules, Hodgson (1997: 679) pointed out that not all situations are driven by existing habits and rules. For example, creativity and novelty may emerge from clashes in rules (endogenous) or be 'uncaused' (exogenous). Agents can also change habits and routines by substituting designed institutions, although there may be limits. Advancing this, Gomez (2008: 83) expands on the term 'designed institutions' as referring to a 'new rule of action' for a given situation (repeated by others). Drawing on a study of a barter market network, Gomez (2008) further develops Hodgson's framework (i.e. actions Y, outcomes Z and new situations X) to incorporate institutional innovation and learning in networks. Gomez describes market forms of exchange as repeated in a market society by routine or 'pre-reflexively' in a 'continuity loop' (Gomez, 2008: 84). Building off Hodgson's model, she adds a lower 'innovation' loop as agents encounter 'new, uncertain, complex situations' to fill institutional gaps (i.e. actions Y^1, outcomes Z^1 and new situations X^1). The evolved institutions experiment in a 'reflective action', and 'skilful actors' then begin innovating and learning. Such activity is shown to be embedded in networks that play a key role in interpretation and decision-making. If a positive response is received, the action is repeated until such activity produces a new 'rule' or 'institution' (or evolved rule from pre-existing rules) for the respective situation. Designed institutions may influence evolved institutions by repeatedly 'forcing reasoning at the moment of action' and may become common habits and routines if behavioural tendencies lead to their action (Gomez, 2008: 250). Advancing Fligstein (2001) and Hodgson (1997), Gomez (2008) cites three necessary conditions for the bottom-up design of institutions: the presence of collective action skilled/resourceful entrepreneurs 'market makers', the participation of interested agents in the early design stages, and third, the presence in the continuity loop of pre-existent institutions that delimit experimentation and facilitate the search for 'new solutions'. Broadening Beckert's theory (1999, 2003), Gomez describes four crucial factors that may contribute to the sustainability of institutional change including 'input legitimacy' (relating to agent participation in the process); mechanisms for 'enforcement of rules' (i.e. local authority); 'resource synergies' in which material benefits of pursuing rules are shared (i.e. transparency on benefits); and clarity on 'transaction and organisational costs' (i.e. transparency on costs). But the conditions that shape actor participation and interaction in these processes remain less certain.

2.3 'Bundles of institutions' in informal developing economies

From a development perspective, the institutional environment – or local conditions – begs greater attention and appreciation in the institutional discourse. Having traversed the key debates on institutional change, and the role of actors and networks, in this final section, I turn to the particular context of developing economies, influencing markets, actor behaviour and institutional development. Traditionally, markets are understood to be sets of institutional mechanisms for exchange, coordination and allocation of resources, goods and services in an economy. Neoclassical economists tend to view markets arising in response to simplistic 'efficiency' objectives in allocating goods under scarcity conditions (e.g. Schotter, 1985). Yet Hollingsworth and Boyer (1997) described markets as just one form of economic coordination. They described evidence from game theory and the 'prisoners dilemma' to show that they are not always in fact the most efficient allocation, particularly where there is asymmetric information, power imbalances, bounded rationality, externalities, restrictions on demand revelation and public goods (Hollingsworth and Boyer, 1997). This is typical in developing contexts. Similarly, Chang (2002) suggests that while markets matters, the market 'is only one of many institutions that make up what many people call the "market economy" '. Harriss-White (2003a) highlighted the role of 'non-state regulative structures' in India, and suggested that there were 'bundles of institutions' in market activity, embedded in broader 'regulating' institutions (Harriss-White, 2003b). In this vein, institutionalism indicates that markets are social constructions, residing alongside (and embedded within) other social, political and cultural institutions, influencing participation and scope of economic activity. Below, I elaborate on the dominance of informal institutions in developing contexts leading to exclusive markets (particularly for women and the poor), power asymmetries, and in some cases, institutional entrepreneurialism (with mixed effects). I also highlight the importance of trust both within the environment, and between actors.

2.3.1 Dominance of informal institutions and power asymmetries

There has been increasing discussion of the complex role of social/cultural institutions in less developed markets. In the absence of formal law and order, informal institutions tend to shape social and economic behaviour. Markets thus persist despite the lack of (formal) controls and regulations. While long-term conflict is deemed to dampen economic activity (with both instability and a lack of controls), a recent study shows little correlation between conflict and enterprise, particularly where conflict has been 'institutionalised' (Ciarli *et al.*, 2009). For example, Somalia has remained engaged in livestock markets amidst years of country chaos. Meanwhile in Afghanistan, informal financial markets linking the country to international markets have prevailed throughout 30 years of conflict. Duffield (2001) and Nordstrom (2004) highlighted how 'state fragility' and 'durable disorder' are generated in a symbiotic relationship between fragile and non-fragile states, challenging the assumption that fragile states are a temporary phenomenon with implications for developing country markets. Such a perspective draws attention to the complex mix of formal and informal social, economic and political structures that prevail within fragile and developing states, permitting the continuation of local economies even where states are weak or absent. Yet the social and cultural aspects of developing and less formal environments still remain poorly appreciated (Albu, 2008), and largely misunderstood (Johnson, 2006). This includes gender-specific household economic relations, and local exchange systems and reciprocity.

In accessing economic participation in less developed and fragile contexts, the dominant influence of social relations and social institutions, and the role of social regulation (as a result of gender, ethnicity and caste) in causing 'exclusion' or 'adverse incorporation' are indeed critical factors. Morrisson and Jutting (2004) argue that social institutions are the single most important factor determining women's freedom of choice in economic activities outside of the household, directly and indirectly influencing women's access to markets and resources. Meanwhile, in the absence of formal institutions, Wood (2003) emphasises the dual role of (informal) social and political institutions, and the constraints that exist for the poor to pursue 'positive action' via the rules embedded in those institutions (Wood, 2003: 457). In a fragile context where immediate survival is critical, there may be heavy reliance on family members or allegiance to other providers (hierarchical) at a cost of 'weak or bonded loyalty', and pervasive clientelism. Such pressures may determine productive strategies (e.g. crop diversification), even when prevailing prices may pay to specialise, in addition to influencing the scope of innovation and cooperation. Wood describes this behaviour as ensuring 'security before graduation' and 'loyalty at any price'.

Entrepreneurs generating informal substitutes

With weak state institutional frameworks – typical in developing country contexts – building on Baumol (1990), Boettke and Leeson (2009) described a situation of 'institutional entrepreneurialism' where entrepreneurs are involved in both productive and non-productive activities. In such environments, Leitmann and Baharoglu (1998) suggest that pressures to control economic behaviour may result in the creation of new informal rules by local governing bodies, which might be costly in terms of resources and collective action. And in some cases, these may include extreme enforcement measures (De Soto, 1987). This challenges the notion that existing institutions always regulate behaviour as suggested in the 'rule-incentive-behaviour causal' framework (Ostrom *et al.*, 1993). Further, entrepreneurs in Leitmann's study were shown to avoid rather than modify formal rules, especially where 'the rules of the game have little bearing on the game', or when there was ineffective enforcement. In fact, formal rules were deemed irrelevant, and informal rules were indicated to create greater incentives and govern behaviour (Leitmann and Baharoglu, 1998: 113). Gomez (2008) points to a whole array of studies, which describes how informal institutions can in fact be created and coexist alongside formal institutions, with positive results (e.g. Platteau, 1994; Uzzell, 1994). Yet the World Bank warns that the development of informal rules and institutions in the absence of formal institutions may bring negative power externalities, as was demonstrated by the rise of the Mafia in Sicily (World Bank, 2002: 175). Naude (2007) cautions particular attention in fragile states with little formal institutions, which may perpetuate negative (informal) institutions and foster unproductive and destructive enterprise. However, this does not consider heterogeneous dynamics within the context, which may generate more varied outcomes in local economic development.

2.3.2 Trust: an outcome and an antecedent of economic activity

Closely linked to social relations and embedded in institutions, appreciating levels of *trust* both within the environment (institutionalised) and between actors is particularly critical in less developed economies. While formal institutions are considered imperative in economic development, Fukuyama (1995: 11) describes their necessary fusion with 'reciprocity, moral obligation, duty toward community and trust'. In formulating economic transactions, trust is thus considered fundamental between actors. Cultural, social and historical contexts play a part in determining trust levels and arrangements, as well as existing social relations (Hollingsworth and Boyer, 1997: 450). Trust is indicated to be associated with sanctions, knowledge on other actors, and a series of norms, providing the basis for assessing trade interaction and shaping economic behaviour in markets. According to Nooteboom (2007: 29), trust is 'both an outcome and an antecedent of relationships'. In this way, trust establishes a foundation for relationships, and may be based on institutions and built from relationships. He differentiates trust from reliability, with reliability incorporating benevolence and based on control, or trust, or both (Noteboom, 2007: 37). Seen as a type of behaviour (Deutsch, 1962) or underlying disposition (Das and Teng, 2001), trust is deemed to have 'instrumental' value in reducing risk and transaction costs of relationships. Several studies have drawn attention to the role of trust in trade and economic structures, including Zucker (1986), Gambetta (1988) and Humphrey and Schmitz (1996).

Trust has been shown to be particularly critical in developing countries where the state has a limited role and there is poor communication (Lyon, 2000), and where highly personalised trust relationships are the norm (Das and Teng, 2001). Often inequitable balances of structural power have a significant influence on the trust-based relationships between powerful commission agents and traders, and smaller dealers and producers. Experience has shown that collective action through associations may improve levels of trust, and producers' bargaining power. And trust is considered to evolve before transaction costs are even negotiated (Maher, 1997). In recent work, Lyon and Porter (2009) contend that personal relationships and institutional based trust are heavily linked to informal social institutions, and underpinned by moral norms. Lyon and Porter draw attention to the dynamic nature of moral norms not only as economies change, but also in response to changes in the political and sociocultural context. Of particular interest in the study was the observation that actors in a post-conflict environment endeavoured to reinstate social norms, and how such norms of behaviour (e.g. reciprocity and obligation) can both assist in reviving economic life in addition to social life. They showed how a range of practical economic relationships and informal institutions emerged with a strong emphasis on trust and moral norms in the absence of appropriate formal institutions such as banks and legal contracts (Lyon and Porter, 2009). Certainly, the socially embedded nature of ties and culture of trust reduces the opportunity for purely self-driven behaviour and is the foundation of emerging and informal economic activity. Yet questions linger for institutional development: how is trust developed and why do some individuals choose to cooperate instead of behaving opportunistically (Gomez, 2008: 115)?

2.4 Concluding remarks

Portes (2006: 251) summarised four major forces leading to institutional transformation and development. These include path dependence and cultural diffusion; and more deep-seated forces of actor-driven change, including 'charisma/charismatic prophecy' with the potential to change the value system and culture, and 'inter-elite and class struggles' with the potential to disrupt power balances. In looking beyond neoclassical theory, this chapter has explored the complex influence of history, sociocultural institutions, habit, power dynamics and social relations in institutional change and development. In vein with these arguments, the chapter has argued for a greater appreciation of the interaction of structure and agency. The particular roles of 'entrepreneurs' and 'skilled actors' were examined, their diverse motivations, power and agency, and collective action through networks. Finally, the specific institutional context of developing economies was discussed. In these environments, the dominance of informal institutions was shown to distort agent behaviour, and the nature and scope of economic activity and institutional development. This tends to lead to more exclusive markets (particularly for women and the poor) and power asymmetries, and necessitates a critical role for agent trust.

Often overshadowed by his earlier work, in *The Theory of Moral Sentiments*, Adam Smith (1759) considered 'economic motivation' as entrenched in the culture and habits of society (Fukuyama, 1995: 18). Mainstream theorist Douglass North (1989: 1324) has acknowledged that it is the 'norms of behaviour' that are perhaps the most influential in human interaction, and a fundamental basis of habitual behaviour and thus require greater understanding. And in more recent discussions, he explores the role of cognition and ideology (North *et al.*, 2003, 2004). Furubotn (1997) described NIE as coming under increasing criticism with the neoclassical-based approach, and reaching a 'watershed' and thus no longer sustainable (Hodgson, 2004). Despite divergences between the various schools of thought, Malcolm Rutherford (1995: 443) suggests that a unifying theme is that institutions are indeed essential in shaping economic behaviour. Yet without a collaborative approach, theories struggle with integrating the influence of non-economic institutions, social structure (social relations and networks), and agency (power, habits and preferences). In particular, deconstructing how these factors shape the *process of institutional change* remains a key challenge. At the frontier of institutional research today, these exciting debates reside at the heart of this study.

As a broad framework, the themes presented in this chapter set the scene for subsequent chapters in this book. In Chapter 3, I further explore the particular research context of Afghanistan. The following three chapters present the research findings, initially delving further into the literature before analysing crucial empirical insights: in the transformation of local norms in women's businesses (Chapter 4), the construction of enterprise institutions (Chapter 5), and the dynamic role of agency (Chapter 6).

References

Albu, M. (2008) *Making Markets Work for the Poor: Comparing M4P and SLA Frameworks: Complementarities, Divergences and Synergies*, Durham, UK: Springfield Centre (for FAUNO).

Archer, M.S. (1995) *Realist Social Theory: The Morphogenetic Approach*, Cambridge: Cambridge University Press.

Bardhan, P. (1989) 'The new institutional economics and development theory: a brief critical assessment', *World Development*, 17(9): 1389–95.

Baron, R.A. (2004) 'Potential benefits of the cognitive perspective: expanding entrepreneurship's array of conceptual tools', *Journal of Business Venturing*, 19: 169–72.

Battilana, J. and D'Aunno, T. (2009) 'Institutional work and the paradox of embedded agency', in T. Lawrence, R. Suddaby and B. Leca (eds), *Institutional Work: Actors and Agency in Institutional Studies of Organization*, Cambridge: Cambridge University Press.

Battilana, J., Leca, B. and Boxenbaum, E. (2009) 'How actors change institutions: towards a theory of institutional entrepreneurship', *The Academy of Management Annals: A Journal of the Academy of Management*, 3(1): 65–107.

Baumol, W. (1968) 'Entrepreneurship in economic theory', *The American Economic Review*, 58(2): 64–71.

Baumol, W. (1990) 'Entrepreneurship: productive, unproductive and destructive', *The Journal of Political Economy*, 98(5): 893–921.

Becker, G.S. (1996) *Accounting for Tastes*, Cambridge, MA: Harvard University Press.

Becker, G.S. and Stigler, G.J. (1977) 'De gustibus non est disputandum', *American Economic Review*, 76(1): 76–90.

Beckert, J. (1996) 'What is sociological about economic sociology? Uncertainty and the embeddednes of economic action', *Theory and Society*, 25: 803–40.

Beckert, J. (1999) 'Agency, entrepreneurs, and institutional change: the role of strategic choice and institutionalized practices in organizations', *Organisation Studies*, 20(5): 777–99.

Beckert, J. (2003) 'Economic sociology and embeddedness: how shall we conceptualize economic action?', *Journal of Economic Issues*, 37(3): 769–87.

Berner, E., Gomez, G. and Knorringa, P. (2009) *Helping a Large Number of People Become a Little Less Poor*, The Hague: ISS.

Bhaskar, R.A. (1979/1998) *The Possibility of Naturalism* (3rd edn), London: Routledge.

Bhaskar, R.A. (1983) 'Beef, structure and place: notes from a critical naturalist perspective', *Journal for the Theory of Social Behaviour*, 13(1): 81–96.

Binks, M. and Vale, P. (1990) *Entrepreneurship and Economic Change*, Maidenhead, UK: McGraw-Hill.

Boettke, P. and Leeson, P. (2009) 'Two-tiered entrepreneurship and economic development', *International Review of Law and Economics*, 29(3): 252–9.

Boettke, P.J., Coyne, C.J., and Leeson, P. (2008) 'Institutional stickiness and the new development economics', *The American Journal of Economics and Sociology*, 67(2): 331–58.

Bourdieu, P. (1977) *Outline of a Theory of Practice*, Cambridge: Cambridge University Press.

Bourdieu, P. (1985) 'The social space and the genesis of groups', *Theory and Society*, 14(6): 723–44.

Bowles, S., Gintis, H., Boyd, R. and Fehr, E. (1993) 'Explaining altruistic behavior in humans', *Evolution and Human Behavior*, 24: 153–72.

Brousseau, E. and Raynaud, E. (2007) 'The economics of multilevel governance', unpublished working paper.

Brouwer, M. (2002) 'Weber, Schumpeter and Knight', *Journal of Evolutionary Economics*, 12: 83–105.

Campbell, J.L. (1997) 'Mechanisms of evolutionary change in economics governance: interaction, interpretation and bricolage', in L. Magnusson and J. Ottosson (eds), *Evolutionary Economics and Path Dependence*, Cheltenham, UK: Edward Elgar.

Casson, M. (1982) *The Entrepreneur: An Economic Theory*, Oxford: Martin Robertson.

Chang, H.-J. (2002) 'Breaking the mould: an institutionalist political economy alternative to the neo-liberal theory of the market and the state', *Cambridge Journal of Economics*, 26(5): 539–59.

Chang, H.-J. (2011) 'Institutions and economic development: theory, policy and history', *Journal of Institutional Economics*, 7: 473–98.

Chang, H.-J. and Evans, P. (2000) 'The role of institutions in economic change', *Proceedings of the 'Other Canon' Group*, Venice, Italy, 13–14 January.

Chang, H.-J. and Evans, P. (2005) 'Role of institutions in economic change', in G. Dymski and S. Da Paula (eds), *Reimagining Growth*, London: Zed Press.

Chantarat, S. and Barrett, C. (2007) 'Social network capital, economic mobility and poverty traps', Munich Personal RePec Archive, unpublished.

Ciarli, T., Parto, S. and Savona, M. (2009) 'Conflict and entrepreneurial activity in Afghanistan: findings from the national risk vulnerability assessment data', *UNU WIDER Discussion Paper for Workshop on Entrepreneurship and Conflict INCORE*, University of Ulster, Northern Ireland, 20–21 March.

Das, T. and Teng, B. (2001) 'Trust, control, and risk in strategic alliances: an integrated framework', *Organization Studies*, 22(2): 251–83.

Davern, M. (1997) 'Social networks and economic sociology: a proposed research agenda for a more complete social science', *American Journal of Economics and Sociology*, 56(3): 287–302.

De Soto, H. (1987) *El Otro Sendero*, Lima, Peru: Instito Liberdad Democracia.

Deutsch, M. (1962) 'Cooperation and trust: some theoretical notes', *Nebraska Symposium on Motivation*, 10: 275–318.

DiMaggio, P.J. (1988) 'Interest and agency in institutional theory', in L.G. Zucker (ed.), *Institutional Patterns and Organizations*, Cambridge, MA: Ballinger.

DiMaggio, P.J. and Powell, W. (1991) *The New Institutionalism in Organizational Analysis*, Chicago, IL: University of Chicago Press.

Dorward, A., Kydd, J., Morrison, J. and Poulton, C. (2005) 'Institutions, markets and economic co-ordination: linking development policy to theory and praxis', *Development and Change*, 36(1): 1–25.

Dosi, G. (1995) 'Hierarchies, markets and power: some foundational issues on the nature of contemporary economic organisations', *Industrial and Corporate Change*, 4(1): 1–19.

Douglas, M. (1986) *How Institutions Think*, Syracuse, NY: Syracuse University Press.

Drucker, P. (1986) *Innovation and Entrepreneurship*, Oxford: Heinemann.

Duffield, M. (2001) *Global Governance and the New Wars: The Merging of Development and Security*, London and New York: Zed Books.

Durlauf, S.N. and Fafchamps, M. (2004) 'Social capital', *NBER Working Paper* W10485.

Edgcomb, E.L. and Thetford, T. (2004) *The Informal Economy: Making it in Rural America*, Washington, DC: Aspen Institute.

Eggertsson, T. (1997) 'The old theory of economic policy and the new institutionalism', *World Development*, 25(8): 1187–203.

Eisenstadt, S.N. (1980) 'Cultural orientations, institutional entrepreneurs, and social change: comparative analyses of traditional civilizations', *American Journal of Sociology*, 85(3): 840–69.

Emirbayer, M. and Johnson, V. (2008) 'Bourdieu and organisational analysis', *Theory and Society*, 37: 1–44.

Emirbayer, M. and Mische, A. (1998) 'What is agency?', *American Journal of Sociology*, 103(4): 962–1023.

Evans, P. (2004) 'Development as institutional change: the pitfalls of monocropping and potentials of deliberation', *SCID*, 38(4): 30–52.

Field, J. (2003) *Social Capital*, London: Routledge.

Fligstein, N. (1996) 'Markets as politics: a political-cultural approach to market institutions', *American Sociological Review*, 61: 656–73.

Fligstein, N. (1997) 'Social skill and institutional theory', *American Behavioral Scientist*, 40(4): 397–405.

Fligstein, N. (2001) 'Social skill and the theory of fields', *Sociological Theory*, 19(2): 105–25.

Ford, J.D., Ford, L.W. and D'Amelio, A. (2008) 'Resistance to change: the rest of the story', *The Academy of Management Review*, 33(2): 362–77.

Friedland, R. and Alford, R.R. (1991) 'Bringing society back in: symbols, practice, and institutional contradictions', in W. Powell and P. DiMaggio (eds), *The New Institutionalism in Organizational Analysis*, Chicago, IL: University of Chicago Press.

Fukuyama, F. (1995) *Trust: The Social Virtues and Creation of Prosperity*, New York: Free Press Paperbacks.

Fukuyama, F. (2003) 'Still disenchanted? The modernity of postindustrial capitalism', *Center for the Study of Economy and Society Working Paper Series Paper 3*.

Furubotn, E.G. (1997) 'The old and new institutionalism in economics', in P. Koslowski (ed.), *Methodology of the Social Sciences: Ethics and Economics in the Newer Historical School: From Max Weber and Rickert to Sombat and Rothacker*, Berlin: Springer.

Galbraith, J. (1969) *The Affluent Society*, London: Hamilton.

Gambetta, D. (1988) (ed.) *Trust: Making and Breaking Cooperative Relations*, New York: Basil Blackwell.

Giddens, A. (1979) *Central Problems in Social Theory: Action, Structure and Contradiction in Social Analysis*, London: Macmillan.

Giddens, A. (1984) *The Constitution of Society: Outline of the Theory of Structuration*, Cambridge: Polity Press.

Gomez, G. (2008) *Making Markets: The Institutional Rise and Decline of the Argentine Red de Trueque*, Maastricht, Netherlands: Shaker Publishing BV (PhD Thesis).

Grabowski, R. (1999) 'Market evolution and economic development: the evolution of impersonal markets', *American Journal of Economics and Sociology*, 58(4): 699–712.

Granovetter, M. (1985) 'Economic action and social structure: the problem of embeddedness', *American Journal of Sociology*, 91(3): 481–510.

Granovetter, M. (1992) 'Economic institutions as social constructions: a framework for analysis', *Acta Sociologica*, 35(1): 3–11.

Greenwood, R. and Hinings, C.R. (1996) 'Understanding radical organizational change: bringing together the old and the new institutionalism', *Academy of Management Review*, 21(4): 1022.

Greif, A. (2006) 'The birth of impersonal exchange: the community responsibility system and impartial justice', *Journal of Economic Perspectives*, 20(2): 221–36.

Hage, R. (1991) *Organizations, Structure and Process*, Englewood Cliffs, NJ: Prentice Hall.

Hamilton, D. (1953) *Newtonian Classicism and Darwinian Institutionalism*, Albuquerque, NM: University of New Mexico Press.

Hamilton, G. (1991) *Business Networks and Economics Development in East and Southeast Asia*, Hong Kong: Center of Asian Studies.

Harriss-White, B. (2003a) *India Working: Essays on Society and Economy*, Cambridge: Cambridge University Press.

Harriss-White, B. (2003b) 'On understanding markets as social and political institutions in developing economies', in H.-J. Chang (ed.), *Rethinking Development Economics*, London, Chicago, IL and Delhi: Anthem Press.

Hayek, F.A. (1948) *Individualism and Economic Order*, Chicago, IL: University of Chicago Press.

Hodgson, G. (1988) *Economics and Institutions: A Manifesto for a Modern Institutional Economics*, Cambridge: Polity.

Hodgson, G. (1997) 'The ubiquity of habits and rules', *Cambridge Journal of Economics*, 21: 663–84.

Hodgson, G. (2000) 'What is the essence of institutional economics?', *Journal of Economic Issues*, 34(2): 317–29.

Hodgson, G. (2003) 'The hidden persuaders, institutions and individuals in economic theory', *Cambridge Journal of Economics*, 27: 159–75.

Hodgson, G. (2004) *The Evolution of Institutional Economics: Agency, Structure and Darwinism in American Institutionalism*, London: Routledge.

Hodgson, G. (2007) 'Institutions and individuals: interaction and evolution', *Organisation Studies*, 28(1): 95–111.

Hollingsworth, J.R. (2002) 'Some reflections on how institutions influence styles of innovation', paper for *Swedish Collegium for Advanced Study of the Social Sciences*, 26 September, available at: http://history.wisc.edu/hollingsworth/documents/Some_ Reflections_on_How_Institutions_Influence_Styles_of_Innovation.htm, accessed 1 December 2012.

Hollingsworth, J.R. and Boyer, R. (1997) (eds) *Contemporary Capitalism*, Cambridge: Cambridge University Press.

Humphrey, J. and Schmitz, H. (1996) 'Trust and economic development', *Discussion Paper No 355*, Brighton, UK: Institute of Development Studies, University of Sussex.

Jackson, W. (2003) 'Social structure in economic theory', *Journal of Economic Issues*, 37(3): 727–46.

Jessop, B. (1997) 'Survey article: the regulation approach', *Journal of Political Philosophy*, 5(3): 287–326.

Jessop, B. (1998) 'The rise of governance and the risks of failure: the case of economic development', *International Social Science Journal*, 155: 29–45.

Johnson, S. (2006) *Making Markets Work for Poor People: The Role of Social Regulation*, Bath, UK: University of Bath.

Knight, F. (1921) *Risk, Uncertainty and Profit*, Boston, MA and New York: Kelley.

Knight, J. (1992) *Institutions and Social Conflict*, Cambridge: Cambridge University Press.

Knorringa, P. and Meyer-Stamer, J. (2007) 'Local development, global value chains and latecomer development', in J. Haar and J. Meyer-Stamer (eds), *Small Firms, Global Markets: Competitive Challenges in the New Economy*, Basingstoke, UK and New York: Palgrave Macmillan.

Kristiansen, S. (2004) 'Social networks and business success: the role of subcultures in an African context', *The American Journal of Economics and Sociology*, 63(5): 1149–71.

Landier, A. (2002) *Entrepreneurship and the Stigma of Failure* (Thesis), Cambridge, MA: MIT Graduate School of Business.

Lanzara, G.F. (1998) 'Self-destructive processes in institution building and some modest countervailing mechanisms', *European Journal of Political Research*, 33: 1–39.

Lawson, T. (1997) 'Realism, explanation and science', in T. Lawson (ed.), *Economics and Reality*, London: Routledge.

Lazear, E. (2005) 'Entrepreneurship', *Journal of Labour Economics*, 23(4): 649–80.

Lazonick, W. (2007) 'Varieties of capitalism and innovative enterprise', *Comparative Social Research*, 24: 21–69.

Legro, J. (1997) 'Which norms matter? Revisiting the "failure" of internationalism', *International Organisation*, 51: 31–63.

Leibenstein, H. (1968) 'Entrepreneurship and development', *American Economic Review*, 58(2): 72–83.

Leitmann, J. and Baharoglu, D. (1998) 'Informal rules! Using institutional economics to understand service provision in Turkey's spontaneous settlements', *Journal of Development Studies*, 34(5): 98–122.

Li, D., Feng, J. and Jiang, H. (2006) 'Institutional entrepreneurs', *The American Economic Review*, 96(2): 358–62.

Lin, N. (1999) 'Building a theory of social capital', *Connection*, 22: 28–51.

Long, N. (2001) *Development Sociology: Actor Perspectives*, London and New York: Routledge.

Lozano, B. (1989) *The Invisible Workforce: Transforming American Business with Outside and Home-Based Workers*, New York: The Free Press.

Lyon, F. (2000) 'Trust, networks and norms: the creation of social capital in agricultural economics in Ghana', *World Development*, 28(4): 663–81.

Lyon, F. and Porter, G. (2009) 'Market institutions, trust and norms: exploring moral economies in Nigerian food systems', *Cambridge Journal of Economics*, 33: 903–20.

Maher, M.E. (1997) 'Transaction cost economics and contractual relations', *Cambridge Journal of Economics*, 21: 147–70.

March, J.G. and Olsen, J.P. (1989) *Rediscovering Institutions: The Organizational Basis of Politics*, New York: Free Press.

Marghlin, S. (1991) 'Understanding capitalism: control versus efficiency', in B. Gustafsson (ed.), *Power and Economic Institutions*, Aldershot, UK: Edward Elgar.

Maseland, R. (2011) 'How to make institutional economics better', *Journal of Institutional Economics*, 7(4): 555–9.

Mogues, T. and Carter, M.R. (2005) 'Social capital and the reproduction of economic equality in polarized societies', *Journal of Economic Inequality*, 3(3): 193–219.

Morrisson, C. and Jutting, J. (2004) 'Changing social institutions to improve the status of women in developing countries', *OECD Development Centre Policy Brief 27*.

Murphy, J.B. (1994) 'The kinds of order in society', in P. Mirowski (ed.), *Natural Images in Economic Thought: Markets Read in Tooth and Claw*, Cambridge and New York: Cambridge University Press.

Naude, W. (2007) 'Peace, prosperity and pro-growth entrepreneurship', *UNU WIDER Discussion Paper No. 2007/02*, Helsinki: UNU-WIDER.

Nelson, R.R. (1995) 'Recent evolutionary theorizing about economic change', *Journal of Economic Literature*, 33(1): 48–90.

Nelson, R.R. (2002) 'Erratum to technology, institutions, and innovation system', *Research Policy*, 31: 265–72.

Nelson, R.R. and Winter, S.G. (1982) *An Evolutionary Theory of Economic Change*, Cambridge, MA: Harvard University Press.

Nooteboom, B. (2007) 'Social capital, institutions and trust', *Review of Social Economy*, 65(1): 29–53.

Nordstrom, C. (2000) 'Shadows and sovereigns', *Theory, Culture and Society*, 17(4): 35–54.

Nordstrom, C. (2004) *Shadows of War: Violence, Power and International Profiteering in the Twenty-First Century*, Berkeley, CA: California University Press.

North, D. (1989) 'Institutions and economic growth: a historical introduction', *World Development*, 17(9): 1319–32.

North, D. (1990) *Institutions, Institutional Change and Economic Performance*, Cambridge: Cambridge University Press.

North, D. (2003) 'The role of institutions in economic development', *ECE Discussion Papers Series*, 2003(2).

North, D., Mantzavinos, C. and Shariq, S. (2004) 'Learning, institutions and economic performance', *Perspectives on Politics*, 2(1): 75–84.

Oliver, C. (1992) 'The antecedents of deinstitutionalization', *Organisation Studies*, 13(4): 563–88.

Ostrom, E. (1990) *Governing the Commons: The Evolution of Institutions for Collective Action*, Cambridge: Cambridge University Press.

Ostrom, E. (2005) *Understanding Institutional Diversity*, Princeton, NJ and Oxford: Princeton University Press.

Ostrom, E., Schroeder, L. and Wynne, S. (1993) *Institutional Incentives and Sustainable Development: Infrastructure Policies in Perspective*, Boulder, CO: Westview Press.

Packard, V. (1957) *The Hidden Persuaders*, London: Longmans, Greens.

Parsons, T. (1937) *The Structure of Social Action*, New York: McGraw-Hill.

Perrow, C. (1986) *Complex Organizations: A Critical Essay*, New York: Random House.

Platteau, J.P. (1994) 'Behind the market stage where real societies exist (part I and II): the role of moral norms', *Journal of Development Studies*, 30(4): 753–815.

Platteau, J.P. (2000) *Institutions, Social Norms, and Economic Development*, Amsterdam, The Netherlands: Harwood Academic Publishers.

Polanyi, K. (1944/2001) *The Great Transformation: The Political and Economic Origins of Our Time*, Boston, MA: Beacon Press.

Portes, A. (2006) 'Institutions and development: a conceptual reanalysis', *Population and Development Review*, 2(2): 233–62.

Powell, W.W. and DiMaggio, P.J. (1991) *The New Institutionalism in Organizational Analysis*, Chicago, IL: University of Chicago Press.

Redmond, W.H. (2003) 'Innovation, diffusion, and institutional change', *Journal of Economic Issues*, 37(3): 665–79.

Roland, G. (1990) 'Gorbachev and the common European home: the convergence debate revisited', *Kyklos*, 43: 385–409.

Roland, G. (2004) 'Institutional change: fast-moving and slow-moving institutions', *Studies in Comparative International Development*, 38(4): 109–31.

Rutherford, M. (1995) 'The old and the new institutionalism: can bridges be built?', *Journal of Economic Issues*, 29(2): 443–51.

Schotter, A. (1981) *The Economic Theory of Social Institutions*, Cambridge and New York: Cambridge University Press.

Schotter, A. (1985) *Free Market Economics: a Critical Appraisal*, New York: St. Martin's Press.

Schumpeter, J.A. (1934) *The Theory of Economic Development*, Cambridge, MA: Harvard University Press.

Scott, W.R. (1991) 'Unpacking institutional arguments', in W.W. Powell and P.J. DiMaggio (eds), *The New Institutionalism in Organisational Analysis*, Chicago, IL: University of Chicago Press.

Smith, A. (1759/2000) *The Theory of Moral Sentiments*, Amherst, NY: Prometheus Books.

Smith, A. (1776/1937) *The Wealth of Nations*, New York: The Modern Library.

Sperry, R.W. (1964) *Problems Outstanding in the Evolution of Brain Function*, New York: American Museum of Natural History.

Sperry, R.W. (1969) 'A modified concept of consciousness', *Psychological Review*, 76(6): 532–6.

Streeck, W. (1997) 'Beneficial constraints: on the economic limits of rational voluntarism', in J.R. Hollingsworth and R. Boyer (eds), *Contemporary Capitalism: The Embeddedness of Institutions*, New York and Cambridge: Cambridge University Press.

Streeck, W. (2002) 'Institutional complementarity and dynamics of economic systems', *Notes for International Seminar Organized by CEPREMAP*, 5–6 April, Paris.

Turner, S. (2007) 'Small-scale enterprise livelihoods and social capital in eastern Indonesia: ethnic embeddedness and exclusion', *The Professional Geographer*, 59(4): 407–20.

Uzzell, J.D. (1994) 'Transaction costs, formal plans, and formal informality: alternatives to the informal sector', in C. Rakowski (ed.), *Contrapunto*, Albany, NY: State University of New York Press.

van Staveren, I. and Knorringa, P. (2007) 'Unpacking social capital in economic development: How social relations matter', *Review of Social Economy*, 65(1): 107–35.

Veblen, T. (1898/1919) 'Why is economics not an evolutionary science?', *Cambridge Journal of Economics*, 22: 403–14.

Veblen, T. (1909/1919) *The Place of Science in Modern Civilization and Other Essays*, New York: Huebsch.

Wagner, J. and Sternberg, R. (2004) 'Start-up activities, individual characteristics, and the regional milieu: lessons for entrepreneurship support policies from German micro data', *Annals of Regional Science*, 38(2): 219–40.

Weber, M. (1904/1930) *The Protestant Ethic and the Spirit of Capitalism* (translated by T. Parson), New York: Charles Scribner's Sons.

Whitley, R. (1992) *Business Systems in East Asia: Firms, Markets and Societies*, London: Sage.

Wood, G. (2003) 'Staying secure, staying poor: the Faustian bargain', *World Development*, 31(3): 455–71.

Woolcock, M. (1998) 'Social capital and economic development: towards a theoretical synthesis and policy framework', *Theory and Society*, 27: 151–208.

World Bank (2002) *World Development Report: Building Institutions for Markets*, Oxford: Oxford University Press.

Zucker, L. (1986) 'Production of trust: institutional sources of economic structure, 1840–1920', *Research in Organisational Behaviour*, 8: 53–111.

3 Afghanistan

Persisting instability, informality and tradition

A country beset by war and unrest, the fragile state of Afghanistan continues to be governed by informality and tradition. Afghans are credited with being remarkably resilient and adaptable, time and again demonstrating their capacity to cope in an adverse environment. In this chapter, the discussion builds on the final section of Chapter 2 to look closer at the dominance of informal institutions, power asymmetries and degrees of trust in the research country context, Afghanistan. To this end, I look specifically at the struggling Afghan state and traditions, the complex nature of social organisation and networks, the conservative Islamic environment intertwined in local politics, and the deeply entrenched cultural rules and norms, especially for women. Turning to the particular character of Afghan markets, I discuss their dynamism yet uncertainty, with markets embedded in social and cultural institutions, skewed by strong power dynamics. This is shown to have critical implications for market participation and growth.

3.1 A weak state and complex people

Labelled a 'rentier state' (Rubin, 1995), since its formation in the eighteenth century, Afghanistan has been predominantly propped up, or dependent on external resources and power with support from British India, the Soviet Union, and now largely the US. According to Maley (2008: 16), achieving political legitimacy has been challenging, with diverse tribes and remote geography, and there have been mixed experiences with 'lengthy periods of rule based on non-legitimate forms of domination'.[1] With a constitution first established in 1921, efforts to bring in new societal laws and reforms with the goal of 'modernisation' have been carried out with varying degrees of effectiveness and sustainability. While the revised 1964 Afghan constitution was deemed to be perhaps the best in the Muslim world, Afghan politics was 'the politics of the intellectuals not the masses' (Rasanayagam, 2005: 40). With little popular support, in the late 1970s, the government was still struggling to promote social change, and to transform and modernise traditional rural society in particular. A number of poorly formulated decrees were issued with the aim of reforming practices related to mortgages and debts, marriage, and land ownership. As before, however, efforts failed and the state shortly disintegrated, 'lacking the capacity to win this battle' (Rubin, 1995: 118). Today, far from being vague or underdeveloped, Afghan laws are argued to be 'precise' with an 'abundance of codifications' under different constitutions (e.g. 1932, 1976).[2] Yet many of them are described to be 'aspirational', as they either do not resonate with the wider context (and are little understood) or there are few 'enforcement mechanisms'. The state is viewed as dislocated from the majority of Afghan lives and livelihoods, with local traditions perceived to be more in tune with the prevailing reality. Rather, it is the interpretation of Islam, and Afghans' embeddedness in a community, group or tribe that defines how Afghans interact in their environment shaping their frame of reference, and how they deal with new situations or 'alien ideology' (Johnson and Leslie, 2004: 63).

With variations in origin, a sense of belonging and religion, Afghanistan has a complex society, reflected in the 'diverse explicit and implicit codes' that organise people's everyday lives (Centlivres and Centlivres-Demont, 2010: 1). Unwrapping Afghan history is imperative to understanding the extent and reach of formal institutions, and the turbulence experienced at the local level in the course of these endeavours. This includes attempts to fragment the tribes under the Amir Abdul Rahman in the nineteenth century, and then later similar efforts during the Russian era in the 1980s, to more recent ongoing destabilisation by the Taliban. This has resulted in both a wariness of central power and outsiders, and a fear of 'inculcation of foreign values on women and families, threatening local order and culture (Brodsky, 2011: 82). It has also led to the phenomenon of local self-rule as a 'defense against the state', leading to Afghans nurturing parallel power networks to protect their interests (Rubin, 1995: 72). Due to war and unrest, over 1979 to 2001, almost a quarter of Afghanistan's population was displaced (over 6–8 million people), mostly to the neighbouring countries of Iran and Pakistan. This experience has had a profound effect on Afghans, and their societal norms and social relations, introducing new ideas and relations but simultaneously leading to a fierce protection of traditional values. With the fall of the Taliban in late 2001, a great number of refugees returned to Afghanistan, bringing with them their differing experiences, largely shaped by an uncertain existence where marginality was the norm, influencing both outlooks and perspectives: 'the kaleidoscope of traditional patterns has been shaken – leadership, women, even children are affected. New voices are being heard, new values emerging, Afghan society will never be the same again' (anthropologist Akbar Ahmed, cited in Centlivres and Centlivres-Demont, 2010: 21). Today, Afghan society carries with it the wounds of 'rupture and crisis' with 'shattered communities spatially fragmented and dispersed' (ibid.). Yet this mosaic of Afghan realities, which now stretches well beyond the borders of Afghanistan, simultaneously reinforces the precarious lives of those still within the country, and moulds evolving transnational Afghan society.

3.1.1 Resilience and adaptability in the face of uncertainty

After three decades of protracted conflict and instability, the Islamic Republic of Afghanistan now stands as one of the poorest and most underdeveloped countries in the world, with some of the lowest human development indicators.[3] Illiteracy is particularly high. In rural Afghanistan, less than 30 per cent of household heads are indicated to be able to read and write. Among female-headed households, this is as low as 12 per cent. Approximately 80 per cent of the population (estimated at 33 million people)[4] live in the rural areas and have been harshly affected by the turbulence, collapse in infrastructure, and fragmentation of the economy, particularly in the two decades prior to the fall of the Taliban (Figure 3.1 charts the transition of the state and economy over this period). This forced many rural communities to seek temporary or permanent refuge in Afghan cities (or to flee to neighbouring Pakistan and Iran). Yet the extraordinary nature of Afghan resilience and their constant adaptability have somehow ensured their survival. The rural sector is still home to the bulk of the poor in Afghanistan (although urban populations are swelling), with almost half of the rural population living on less than $1 per day.

It is necessary to appreciate the country geography, and local conditions, to better understand the nature of the Afghan people. A mountainous and landlocked country, Afghanistan is nestled between the frontier of Asia and the Middle East, bordering China, Tajikistan, Uzbekistan, Iran and Pakistan. With contrasts in altitudes and terrains, the Afghan landscape is characterised by 'a combination of remoteness and accessibility, stability and resilience, and marginality and diversity' (Pain, 1996 in Pain, 2007). Agriculture and animal husbandry are the major means of securing livelihoods, generally at a subsistence level with rudimentary technology, alongside (increasingly) necessary migrant labour (inside and outside of the country). Extreme climatic conditions engender frequent hazards such as snow, drought and floods, and access to markets is often difficult. This is exacerbated by a lack of adequate roads and transport. While some traditional support systems function reasonably well at a community level (e.g. the maintenance of water channels and mosques), government-provided services – including healthcare and education – remain limited (although they are now improving). Yet despite this unpredictable and challenging context, Pain (2007) points out that 'Afghans have been anything but passive and static, adopting brilliant, innovative and unorthodox strategies to secure food, livelihoods and stability in a shifting and insecure environment'.

Since an internationally-backed government came into power in 2001–2002, large-scale reconstruction and development efforts have been rolled out in Afghanistan under an ambitious state-building agenda. Assistance to rural areas has been transitioning from short-term emergency/recovery programmes to longer-term development (where possible). The flagship government-led National Solidarity Programme (NSP) has been notably successful at promoting participation in reconstruction at the community level through the establishment of Community Development Councils (CDCs), endeavouring to link communities to formal government structures.[5] Yet (formal) governance and the rule of law still remain weak, with recurring regionally based conflict. Meanwhile, the abject poverty, persistent unemployment and high levels of opium poppy cultivation[6] are fuelling instability and frustration in other parts of the country. At the time of the research, despite several years of intensive aid and international military support, the Western-backed government had largely lost public credibility due to endemic corruption, and the lack of visible progress in terms of basic social and economic development. With continuing insecurity and lawlessness, and political instability

Period	The state	The economy
Pre-war	• Buffer state • Rentier state • Centralised but weak, limited power and legitimacy	• Rural subsistence economy • Bifurcation of urban and rural economies • Afghan Transit Trade Agreement (ATTA) – early foundation for cross-border smuggling economy
Proxy civil war (1972–1992)	• Expansion of state institutions with Soviet support, but remit limited to urban areas • Refugee warrior communities in Pakistan and Iran • Growth of political parties • Alternative rural power structures (commanders)	• Deliberate targeting of infrastructure in the countryside by Soviets • CIA/ISI arms pipeline • Monetisation of the economy • Growth of smuggling networks with Pakistan
Fragmentation (1991–1995)	• State collapse • Expanded role of regional powers • Growth of regionalised conflict • Aid community as surrogate government	• Decline of superpower largesse • Increased importance of internally generated resources • Expansion of opium and smuggling economics • Fragmentation/'peripheralisation' of the economy
Taliban (1995–2001)	• Taliban attempts to establish monopoly over means of violence (and predation) • Growing strength of transnational religious networks • International isolation (e.g. sanctions)	• Consolidation and expansion of war economy (e.g. in 1999, 75 per cent of global opium production) • Transport and marketing corridor • Growing political and economic importance of transport and trading sector

Figure 3.1 The evolving Afghan state and economy 1970s–2001

Source: Bhatia and Goodhand (2003)

and uncertainty, in addition to increasing levels of wealth differentiation, the situation remained perilously fragile, straining Afghan resilience and adaptability.

3.1.2 Diverse tribes and elaborate social organisation

Looking closer at the character of the Afghan people, at a crossroads of Asia, it is difficult to situate this diverse nation either in Central Asia, the Indian subcontinent or the Middle East (Marsden, 1998: 11). A patchwork of ethnicities, languages and cultures, Afghanistan's population comprises several distinctive social groups. Similar to peoples in the Arabian peninsula, the largest and dominant tribe are the Pashtuns (38–63 per cent). Other large groups include the Tajiks (12–25 per cent), the Hazaras (8–19 per cent) and Uzbeks (6.3–9 per cent). Meanwhile, minorities include Turkmen (2.5–3 per cent), Aimak, Baluch and Brahui, Nuristani and Kuchi (Giradet and Walter, 2004). The Pasthuns have been the predominant leaders in Afghanistan, and are known for their strong social cohesion. Contrasting to the other tribes, they have a 'complex criteria of ethnic identity' (Entezar, 2007: 154). In particular, they are known for their clearly defined code of honour, '*Pashtunwali*', a legal and moral value system determining social order and personal responsibilities (ibid.). Beyond the Pashtuns, Johnson and Leslie (2004: 52) describe ethnicity in Afghanistan as both 'complex and fluid', and as 'social and political constructs' changing according to perceived pressures. This is particularly evident among the Hazara and Tajiks in the Central Highlands.

Reflecting the linguistic, ethnic and geographical heterogeneity of the people, social organisation is complex and elaborate in Afghanistan, highlighting the importance of bonds and reciprocity (Maley, 1998: 5). Traditional trust and interconnected networks of kinship, friendship, ethnicity and regional affiliation make up the core of this intricate web of Afghan social relations. In particular, tribal-based *qawn* and religious *ulema* networks are the informal norm-based social networks in Afghanistan that influence societal interaction and relations. Olivier Roy (1994) describes the *qawn* as 'any segment of the society bound by close ties . . . extended family, a clan, an occupational group, or a village'. Based on kinship and client-patron relations, the *qawn* acts a solidarity group, which 'protects its members from encroachments from the state and other *qawns* and includes the sense of lively competition between contenders for local supremacy' (ibid.). Inevitably, with such high levels of risk and vulnerability in Afghanistan, these relational ties have tended to dominate both social and economic behaviour. In the absence of a strong state, studies indicate that traditional relational networks and associations may in fact thrive (rather than break down), as people depend on them for trust and solidarity (Nordstrom, 2000). In the context of chronic conflict and instability in Afghanistan, people have indeed depended on these networks and relations for their very survival (Bhatia and Goodhand, 2003).

Extensive research by local study groups and think-tanks has explored evolving Afghan family relations and networks. Far from the erosion of social networks over the conflict years (World Bank, 2001), Pain (2007) suggests that evidence has pointed to the consolidation of informal networks and connections, in part due to state failure to provide social protection. Afghan resilience and survival over decades of conflict has been greatly attributed to the formation and development of both 'strategic family alliances', and relations with more diverse groups, 'solidarity networks'. Yet while the latter may be viewed as strengths, they can also be weaknesses, as they have been known to fracture when groups are set against groups. The changing context has influenced the existence and development of group ties, with the periodic erosion of social relations, and the emergence of new networks. In particular, war and displacement have precipitated new forms of affiliation and identity with the development and emergence of political parties, resistance groups and Islamic organisations (Collective for Social Science Research, 2006b). Beyond the influence of local and regional politics, Pain and Lautze (2002) highlight the impact of the Taliban religious restrictions on women, which led to the establishment of an underground network of schools, spurring new social networks and relations between women.

Social capital, reciprocity and collective action

The nurturing and development of social relations and networks is viewed as essential for building social capital (as described in Chapter 2) and securing sustainable livelihoods (Scoones, 1998). Social capital – in the form of networks of reciprocity – is considered to be strongest in the rural areas in Afghanistan, although a recent study found that there was considerable variation in the strength of urban social capital, both between and within cities (Beall and Schutte, 2006). Overlapping family, ethnic and neighbourhood connections has ensured the prevalence of social networks and patterns of reciprocity, which act as social nets and support mechanisms 'indispensable to maintaining existing livelihood opportunities'. Yet while these relations have facilitated information sharing on work opportunities, they have not (generally) permitted families to rise above poverty (ibid.). Motivated more by survival (and solidarity or even pleasure), poor and vulnerable people were shown to spend significant periods of time developing and protecting these social assets, through visiting relatives, attending festivals together, and supporting family at weddings and funerals (ibid.). Cultural social agreements such as *ashar* (communal, reciprocal work, typically around life-cycle events), and *pandusi* (e.g. agreements in livestock caring while family members are away) also support 'cooperative' self-help. But the research suggested that social networks could be vulnerable to over-use. It was further suggested that the urban poor do not seem to have much bridging capital between heterogeneous (and more powerful) groups, with networks existing more on a homogenous survivalist level, barely reaching beyond the neighbourhood (ibid.). For example, establishing '*wasita*', or relations to powerful people, is said to remain a challenge, even in collective action efforts.

3.1.3 Migration and transnational links shaping livelihoods and trade

Conflict, poverty and drought have scattered the humble and unlettered, as well as the better off and educated, across the face of the globe . . . these experiences have helped to hone the already robust coping and survival mechanisms of members of the Afghan rural population to develop a keener edge and have exposed them to livelihood opportunities of which they were previously ignorant.

(Fitzherbert, 2007: 30)

Going beyond a frozen 'preserved, distant and distinct society', to understand Afghan evolving culture and livelihoods, it is crucial to elaborate on the influence of Afghan migrations (Centlivres and Centlivres-Demont, 2010: 2). The migration experience has led to the extended networks of families and relations, and the development of 'multi-locational' households (Pain 2007). Stigter and Monsutti (2005) observed that the traditional social networks have been broadened with the emergence of *regional and transnational networks* of families and relations. This has brought Afghans in close contact with those beyond their immediate and extended groups, influencing their 'social, cultural and economic life'. Historically, trade relations and seasonal migration are seen as having deep roots in Afghanistan, and the role of migration has been shown to be significant, with many Afghans involved in migrant work in Iran and Pakistan in the 'pre-1978' years (ibid.). However, migration became a more critical strategy of rural households during the conflict years, both for security and economic opportunity (inside and outside the country). In the Soviet era (1980s), a significant diaspora of Afghans was established in Central Asia and the West. In this same period, the Afghan city populations also swelled, as rural populations sought safety and access to resources, linking rural communities with urban areas. During the 1990s, further families migrated to Pakistan and Iran. In these years, regional refugee populations were in a 'dynamic state of flux' (Pain and Lautze, 2002), with constant movement of members in and out of Afghanistan seeking work during times of drought and stress (the outflow of Afghans was so high that labour was considered Afghanistan's primary export; Bhatia and Goodhand, 2003).

Refugee and migratory movements have facilitated access to skills, technology and financial capital; and the growing remittance economy has helped sustain rural households in particular. Networks have also created innovative transnational opportunities for education, employment and trade. One respondent described the family livelihood strategy as an 'octopus model' (ibid), with family members deployed to 'available' employment activities across family ties that were most suited to their status/skills (i.e. gender, qualification and occupation). Families described deliberately nurturing and exploiting as large a network as possible across family, political and commercial players (ibid.). For example, in the eastern city of Jalalabad, Afghans were shown to visit/keep up with their relatives in neighbouring Pakistan to access information on job opportunities, and to ensure accommodation during search for migrant labour (Schutte, 2006). Fitzherbert (2006) suggests that traditional trade information networks (e.g. market prices) have also been 'enhanced, strengthened and expanded' as a result of the diaspora, and boosted by the recent mobile communications revolution.[7] Transnationalism now 'permeates the nature of Afghans' settlement patterns, livelihoods and support networks', with relations established not only with families, kinship groups and political affiliates, but also with international counterparts for social and economic gain (Collective for Social Science Research, 2006a). For example, Afghan diaspora in the neighbouring Pakistani city of Peshawar engage in thriving cross-border trade, and also help family members access work in situ, or beyond (e.g. Iran, Europe and Australia). And networks have been shown to also extend to non-Afghans (e.g. Pakistani links in the carpet trade).

3.2 Society, religion and politics

To develop a deeper perspective of Afghan livelihoods however, it is necessary to appreciate more fundamental sociocultural dynamics, the influence of religion and the nature of local governance. Afghanistan still remains highly illiterate outside of the cities, with less than a third of its overall population able to read and write. As common in traditional and largely oral societies, both Afghan men and women tend to learn 'modes of behaviour, rules and customs as they are communicated and passed down the generations' (Brodsky, 2011: 100). In this situation, both tradition and religion continue to play strong roles in Afghan lives, as families navigate persisting uncertainty across physical, social and economic spheres. Aside from a handful of Hindus and Sikhs (less than 1 per cent), Afghanistan is a predomi-nantly Muslim country (mostly of the Sunni branch),[8] practicing the five pillars of Islam: the profession of faith, daily prayers, alms (*zadat*) for poor people and clerics, fasting during the month of Ramadan, and (if possible) during their lifetime, performing the *haj* pilgrimage to the holy city of Mecca. Yet the Islam of Afghanistan has its own character, intermingled with their rich history and culture, including the poetry of Persia (Rubin, 1995: 38). This localised form of Islam has become a 'source of universal values and ethics that give life a transcendent meaning' (Rubin, 1995: 39), and is the lens upon which Afghans view and comprehend their world, shaping societal behaviour.

As a religious society, the current formal laws in the Afghan constitution are a mix of both Islamic and modern law, approved by religious scholars.[9] Yet, as indicated earlier, with little government reach outside of the cities, informal institutions tend to persist, particularly those that remain closer to traditional societal norms and values. At the provincial and district level, formal institutions are thus often extremely limited in their capacity, and (formal) justice systems remain weak with 'widespread dissatisfaction among the people' (ibid.). As a result, for common disputes and local affairs, religious clerics and strongmen tend to still assume traditional roles.

3.2.1 Sociocultural dynamics shaping power and agency

Afghan cultural norms, values and power relations are heavily embedded in traditional structures of language, folklore and religion. These include proverbs, poems and traditional storytelling, and local interpretations of Koranic texts and *hadiths*. Mills (1991) examined rhetoric and politics in Afghan traditional storytelling with themes underscoring gender and sexuality, religion, and public and private social control. Such (often humorous) stories are used to regulate society and individual behaviour, and provide guidance for local people to manage their lives. Drawing on Geert Hofstede's extensive work on culture (e.g. Hofstede, 1980), Entezar (2007) elaborates on critical cultural dimensions of Afghan society – embedded in prevailing norms, values and habits – that shape the traditional Afghan world view, and how people think and behave. In particular, Entezar highlights dynamics of power, uncertainty and religion, and 'collectivism' (i.e. tendencies towards group-orientated behaviour).

Afghans revere wealthy and well-connected powerful people, often from dominant families. 'Who you know' (*rawabit*) is crucial. These individuals may be formal government appointed rulers, as well as local informal commanders[10] and community leaders. With little formal law and order, however, Afghanistan is still ruled heavily by traditional decision-making bodies (Entezar, 2007: 38). These forums resolve many disputes between families, in communities and between tribes, and are often perceived as 'less corrupt, more convenient and less expensive' than government courts. The importance of consultation is articulated within the Koran, and often part of traditional customs in tribal societies such as Afghanistan. In vein with Hofstede's theory, Entezar describes Afghan society associating power with old age or seniority, and charisma. Older people are both trusted and respected, and have greater potential for social power and prestige. *Asqsaqal* or grey beards' advice and consultation are sought for their experience, and they often play a critical role in resolving disputes between individuals, families and tribes. Charismatic individuals are also highly respected for either their 'deeds or leadership skills' (ibid.) Entezar describes the added importance of being religious, and this may often be associated with charisma. Entezar draws attention to the perceived authority (and strength) and power of individuals and their capacity to enforce societal rules and keep control. In this regard, Afghans traditionally respect the authority of 'people' more than the authority of the rules themselves.

Second, Entezar (2007) highlights Hofstede's theory of uncertainty and fear, with societies typically drawing on three potential mechanisms to cope with this, namely technology, law and religion. In traditional Afghan society, the latter remains the most significant. While formal laws, rules and regulations are made, they 'are patchy and unevenly enforced' (Entezar, 2007: 61). This is due both to the persisting weaknesses (and reach) of formal government in Afghanistan, and the dominance of local systems embedded in religion and traditional structures. In particular, the strong authority of religion in daily lives means that the 'average Afghan accepts divine will' (Entezar, 2007: 64), and 'God is both a source of comfort and of fear' (Entezar, 2007: 66). This translates into a sense of fatalism, in the 'temporary nature of life on earth' (ibid.). Finally, Entezar also emphasises the prevalence of 'collectivism' in Afghanistan – rather than individualism – where individuals are embedded into cohesive in-groups 'which protect them in exchange for their unquestioning loyalty' (Entezar, 2007: 75), underscoring the importance of social relations mentioned earlier. In collectivist societies, the family, ethnic group and other social organisations are perceived as crucial for both 'protection and advancement'. In particular, Afghans tend to relate to their ethnicity (race and language), Islamic sect (Sunni or Shia), and regionalism (place of birth) in forming their identity and deriving their agency.

3.2.2 Local power structures and collective action

Further examining local power structures, Rubin (1995) draws attention to the nature of kinship, *qawn*, tribe and ethnicity to unwrap societal relations, and social control and collective action. Roy (1994) expands on the composition of Afghan traditional elites, including the *khan*, (or *mawlawi* or *hakim*), who is a powerful landowner and head of a *qawn*, and clerics that are often trained at high levels. There may also be elected community heads (*maliks*), and government-designated representatives (*arbabs*, or in cities, *wakils*). Made up of different *qawns*, village politics is typically intertwined in wrestles for power between the local *khans* (leaders of *qawns*), who skilfully draw on wealth and kinship ties for local support and resources to gain power (Rubin, 1995: 41). Influenced by social relations (as a result of kinship, production and religion), a leader's 'resources' may include the ownership of assets, family connections and outsider relations, as well as Islamic knowledge and charisma (ibid.). In the same way that common people draw on these resources for their livelihood strategies, leaders thus draw on them for social control and collective action (ibid.). *Khans* aim to be perceived as 'bigger' than their rivals, and to obtain and then distribute resources from the state or market (derived from patronage, trade or smuggling) (ibid.). As wealthy men, *khans* then gain 'clientele' through providing loans and employing local people as tenants on their land. Villagers tend not to perceive wealth (or power) as an oppressive force, however, since *khans* often redistribute wealth through patronage, and through creating public goods such as infrastructure and protection (ibid.). Village power tends also not to be individually or family situated, but more fluid across 'networks of influence' (ibid.). Notably, *khans* can be both allies of the state or competitors of social control.

Meanwhile – with no formal religious hierarchy in *Sunni* Islam – religious leaders are locally appointed mullahs, belonging to each village. More senior religious scholars form part of regional *ulema*. Crucially, perceptions on the mullah vary across regions and tribes. Pashtuns in the east may even see local mullahs as an object of mockery, particularly if they try to intervene in village affairs (Rubin, 1995: 39).[11] Yet while they may be reduced to 'second-class actors' in some villages (particularly after the fall of the Taliban), research by CPAU (2007) suggests that there remain three core matters that mullahs still have significant control and influence, and over which they can 'rouse public support'. These include apostasy, women (and issues related to honour), and the presence of foreigners (specifically foreign troops). The elite may thus increasingly view mullahs as a minor authority or even irrelevant, but the mullahs themselves regard their own role in community life as potentially strong, with support from local people – 'ordinary people are listening to us' (ibid.). They see themselves as protectors and advisors of the local village culture and religion. Further, mullahs have useful and important allies. These include the 'religious teachers' in the community, straddling both male and female societies (the male *kaari* and female *kaaria*). In addition, traditionally, the mosque is seen as the heart of village life, a place for prayer and religious rituals, as well as a place for teaching, community meetings and receiving guests (CPAU, 2007: 22). Yet perceptions on the role of religion may now be changing, even more for the common villager. For some, the religious dimensions of the ongoing conflict – or foreign experience – have created a desire for the separation of religion and village affairs (ibid.). The 'changing power structures' and 'increasing wealth' of elites is further decreasing the dominance of the mosque in some locations. At times, *khans* have also been known to compete with religious leaders. Yet Giustozzi (2007: 44) argues that due to the (ongoing) fragmentation of communities, the clergy can still pose a considerable force with a 'supra-communitarian network', particularly in more remote and unstable areas, and have a strong role in collective mobilisation and action.

3.2.3 Traditional decision-making and conflict resolution

Taking a closer look at traditional decision-making and community rule, the *khans* tend to oversee local village day-to-day affairs, typically resolving 'recurrent disputes involving women, money and land' (Rubin, 1995: 43). Religious leaders can also act as mediators when disputes remain unresolved, or in times of crises across tribes and *qawns* (and, if required, can mobilise people for 'protest or revolt') (Rubin, 1995: 44). Traditional local decision bodies include *shuras* or councils, and *jirgas* or assemblies.[12] The *shura* is the village-based council, and is an informal gathering of senior, influential and well-respected men of the community that convene as necessary on important community affairs. They are also involved with traditional conflict resolution. In addition to local elders, this body tends to include powerful figures such as landowners and commanders, the village *arbab* (head), and the mullah(s). According to CPAU (2007), changes to this circle have occurred in the last 30 years of conflict and unrest with a more prominent role for commanders and warlords during the height of instability. This then receded after 2001, but is now notably growing again in some areas. Meanwhile, religious leaders saw their influence increase during the religious-fueled Taliban years and generally also decline again since 2001. In matters of conflict resolution and justice, traditional village *shuras* typically apply to a mixture of practices usually including *sharia* law, *maraka* customary law (*urf*), and in Pashtun areas, *Pashtunwali* (CPAU, 2007: 24). Formal authority is still rarely sought due to its ineffectiveness, slowness and corruption (ibid.).

In recent years, the government has attempted to facilitate the establishment of more formal village-based authorities, with the initiation of government-supported Community Development Councils (CDCs). These organisations comprise elected members of the community (with an appointed head, deputy and treasurer). First introduced in 2003–2004 for community development projects, these bodies are gradually now being transformed into politically oriented local village councils. Even with formal democratic elections, in reality this council has (still) been composed of traditional village elders and the village mullah. And while local commanders may not be part of the new CDC (by choice), in practice, they still influence all crucial decision-making and play a lead role in resolving community issues. In recent years, where possible, there is now also a separate women's CDC subcommittee, also elected by the community (women). This body usually includes senior elders' wives and the wife of the main mullah. The women's CDC tends to meet separately, and communicates with the village men either through written messages, or through the leaders' wives. The power and influence of this group may vary as a result of their experience and education, and the local village subculture.

3.3 'Zan, zar and zamin': honour and women

Known collectively as *namus*, the mantra '*zar, zan* and *zamin*' (woman, gold and land) is the tribal code that calls upon Afghan men to protect and support their family and kin. In particular, Afghan men perceive their womenfolk as the 'repository of their honor' (Rubin, 1995: 24). For Pashtuns, their specific code of honour, *Pashtunwali*, embodies this explicitly through related customs, traditions, heritage, customary law, and social relations (Atayee, 1979). Linked to notions of honour and protection, and as a strongly patriarchal society, women fall under the male hierarchy of domination (with senior men controlling more junior men) in the Afghan family structure of organisation and control. This 'protection' has led to women's marginalisation in all public spheres, constraining their social, economic and political life, and affecting their skills and capacity development, and potential societal roles. Restraint on their mobility inhibits basic social exchange, access to information and services, and prevents women's organisation in civil society and markets. As a result of these limitations, women's lives tend to be characterised by inequality 'not only legal and cultural, but also biological and physiological, insofar as inequality encompasses health, life expectancy, and diet, as well as history, tradition, and balance of power' (Centlivres and Centlivres-Demont, 2010: 55). Rubin (1995: 24) describes this protection and control as manifested in the social custom of women's *purdah* (segregation and seclusion of women) and related *chadri* (veiling), and highlights variations in ethnic group, social class and location (with rural and urban differences).

While restrained and secluded, women are still traditionally perceived as economically productive and 'indispensable' members of the household (ibid.), but work usually takes place within the confines of the home. Women's chores thus go beyond childcare and cooking, and may include pastoralism, vegetable gardening, harvesting, food processing and textiles (spinning, carpet weaving, embroidery and tailoring). Centlivres and Centlivres-Demont (2010: 57) describes Afghan life divided between the public and private realm, with women's worlds falling into the latter. It is in this domestic domain that women are supposed to 'expend their energies, thrive, be supported, cherished and honored' (Azarbaijani-Moghaddam, 2009: 64). Within this sphere, women are able to exert influence and have power, even means of resistance. While under male domination, there is also a secondary female hierarchy in the family setting, with mothers-in-law having authority over daughters-in-law. Female solidarity against men is rare, however. Rather, 'collusion and conflicts' occur between the women themselves, particularly since traditional relations between a mother and son preclude the son siding with his wife (ibid.).

3.3.1 'Makr-i-zan' Afghan women's tricks . . . 'Seven steps ahead of the Devil'[13]

Paradoxically, Afghan women are at once honoured and protected, and at the same time traditionally portrayed in folklore as unreliable, or at worst 'tricksters'. Unwrapping these contradictory attitudes towards women, Brodsky (2011: 74) describes oppressive and suspicious male behaviour as based on conservative interpretations of Islam intermingled with Afghan tribal and ethnic customs (particularly *Pastunwali*).[14] Both within Middle Eastern cultures and in Afghanistan, less trusting and antisocial perceptions of women are reflected in language and literature. However, in Afghanistan, storytelling of women's tricks may be unfavourable but they can also have 'pro-social outcomes' (Mills, 2011: 63). In day-to-day life however, Entezar draws attention to gender dynamics in Afghanistan and the embeddedness of discriminatory gender norms, values and roles in local language and grammar, literature, education, religion and social organisations (Entezar, 2007: 113). In language, for example, actions related to women are often in the passive voice. Women are often also defined in relation to men (e.g. the mother of Rasoul). In traditional Farsi proverbs, many are cited as being 'slanderous' against women, describing them as sex objects, property, or evil (e.g. 'women have [even] fooled the Satan') (Satari, cited in Entezar, 2007: 117). Meanwhile, in poetry and folk literature, there is much that indicates women are not to be trusted or lack value:

> Don't ever listen to women; try to always keep them silent; they defy logic and religion . . .
>
> (Poet Nasir Khusraw, cited in Entezar, 2007: 115)

In contrast, Islam enshrines equality between the sexes in the Koran, through articulating women's rights, for example, to education and property (Abdul Azeem, 1999). Yet within the Afghan context, ancient cultural attitudes and practices persist – often above religious ideals – due to high levels of illiteracy. Both the educated, and the law, have endeavoured to bring the society closer to the ideals of the Koran however. For example, the Afghan civil code of 1978 is based on *sharia* law (Islamic law), and stipulates that widows may receive one-eighth of the property of their husband, or one-fourth if they have no children. But local social norms mean that she may not often claim her entitlement (in customary practices, widows are expected to marry their brothers-in-law to keep property in the family). Few women thus own land, and if they do, have little access to it. Traditionally, women themselves may also be treated as property and are used to settle feuds (*badal*).

3.3.2 Nuanced and heterogeneous realities

Doubleday (2006) sought to look beyond the stereotype of Afghan women as 'subjugated, powerless and invisible beings' to highlight their creativity, resistance, power and heterogeneous reality. She drew attention to a minority group of women at the margins of society practising as professional musicians and dancers in the late 1970s. She emphasised the strength of women to women relationships in helping one another and sharing burdens (Doubleday, 2006: 13). She looked at the power that women exerted in family rituals. She also discussed more austere versions of *purdah*, induced by controlling husbands (Doubleday, 2006: 106), and some positive outcomes, including the security it provided for nurturing family and community networks (Doubleday, 2006: 218). Traditionally, women's relations remain within the family, and they have no direct access to the economic life of the marketplace and beyond. Yet in some cases, women do manage to build informal economic exchanges from the confines of their backyards while veiled, thus promoting their work and facilitating sales in situ (Centlivres and Centlivres-Demont, 2010: 59). In urban life, 'the risks and unknowns' have often led families to increase *purdah* restrictions (ibid.). This is argued to have been exacerbated by the development of a 'modern economy' accentuating traditional activities related to production and domestic life, further contributing to the segregation of women (Centlivres and Centlivres-Demont, 2010: 62). Indeed, Rubin (1995: 24) highlights the prevalence of veiling in the urban context to preserve tradition (in conservative families), perhaps in the face of perceived 'Western culture'.

Looking beyond the outcomes of Afghan women's structural inequalities, Pain and Grace (2011: 263) argue that there are two classic potential traps to assessing women's lives and work. The first is in comparing and contrasting Afghan women's lives (and what they have) with men's lives. And the second is in dwelling on women's capacity to act as 'autonomous economic agents'. In vein with Doubleday (2006), instead they suggest that it is critical to look at how women find power to act within such constraints, to give both 'meaning and satisfaction' to their lives. They cite the variability to act, and thus *purdah* manifestations, as depending on factors such as age, marriage status (unmarried, married, widowed), children, sex of children, and the wife status/position in a polygamous household. Meanwhile, Wright (2010: 14) further underscores the situation of local politics and perceived environmental security by families, as further determining women's allowances and restrictions. In addition, the increased need for male dignity – as observed in the Afghan refugee camps – was also shown to motivate a reinforcement of women's *purdah* (Centlivres and Centlivres-Demont, 2010: 78). Expanding upon these various pressures, Pain and Grace (2011) draw attention to the dynamic state of Afghan culture, with change induced by contextual conditions such as war and insecurity, nature of male migration for work (with increasing responsibilities for women), and women's access to education. They also underscore the difference between the ideal and practice. In poorer households, (older) women may have increased public-facing roles in agriculture and farming within the household and outside.[15] In general, during the course of their life (and with seniority), women's mobility, and influence and authority within the household and in decision-making, does tend to improve, particularly in the case of older widows (Smith, 2011: 164).

3.3.3 Resistance and change

> We have a voice, so why should we remain silent? Why should we choke our throats when we can sing in harmony?
>
> (Nahid Sultan, cited in Kator, 2011: 363)

Yet while it is important to appreciate how women act 'within constraints', it is equally critical to learn how women may actively negotiate and overcome such constraints, outside of life variations and the pressures of war. Contrary to women's depiction in the Western press as 'silent' victims, Afghan women in fact have a 'long history of spirited resistance and resilience' (Brodsky, 2011: 76). Personal narratives and stories are a typical way that women share their experiences, often articulating the suffering and hardships that they face to gain community (or other women's) respect (Brodsky, 2011: 99). Women also resist through more subtle means such as poetry. For Pashtun women in particular, poetry and songs are their well-known language of resistance (Majrouh, 2003). Meanwhile, Centlivres argues that women's slavery can translate into men's slavery in the power that women hold to (potentially) threaten male honour through such means as humiliation, although this can have fatal consequences (Centlivres and Centlivres-Demont, 2010: 62). Women can wield such power in the domestic sphere through, for example, the preparation of mediocre meals, or sending their husbands back and forth to the bazaar (Centlivres and Centlivres-Demont, 2010: 57). As a form of solidarity, women also have their own cultural traditions such as the annual spring festival of *Samanak*, where women gather together for a celebratory meal, and share and exchange the joys and challenges of their lives. Other forms of gently resisting discriminatory attitudes and practices include drawing on progressive verses of the Koran, in particular its emphasis, for example, on equal rights to education, etc. (Mills, 2011: 71). More extreme forms of (less positive) protestation include self-immolation and suicide (common in the western city of Herat).[16] Suicide is described as the ultimate (and most tragic) act of resistance, going against both tribal codes and Islam (Majrouh, 2003).

Social change from above

Towards more fundamental change in women's rights, Afghan history has demonstrated the challenge of enforcing societal change 'from above' in various lawmaking efforts, as indicated earlier. In the 1920s, the incumbent King Amanullah visited Europe with his wife, Queen Soraya. Witnessing the liberal European societies of the time, they rushed back to Afghanistan to 'modernise' their country. In Amanullah's reform programme (1919–1928), Queen Soraya pushed for women's emancipation in particular. Similar to other regional leaders of the time (e.g. Mustafa Kemal Ataturk in Turkey and Reza Shah Pahlavi in Iran),

Amanullah appreciated the link between a nation's development and women's status (Le Duc, cited in Centlivres and Centlivres-Demont, 2010: 64). Disconnected from the Afghan reality, though, he introduced radical new laws to 'liberalise' Afghan women, forbidding the wearing of the *burka* in public places and declaring 'equal rights' between men and women.[17] Girls' education was then initiated in 1921. And in the same year, the first women's magazine was founded by Queen Soraya, the weekly *Irshad-e-Naswan*, 'The Guide for Women' (yet the publication only notably lasted until 1925). In pushing through such laws, Amanullah went against the *ulemas* and tribal leaders that pursued Islamic and tribal codes. A massive backlash followed, led by core members of the clergy (mullahs). The authorities reacted violently and purged lead protestors. Laws were then enforced in cities, and urban-based social change was gradually generated over the next few years. Yet in practice, change was only pursued by the upper classes. For the most part, traditional attitudes remained, with strong levels of opposition. The laws were perceived as 'an unbearable transgression of the social and divine order, a conspiracy against the fundamental notions of male honor and divine laws, in which the tribal code and religious law are closely connected' (Centlivres and Centlivres-Demont, 2010: 66). Ultimately, this resulted in Amanullah rescinding most of the social reforms. He was then finally overthrown in 1929.

Thirty years later (1959), the secularist Prime Minister Daud tried again to bring in social reform, and finally succeeded in bringing in laws related to the voluntary removal of the veil (using Islamic scholars citing that the veil had no justification in Islamic law). Yet government literature (e.g. textbooks) that aimed to support social change depicted Western-inspired illustrations of family life that were far removed from the Afghan reality (Centlivres and Centlivres-Demont, 2010: 66). With this association, they possibly created a lingering dichotomy of (Western/non-Islamic) modernity versus (Afghan/Islamic) tradition. By the 1970s, however, there was apparent short-term success, with over 40 per cent of Kabul women boasting both formal education and working outside of the house (Rubin, 1995: 79). But these progressive practices were not mirrored by local attitudes, which still remained conservative (Knabe, 1977), particularly outside of the elite circles, and there remained a distinctive 'cultural rift' between the capital and the rest of the country (ibid.). The subsequent Soviet occupation (1979–1989) attempted to push the women's rights agenda further – particularly in the workplace and education – through a top-down approach, but efforts were largely again confined to urban centres[18] (and general support was also lacking). These communist-driven decrees were considered un-Islamic, and the regime labelled as non-Muslim. Once more, religious and tribal communities vociferously objected to these, and to other progressive laws on land and property. The reforms became associated with Western ideals and hence deemed anti-Islamic (ibid.). Subsequent civil war in the 1990s then pushed out progressives, and re-ushered in conservative attitudes towards women. Small gains that had been made were undermined as Mujahedeen (resistance) fighters wrestled for control. Finally, the extreme fanaticism of the Taliban regime in the late 1990s forced a return to 'traditional' (strict Koran-abiding) practices, particularly in the more 'modern' urban areas. While highly conservative and oppressive, it is often overlooked that the Taliban sought to bring the society closer to the Islamic ideal, going beyond discriminatory customary practices, for example in the areas of property and inheritance (Centlivres and Centlivres-Demont, 2010: 81). Since 2001 and the fall of the Taliban, the aid community has endeavoured to re-champion the rights of women to usher in broad social change, and in fact has almost completely framed their efforts under this cause of 'women's emancipation'. Efforts have included renewing and updating legislation[19] and through Afghanistan becoming signatories to global conventions.[20]

Emerging social change from below

Yet instituting radical change solely through legislation, and so far removed from the average reality, has shown both its challenges as well as limitations in Afghanistan. In terms of more grass-roots action, and beyond just 'resistance and resilience', women's rights efforts are now gathering pace, although these initiatives still remain largely rooted in cities (and notably in city mentalities). Since 2001, many (urban-based) women's civil society organisations have sprung up to campaign for women's rights, but their 'global rights' message often appears alien to village women.[21] As an extreme reaction to Afghan women's rights, a controversial resistance movement known as the Revolutionary Association of the Women of Afghanistan (RAWA) emerged out of Pakistan in the 1980s. This group has sought to fight for women's rights but is often perceived as a radical feminist group that does more harm than good. In general, while the new urban generation is more open to progressive values, traditional values still persist in the older generation and in the rural areas. Further, rights are also often still associated as 'Western' and thus un-Afghan/Islamic. These perceptions have arguably been exacerbated by the large Western presence and their explicit agenda of women's 'emancipation', and Afghanistan's cultural fragility after years of war and turbulence.

3.4 Dynamic but distorted Afghan markets

> There are strong arguments for private sector, market-led growth in Afghanistan, with few exceptions there is little actual discussion of the market itself, other than price determination.
>
> (Pain and Lister, 2007: 239)

Amidst this instability, uncertainty and conservatism, the discussion turns now to the nature of Afghan markets, and the participation of marginalised groups such as women. Evidence from mountain economies suggests that 'movement and exchange' are an integral part of the typical livelihood systems in these challenging environments, with business thriving along well-trodden routes (Viazzo, 1989). Afghanistan indeed has a long tradition of trading and market activity, although customary trade systems remain deeply embedded in informal social relations and patronage. Often Afghanistan's economy is portrayed as merely 'traditional', relying on subsistence-based agriculture and antiquated techniques, but this misses the 1960s global market orientation of major export sectors such as dried fruit (particularly raisons) and karakul lambskins (Christoplos, 2004), and significant investment in intensive agriculture in the South. Incorporating these developments, the agricultural systems should be rather characterised as both diverse and adaptable to 'episodic development interventions, recurrent drought, periodic conflict and the regional politico-economic situation' (ibid.). In recent decades of war, institutions, infrastructure and market structures were weakened or destroyed in Afghanistan, exacerbating traditional market dynamics described in Chapter 2. With continued market informality, limited government control and a context of risk, this has led to the evolving 'distorted' nature of Afghan business.[22] Despite this, commodity markets have proven remarkably resilient. Christoplos attributes this to experience over years of 're-establishing business when opportunities have arisen amid recurrent crises and periods of recovery' (ibid.).

According to Goodhand (2004), three types of economy have tended to emerge in Afghanistan over the major years of conflict (1979–2001). He describes these as the combat, shadow and coping economies – each with its own dynamic and patterns of change (Figure 3.2). These have enabled different groups to 'wage war, profit, cope or survive' (ibid.). The combat (or war) economy includes the trading of economic resources used to sustain the conflict, and war-induced strategies deployed to disempower specific groups. The shadow (or black) economy relates to those involved with profiteering on the fringes of the conflict. Finally, the coping economy describes the majority, striving to simply maintain their asset bases. In the absence of a strong state and legal framework, conflict 'opportunistic' entrepreneurs (mostly from traditional business families) have tended to be involved in 'low-risk, quick return activities' with profits generated outside the country (Bhatia and Goodhand, 2003). For those in the coping economy, labour has been a major activity. Collinson (2003) indicates that there is a complex relationship between so-called war economies, shadow economies, and coping and survival economies (e.g. within extremely poor societies), which affect local vulnerability (e.g. access to resources and local power relations) and people's links with wider economic and political processes. While the government has made concerted efforts to regulate the economy in recent years, informality and illicit trade persist, particularly in the conflict-ridden south of the country. In lucrative and illicit sectors, war and conflict have even facilitated business. Afghanistan is now the largest global supplier of opium, accounting for over 90 per cent of world production (Ward *et al.*, 2008).

3.4.1 Markets shaped by informality and uncertainty

Despite the ongoing conflict in Afghanistan, entrepreneurial activity is for the most part 'ubiquitous' in the country, (Ciarli *et al.*, 2009), and business is thriving, particularly among dominant trading families. There is an underlying assumption that all entrepreneurship is productive and will facilitate prosperity and peace. Yet findings from Africa suggest that entrepreneurship may not always generate economic growth and development, as previously suggested by Baumol (1968). Pain (2007) suggests that traditional markets in Afghanistan cannot be disentangled

	The war economy	The black economy	The coping economy
Key actors	Commanders, 'conflict entrepreneurs', fighters	Profiteers, transport mafia, businessmen; 'downstream' actors (truck drivers, poppy farmers)	Poor families and communities (the majority of the population)
Motivations and incentives	To fund the war effort or achieve military objectives Peace may not be in their interest as it may lead to decreased power, status and wealth Fighters may have an interest in peace if there are alternative sources of livelihood	To make profit on the margins of conflict Entrepreneurs profit from the lack of a strong state and a highly liberal economy Peace could be in their interest if it encourages long-term investment and licit entrepreneurial activity	To cope and maintain asset bases through low-risk activities, or to survive through asset erosion Peace could enable families to move beyond subsistence
Key activities and commodities	Taxation of licit and illicit economic activities (opium, smuggled consumer goods, lapis and emeralds, wheat, land tax) Money, arms, equipment and fuel from external state and non-state actors Economic blockades of dissenting areas Destruction of means of economic support Asset-stripping and looting	Opium economy Cross-border smuggling Mass extraction of natural resources (timber, marble) Smuggling of high-value commodities (emeralds, lapis, antiquities, rare fauna) *Hawala* (currency order and exchange system) Aid manipulation	Diverse livelihood strategies to spread risk Subsistence agriculture Petty trade and small businesses Agricultural wage labour Labour migration and remittances Redistribution through family networks Humanitarian assistance
Impacts	Disruption to markets and destruction of asset bases Violent redistribution of resources and entitlements Impoverishment of politically-vulnerable groups Out-migration of educated people	Concentrates power and wealth Undermines patron–client relationships, increasing vulnerability Smuggling circumvents Pakistan's customs duty and sales tax, affecting revenue collection and undercutting local producers Increased drug use	Coping may reinforce social networks, but survival may lead to negative or regressive coping strategies Lack of long-term investment Long-term effects on human capital – lowering levels of health, education, etc.

Figure 3.2 Afghanistan's sub-economies

Source: Bhatia and Goodhand (2003)

from the nature of the current context of the Afghan state and society governing their behaviour, both in the problematic formal regulation and extraction of 'bureaucratic rent' and in the non-economic forces of control, embedded in social and cultural institutions. Characterised by informality and power distortions, understanding Afghan markets thus requires looking at how the trade is embedded, assessing the distributional spread of income and profits, and identifying control mechanisms within the chain (ibid.). It is also essential to consider the context of risk/distrust, which leads to the perpetuation of predictable trade linkages (Ritchie and Fitzherbert, 2008).

Facilitating private sector led development is viewed as the key strategy to accelerating Afghanistan's socio-economic development. Priority sectors have been selected (both for export and import substitution),[23] and value chain development promoted by major donors. A great deal of effort is being channelled into strengthening and developing markets with varying degrees of success. Markets are assumed to be open and free, and there is an almost complete ignorance of non-economic dimensions (Pain and Lister, 2007). All that is conceived to be required to jump-start markets is 'entrepreneurship' support. Little discussion is held on the market itself, or the underlying institutions, beyond the basic nature of exchange (e.g. influencing supply and demand through competitive pricing and efficiency). While some recent efforts have been made to formalise trading, poor enforcement, continued uncertainty and discriminatory social institutions result in power asymmetries and high transaction costs, mostly borne by producers (including the identification of trustworthy suppliers/buyers, and costs associated with negotiation, measuring, transfer, monitoring and contract enforcement; Christoplos, 2004). This has led to the evolving skewed nature of Afghan business, where trading remains dominated by powerful and traditional players. It is argued that current (inequitable) economic growth in Afghanistan may not necessarily lead to improved broader political governance (and institutional development) as many policymakers suggest. In fact, current market functioning may indeed have a negative impact on political governance and state building (Pain and Lister, 2007). It may also lead to 'unproductive' economic growth and social discontent.

3.4.2 Trading elite, regionalism and evolving politics

While traditional trading systems have thus prevailed over the conflict years, changes to power dynamics have influenced the nature of the trading networks and the type of goods exchanged, with increasing numbers of Pakistani middlemen involved in trade networks in the south of the country. Trade networks that previously extended to Central Asia now predominantly go through Pakistan (Bhatia and Goodhand, 2003). Pain and Lister (2007) contend that the business elite is strongly connected to local and national military, and political power holders, facilitating tax exemptions, security and access to contracts (e.g. construction sector), and channels to launder money. According to Bhatia and Goodhand (2003), though, this was not always the case. In the 1950s, the Afghan merchant class was politically weak and heavily taxed. Yet in the 1980s and 1990s, the transport businessmen in Pakistan border cities (Peshawar and Quetta) had close links to the political players – chiefly as a result of ties to military groups – and trade routes became increasingly oriented towards Pakistan (particularly in the east), and embedded in local power dynamics. Today, 90 per cent of Afghan carpets are still channelled through Pakistan where they complete the final processing (cutting and washing) (and are branded 'made in Pakistan') and exported. Across traditional (and new) sectors, high levels of integration currently exist within business chains, and deals are still largely conducted on the basis of 'personalized client and social relation-ships', which are grounded in ethnicity, family relations, history and religion (Pain and Lister, 2007: 244). While specific ethnic groups and families tend to dominate particular sectors (e.g. carpet trading and Pashtuns), Pain and Lister (2004) suggest that export traders may also be involved in several emerging sectors, leading to the dominance of business by a limited number of traders. Business elites tend to be able to freely manipulate prices, access credit and make payments in cash, and enjoy political power. Paterson (2006) suggests that new high-level entrants may indeed be possible, but only with 'influential sponsorship'.

3.4.3 Traditional market regulation: sociocultural institutions and gender

> Afghan markets are characterized by informality and non-competitiveness with high social exclusionary elements that influence the way that markets work: governing trade, distributional outcomes and power structures.
>
> (Pain and Lister, 2007)

As described in Chapter 2, there has been increasing discussion by development theorists about the complex role of social/cultural institutions (i.e. norms, values) in 'market-oriented' development and the role of social regulation (as a result of gender, ethnicity and caste) in causing exclusion or 'adverse incorporation' (Johnson, 2006). Harriss-White (2003) highlighted the dominance of 'non-state regulative structures' in developing environments, with markets comprising *'bundles of institutions'* embedded in broader 'regulating institutions'. The role of 'non-state regulative structures' is in fact critical to understanding markets in the deceptively thriving and dynamic non-formal Afghan economy. Sociocultural institutions largely determine access to land, resources and services, influencing both market competition and participation. Multi-sector research (such as in the construction industry) supports the view that markets are characterised by informality, with indications of non-competitiveness and high social exclusionary elements that influence the way that markets work (governing trade, distributional outcomes and power structures; Paterson, 2005, 2006).

Despite development efforts, according to Pain (2007), the social regulation of markets in Afghanistan is still heavily driven by ideological norms and institutions, with gender specific roles. Prevailing cultural practices and tradition (such as the norms of *purdah*) constrain women's movement outside of the domestic sphere, and their potential contribution as social and economic actors. As a result, women have almost no physical access to markets (over 70 per cent cannot visit markets freely), unless accompanied by a *maharam* (a male member of the family) and often in conjunction with an 'event' (visit to clinic, funeral, wedding; FIFC, 2004). Wealthier (traditional) households tend to abide by this custom, while poorer and landless households may permit more mobility for women due to urgent needs. Widowed women and old women are also exceptions to the rule, and generally have good mobility. The National Risk and Vulnerability Analysis survey (NRVA, 2004) showed that the majority of women involved in income generation do so from within the home (e.g. carpet weaving, embroidery and tailoring). Hence, women are present at the production level, but are almost absent at the other levels along the chain. Research suggests that income generation choices may also be limited for women, with socially acceptable participation in traditional sectors such as handicrafts and food processing, or if the women are educated, in teaching. Access to income-generating activities can also be ethnically selective (e.g. carpet production) with long-term links between particular communities and traders. There are thus significant variations in women's access to income-generating opportunities related to age, marriage status, wealth, educational levels and ethnicity (Kerr-Wilson and Pain, 2004).

3.4.4 Markets and risk: the Faustian bargain?

> Risk due to institutional uncertainty is a key factor that locks households into dependent, client-based relations.
>
> > (Pain, 2007)

It is argued that formal institutions may improve market efficiency and participation, yet it is unclear whether the more marginalised and vulnerable producers will manage to compete due to the traditional bounded nature of 'trust and market-based relations' (Christoplos, 2004). The persisting context of uncertainty and risk in formal institutions is indicated to lead the poor to nurture and maintain strong patron-client relations, prioritising immediate survival over new opportunities and future prosperity. And thus market forces may not necessarily create competitive pressures for rising above the status quo (Christoplos, 2004). The context of risk is considered to be a structural/institutional element in Afghan livelihoods, beyond external shocks (drought) but entrenched in inequality, class, power dynamics and social exclusion (Wood, 2004: 69), affecting access to employment, assets and resources, and influencing degrees of poverty. Wood uses the concept of 'adverse incorporation' to describe the behavioural imperatives of 'risk aversion' in the present, in favour of short-term security (Wood, 2003). Patron-client relations play a major role in facilitating access to land, inputs, credit and markets, but also in providing protection (Ritchie and Fitzherbert, 2008). According to Pain (2007), it is not enough to speak of markets being embedded in social relations, in how the poor achieve welfare and well-being in a weak state context. It is also crucial to appreciate that formal labour markets are often lacking, and that there is an absence of social protection measures. And Pain adds a further dimension (beyond state, market and family), citing Gough *et al.* (2004) (and their adaptation of the

Esping-Anderson Model for developing country contexts) highlighting the role of the 'community' in determining social relations and identities, and providing a means to achieve security. These various dynamics shape labour opportunities and gender roles in the household, community and market.

Thus, Pain and Lister (2004) suggest caution in the extent that market-based growth can reduce poverty (although the opium economy has been shown in fact to have positive multiplier effects). Markets are considered risky for the poor in Afghanistan. Smaller market players may be trapped at a 'micro level' of activity or constrained by marginalisation – for example, as Wood (2006) indicated, agricultural or craft producers can be locked or tied into traditional relationships with middlemen that are formed on the basis of personal trust, with small margins (Paterson, 2006). These are often gender-biased (household men tend to hold the relationships), and characterised by indebtedness. The latter is illustrated in a study on the carpet sector, where carpet-weaving households are typically trapped in a cycle of debt: 'the middleman provides a loan to tide the household over until the carpet is sold. Once the carpet is sold, the household repays the loan from the profit, and once more needs a loan' (Pain and Grace, 2004). Yet, at the same time, for both small and large market players, personal contacts and trust were considered critical and often enabling. These ties were highlighted as crucial in both setting up, and expanding a business, in research across six Afghan sectors (Paterson, 2006). And it was suggested that such relations acted as a 'compensation for the absence of formal credit or insurance systems'. Close relations have been shown to lead to cooperation amidst traders, and collaborative rather than competitive behaviour in certain markets (e.g. among fuel traders with a single supplier, who loan money to each other in times of difficulty; ibid.). More traditional patronage relationships and systems may also help in reducing risk, particularly in transit, where theft, seizure and bribes are commonplace (Pain and Lister, 2004). However, local politics and relations can equally influence how businesses grow: many rural small- and medium-sized enterprises choose not to expand formally because they fear being 'noticed' and 'coerced by corrupt elements' (Parto *et al.*, 2007). But Paterson (2006) suggests that high levels of close support networks were generally a 'positive force allowing poorer people to become entrepreneurs' (World Bank, 2001). But such support networks and relationships of trust may limit access for excluded groups such as women, and constrain trading partner choices (influencing related benefits) in the risky and unpredictable context of Afghanistan.

Going beyond the status quo?

With an influx of Afghan disapora coupled with the booming aid/war economy, in the past decade, there has been significant economic growth in Afghanistan. Evidence suggests that sectors are growing, but the challenge remains in facilitating an increase in participation in markets with benefits of more widely distributed growth (Pain and Lister, 2007: 249). The prevailing business environment may be characterised as an 'oligopoly', and this is predicted to lead to increased social inequality (Pain and Lister, 2007: 246). While the government has attempted to regulate markets through new tax and tariff laws, the enforcement of the laws remains weak and poorly communicated information has created further confusion. With the continued alliance of business to the government, such regulation faces strong opposition. Pain and Lister suggest that while a broader political strategy should promote good governance decoupled from business, key smaller steps that incorporate (formal) institutional building and educational initiatives can improve the local market situation, and foster more democratic markets.

Reflecting on current market dynamics for women, several new women's-led businesses and associations have emerged in recent years with donor support.[24] But these remain predominantly in the urban areas, typically with existing business families (or those with political connections). For the most part, Afghan women struggle to go beyond the status quo, due to prevailing norms and attitudes, restricting their mobility, the development of skills/knowledge and their participation in the marketplace. However, selected rural enterprise initiatives are now showing promise at tackling these more deep-seated issues. While still being trialled by NGOs, the relatively new phenomenon of the Indian-modelled self-help groups (SHGs) has proved successful at precipitating women's micro 'businesses' at the community level, particularly in the more liberal Tajik and Hazara areas in the north, west and central regions. Support to literacy, group microcredit and new social linkages have permitted the development of simple economic activities (as a group or between several members), and encouraged older (and more mobile) women to initiate basic trading activities such as buying/selling garments to relatives in neighbouring villages (Ritchie, 2009). Despite the modest economic impact at the household level (in the short term), the experience has been shown to promote attitude change towards female involvement in enterprise, social exchange beyond the confines of the family (for women), and enhanced community networks.

3.5 Concluding remarks

Drawing this chapter together, the discussion has examined the challenging context of Afghanistan across sociocultural, political and economic dimensions, providing country depth to the more general characteristics of developing contexts introduced in Chapter 2. In particular, it has looked at the perennial struggle of state building in Afghanistan, and highlighted the persistence of informal institutions governing turbulent Afghan lives.[25] Yet the discussion emphasised the remarkable nature of Afghan resilience and adaptability in the face of both geographical and political uncertainty (and adversity). In unwrapping traditional structures, the significance of dynamic tight-knit relations and ethnic/family networks were highlighted straddling well beyond the borders of Afghanistan. As a strongly collectivist society, clan networks are perceived as crucial for both 'protection and advancement'. Entrenched in tradition, risk and informality, the nature of sociocultural dynamics in Afghanistan was emphasised with implications for power and agency. Looking beyond the state, the shifting influence of local power structures and religion in traditional governance was examined and the emergence of new structures. Dominating the culture and intertwined in codes of honour, the discussion looked at the particular situation of Afghan women: their bounded world; and their entrenched discrimination, permeating both social norms and language. Yet it drew attention to their nuanced reality, and the scope of resistance and social change. Finally, the discussion turned to vibrant but distorted Afghan markets. Markets were shown to be characterised by informality and uncertainty. Deeply embedded in social and cultural institutions, with strong power dynamics, markets are tightly regulated by social norms and relations. This poses particular constraints for women in their choice of sector, level of activities, organisation and market interaction, although new micro trends may be emerging at the community level through women's self-help groups. In general, markets remain controlled by few players with strong links to power holders. Constraints for the poor were described in terms of institutional and relational barriers, exacerbated by the insecure environment, influencing the scope of their participation and economic development. On the fringes of modernity, the war-stricken context of Afghanistan remains stubbornly governed by tradition and informality and anchored in uncertainty and risk. Yet it continues to shape and be shaped by the dynamic and innovative lives within.

Notes

1 Drawing from Max Weber, Maley described 'legitimate rule' – the relationship between rulers and ruled that is based on the consent rather than coercion – to include tradition (e.g. monarchy), charisma, and legally rational roots of legitimate authority.

2 Interview with United States Institute for Peace, Kabul (2011).

3 At the time of the research, Afghanistan was ranked 174th out of 178 countries on the Human Development Index (CPHD, 2007). Average life expectancy currently stood at just 44.6 years (at least 20 years lower than in all neighbouring countries), the literacy rate for the total population was just 28.1 per cent (for men 43.1 per cent, and for women 12.6 per cent) and child mortality rates were among the highest in the world (151.95 deaths per 1,000 live births) (CIA World Factbook, 2009). Up to one in eight women was described to die in childbirth (Womankind, 2006).

4 CIA World Factbook (2009).

5 Considered the Afghan government's flagship programme, the National Solidarity Programme (NSP) was a major countrywide initiative over 2003–2011 that provided block grants to communities to enable them to plan, prioritise, implement and finance their own development projects. By 2011, the NSP had mobilised over 26,000 communities in all 34 provinces and had disbursed over US$827 million as block grants to communities (predominantly for locally led community infrastructure projects; MRRD, 2011).

6 At the time of the research, Afghanistan still remained the largest global producer of opium, and this dominated the Afghan economy, comprising approximately 30 per cent of non-drug GDP (Ward *et al.*, 2008).

7 Fitzherbert (2006) highlights the remarkable local adoption of mobiles in Afghanistan, even by the 'illiterate stall holder in the bazaar and farmer behind the bullock', with 'truly astonishing alacrity'.

8 Sunnis make up 85 per cent of the population, with the minority subscribing to the Shia faith (CPAU, 2007: 10).

9 Notably, many of the *Ulema* have graduated from the renowned Al-Azhar University in Egypt (CPAU, 2007: 41).

10 Commanders are local influential strongmen that are often large landowners.

11 Islam traditionally does not view 'priestly specialists' as 'mediators between the individual and God'.

12 For example, tribal councils, *jirga-ye qawmi*, religious ulema councils, *shuray-e ulema*, and provincial councils, *shuray-ye wilayti*.

13 Brodsky (2011).

14 This is the cultural code of conduct of the Pashtuns that confines women to their homes and subordinates women under the control of men (Brodsky, 2011: 74).

15 In rare cases, women also work as daily labourers (unpublished field interviews of author for Oxfam food security research, Afghanistan, 2011).

16 In Herat, the progressive refugee experience in Iran has left many young women unable to cope with Afghan patriarchal expectations (e.g. forced marriages, strict *purdah*).

17 The first legislation on women's rights was instated in 1923–1924, and related to engagements and marriages with the bride's consent required for marriage (20 Aqrab 1302/11 November 1923, Article IV) (Centlivres and Centlivres-Demont, 2010: 65).

18 For example, Decree Number 7 stipulated 'equal rights for both men and women in political, cultural, social and civil affairs . . . to do away with unjust, patriarchal and feudal relations between husband and wife and to consolidate family ties' (Centlivres and Centlivres-Demont 2010: 73).

19 For example, the current Afghan constitution stipulates the following articles related to women's rights: Article 24 (Liberty is the natural right of human beings. This right has no limits unless affecting the rights of others or public interests, which are regulated by law), Article 39 (Every Afghan has the right to travel or settle in any part of the country except in the regions forbidden by law), Article 43 (Education is the right of all citizens of Afghanistan, which shall be provided up to the level of the B.A. (lisâns), free of charge by the state), Article 44 (The state shall devise and implement effective programs for balancing and promoting of education for women, improving of education of nomads and elimination of illiteracy in the country), Article 48 (Work is the right of every Afghan). Interview with United States Institute for Peace, June 2011.

20 These include the Convention on the Elimination of All Forms of Discrimination Against Women (CEDAW).

21 Author interviews in Herat, 2010.

22 The traditional *Harwala* finance system (across Afghanistan and the region) seems to be an exception to this, however, as an informal but effective and reliable market system transcending local social relations and politics: 'money dealers, or hawaladers, provide a well-organised, convenient and cost-effective means of making international and domestic payments' (Maimbo, 2003).

23 For example, Afghan exports include dried fruit and nuts, carpets and cashmere, while imports include vegetable oil, poultry products, dairy products, wool, bottled water and soap/detergents (unpublished overview by Afghanistan Ministry for Rural Rehabilitation and Development, 2007).

24 It is important to note that even under the Taliban years at the end of the 1990s, there were exceptional cases of Afghan women entrepreneurs (Lemmon, 2011). But these women tended to stem from urban-based families that were more liberal and educated, and the challenge was rather in navigating the strict Taliban context (rather than family/social group values).

25 While not democratic, Wunsch and Olowu (1995, 2004) have elaborated on the existence of such self-organising capabilities in Africa and multiple (informal) governing authorities at different levels, and draw attention to their strength. Ostrom and Ostrom (2003) describe the multiple layers of governing authorities as 'polycentricity'.

References

Abdul Azeem, S. (1999) *Women in Islam*, Cairo (publisher unknown).

Afghan Ministry of Rural Rehabilitation and Development (MRRD) (2011) *National Solidarity Programme* (Brochure), Kabul: Islamic Republic of Afghanistan.

Atayee, I. (1979) *A Dictionary of the Terminology of Pashtun's Tribal Customary Law and Usages* (translated by A. Mohammad Shinwary), Kabul: International Centre for Pashto Studies, Academy of Sciences of Afghanistan.

Azarbaijani-Moghaddam, S. (2009) 'The arrested development of Afghan women', in J. Their (ed.), *The Future of Afghanistan*, Kabul: USIP.

Baumol, W. (1968) 'Entrepreneurship in economic theory', *The American Economic Review*, 58(2): 64–71.

Beall, J. and Schutte, S. (2006) *Urban Livelihoods in Afghanistan*, Kabul: AREU.

Bhatia, M. and Goodhand, J. (with Atmar, H., Pain, A. and Suleman, M.) (2003) *Profits and Poverty: Aid, Livelihoods and Conflict in Afghanistan*, London: Overseas Development Institute (ODI), available at: www.odi.org/publications/319-profits-poverty-aid-livelihoods-conflict-afghanistan, accessed 1 December 2012.

Brodsky, A.E. (2011) 'Centuries of threat, centuries of resistance: the lessons of Afghan women's resistance', in J. Heath and A. Zahedi (eds), *Land of the Unconquerable: The Lives of Contemporary Afghan Women*, Berkeley, CA and London: University of California Press.

Center for Policy and Human Development (CPHD) (2007) *Afghanistan Human Development Report 2007*, Kabul, Afghanistan: Center for Policy and Human Development, Kabul University.

Centlivres, P. and Centlivres-Demont, M. (2010) *Afghanistan on the Threshold of the 21st Century: Three Essays on Culture and Society*, Princeton, NJ: Markus Wiener Publishers.

Christoplos, I. (2004) *Out of Step? Agricultural Policy and Afghan Livelihoods*, Kabul: AREU.

CIA World Factbook (2009) Available at: www.cia.gov/library/publications/the-world-factbook/geos/af.html, accessed 11 September 2009.

Ciarli, T., Parto, S. and Savona, M. (2009) 'Conflict and entrepreneurial activity in Afghanistan: findings from the national risk vulnerability assessment data', *UNU WIDER Discussion Paper for Workshop on Entrepreneurship and Conflict INCORE*, University of Ulster, Northern Ireland, 20–21 March.

Collective for Social Science Research (2006a) *Afghans in Peshawar: Migration, Settlements, and Social Networks*, Kabul: AREU.

Collective for Social Science Research (2006b) *Afghans in Quetta: Settlements, Livelihoods, Support Networks and Cross-Border Linkages*, Kabul: AREU.

Collinson, S. (2003) 'Humanitarian action in conflict: implementing a political economy approach', *HPG Briefing 8*, London: Overseas Development Institute.

CPAU (2007) *The Role and Functions of Religious Civil Society in Afghanistan*, Kabul: CPAU.

Doubleday, V. (2006) *Three Women of Herat*, New York: Tauris Parke Paperbacks.

Entezar, E. (2007) *Afghanistan 101: Understanding Afghan Culture*, Bloomington, IN: Xlibris Corporation.

FIFC (Feinstein International Famine Center) (2004) *Human Security and Livelihoods of Rural Afghans 2002–2003*, Medford, MA: FIFC Tufts University.

Fitzherbert, A. (2006) *Market Information System (Report for Support to Strategic Planning in Sustainable Rural Livelihoods)*, Kabul: Ministry of Agriculture.

Fitzherbert, A. (2007) 'Rural resilience and diversity across Afghanistan's agricultural landscapes', in A. Pain and J. Sutton (eds), *Reconstructing Agriculture in Afghanistan*, Rugby, UK: FAO and Practical Action.

Giradet, E. and Walter, J. (2004) *Crosslines Essential Field Guides to Humanitarian and Conflict Zones: Afghanistan* (2nd edn), Geneva: Crosslines.

Giustozzi, A. (2007) *Koran, Kalashnikov and Laptop: The Neo-Taliban Insurgency in Afghanistan*, London: Hurst & Company.

Goodhand, J. (2004) 'From war economy to peace economy? Reconstruction and state-building in Afghanistan', *Journal of International Affairs*, 58(1): 155–74.

Gough, I., Wood, G., Barrientos, A., Bevan, P., Davis, P. and Room, G. (2004) *Insecurity and Welfare Regimes in Asia, Africa and Latin America: Social Policy in Development Contexts*, Cambridge: Cambridge University Press.

Harriss-White, B. (2003) 'On understanding markets as social and political institutions in developing economies', in H.-J. Chang (ed.), *Rethinking Development Economics*, London, Chicago, IL and Delhi: Anthem Press.

Hofstede, G.H. (1980) *Culture's Consequences: International Differences in Work-Related Values*, Beverly Hills, CA: Sage.

Johnson, C. and Leslie, J. (2004) *Afghanistan: The Mirage of Peace*, London and New York: Zed Books.

Johnson, S. (2006) *Making Markets Work for Poor People: The Role of Social Regulation*, Bath, UK: University of Bath.

Kator, A. (2011) 'Hopes and dreams: interviews with young Afghans', in J. Heath and A. Zahedi (eds), *Land of the Unconquerable: The Lives of Contemporary Afghan Women*, Berkeley, CA and London: University of California Press.

Kerr-Wilson, A. and Pain, A. (2004) *Three Villages in Laghman: A Case Study of Rural Livelihoods*, Kabul: AREU.

Knabe, E. (1977) 'Frauenemanzipation in Afghanistan. Ein empirischer Beitrag zur Untersuchung von soziokulturellem Wandel und sozio-kultureller Beständigkeit', *Afghanische Studien Bd. 16*, Meisenheim am Glan, Germany: Verlag Anton Hain.

Lemmon, G.T. (2011) *The Dressmaker of Khair Khana*, New York: HarperCollins.

Maimbo, S. (2003) 'The money exchange dealers of Kabul: a study on the Hawala system in Afghanistan', *Working Paper 13*, Washington, DC: International Bank for Reconstruction and Development, IBRD, World Bank.

Majrouh, S.B. (2003) *Songs of Love and War: Afghan Women's Poetry*, New York: Other Press.

Maley, W. (1998) *Fundamentalism Reborn? Afghanistan and the Taliban*, Lahore, Pakistan: Vanguard Books.

Maley, W. (2008) 'Building legitimacy in post-Taliban Afghanistan', in *State Building, Security, and Social Change in Afghanistan: Reflections on a Survey of the Afghan People*, Kabul: The Asia Foundation.

Marsden, P. (1998) *The Taliban: War, Religion and the New Order in Afghanistan*, London: Zed Books.

Mills, M.A. (1991) *Rhetorics and Politics in Afghan Traditional Storytelling*, Philadelphia, PA: University of Pennsylvania.

Mills, M.A. (2011) 'Between covered and covert: traditions, stereotypes, and Afghan women's Agency', in J. Heath and A. Zahedi (eds), *Land of the Unconquerable: The Lives of Contemporary Afghan Women*, Berkeley, CA and London: University of California Press.

Nordstrom, C. (2000) 'Shadows and sovereigns', *Theory, Culture and Society*, 17(4): 35–54.

NRVA (2004) *Report on Findings from the 2003 National Risk and Vulnerability Assessment (NRVA)*, Kabul: WFP.

Ostrom, V. and Ostrom, E. (2003) *Rethinking Institutional Analysis: Interviews with Vincent and Elinor Ostrom*, Mercatus, VA: George Mason University.

Pain, A. (2007) 'Rural livelihoods in Afghanistan', in Pain, A. and Sutton, J. (eds) *Reconstructing Agriculture in Afghanistan*, Rugby, UK: FAO and Practical Action.

Pain, A. and Grace, J. (2011) 'Rural women's livelihood: their position in the agrarian economy', in J. Heath and A. Zahedi (eds), *Land of the Unconquerable: The Lives of Contemporary Afghan Women*, Berkeley, CA and London: University of California Press.

Pain, A. and Lautze, S. (2002) *Addressing Livelihoods in Afghanistan*, Kabul: AREU.

Pain, A. and Lister, S. (2004) *Trading in Power: Politics of 'Free' Markets in Afghanistan*, Briefing Paper, Kabul: AREU.

Pain, A. and Lister, S. (2007) 'Markets in Afghanistan', in A. Pain and J. Sutton (eds), *Reconstructing Agriculture in Afghanistan*, Rugby, UK: FAO and Practical Action.

Parto, S., Paterson, A. and Karimi, A. (2007) *Enabling or Disabling: The Operating Environment for Small and Medium Enterprises in Rural Afghanistan*, Kabul: AREU.

Paterson, A. (2005) *Understanding Markets in Afghanistan: A Study of the Market for Petroleum Fuels*, Kabul: AREU.

Paterson, A. (2006) *Going to Market: Trade and Traders in Six Afghan Sectors*, Kabul: AREU.

Rasanayagam, A. (2005) *Afghanistan: A Modern History*, London and New York: I.B. Tauris.

Ritchie, H. (2009) 'Hand in Hand Afghanistan organisation external progress review and lessons learnt report, mass mobilisation into entrepreneurship project (through SHGs)', Balkh, Afghanistan, unpublished.

Ritchie, H. and Fitzherbert, A. (2008) *The White Gold of Bamyan: A Comprehensive Examination of the Bamyan Potato Value Chain from Production to Consumption*, Kabul: Solidarites.

Roy, O. (1994) *Afghanistan: From Holy War to Civil War*, Princeton, NJ: Darwin Press.

Rubin, B. (1995) *The Fragmentation of Afghanistan: State Formation and Collapse in the International System*, New Haven, CT: Yale University Press.

Schutte, S. (2006) *Gaining Some Ground: Urban Livelihoods in Jalalabad*, Kabul: AREU.

Scoones, I. (1998) 'Sustainable rural livelihoods: a framework for analysis', *IDS Working Paper 72*, Brighton, UK: IDS.

Smith, D.J. (2011) 'Between choice and force: marriage practices in Afghanistan', in J. Heath and A. Zahedi (eds), *Land of the Unconquerable: The Lives of Contemporary Afghan Women*, Berkeley, CA and London: University of California Press.

Stigter, E. and Monsutti, A. (2005) 'Transnational networks: recognising a regional reality', *AREU Briefing Paper*, Kabul: AREU.

Viazzo, P.P. (1989) *Upland Communities: Environment, Population and Social Structure in the Alps since the Sixteenth Century*, Cambridge: Cambridge University Press.

Ward, C., Mansfield, D., Oldham, P. and Byrd, W. (2008) *Afghanistan Economic Incentives and Development Initiatives to Reduce Opium Production*, Kabul: DFID, World Bank.

Womankind Worldwide (2006) *Taking Stock Update: Afghan Women and Girls Five Years On*, London: Womankind Worldwide.

Wood, G. (2003) 'Staying secure, staying poor: the Faustian bargain', *World Development*, 31(3): 455–71.

Wood, G. (2004) 'Informal security regimes: the strength of relationships', in I. Gough, G. Wood, A. Barrientos, P. Bevan, P. Davis and G. Room (eds), *Insecurity and Welfare Regimes in Asia, Africa and Latin America*, Cambridge: Cambridge University Press.

World Bank (2001) 'Afghanistan', *World Bank Approach Paper 23*, Washington, DC: World Bank.

Wright, R. (2010) *NonZero: History, Evolution and Human Cooperation*, London: Abacus.

Wunsch, J.S. and Olowu, D. (eds) (1995) *The Failure of the Centralized State: Institutions and Self-Governance in Africa*, San Francisco, CA: ICS Press.

Wunsch, J.S. and Olowu, D. (2004) *Local Governance in Africa: The Challenges of Democratic Decentralization*, Boulder, CO: Lynne Rienner Publishers.

4 Transforming norms towards unlocking societal barriers

Turning to the empirical research in Afghanistan, this chapter looks at the first set of key findings from the case studies: the initial transformation of *purdah* norms, permitting the start of the three women's enterprises. Building off Chapter 2, the discussion begins by expanding on the relevant literature on social norms, drawing particular attention to codes of honour, religious-based values and economic development. It discusses the general emergence of social norms, their maintenance and effects, and their transformation. Within the context of Afghanistan (Chapter 3), it then describes the specific characteristics of the norm of *purdah*. Exploring the case studies, the process of transformation of *purdah* in the women's enterprises is then presented, looking carefully at the role of core actors and the influence of the local context. In the cross-case analysis, the discussion assesses critical aspects of the transformation process and the evolving nature of heterogeneous *purdah* norms. It also looks at resulting outcomes in terms of power, trust, cooperation, and networks; and emerging new values and preferences.

4.1 Social norms, values and their persistence

Embedded in beliefs, history and cultural experience, and relative to specific sociocultural settings, social norms are described by sociologists as being informal institutions that govern and guide human behaviours in social encounters (Parsons, 1951). Norms tend to generate uniformity of behaviour within designated social groups, but can vary across groups (Peyton Young, 2007). Distinguished from personal norms – relating to beliefs and values about one's self – social norms refer to society's beliefs, and expectations. Social norms usually arise out of to 'situations in which there is an inherent conflict between individual and collective interests' (Biccheri, 2010: 298). The literature on social norms distinguishes between 'descriptive norms', which pertain to people's perceptions of typical behaviour in specific situations, and 'injunctive norms', referring to people's perceptions of behaviour that is commonly approved or disapproved of within a particular culture (Schultz *et al.*, 2007). Studies have highlighted how perceived norms can affect various behaviours, for example workplace absenteeism and conflict (e.g. Hofstede *et al.*, 1980, 2010). While sociologists have theorised that people follow norms to avoid sanctions, norms may also generate positive effects.

Seabright (2010) elaborates on rules of behaviour or social norms that help us deal with strangers through permitting trust and social cooperation.

Norms may be used to promote and assign specific roles at different levels n society. Building off earlier work by Durkheim (1912), Weber (1924) and Berger and Luckmann (1966), Scott (2004) cites Meyer (1970), who described 'social order' as a significant product of social norms, with norms often linked to particular sub-groups of actors that are expected to act within certain boundaries. Such behaviours are argued to be socially constructed rather than socially influenced. Meanwhile, closely associated to norms – and further influencing them – are 'values', pertaining to beliefs about what should be judged as right or wrong. Also related to norms are more engrained 'habits' that are described as 'a more or less self-actuating disposition or tendency to engage in a previously adopted or acquired form of action' (Camic, 1986, cited in Hodgson, 1997: 664). Norms and habits influence whom and what are included in different types of decision-making, how information is processed and structured, and what action is taken (Shepsle, 1986, 1989). Drawing on insights from Dewey (1922: 40), Hodgson (2004: 656) described social institutions, or norms, as both reflecting and shaping preferences and dispositions. Figure 4.1 endeavours to capture values, social norms and habits; embedded in deeper beliefs, history and cultural experience; and associated to preferences and dispositions.

4.1.1 Unwrapping dynamics and dimensions of social norms

Going beyond social norms as mere optimising behaviour (e.g. Arrow, 1971), Elster (1989: 99) elaborates on nuances of norms. He defines social norms as 'non-outcome oriented' prescriptive rules, that are either unconditional or, if conditional, 'not future-oriented'. For norms to be social, he maintains that they must be shared by other people and 'partly sustained by their approval and disapproval'. They may also be sustained by the 'feelings of embarrassment, anxiety, guilt and shame that a person suffers at the prospect of violating them' (ibid.). Yet external sanctions may not be required for norms to be effective, particularly when they have been 'internalized', since 'shame or anticipation of it is a sufficient internal reaction'. In contrast, a person that obeys a norm may also be fuelled by 'positive

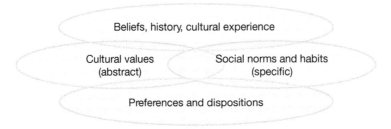

Figure 4.1 Unwrapping values, norms and habits

Source: Author's own illustration

emotions, like anger and indignation'. Yet he adds that social norms can also permit 'considerable scope for skill, choice, interpretation and manipulation'.

Further to this, and disputing notions of either 'self-interest' or the 'collective optimality of norms' (Arrow, 1971), Elster (1989) suggested that not all norms make everyone better off, and that norms that would improve the situation for all are not pursued; and even if they do improve people's welfares, they do not account for their existence. Elster suggests that social norms should be separated from private norms, which are self-imposed rules; from moral norms, in that social norms do not necessarily bring benefits; and from legal norms, in that the general community enforces social norms and that they are not always in self-interest. Elster further argues that social norms are different to 'habits', which are not enforced by others and do not bring feelings of guilt and anxiety if violated. Yet shared habits may be closely linked to rules and norms (as indicated by Hodgson, 1997), and the latter may not always hold true (for example, there may be a sense of guilt if the 'habit' of wearing a headscarf in Muslim cultures is not followed correctly or appropriately). In looking across cultures, Elster describes different perspectives on established social norms with some societies labelling certain behaviour as a 'compulsive neurosis', which others may perceive/accept as quite normal. He cites examples of social norms, including those of asocial behaviour, related to use of money, reciprocity, retribution, work, cooperation and distribution. Meanwhile, going beyond differentiations between types of norms (and habits), and looking at links to more formal institutions, Axelrod (1986 in 2006: 61) indicates that social norms and formal laws can be mutually supporting, and this can strengthen their abidance.

Emergence, maintenance and effects

Looking closer at norm dynamics, Horne (2001: 26) describes social and technological change as precipitating change in social norms, affecting the distribution of the costs and benefits linked to certain behaviours and perception of the continued relevance of such practices. She highlights the content, distribution and enforcement of norms as a function of negotiation, distribution of the cost/benefits of a behaviour, and the control capacity of the group. She maintains that norms are more consistent among those who experience similar costs and benefits, and thus in common social positions. Kandori (1992) suggests that communities play a strong role in norm development and enforcement. Social norms may be enforced either formally (e.g. through sanctions) or informally (e.g. through verbal reprimands such as warnings and non-verbal communication cues). And while some norms may be deliberately introduced, Platteau (2000: 325) argues that moral norms (emphasising honest behaviour) tend to evolve spontaneously within commonly interacting groups. Meanwhile, norms that are counter to the overall prevailing society or culture may also be transmitted and maintained within small subgroups of society (e.g. Crandall, 1988). Groups internalise norms by accepting them as reasonable and proper standards for behaviour within the group. Once firmly established, a norm becomes socially acceptable, and a part of local culture, and is then more difficult to change. Knight (1992: 188) cites much resistance to intentional change as a result of 'distributional factors', but also describes 'ideological and cognitive factors' in reaction to intentional change and external enforcement. Platteau (2000: 21) looked at the nature of the socialisation process, and the related persistence of 'dysfunctional arrangements' or even so-called 'revolting' social norms that may be embedded in the culture and linked to local beliefs. Platteau (2000: 308) also drew attention to role models that through their behaviour, boosts 'the salience of the relevant norm' (Darley and Latane, 1970: 85). And the reputation of these norm proponents may also boost their enforcement. There has been much analysis of norms in game theory, looking at issues such as norm emergence, fairness, cooperation and compliance (e.g. Bicchieri, 2006), shedding light on behaviour and conditionality, although there tends to be assumptions about agent motivations and interests.

4.1.2 Cultural influences on social norms: honour codes and religion

Unwrapping societal influences further, social norms may often reflect specific cultural codes. Elster (1989) suggests that the phenomena of envy and honour are worth special study. Appiah (2010) writes extensively about honour codes in different societies and moral revolutions, looking closely at the psychology of honour. He cites examples such as English duelling, foot binding in Japan and family honour codes in Sicily. He discusses the connection with identity, status and prestige. Integrating self-perception in the pursuit of honourable behaviour, Wikan (1984: 638) draws attention to Pitt-Rivers, who defines honour as the value of a person 'in his own eyes', but also in 'the eyes of his society': 'It is his estimation of his own worth, his claim to pride, but it is also the acknowledgement of that claim, his excellence recognized by society, his right to pride' (Pitt-Rivers, 1965: 21). In this way, honour is associated with self-regard and social esteem. Honour and the related notion of shame are often seen as opposing sides of the same coin, Wikan (1984) disputes this, and highlights conceptual differences with shame described as 'experience-near' and reflecting the individual's point of view (as applied to an act). This is in contrast to honour, which is described as a 'construct of the analyst' (an aspect of the person). Bourdieu (1977: 15) further differentiated between a point of honour as 'mental dispositions, schemes of perception and thought', and a sense of honour to be 'nothing other than the cultivated disposition ... [enabling] each agent to engender all the practices consistent with the logic of challenge and riposte'. Related to norms of honour and pride (and an avoidance of 'shame'), Kim and Nam (1998) explored the pervasive notion of 'saving face' in Asia, with individuals endeavouring to retain social respect, particularly in more traditional societies.

Yet, from a spiritual standpoint, religious beliefs, values and ideals may also have a strong influence on social norms. Religion refers to a 'belief in the existence of an invisible world, that is distinct but not separate from the visible one, and that is home to spiritual beings or entities that are deemed to have effective powers over the material world' (Ter Haar, 2011: 11). Embedded in culture, religion may also be understood as a 'shared set of beliefs, activities and institutions premised upon faith' (De Jong, 2011: 112). Towards exploring the manifestations of religion in society, the anthropologist Clifford Geertz (1973) describes religion as encompassing '(1) a system of symbols to (2) establish powerful, pervasive, and long-lasting moods and motivations in men by (3) formulating conceptions of a general order of existence and (4) clothing these conceptions with such an aura of factuality that (5) the moods and motivations seem uniquely realistic'. Symbols thus induce dispositions – tendencies, capacities, propensities, skills, habits, liabilities and proneness – that influence moods and motivations (Geertz, 1973: 95). Geertz described the religious perspective on the world as contrasting to the 'common-sensical', the 'scientific' and 'aesthetic', in moving beyond reality, questioning reality, taking on wider, non-hypothetical truths and deepening 'fact . . . to create an aura of utter actuality' (Geertz, 1973: 112). Ter Haar (2011) draws attention to religious ideas and attitudes, and links to social trust and cohesion. She looks in particular at religious ideas and beliefs, religious practices and rituals, and religious organisation and community. Such spiritual orientated dynamics play strong roles in more traditional societies, where the role of religion is often significant in shaping world views. For book religions, life values and world views are typically based on a specific holy script such as the Bible (Christianity), Koran (Islam) and the Torah (Judaism). Yet it is important to highlight that the local version of a world religion may in fact be a mix of local customs and their own interpretation of the religion, particularly in less literate societies where the faith is transmitted by oral means (Ter Haar, 2011: 13). Ter Haar emphasises the role of religious leaders in (positively and negatively) shaping people's attitudes towards concepts such as development and progress, and potentially having the power to bring about social change.

4.1.3 Economic development: cultural systems as barriers and resources

Due to the complexity of the economic environment, social norms, customs and habits tend to guide economic behaviour. Originally, Max Weber drew attention to the connection between religion and economic development (Weber, 1904), with Protestantism associated with pro-economic growth (and a hint of reverse causality; De Jong, 2011: 137). While sociologists have tended to study norms to understand their social functions and how they motivate people to act (e.g. Durkheim, 1895; Parsons, 1937; Hechter and Opp, 2001), economists have been interested in adherence to norms, mechanisms of change and how this influences market behaviour (e.g. Peyton Young, 1998). Chapter 2 highlighted the link between cultural beliefs, values and moral norms, and economic behaviour and institutional development (e.g. Platteau, 1994, 2000; Chang, 2005). According to Hayami (2001), understanding the traditional culture or a value system is an important foundation for economic modernisation. Platteau (2000: 189) elaborates on norms that may 'slow down entrepreneurship and capital accumulation', particularly prevalent in traditional environments. He cited Hirschman (1958), who argued that there were two contrasting types of traditional society: those that were 'group-focused', which were 'inimical' to economic development, and those that were 'ego-focused' and thus harmful to structures such as cooperatives and entrepreneurship. Both posed barriers to economic development. In processes of change, Plateau (2000) explored two prevailing views on the natural or delibreate transformation of norms (and related values) in economic development and growth. The first is through 'experience' in 'evolution', with slow change over time. The second is through the purposeful transformation of institutions by an 'outside' agent (in vein with Rostow, Kuznets, Bruton, Meier and Baldwin). He highlights Marx's view of growing tensions as a 'new order' is ushered in; and the potential resistance of power holders, which can ultimately culminate in a revolution (ibid.).

Taking a more nuanced view, De Jong (2011) looked in particular at religious values and economic growth. He suggested that religion has two different influences on society: first in terms of the practical participation in 'social activities', which can generate networks that can stimulate economic growth (but time spent can also reduce income generation time), and second in terms of emerging 'values', which can influence preferences and behaviour. He suggests that political and economic reform in economic development may be more successful if it is in tune with the existing religious framework. And arguably, within such a framework, there may also be subtle opportunities for introducing new/progressive ideas. Yet he draws attention to politics in the misuse of some religions. Citing Platteau (1997), he argues that political actors have manipulated religions such as Islam, with rulers creating internal divisions to reduce the risk of political opposition (De Jong, 2011: 125). With a lack of a central interpretation, Platteau (1997: 125) believes that Islam in particular has been more open to abuse by local rulers (e.g. with rulers selecting religious leaders that they liked the most that can perpetuate the status quo). Such politically vulnerable religious authority can pose problems for facilitating broad and durable change. In general, however, religious adherence is argued to be positive for society in improving trust in local governance institutions and law abidance (Guiso *et al.*, 2003, cited in De Jong, 2011: 127). For economic development in particular, religion has often been perceived as an obstacle to development and change, but for many peoples there is also great value attached to religion, and thus it should be considered a resource, and a 'stone on which to build' (ibid.). Ter Haar (2011: 23) suggests that existing evidence indicates that no specific religious tradition can be described as 'pro or anti growth', she called for more studies to look at religious values (and their various types) that may influence economic behaviour at a macro and micro level.

4.1.4 Transforming norms: actors and strategies

Towards understanding cultural dynamics and change, theories in cultural persistence and evolution have looked at collective-level patterns over time (e.g. Boyd and Richerson, 1985). Norms are maintained through interactions between actors, and in public representations such as discourses, texts, and institutional rules (Sperber, 1996). Yet some of the same mechanisms that contribute to persistence may figure in cultural change (e.g. the use of sociocultural ideas). Taking a deeper cognitive approach, Appiah (2010) describes ways of overcoming norms, such as those related to honour, through 'collective shaming', which necessitates 'insiders and outsiders if it is to work'. This indicates that changing underlying values, attached to respective norms, can precipitate change. In particular, where there is a supply of activists who challenge a norm, this creates the opportunity for progressive authorities to respond and adapt. Coined by Sunstein (1996) from the field of law, the term 'norm entrepreneur' describes actors with an interest in changing social norms, in vein with later broader notions of 'institutional entrepreneurs' described in Chapter 2 (Li *et al.*, 2006; Battilana *et al.*, 2009). Sunstein identified a category of people, whom he calls *norm entrepreneurs*, who are interested in changing social norms, and initiate new behaviours. If they are then successful in their endeavours, they can produce what he calls *norm bandwagons* and *norm cascades*, which may lead to substantial changes in norms across social groups. In this case, further actors will adopt the new behaviour seeing that authorities approve. As new norms are institutionalised, there may be tipping points as new beliefs and practices are adopted. Similarly sociologists argue that analysing norm change requires looking at the different actors within the respective environment, in particular change agents and their attributes, motives and roles in the change process (Hechter and Opp, 2001).

In assessing norms and change in local development, there appear to be several dimensions of potential interest. First, what are the particular motivations for norm change, and how do people garner support for the new norms within their cultural groups? Second, what enforcement mechanisms are used for norm violation, for example through prior threats or promises, as well as sanctions? Third, how are new beliefs or behaviours spread within and across groups – including through group interactions, collective action or more complex social network structures – and how do they ultimately gain consent and become normalised? Studies on rumours and storytelling suggest that close associations with local beliefs and practices can facilitate adoption and transmission (e.g. Sperber, 1996). Yet charisma can matter too, with the influence of particular individuals involved in championing the new norm. And fourth, how are social learning and social network mechanisms influenced by cultural or political factors (e.g. Weber and Dacin, 2011)? Further to this, norm diversity within a population may also warrant examination, to appreciate differences existing between elites and the majority, and the underlying factors that are driving this. Finally, it is important to look at aspects of norms that influence their stability. For example, Zucker (1991) shows that institutionalisation can aid their stability. Meanwhile, Knight (1992) suggests that the embeddedness of norms in ideology can make them more resistant to change, underscoring notions of 'institutional stickiness' (Boettke *et al.*, 2008). In general, among social scientists, anthropologists and economists, it is clear that there is still much interest in better understanding the roles of belief, trust, cooperation and power in the evolution of social norms, their persistence and processes of change.

4.2 Afghan norm of *purdah*: entrenched in religion and culture

As described in Chapter 3, traditional Afghan *purdah* norms mean that women's lives remain heavily restricted outside of the private realm.[1] Manifested by segregation, seclusion, modesty and 'coveredness', the practice of *purdah* influences the scope of women's mobility and social interaction (due to the pressure to avoid being 'seen' by non-family men). This shapes all potential aspects of women's social, political and economic life in Afghanistan. *Purdah* is considered to be embedded and bound up within local cultural codes (honour and shame) and traditional social habits. It is also notably associated with Islam, although there are no explicit verses that require women to be kept from public view (only descriptions of 'modesty of dress'; Ahmed, 1992: 55).[2] For Pashtuns, the tribal law of *Pashtunwali* adds a further (sub)cultural dynamic to *purdah*, beyond typical Afghan norms and religious influences. As an all-encompassing way of life, *Pashtunwali* has a 'complicated' relationship with Islam, with the former embedded in honour, and a person's integrity, and the latter related to moral behaviour (Kakar, 2005). *Pashtunwali* includes an emphasis on chivalry (in being honourable in oneself to uphold the honour of one's tribe) (*ghayrat* or *nang*), as well as maintaining traditional gender boundaries in the defence of the honour of women (*namus*, or the practice of *purdah*; Kakar, 2005: 3–6; Rzehak, 2011: 9–10). The collective cultural concept of *namus* – '"honour", "reputation", "esteem", "conscience" and "chasteness"' (Rzehak, 2011) – in fact relates to ensuring dignity for men and women through women's seclusion and protecting gendered space. And thus *purdah* for Pashtun tribes translates into a means of controlling women as well as controlling men: if an unrelated man enters a woman's area of the compound, he can be both beaten and expelled from the community (Kakar, 2005: 5). Yet *purdah* practices differ even between Pashtun groups, with nomadic tribes tending to be more relaxed than conservative landowning or urban Pashtuns (*qalang*).

Overall, strict interpretations of *purdah* across all social groups in Afghanistan tend to confine the women to the household limiting the extent of women's public life, access to services and resources, and engagement in economic activities. Drawing attention to family preferences, Mills (2011: 61) describes *purdah* as 'an ethic of privacy and sexual exclusivity for the honour of her family'. She also adds that *purdah* practices may be related to the expected wishes of her *maharam*, her male accompaniment. In conservative *qalang* Pashtun households, physical space within the family compound is highly gender segregated, and only older women and female children may move between the different spaces, or leave the house unveiled (Kakar, 2005). Where such communities have been displaced to cities, *purdah* practices may become even more austere, as families are forced to live close to one another, and female-only domains are tightened (ibid.). Even in these urban settings, the honour of a man is entrenched in the honour of his women family members. Yet while Afghan women are secluded, they may still have domestic authority (particularly in Pashtun households). This may include, for example, managing the household expenses and matchmaking, and (for older women) assisting in blood-feud conflicts (Rzehak, 2011: 10). Mills draws attention to the less positive side of *purdah*, which can feed legends and gossip about women and their potential involvement in illicit activities. In general, it is indicated that *purdah* norms vary with individual motivations, in addition to age, marital status,

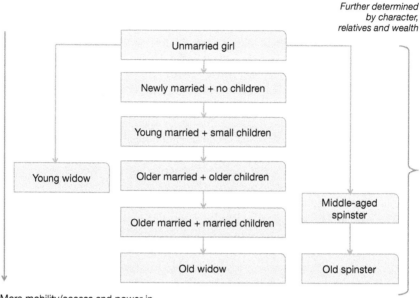

Figure 4.2 Layered reality of *purdah* on Afghan women

Source: Author's own illustration

children, husbands and relatives and wealth (as conceived in Figure 4.2); with family men having 'the final word as regards freedom of movement' (Doubleday, 2006: 13).

4.3 Transformation of 'layered' *purdah*

> We have changed a great deal but our culture [and religion] remains strong.
> (Female entrepreneur, interview 2011)

Moving now to core findings from the research case studies, the discussion returns to the three women's enterprises in Afghanistan, introduced in Chapter 1. In order for the women to participate in activities outside the home, and ultimately group enterprise, the associated NGOs, both initiated, and led the initial reform of the cultural barrier related to *purdah*. Before the project, target women were typically involved in homebound activities in their respective communities and pursued a strict form of *purdah* (with variations depending on age, marital status, etc.). These activities included domestic chores and child-rearing; and in some cases, the production of basic handicrafts, tending basic kitchen gardens and the harvesting of perennial horticulture. Women were able to visit close family households, and to attend the weddings of close relatives. Some women were able to visit the local market with their *maharams* (male relatives). Lead women had notably more of a mixed background of mobility, including a few educated women that had been involved in teaching and/or doing family errands. Yet they still tended to have had little market interaction.

The expansion of cultural norms (*purdah*) was thus fundamental to allow the various women the mobility to leave their homes several times a week to attend meetings and training, and to eventually work in joint production (outside of the home) and for some, to engage in marketing. In each case, in the first period of the project, much effort was channelled into this primary transformation of *purdah*, led by the NGO in negotiation with local power holders and target households. For the lead women or entrepreneurs, there tended to be a greater degree of pre-project mobility (yet still limited to the community). For the worker women, however, there was a significant need to negotiate with their families to simply leave the house. Three specific stages were evident in the transformation of *purdah*. First, there was a preliminary phase in which a new reformed *purdah* institution was conceptualised and introduced, precipitated by the need/interest to engage in activities outside the domestic sphere. Following the approval of this tentative new version of *purdah*, there was a secondary phase of experimentation in the practical reshaping of the proposed institution. Finally, there was a third phase, marked by the stabilisation and 'operationalisation' of the reformed institution of *purdah*, with approval for replication within agreed groups (with variations of new *purdah* practices).

4.3.1 Case 1: changing attitudes through strategic religious education

The discussion looks initially at the first case study: the rural-based women's food processing business in western Afghanistan (situated across 36 villages, with two villages examined in this study, Case 1a and Case 1b). In this case, the broadening of *purdah* was crucial to allow target women to attend initial meetings and training, and to then engage in joint village production. Later, additional negotiations were required to permit a few lead women to engage in marketing and city networking.

Case overview

With an interest in women's village enterprise, the facilitating NGO tentatively approached several preselected rural communities that were accessible, but were marginalised (i.e. had little outside support).[3] The NGO coordinated with the community leaders – including village chiefs, the community council and religious clerics – to determine local interest in women's food processing. With the eventual support of some of the community leaders (and women's families), and extensive negotiation of conditions for women's participation, suitable women[4] were put forward that were interested to collaborate in joint enterprise, and had the support of their families. A total of 15–20 women were then selected by the community leaders in each village. Women tended to come from the middle of the community, although a few leaders' wives were also included 'to control the group'. As described in Chapter 1, lead women (for this study, the 'entrepre-neurs') were elected by the group themselves.[5] The strength of character (and interests) of these entrepreneurs proved crucial in the initial challenging phases of the project, particularly as new practices were introduced and resistance was faced from within their families and the community.

In the early part of the project, the NGO concentrated its efforts on mobilising the women into self-help groups (see earlier), as a foundation for cooperative work. Yet perhaps more importantly, they also conducted a community-wide campaign of progressive Islamic religious education (including the 'right' of women to be involved in business). The women were then recipients of extensive training in food processing and literacy (most women were illiterate), and a production centre was established in the village. These new technical skills significantly aided the *purdah* transformation, since the women were then perceived to be no longer just typical village women, but professional actors (with new 'modern' skills). Selected (more mobile) women received advanced training in 'marketing' (sales agents).

For the producer women, basic negotiation with the *shura* and the women's families was needed for them to participate in trainings and meetings, and to engage in production in the village food-processing centre. For the entrepreneurs however, further effort was required in this initial expanded version of *purdah*. While there tended to be a greater degree of pre-project mobility for these women (since they were older and/or widows), there was still a need to broaden their allowances to permit a greater degree of flexibility on movement (including locations that they may visit); and meetings with non-family men, within and outside of the community. Exploring the transformation process closer, below I elaborate on the three specific phases characterising this process:

Introduction of concept of new 'purdah' institution

In the opening phase of the project, the external NGO initially consulted with the local leaders to discuss the concept of intervention in enterprise development with women (from poorer families and widows). With an obvious need for participating women to extend their mobility, the NGO introduced the preliminary 'idea' of the need for a change in *purdah* practices to allow women's engagement in regular (economic) activities beyond the home. There was much protracted discussion in this phase among the local power holders in the village (including religious authorities) and families. An agreement was finally reached permitting certain women to partake in the project under prescribed conditions. Criteria for participation included household poverty and vulnerability, the immediate family approval, and the agreement by the women themselves. Most of the women that were permitted by their families were indeed from poorer and more needy households – the husbands forbade them in richer households![6] Yet it appeared that local power dynamics also influenced this selection, with a few *shura* wives strategically included as a means of keeping the group 'in check'. The power holders further identified possible lead women that were both responsible and more mobile (i.e. widows, and older women with less conservative families). The NGO endeavoured to check the proposed lists and finalised the target group. The NGO then negotiated the initial new conditions of *purdah* for the selected women. These tentative guidelines stipulated that the women would gather in the house of one of the senior women for their meetings, and the male trainer (if permitted) would need to operate 'from behind a curtain' to avoid any direct interaction with the women!

Taking a closer look at the research villages, in Case 1a, the NGO initially presented the project to the village elders, and emphasised that they were an Afghan organisation (i.e. they were not foreigners),[7] and that male staff would not directly interact with the village women. However, the villagers were not easily convinced. The NGO privately consulted with 'strong' members of the *shura,* but they continued to face tough resistance. A large community meeting was then held to further discuss this idea. This gathering included the *shura,* all of the community elders, and the village mullahs, together with the NGO. The community finally agreed to the project on two conditions: if trainers were women only, and if there were no foreigners (even as visitors). Twenty women were subsequently selected for the project, in line with the project criteria. And a calm, level-headed and religious woman was elected to lead the overall group (the 'entrepreneur' for this research) (with the approval of the *shura*). Meanwhile, in Case 1b, the project was once again presented to the *shura* by the NGO, with the support of the persuasive project coordinator. After much discussions over several meetings (but with less resistance than Case 1a), there was agreement to let the project start, with conditions in this case, prescribed almost entirely by the mullah! These conditions included again the preferential use of a female trainer, and strict abidance by 'Islamic' codes (such as maintaining segregation in their work, and 'appropriate' *purdah*). Twenty women were again chosen by the community for the project, according to the agreed criteria. In this case, an older widow was elected as the head of the group, with the approval of the *shura* (after the initial choice dropped out), as she was perceived to be 'strong enough' to manage the group.

Of note – particularly in this early phase – was the NGO's comprehensive religious strategy through both explicit means (progressive religious education) – 'Islamic education is a must' – as well as more subtle strategies (e.g. adherence to religious dress and rituals). The latter tactic was employed to gain the trust and confidence of the communities, enhancing local receptivity to new ideas on women. Such strategies were particularly critical in villages that were considered more fragile, distrustful and resistant to change. Staff comprised both male and female employees. And together they were instrumental in mobilising the community, and opening up a dialogue about women's roles in social and economic life. Senior male employees were known in particular for their 'strong Islamic faith' and behaviour, and this gave them much respect. In terms of their physical appearance, the project coordinator kept an appropriate beard (i.e. in keeping with Islamic traditions), and while in the villages wore a skullcap and the dress of a pious and religious man. The villages were reportedly very impressed with this! The staff also adhered to local religious practices in respecting rituals, and recited the Koran prior to training. As they initiated discussions on women, they then drew on progressive messages from within the Koran and the book of the *hadiths*. More extensively, during subsequent project phases, the NGO then pursued broader community-wide religious education (introducing such messages to other village households). Meanwhile, the senior female employee of the NGO originally stemmed herself from one of the project villages (from an educated family), and was very familiar with village traditions. In vein with the strategies of the men, she also drew on extensive religious stories and Koranic verses, compiling basic anecdotes for the village women. With her assistants, she was predominantly involved in all group activities from establishing new groups, technical training, marketing, and facilitating monthly office meetings with the representatives, and integrated these basic religious messages into her daily work. A local female district head elaborated on the importance of 'educating through religion' (or promoting social change through religion), as opposed to the formal law:

> If you introduce the law or women's rights [Afghan or international], village people become mad and say that 'this does not belong to our village or our culture', and then they become even more strict!
>
> (Local female district head)

Transforming institution: shaped/elaborated through experimentation

Following the introduction of the new *purdah*, in the second stage of the transformation process, the lead women (the entrepreneur and her deputies), in negotiation with the village leaders, proposed the 'trial conditions' of the reformed institution of *purdah* (i.e. where the women could go, type of dress and trainer rules); and importantly, for which women. With the husband and family permission, the women then started to participate in the group training on food processing. Basic production of food stuffs (e.g. tomato paste and chutneys) was also initiated in the village centres. In the face of continuing local distrust, lead women advocated for the women's new roles, and tried to promote these where possible in the three social forums that they had access to, namely, within the confines of their families, in the women's village council (CDC) and at wedding parties. To encourage more conservative families, lead women also visited actual family homes. Meanwhile, difficult community elders continued to reject this new form of *purdah*, and created problems in the village council:

> Some of the stricter elders were complaining '*Women are going outside . . . and this is a foreign imposed programme!*'
>
> (Entrepreneur, Case 1a)

Yet with strong beliefs in the project, more liberal leaders debated with these resisters within the council. In one village, the conservative elders tried to halt all activity related to the project (Case 1a). The local mullahs further criticised the

NGO and suggested that they were 'pushing the women out of their homes', and that the project was 'against Islam and a great shame for the people'! Meanwhile, the common village people (both from within and outside of the community) created trouble through rumour-mongering, and intimidation at social gatherings. Once again, the progressive *shura* members (particularly the husbands of some of the women) tried to counteract such behaviour through drawing on positive religious messages. To further garner local acceptance, lead women also tried to demonstrate exemplary behaviour, and pious, if necessary. This trial phase was particularly reliant on the entrepreneur's charisma and persistence in encouraging the other women and championing their new *purdah* practices, and obtaining support from female and male power holders. At an overarching village level, however, the NGO was instrumental in providing higher-level support, through employing both religious/educational initiatives, and storytelling (describing their experience in other communities, both in and outside of Afghanistan). In particular, this required negotiating with conservative and controlling local elders that both curtailed the further development of progressive forms of *purdah* and levels of access. In some difficult cases (Case 1a), this meant that tight restrictions remained, and only the lead women had access to more flexible variations of *purdah* (i.e. the liberty to meet at any time and to visit new households).

As indicated, overcoming incessant gossip, distrust and intimidation were some of the major challenges during this phase. Local anecdotes illustrate this further. In each village, key events tended to mark this period. In Case 1a, for example, as the women became active in production, there were suddenly rumours that in a neighbouring village centre, there was a male NGO staff trainer with young girls, and this caused quite a stir. The mullah reacted swiftly and uncompromisingly, and suggested that all centres should be closed! Yet with courage (and cleverness!), the group head played a double game. She suggested a reversion to extreme 'Taliban' (*purdah*) codes:

> I will stand at the gate and stop all women's movement!
>
> (Entrepreneur, Case 1a)

This was naturally considered too harsh! Alternatively, the entrepreneur suggested that they should let them reopen their centre, and if bad behaviour was then indeed observed, the centre could then again be closed. Meanwhile, in Case 1b, when the production was just beginning to get underway, as a way of intimidating the women, a letter was posted in the mosque, which threatened to 'kill the people who worked with the NGO'. The entrepreneur was also specifically warned:

> I was at home busy on some tailoring and I could hear the dog barking. A letter was then posted under the door. The letter said: 'you are taking salary from an [foreign] organisation: we give you 20 days to close the centre and cut ties with NGOs. If you don't do this, we will kill your husband and children'. I was so worried about this threat that I kept it quiet throughout Eid

[religious festival]. Finally, I told my husband and he laughed. He said '*these people are not educated! And they are suspicious of foreigners [non-local people] and mistrustful*'.

(Entrepreneur, Case 1b)

The NGO summed up this situation: among the common villagers (particularly the less educated), there was both a pervasive 'fear of foreigners', and of 'change' (particularly in women's roles according to Islam). Despite her husband's assurances, the entrepreneur in Case 1b was duly terrified for herself, her family and the women workers, and spent several sleepless nights worrying about it all. Her village had experienced excessive violence in the past, which she had seen with her own eyes under the Soviet era, and this fed into a prevailing sense of uncertainty of outside ideas (particularly for the older generation). Eventually, she sought advice from an influential local commander. And with much relief, this led to the significant 'high-level' promotion of their work:

I decided to go to see a powerful community man (commander) and to ask his advice. The commander stood up at the mosque and promoted the women's work! He then spoke with the mullah. He is a very influential man! After that, he held a meeting with the male *shura*.

(Entrepreneur, Case 1b)

With this critical backing, the male *shura* and NGO quelled local rumours and gossip through a re-clarification of the project, and the reiteration of progressive Islamic messages.

'Operational' institutional arrangements with potential for 'replication'

In the final stage of transformation, once new norms had been trialled and agreed, entrepreneurs and women settled into their new *purdah* norms, and resistance subsided (less gossiping and threats). These norms included new levels of mobility to move between their own houses and the centre at designated times of the day, and to officially work outside of their houses. While the roles remained dynamic (with boundaries being subtly pushed on dress, extent of mobility), it was clear that there was a new period of 'stability', with the majority of local elders and community members accepting these 'new' norms for selected women.

Further purdah transformation (ongoing)

With the official start of the enterprise and the establishment of related routines (as discussed in the next chapter), women began to get involved in more permanent production commitments, and for selected women, new public-facing duties beyond the realms of the village (such as marketing and attending NGO workshops). Participation in these new activities necessitated a return to the trialling stage 2 above. And further allowances on *purdah* required renegotiation with the community power holders, led by the NGO together with the entrepreneurs. Yet once these progressive *purdah* habits were put into practice and visible, renewed concerns were generated. Many questions were abruptly asked in the enterprise village on the 'need' for women to get involved in any enterprise activity, particularly in stricter and low-trust communities. The NGO explained that it was a condition of their funding! But they endeavoured to reinforce the acceptability of the women's new practices once again through extensive religious messages. The challenges of gaining local support for evolving *purdah* practices – particularly as groups needed to market their products – were illustrated in each village. In Case 1a, for example, as the group started to make significant money through the marketing of products, the entrepreneur received a 'night letter' (a warning message) – similar to the earlier scenario in Case 1b – threatening her and her family if the women continued their work with 'foreigners'. Meanwhile, in Case 1b, when the women indicated that they wanted to begin marketing, this was considered to be a major village matter: this activity would take certain women beyond the (safe/acceptable) realm of the village! A community-wide *shura* meeting was promptly called to discuss this critical step, and preliminary conditions were eventually agreed, permitting some of the older women or widows to participate in this activity. These initial conditions included the wearing of the *hijab* (full body cover), and travelling with a *maharam*. Pressures on *purdah* boundaries eventually penetrated beyond the realms of the group. As the women's new business practices were normalised into village life, other local women also endeavoured to participate in new mobile practices, further demanding a change in *purdah* norms. These situations led to a renewed period of resistance with a resurgence of gossiping and intimidation, threatening again, even initial gains made (with the original women). The support of the NGO was considered critical in overcoming these hurdles, particularly in providing continued reassurances to the *shura* that new practices were still in keeping with Islam.

In summary, the process of *purdah* transformation in Case 1 has illustrated the complexities of women's norm change in rural women's groups (in two villages), prompted by enterprise. This process has involved an external NGO, local power holders and the entrepreneurs (and active women); and specific emphasis was given to religious education. Ultimately, however, the broader percolation of new ideas on women's practices has also triggered more widespread socio-economic change, particularly in Case 1b.

4.3.2 Case 2: changing attitudes through designated champions and skills

Looking forward to Case 2, the discussion now considers the rural women's vegetable business situated in central Afghanistan (based across nine villages, with two villages once again examined for this study, Case 2a and Case 2b). As indicated in Chapter 1, this was supported by an international NGO together with a local NGO (hereafter the 'NGO' unless specified). Similar to Case 1, the broadening of *purdah* was necessary to allow selected women to attend meetings and training (within the village), and in this case to work more publicly outside on their family land. Later, further negotiations were required to permit a few selected women to engage in city marketing.

Case overview

As in Case 1, with a strong interest in (rural) women's economic development, the NGO team initially approached several preselected communities that were accessible, and where no other NGOs were currently working. Once again, they coordinated with village leaders – including village chiefs, community council and religious clerics – to determine local interest in the establishment of a women's vegetable enterprise. These discussions took place over several weeks. With the eventual (tentative) support of the community leaders and families, selected women were proposed as participants for the project (200 women in each community).[8] Community leaders then approved a strong and respected woman as the business head – the 'Village Facilitator', or for research purposes, the 'entrepreneur' – and 10 capable women as 'lead farmers'.[9] The NGO concentrated its initial efforts – as in Case 1 – on mobilising the women farmers into self-help groups, led by the lead farmers. The women farmers were then recipients of extensive training in horticulture, literacy and basic marketing. Meanwhile, selected women (older, widows) received advanced training in marketing ('sales agents').

Once again, initial *purdah* changes necessitated a complex process of negotiation. For the producer women, negotiation with the *shura* and the women's families was needed for them to participate in trainings and meetings, although production still remained homebound (in their gardens). For the entrepreneurs, lead women, and later sales agents, further initial effort was channelled into this primary transformation of *purdah*, led by the NGO. While for these senior women, there tended to be a greater degree of pre-project mobility (as in the previous case), there was still a strong need to broaden this, both within the village setting, and later outside. This was required to permit greater flexibility on movement, for example on agreed locations that they may visit, and on holding meetings with non-family men within and outside the community. To support the project, and particularly the sensitive nature of the work with women, the NGO deliberately identified a key 'champion' in the local *shura* to assist with project coordination and troubleshooting.[10] As in Case 1, three phases were evident in this primary transformation of *purdah*.

Introduction of concept of new 'purdah' institution

At the start of the project, the NGO initially met with the local community *shura* to propose the concept of intervention in enterprise development with village women, and discuss practical considerations. Various visits were then conducted over a period of several weeks. There was much discussion at this stage between the NGO and the *shura,* and among the *shura* members in consultation with religious authorities. Finally, the NGO team managed to obtain an agreement to permit certain women to partake in the project under specific prescribed conditions. Using different tactics to Case 1, persuasion was in part financial – both the entrepreneur and lead women would be remunerated by the NGO. To guarantee the participation of women and readiness to work, the NGO requested a signed formal contract with the community head. The community leaders then identified an overall business head, the village facilitator, and suitable lead women from different village clans (widows, older with less conservative families) to be lead farmers. From within their respective clans, lead farmers then selected (farmer) women from appropriate and interested households to join their respective farmer groups. The NGO staff negotiated the initial new (various) conditions of *purdah* for the selected women. These stipulated that the women farmers would need to be gathered in the house of the lead farmer for training, but production would remain within each individual's home compound. For the entrepreneur and lead women, special additional agreements were granted for them to leave their homes to attend meetings within and outside of the community (if possible).

In Case 2a, after the initial introductory meetings, the village leader (*arbab*) remained stubbornly suspicious of the INGO's intended activities, as it was rare for foreigners to approach the village. He was particularly keen to understand the 'real' objective of their work (with memories of the Russians)![11] In contrast, the more progressive head of the *shura* strongly believed in the concept of the project from the outset, and felt this to be a great opportunity for their village. He described how he made concerted efforts to go from house to house to explain the project directly to the village people. He also described sitting in the *shura* and extensively discussing 'foreign culture', and encouraging the sceptical *arbab* who was illiterate! At a secondary power level, the women's council in the village (CDC subcommittee) was tasked with initially proposing appropriate women for the project. Women were put forward that were strong and reliable, able to voice their opinions (i.e. to speak publicly), and importantly, known as good Muslims. The list was then submitted to the *shura* for approval. Initial agreements on *purdah* included new basic levels of mobility for women farmers to attend meetings, and to work as planned (in their home compounds but outside). More extensive levels of mobility were required for the entrepreneur and lead farmers in order for them to attend broader meetings, visit households and make city visits.

Meanwhile, in the early phases of the more challenging Case 2b, there was a series of 'difficult' meetings between the *shura* and the NGO staff. Following tentative agreement to participate in the project, the male *shura* then held a village meeting in the mosque to introduce the project concept to the local men and to gain their consent. Upon obtaining the majority support, and the public go-ahead for the project, the mullah issued caution that the women should only work if practices remained 'within the culture'. Lead women were then predominantly selected by the male *shura* from local village clans. Particular emphasis was placed on identifying strong religious women that could act as community role models. Lead women then gathered local women from appropriate and interested households within their clans into their respective farmer groups. Initial agreements on *purdah* included new basic mobility for the women farmers (as in Case 2a), slightly more mobility for lead farmers (less than in Case 2a), and more extensive mobility for the entrepreneur.

Transforming institution: shaped/elaborated through experimentation

Following this tentative introduction of new forms of *purdah*, in the second stage, the entrepreneur – together with lead women (only in Case 2a where the entrepreneur permitted such involvement) – coordinated with the village leaders to elaborate on the conditions of the reformed institution of *purdah*: where each of the different types of women could go, how often, and their type of dress. Further rules were then issued regarding trainers (i.e. they should be 'respectable' Islamic women). With the husband and family permission, the women then started to participate in their respective groups, and attend initial training on vegetable farming. Yet with obvious local distrust, lead women endeavoured to promote the women's new practices where possible (e.g. within the confines of their families, in the women's council and at wedding parties). To encourage more conservative families, lead women also visited actual family homes (as in Case 1). Similar to the previous case, certain power holders continued to reject this new form of *purdah,* particularly for the lead women. Meanwhile, other village people (both within and outside of the com-munity) created trouble through spreading gossip, and intimidating the women and their families. Progressive *shura* members tried to contain such behaviour through drawing on positive religious messages. Reinforcing the project, the local NGO endeavoured to support the women's new practices at this trial stage (and the effort of local champions) through extensive religious reassurances, and with close consultation with the families and elders.

As before, overcoming rumours, distrust and intimidation were once again the major challenges during this phase.[12] This is illustrated in the case villages. In Case 2a, in the early stages of the project, local people still remained sceptical about the women's new farming activities, and the women themselves were nervous. The NGO drew from progressive passages from within the Koran to support these 'new ideas' about women's roles:

> The NGO gave us a lot of messages about the Koran – about women's rights in the Koran, their equality to men, our use in society and particularly Khadija – she had a lot of sheep, a lot of work and she married the Prophet!
>
> (Woman farmer, Case 2a)

To further convince the people, the lead *shura* member also described employing a 'religious policy', and promoting the work with 'messages from the Koran'. He further recounted stories about his experience with women in employment in other Islamic countries. He used these anecdotes to support more progressive ideas of both men and women working and supporting the household:

> I went from house to house explaining the project and telling stories. I then sat in the *shura* and explained to the elders who these foreigners were and

how they were helping us. I suggested to the mullah that work is for both men and women, and that men and women can work together.

(*Shura* leader, Case 2a)

Departing from tradition, the mullah also described reiterating this 'new message' from the *shura* leader in the mosque. And he actively encouraged families to allow both men and women to work to support the household.

Meanwhile, in Case 2b, to gain village wide support for project activities, the selected champion *shura* member – who worked in the city and had extensive experience abroad – promoted the project within the sphere of the *shura* and with participating families. He emphasised that the women's new work was both good and useful, and would bring economic benefits to local families. And he described the NGO staff as honourable people (and thus the village people should not be afraid of cultural disrespect). To quell the so-called 'illiterates', and convince the main troublemakers, the *shura* leader described telling (and retelling) stories from the *hadiths* and the Koran explaining how women should work (like men):

Our God says that during the night you must sleep but in the day you must work and find a salary . . . Allah says that if you are free from prayer, find your salary and food.

(*Shura* leader, Case 2b)

As in Case 2a, the *shura* leader also drew on stories from his own lifetime and experiences, such as the five years that he spent in Iran, integrating these with religious reassurances:

I persuade people by highlighting the nature of the women's work as good and within our culture's boundaries and I tell them not to be afraid to let their women participate . . . I highlight the economic benefits, and explain that the foreign people are good people . . . I tell stories from my own experiences in Iran where both men and women alike work and are still good Muslims . . .

(*Shura* leader, Case 2b)

Notably, in a similar fashion to the strategies of these designated champions, another local NGO that was working in the research villages[13] described advising his team that 'for every two hours of training in the village, they must dedicate at least twenty minutes to discussing relevant messages from the Koran!'[14]

'Operational' institutional arrangements with potential for 'replication'

As in the first case, once new norms had been trialled and agreed, entrepreneurs and women settled into their new *purdah* 'norms', and resistance subsided (less gossiping and threats). These norms included new boundaries on mobility to work outside, to attend meetings at certain times of the day, and for selected women to travel to the city. Roles remained dynamic (with boundaries being subtly pushed, particularly by lead women), but a new period of stability was observed, with the majority of power holders and community members accepting these 'new' women (and variations between the women). In both Cases 2a and 2b, the enterprise women emphasised the significance of this 'accepted' change to their habits and lives:

> We came from darkness into light . . . and became active in our lives. Our lives have been transformed at home and in the community. Even neighbouring communities that were once gossiping about us, and our new habits, are now jealous when we meet them at wedding parties and hear of our [respectable and successful] activities . . .
>
> (Women farmers, Case 2b)

Further purdah transformation (ongoing)

Yet as the business evolved, this prompted renewed nervousness. In particular, the start of designated women getting involved in new activities beyond the realms of the villages (such as marketing in the city) led to an abrupt return to Stage 2. These practices required further negotiation with power holders by the NGO and entrepreneur. As in Case 1, this prompted many questions to be asked on the 'need' for women to get involved in any activity. The NGO explained that women's empowerment was one of the aims of the project! A period of resistance was once again observed, with a resurgence of gossiping and intimidation related to all of the women's work, threatening even initial gains made. Yet in Case 2a, while there was some initial anxiety attached to selected women engaging in city marketing, families and leaders became 'encouraged' once they could see this new behaviour with their own eyes (particularly as this was led by the much-respected village entrepreneur, giving assurance to the new *purdah* boundaries). Experience and financial results proved also to be persuasive factors, with families later even boasting about the women's new work, techniques learnt and economic dividends. Villagers reported changing their 'entire' ideas about women's work beyond participating women, particularly work for 'widows and jobless families'. Meanwhile, in Case 2b, while the entrepreneur secured permission for herself to travel beyond the village for meetings and successful exhibitions, tighter restrictions were placed on the other women by their families, and this was reinforced by the entrepreneur herself. The mullah also warned against travel, re-emphasising that their 'culture forbids this'. Yet the progressive *shura* member endeavoured (again) to resist these conservative elements, and pushed for permission for other lead women to travel if they wore a *chardari* and, if required, took a *maharam*. Eventually, some of the lead farmers were approved to attend important workshops in the NGO city office with extensive persuasion by the NGO, and then were permitted to tentatively begin marketing. Across both Cases 2a and 2b, the NGO described the village people as generally 'thirsty for change' but simultaneously terrified of losing their culture, and of what their neighbours might say.

In summary, in Case 2, the process of *purdah* transformation has again illustrated the challenges of gradually changing women's norms, prompted by enterprise, but in this case across a larger group of women (in two research villages). Key actors involved included the external NGOs (local and international team), local power holders and the women themselves. Specific emphasis was placed on identifying village champions (to address sociocultural issues) and channelling new skills. Similar to Case 1, the new women's practices have also unleashed new ideas on women in Case 2a, but less so in conservative Case 2b.

4.3.3 Case 3: changing attitudes through designated champions and charisma

Finally, I turn to Case 3, the small urban-based women's electronics business situated in Kabul City. Once again, changes to target women's norms were imperative to allow them the freedom to participate in the project meetings and training. Later, further negotiations were needed to permit the women to 'work' in the designated production centre in the community, and eventually to travel to the middle of the city for work.

Case overview

At the project outset, the NGO selected the urban-based community area for its extreme poverty and the notable lack of other NGOs. While the community were initially welcoming, upon discovering the project was for women, the NGO faced a series of 'difficult' meetings with the local leaders of the *shura* (including religious clerics) and *wakil* (neighbourhood head) to further explain and justify the project concept, and their desire to support women in enterprise. These discussions spanned over several weeks. Finally, after extensive negotiation, the NGO obtained agreement by the elders to start the project, and the NGO was permitted to carry out a survey to determine poor, vulnerable and willing families. In this initial assessment of 450 families, 50 families[15] were selected for possible participation in various enterprise initiatives (including electronics, as well as jewellery, catering and mobile phone repair). Women from these families were then invited to a meeting to outline the project activities. At this point, many families still rejected the project concept and further requested payment for women's participation! Finally, interested women were selected for the electronics project in particular, and their names were agreed by the community *shura*. A total of just 13 women was then mobilised to attend an initial nine-month-long literacy training course before potential participation in the electronics business. Following this, the technical training was facilitated. At this point, the entrepreneur was elected by the other women to head the group (for her 'strength of character' and 'confidence'). As a Tajik, she was also from an ethnic group that permitted more (general) mobility for women than typical Pashtuns.

As before, early revisions of *purdah* were led by the NGO in negotiation with the community *shura* (in particular through the local leader or *wakil*) and target households. Yet while the *wakil* was instrumental in coordinating with the *shura*, he was notably motivated by a small financial contribution from the NGO, as the designated 'community facilitator' for the project. In this case, *purdah* negotiations differed markedly between the various women. The entrepreneur tended to have a greater degree of pre-project mobility than the other women, both as a Tajik and due to her strong character. Yet there was still a need to broaden 'her habits', both to allow greater flexibility on her movement and to permit her to hold meetings with non-family men within the community. Meanwhile, for the other women, extensive negotiation was required with their families to permit simple mobility for them to move outside of the home. This appears to have been exacerbated by the tribal code of *Pashtunwali*, necessitating a stricter form of *purdah*. As with the other cases, three stages were evident in this primary transformation:

Introduction of concept of new 'purdah' institution

Once again, at the beginning stages of the project, the NGO initially met with the local city *shura* to discuss the potential participation of women in enterprise development. There was much discussion in this phase with conservative elders (including religious leaders), necessitating a series of meetings with the NGO. A final agreement was reached to permit certain women to partake in the project under prescribed conditions. Criteria for selection included those from poor households and widows, (immediate) family approval, and agreement by the women themselves. The power holders authorised the final list of women from appropriate and interested households. As necessary, the NGO negotiated the basic *purdah* 'norm' changes required for the women's initial participation (i.e. to attend training outside of the home in the community centre). Yet these new practices were subject to various conditions posed by the religious leaders, including initial rules on training. For example, the door of the training room would need to be kept open, and the women would need to be gathered in the house of one of the lead women.

Looking closer at this protracted process of negotiation – and perhaps more so than in the previous cases – nervous *shura* members and husbands put up significant resistance to women's participation and new *purdah* allowances (even if the women themselves agreed). While there was anxiety of going against Islam, greater concerns included their (unspoken) fear of breaking the Pashtun honour code of *Pashtunwali*. This led to pervasive distrust within the community of the women's new proposed practices and activities. In addition, the fractured nature of the neighbourhood, largely made up of displaced and disconnected rural families, compounded the general feeling of uncertainty, and a sense of not fully knowing one another:

> We had a neighbour and he was a known *hafiz* (religious scholar) and a teacher in English . . . but he turned out to be a radical, and then became a suicide bomber.
>
> (Woman worker)

In the midst of these extended discussions and conflict, and with no clear decision made, out of desperation, the NGO representative decided to go to the mosque himself to speak with one of the leading local mullahs, who was known to be open and educated. He explained clearly that the project was respecting the religion and culture. Finally, after a long debate on the role of women in Islam, the mullah agreed to the project on the strict conditions that only women were participating, and that the training would be 'open' for anyone to witness what was going on inside! A further meeting was called with the elders, and after more discussions there was an agreement to permit the project to continue (although many of the conservative elements remained afraid of NGO interventions in general, and a 'foreign' culture disrespecting their women).

Transforming institution: shaped/elaborated through experimentation

After the introduction of new potential *purdah* arrangements in negotiation with the elders, the entrepreneur and her deputies proposed the specific conditions of new practices – where the women could go, type of dress, and trainer rules. With the husband and family permission, the women started to participate in the group, and initial trainings on electronics. The entrepreneur advocated for these new roles, and tried to promote these new roles within the confines of her family, and at local events such as wedding parties. As in previous cases, to encourage more conservative families, the entrepreneur also visited actual family homes.

Meanwhile, difficult power holders and families continued to reject this new form of *purdah* and created problems in the village council. Similar to previous cases, this phase was characterised by several 'events'. For example, at one point, local people exacerbated ongoing discussions through spreading malicious rumours about the women (and even speculating their involvement in prostitution!). Security issues in the city created additional tensions. The *wakil* debated extensively with the resisters during this phase, coping with each and every setback. In addition to close coordination, the NGO was instrumental in tackling these issues through disseminating progressive religious as well as human rights messages, and using economic arguments to keep the *shura* and families on side:

> During these early days, I kept the *shura* informed as I was worried to lose their trust . . . and then for all activities with the women to be halted. I also put a great deal of effort into gaining the family support, and persuading them that through this work, the women would become active and know more about religion too.
>
> (NGO male staff)

Yet there continued to be considerable distrust of the foreign NGO, and their work with the women. While religious messages were useful, more fundamental issues on respecting *Pashtunwali* remained, and thus religious 'rights' messages held little weight. Despite this, the charismatic Afghan NGO staff member persisted, eventually gaining the trust of the women 'like a father':

> Our husbands were not initially convinced and thought that these people
> [the NGO] were socialists but we were not afraid . . . We saw him and trusted
> him.
>
> (Women workers)

At the same time, the entrepreneur endeavoured to continue to support the women
through regular household visits, encouraging the families as best she could. As
indicated, major bottlenecks in this phase included conservative and controlling
local power holders and husbands, which delayed and curtailed the development
of progressive forms of *purdah*. While the increasingly confident entrepreneur was
permitted certain flexible allowances, fairly tight restrictions remained on the rest
of the women.

'Operational' institutional arrangements with potential for 'replication'

With the (semi) successful trialling and implementation of new norms, community
resistance subsided (less gossiping and threats). These revised norms included
expanded levels of mobility to attend meetings at the community centre at
designated times of the day, and to begin to work outside of the house. While
purdah boundaries remained fluid (as in previous cases), there was a new period
of semi-stability with the majority of power holders and community members
accepting these 'new' women. The women described the dramatic effects of this
change:

> Before the business begun, we were mainly at home doing household chores.
> Our new 'habits' have impacted upon our own lives both in terms of our
> activities and our sense of worth, influencing perceptions in our own families,
> and within our community [of women's capacities].
>
> (Women workers)

Further purdah transformation (ongoing)

Once the business was formally started, the NGO proposed the relocation of the
business to a women's leisure/commercial park in central Kabul (to facilitate
networking and marketing). This was considered a major step that would take the
women beyond the safe and controlled context of the community, and thus
precipitated a swift return to stage 2 above. New allowances on *purdah* were
required, and a renewed period of extensive negotiation with power holders –
championed by the NGO and entrepreneur – ensued. As in previous cases, many
questions were suddenly asked on the 'need' for women to travel or to work
at all. At this stage – and quite dramatically – one-third of the women dropped
out due to mounting pressures to remain close to home (from both family and
conservative elements). Others were subjected to increased family intimidation.
A resurgence of local gossiping related to the women working outside of the
house threatened even initial gains made in the women's mobility. Eventually,

the remaining women managed to overcome the resistors with extensive support by the NGO, and they continued to participate in the enterprise. Notably, during this time, the entrepreneur and her family also decided to move to a more progressive city neighbourhood, possibly to escape the clutches of the controlling authorities.[16]

Overall, in Case 3, the process of *purdah* transformation has further highlighted the various uncertainties and complexities tied up with women's norm change, prompted by enterprise, and in this case within a small group of urban women. Again, this process has involved an external NGO (international), local power holders and the women themselves. Specific emphasis was placed on identifying community champions (to address sociocultural issues) and employing charisma. Yet strong tribal codes have complicated the nature and breadth of transformation, as well as contextual uncertainty, and further potential effects (i.e. broader socio-economic empowerment).

4.3.4 Examining new dynamics of language and power in norm change

As the findings suggest, across the cases, changes to *purdah* were heavily influenced by the use of Islamic messages, storytelling and individual/collective power. To facilitate the initial process of change, key Koranic verses were deliberately highlighted by the NGOs regarding women's rights, with the emphasis that the teachings of Islam must be respected over local (more discriminatory) traditions and customs. This was discussed carefully with community power holders and the women themselves. These themes specifically emphasised the importance of *equal rights* between men and women, *seeking knowledge* and *the right to employment*. For example, the NGOs explained that it was acceptable for Muslim women to leave the house if their guardians or husband permitted them, and if they were covered and conducted themselves according to Islam (ensuring modest dress, and avoiding looking, unnecessarily, at non-family men). Further to this, in terms of education, the NGOs drew attention to a strong emphasis on seeking knowledge and learning as an 'obligation in Islam'. And thus, learning new skills and literacy in the project was in line with being a 'good Muslim':

> Say (unto them, O Muhammad): Are those who know equal with those who know not? But only men of understanding will pay heed.
>
> (Koran, 39:9, translation by Pickthall, 1938)

Finally, in terms of employment, the NGOs highlighted Islamic support for women working outside of the home if 'Islamic rules' were respected, both in terms of the nature of the work (the work was moral and appropriate, and there was gender segregation), and in terms of obtaining her husband's consent (i.e. it did not interfere with her duties as a wife and mother).

Expanding upon this in the cases, the producer women in Case 1 were breathless with excitement, as they shared specific written passages in the back of their enterprise books (as given by the NGO). These related to key Koranic messages on the importance of education, knowledge and equality, as well as women's involvement in business. In particular, the role of Khadija, Prophet Mohammed's wife (who was a businesswoman) was highlighted (and how she supported the Prophet 'when he had nothing'). These were used to encourage one another in their own work, as well as to help in 'convincing their families' towards (re)shaping ideas and attitudes about women. They also noted down other positive stories related to trust in women, the frivolousness of gossip, and the importance of being a good Muslim, and emphasised:

> If you do honest work and are a good Muslim, then your conscience is clear
> ... We accept these changes, and so should the community because they are
> within the frame of Islam ... Men and women should work side by side ...
>
> (Women workers, Case 1)

Yet in extreme cases, where local people had a 'very dark idea about women', NGO female staff described needing to (initially) employ more basic messages of 'humanity', even justifying their own work:

> [In difficult situations] ... I would need to initially say 'I am a woman, and
> a mother. I want to support my husband and family ...'
>
> (NGO female staff, Case 1)

While arguably less structured than in Case 1, the staff in Cases 2 and 3 similarly drew on messages from the Koran in 'Islamic training' sessions, relating to women's rights, capacities and their potential to take on responsibility. Through these Islamic messages and stories, the NGOs introduced a new 'narrative' regarding women as *equal to men and worthy*, both *capable and responsible*, and as *potential household and community contributors*. These themes were then strategically adopted and reinforced by the women themselves, as well as by liberal power holders, to support the evolving change in *purdah* norms.

Reflecting on (changing) power dimensions, embedded in this new narrative and emerging new norms, was arguably a new subtle 'invisible' dynamic of power conferred to respective women (Gaventa, 2006). Yet the degree of this new power, and for which women, was heavily dependant on emerging 'visible' (political power) and 'hidden' power (by more dominant actors). These dimensions were shaped by the capacities of the NGO, the nature and strength of the power holders (resistors and promoters), and perhaps most significantly the charisma and interests of the entrepreneurs. In terms of the 'power' of the NGO, it is worth noting that in Case 1, the NGO coordinated directly with the power holders as a whole (i.e. they had no designated champions). But in Cases 2 and 3, the NGOs felt that it was necessary to deliberately employ charismatic village elders or local representatives to support their cause – perhaps since the NGOs felt that they themselves were less credible religious experts (and thus less powerful in this regard).

4.4 Discussion

Going beyond static descriptions in the literature (e.g. Doubleday, 2006; Mills, 2011), the research has examined dynamic transformations of Afghan *purdah,* generating new insights into *norms* and change processes. Building off Gomez (2008) and one particular set of actors or 'institutional entrepreneurs' (Li *et al.,* 2006; Battilana *et al.,* 2009), the process of transformation of *purdah* has involved the interaction of a multitude of both skilled and less skilled actors including NGOs, entrepreneurs and power holders, further shaped by the local context. Incorporating both exogenous (e.g. Fligstein, 2001; Appiah, 2010) and endogenous elements (Aoki, 2001), the institutional process is indicated to take place in three specific stages. The initial phase was distinguished by the introduction of the revised concept of *purdah* by an outside group, the NGO. This was followed by a period of local experimentation in the face of 'uncertainty', as theorised by Beckert (2003), in the trial and error of *purdah* and its reshaping towards new agreed solutions. Finally, the process culminated in reaching a renewed point of stability with local legitimacy (Jacoby, 2001). At this point, the norm of *purdah* returned to a more gradual evolving state (yet with potentially changed momentum). The institutional change process was characterised by varying actor skills and interests, degrees of trust and cooperation (between the actors), power dynamics, and the use and development of new relations and networks (particularly within the enterprise and the community).

4.4.1 Complex institutional change processes: from concept to dissemination

In all of the cases, the initial introduction of more progressive forms of *purdah* was led by an external NGO, in negotiation with the local authorities. The entrepreneurs then were involved with reshaping these new practices, with the assistance of senior women. Once new norms had been trialled and agreed, in the final stage, new *purdah* norms were then put into practice, although these remained dynamic. There were dual motivations for norm change: the fundamental 'conceptual' (social) need for women to move beyond the home, in order to facilitate the ultimate (economic) goal of initiating group enterprise. The trigger for considering the initial change to the social institution was the proposed 'new' behaviour by an outside group, typically framed through existing religious references. This clearly indicates that a 'lower order' (social) institution needs to be transformed (e.g. *purdah*), before 'higher level' institutional processes can begin (enterprise institutions).

The nature of *purdah* change varied across the cases, both in terms of process and outcomes. In Case 1, the NGO involved with the initial introduction of the new revised *purdah* took a strategic approach to changing attitudes and practices, with a particular focus on religious education. In Case 1a, the subsequent reshaping of *purdah* was then quietly pursued by the determined entrepreneur with the support of active workers. Yet the conservative village authorities remained suspicious and difficult. This ultimately led to restrictions on the wider adoption of more progressive *purdah* practices. In Case 1b, the reshaping of *purdah* was more openly pursued by the tough, older entrepreneur and her assistants. The village authorities were initially strict but became more relaxed as new practices were adopted. Meanwhile, in Case 2, the NGO was initially clumsy with tackling new revised forms of *purdah*, but then efforts were rechannelled through a designated village project champion with key religious messages and concerted efforts in women's skills development generated tangible financial results. In Case 2a, the educated entrepreneur had a strong influence on the open-minded village authorities on both initial and evolving attitudes and practices. New ideas were then further reinforced by quick dividends. In Case 2b, the controlling entrepreneur used the strict village authorities to her own ends in ensuring more exclusive evolving attitudes and practices (mostly for own benefit). Finally, in Case 3, the NGO struggled with the dual combination of strong social (*Pashtunwali*) and religious barriers, in addition to contextual uncertainties. Charisma and religious messages were employed by the NGO to convince authorities. Yet conservative elements persisted, constraining the mobility of worker women. The strong (but controlling) entrepreneur reinforced ideas on basic *purdah* revisions, but distanced herself from the rest of the group. This ultimately created a widening gap over time between her *purdah* allowances and those of the rest of the women. In summary, the research cases demonstrate the varied nature of *purdah* transformations, influenced by both actors and local conditions with different emerging outcomes.

Diverse actors, strategies and conditions influencing norm development

The various research findings highlight pertinent insights into the different actors involved in the transformation of norms, and their strategies (particularly illustrated in the village ethnographic exercises). Going beyond Kandori (1992), actors both within and outside of the community have influenced norm development and enforcement. This has been further tempered by local conditions. Building off Battilana *et al.* (2009) and Gomez (2008) (as described in Chapter 2), a range of actors have acted as 'institutional entrepreneurs', but have been motivated by differing interests, with varying capacities and roles in the change process (Hechter and Opp, 2001). These include the NGO, the local power holders and entrepreneurs. Diverse strategies for norm revision and renegotiation have also been observed. For example, the use of progressive religious messages and associations (Sperber, 1996) has been employed to facilitate new ideas around beliefs, leading to the reinterpretation of religious texts. This corroborates with theories of De Jong (2011) and Ter Haar (2011) that such beliefs may be both a barrier and a resource in local development, going beyond the perception that traditional ideas act only as a hindrance to development (e.g. Lewis, 1955). Knight (1992) and Boettke *et al.* (2008) also indicated that if norms remained close to (or associated with) ideological ideas, they would be more resistant (or hold more weight). In the cases, the association of new norms to evolving cultural ideas (embedded particularly in religion) has indeed strengthened new norms, and permitted their ongoing evolution. In addition, actor strategies endeavoured to use charisma (often linked to religion) and role models (Darley and Latane, 1970; Platteau, 2000), as well as local rituals of dress and behaviour (prayers), and to work through prevailing moods and motivations (Geertz, 1973) in order to reinforce new ideas, meanings and community learning (Weber and Dacin, 2011), particularly in conservative environments. Ultimately, this has enabled the generation of a new narrative regarding the women, facilitating *purdah* norm change. Yet these ideas are still strongly linked to religion, providing a 'stone on which to build' (Ter Haar, 2011).

In particular, it is significant to elaborate on the specific role of the NGO, and the effect of their strategies, particularly in boosting the agency of other actors. In Case 1, the NGO championed progressive religious messages through both religious education, and used solemn dress and prayers to facilitate receptivity to ideas. Meanwhile, in Cases 2 and 3, there was more emphasis on identifying local respected (religious but liberal) power holders as champions to support the women's enterprise and new practices. These NGO strategies boosted the capacities of the entrepreneurs with varying effect. While they were effective in Case 1b in strengthening the entrepreneur and the women's work, in Case 1a strict power holders constrained change processes beyond the entrepreneur, limiting the broad adoption of new norms. Meanwhile, in Case 2a, the NGO strategy was reinforced through an educated entrepreneur and progressive authorities. But in Cases 2b and 3, efforts were held back by both controlling entrepreneurs and conservative authorities. While the NGOs themselves were not of course disembedded from the local religion (as Muslims themselves), in interacting with the communities, there was a conscious effort to draw on an overt religious approach to appear more credible and to channel business ideas through this medium. This has arguably strengthened evolving new norms (particularly in Case 1). Yet in Case 3, beyond the entrepreneur and power holders, limitations on the effectiveness of the NGO were observed, and the efficacy of such religious strategies. In this case, the norm of *purdah* was also deeply entrenched in norms of honour (*Pashtunwali*), typical in *Pashtun* communities. These more ideological issues proved more difficult to overcome, with their arguably more challenging association to identity, status and prestige (Appiah, 2010) and social respect (Kim and Nam, 1998). And the local situation was notably exacerbated by a context of uncertainty. These combined factors led to protracted resistance in Case 3, particularly among less educated groups.

Reflecting on these findings, Hechter and Opp (2001) emphasised the importance of studying actors in the process of change in social norms. However, the research indicates that it is the combined influence of the environment and actor strategies that have impacted upon *purdah* outcomes, the stability of the new (evolving) *purdah*, and replication (i.e. the potential of *purdah* norms to be copied and adopted by broader group members). Where there are respected and capable actors and supportive local conditions, *purdah* transformation is evolving with stability

Table 4.1 Purdah transformation influenced by environment and actors

Case number	Environment/ power holders	Core NGO strategy	Entrepreneur characteristics	Purdah transformation for enterprise women	Stability of evolving purdah	Local replication
1a	Strict, closed	Religious education	Determined, strong, open	Slow, strongly controlled	High	Controlled
1b	Becoming more progressive and open	Religious education	Tough, older, open	Slow, initially strongly controlled	High	Among confident women
2a	Progressive and open	Designated champions and skills	Educated, open	Medium-paced with light control	High	Among confident women
2b	Strict, closed	Designated champions and skills	Controlling, powerful	Constrained beyond entrepreneur	Low	Limited
3	Strict, closed, uncertain	Designated champion and charisma	Controlling, self-oriented	Constrained beyond entrepreneur	Medium	Limited

and replication is possible (e.g. Cases 1b and 2a). Yet where power holders, entrepreneurs or NGOs are controlling or weak and the environment is less open, *purdah* transformation is constrained, affecting the stability of evolution and local replication, particularly evident in Cases 2b and 3. Table 4.1 summarises environmental and actor influences on *purdah* transformation, stability and replication across the cases.

4.4.2 Examining nature of evolving purdah rules across cases

To further unwrap findings, it is instructive to take a closer look at the nature of evolving *purdah* rules in each case. In Case 1a, *purdah* rules were progressive for the entrepreneur and senior workers (i.e. good mobility with negotiable terms and less restrictions), but stubbornly constrained for the rest of the women with limited flexibility (particularly with regard to work hours, meetings and village locations). In Case 1b, *purdah* rules were again progressive for the entrepreneur and senior workers, but less constrained than in Case 1a for the rest of the women (i.e. more flexible work hours and village mobility). In Case 2a, *purdah* rules were once more progressive for the entrepreneur and senior workers, and similar to Case 1b for the rest of the women but with growing degrees of flexibility. Meanwhile, in Case 2b, *purdah* rules were only notably progressive for the entrepreneur – particularly in a strict environment – but highly constrained for senior workers and the rest of the women, with limited flexibility. Finally, in Case 3, *purdah* rules were again progressive for the entrepreneur, but constrained and inflexible for the rest of the women (and strictly monitored by the power holders, particularly the worker women's husbands). Reflecting on these findings and above discussions, it is indicated that the nature of evolving *purdah* is clearly shaped by the entrepreneurs (and to some extent, the senior workers). And the entrepreneurs' behaviour is both influenced/moderated by the local environment and authorities. In particular, in the cases of more controlling entrepreneurs (such as Cases 2b and 3), progressive *purdah* was reserved for themselves, with little participation by the other women (in contrast to Cases 1b and 2a). Yet where there were strict authorities in more difficult and uncertain contexts (such as Case 1a, as well as Cases 2b and 3), both the extent of participation in progressive *purdah* forms and the flexibility of evolving *purdah* were shown to be constrained (beyond the entrepreneur).

Power and interests determining norm scope, adoption and change

The emerging nature of rules, and their related dynamics, has influenced norm scope, adoption and change. Elster (1989) suggested that social norms are neither collectively optimal nor solely promoted or pursued out of self-interest. Exploring this perspective in the case studies, it is clear that both power and interests have influenced norm emergence, and resulting norm dimensions (scope, adoption, enforcement and flexibility). Further to this, Fligstein (2001) theorised that actor learning within networks precipitated 'new paths of action'. Yet such learning may be hindered by powerful entrepreneurs, or by other actors, affecting resulting 'paths of action'. Where authorities have been supportive and entrepreneurs open, there is a healthy participation in *purdah* rules with light oversight by the authorities. Where authorities have been controlling, this has constrained the further development of *purdah* rules and participation by workers, although the entrepreneur and her supporters may be able to partly navigate around this (e.g. Case 1a). In cases where both entrepreneurs and authorities have been controlling (e.g. Cases 2b and 3), this has led to exclusive and constrained *purdah* rules with little participation by other women in rule shaping, monitoring and change.

As indicated, institutional change has in fact generated layers of *purdah* norms (or multiple manifestations), with the degree of self-interest embedded in new norms influenced by powerful actors. Crandall (1988) described the existence and transmission of norms 'counter to the prevailing society'. All of the cases have demonstrated the departure from the typical *purdah* norms in the community (with the approval of the authorities), with new layers of norms created for selected circles of women. And in Case 2b, there was acceptance of a new extremely liberal form of *purdah* for the entrepreneur only. Yet in Case 3, where the entrepreneur had negotiated more extensive *purdah* norms, local pressures and mistrust led to the decision of the entrepreneur to leave the community. This was in part motivated by self-protection, and the widening of *purdah norms* between herself and the rest of the women. Table 4.2 describes these emerging *purdah* rules, and their dynamics, across the cases.

4.4.3 Outcomes of evolving purdah: new relations, values and preferences

In the research cases, new *purdah* norms have generated new ideas on women's roles, precipitating new relations, trust and cooperation between women in the community. These 'breakthroughs' in norms (Kuznets, 1968) have permitted the subsequent participation in economic activities (see the next chapter). Yet it is worth mentioning that beyond the research communities, there have been diverse experiences of *purdah* transformation in other participating villages (Cases 1 and 2), particularly where there was heightened local instability (and conflict) and (less capable) actors clashing with uncertain resolutions.[17] In the research cases, new emerging norms and relations have permitted both new practices, and the development of new networks. In Cases 1a, 1b and 2a – where entrepreneurs display interests in collaboration with other women, or are *'public-spirited'* – new networks have provided a web of women that are prepared to champion evolving practices and new routines, strengthening their stability and enabling their ongoing evolution. Specifically, this has aided the women's interaction with power holders and enabled the women to garner public support. In Case 1a, these networks have created a strong defence against the power holders and conservative attitudes, permitting new and slowly evolving *purdah* practices, although the network of women remains tight, with controlled participation constraining further diffusion of practices and their natural evolution. Meanwhile, in Cases 2b and 3, such networks were deliberately limited or undeveloped, with power remaining in the

Table 4.2 Evolving *purdah* rules: scope, shaping boundaries, enforcement and change

Case number	Entrepreneur	Assistants/senior workers	Workers	Who shapes rules	Who monitors/enforces	Who can propose change/flexibility
1a	Few restrictions in village / Frequent city visits	Agreed working time/meeting time/other duties as required / Some city visits with *maharam* or other women	Agreed working time/meeting time / Limited city visits with *maharam*	Entrepreneur/senior workers	Entrepreneur with senior workers / Village authorities	Entrepreneur with senior workers / Limited flexibility
1b	No restrictions in village / Frequent city visits	Agreed working time/meeting time/other duies as required / City visits with *maharam* or other women	Flexible working time/meeting time / Some city visits with *maharam*	Entrepreneur/senior workers	Entrepreneur with senior workers / Light oversight by village authorities	Entrepreneur with senior workers / Medium flexibility
2a	No restrictions in village/city	Agreed working time/meeting time/other duties as required / City visits with *maharam* or other women	Flexible working time/meeting time / Some city visits with *maharam*	Entrepreneur/senior workers	Entrepreneur/senior workers / Light oversight by village authorities	Entrepreneur/senior workers / Medium flexibility
2b	No restrictions in village/city	Agreed working time/meeting time / Limited city visits with *maharam*	Agreed working time/meeting time / Limited city visits with *maharam*	Entrepreneur	Entrepreneur / Village authorities	Entrepreneur / Limited flexibility
3	No restrictions	(None)	Agreed working time/meeting time	Entrepreneur	Entrepreneur / Local authorities (and families)	Entrepreneur / Limited flexibility

Table 4.3 *Purdah* practices shaping new community values and preferences

Case number	Environment	Entrepreneur interests	Women's values/preferences	Power holder values/preferences regarding women
1a	Strict	Public-spirited	New ideas on public roles among elite and confident women	Control evolving status quo for agreed women, some interest in basic women's empowerment
1b	Open/progressive	Public-spirited	New ideas on public roles	Increasing interest in women's empowerment and public roles
2a	Open/progressive	Public-spirited	New ideas on public roles	Increasing interest in women's empowerment and public roles
2b	Strict	Individually oriented	New ideas on public roles among elite	Maintain status quo except for strong women
3	Strict, uncertain	Individually oriented	New ideas on public roles among elite	Maintain status quo except for strong women

hands of more '*individually oriented*' entrepreneurs that were more focused on their own interests. The combination of the controlling entrepreneur and a strict environment has led to more exclusive *purdah* practices, and constrained emerging new institutions and their adoption.

As described in Chapter 2, Hodgson (1997, 2003) argued that a hidden feature of institutions was their capacity to mould individual habits and dispositions ('reconstitutive downward causation'). With new *purdah* practices or habits ('propensities' to behave in certain ways; Hodgson, 2003: 164), the women's values and preferences have changed, with new ideas on their life roles and aspirations, going beyond the household to potentially public-facing activities in the economic, social and political realms. As discussed in the next chapter, this permitted the unleashing of the women's enterprise. Yet the realisation of these new preferences and attitudes has been largely controlled by the entrepreneur, or local authorities. In Cases 2b and 3, entrepreneurs have deliberately ensured that more open *purdah* practices are not shared with other women. While in Case 1a, the authorities have kept a lid on *purdah* practices although the entrepreneur has managed to navigate around this for selected women. Meanwhile, new women's *purdah* practices have also fostered new values and preferences in progressive power holders, particularly in Cases 1b and 2a, with increasing interest in women's education and public roles in the community. This included promoting girls' school education (and discouraging early marriage), and encouraging active participation in the women's council (and raising the power of this platform within the community).

Table 4.3 summarises emerging new values and preferences as a result of *purdah* transformation, with the most progressive change in preferences indicated in more open and progressive environments with *public-spirited* entrepreneurs. Meanwhile, in strict environments with *individually oriented* entrepreneurs, new preferences regarding women's roles were largely confined to the elite.

4.5 Concluding remarks

Koford and Miller (1991) highlighted the significance of cultural change in economic systems. Looking into the research cases, this chapter has endeavoured to carefully examine the initial 'revolutionary' transformation of the women's norm of *purdah*, permitting subsequent engagement in enterprise. Following a review of the pertinent discourse on norms, economic development and change (advancing insights from Chapter 2), the discussion highlighted key stages in the transformation process, identifying triggers and events, the strategies of core actors, and the varying influence of the local context. Horne (2001) described the emergence of norms as a function of negotiation, existing interests and structure, and the control capacity of the group, with greater consistency in emerging norms of those in similar social positions. Precipitated by close association to new ideological and cognitive ideas (Knight, 1992), the research has indicated diverse actor negotiation in the transformation of (heterogeneous) *purdah* norms of selected women in view of new (emerging) interests, with control dynamics situated both within the group (the entrepreneurs) and the environment (local power holders), and moderated by a third party, the NGO. Building on Hechter and Opp (2001) and insights on agency from Chapter 2 (e.g. Beckert, 1999), the research examined the role of different actors in the change process, yet it also appreciated variations in local conditions. Initiating the process, the NGOs introduced the early reformed version of *purdah* in negotiation with the local power holders. The entrepreneur and her allies were then involved with trialling these preliminary practices, and formulating variations of the new *purdah*. Taking a broad perspective in this research, the notion of 'institutional entrepreneurs' (DiMaggio, 1988; Sunstein, 1996) may be applied to each of these actors that influence norm development. Thus, this includes the NGOs in initiating new norms and the entrepreneurs in shaping norms, as well as the power holders in articulating norm boundaries. Yet these institutional entrepreneurs have demonstrated mixed objectives and interests, and different capacities, affecting levels of trust, power dynamics and cooperation. This has influenced the scope of norm development, and broader learning, diffusion and adoption processes. Since the norms were strongly tied up with religion and world views, progressive religious ideas have proved fundamental in strategies permitting change, and the involvement of power holders was not only necessary, but shown to strengthen resulting norms and enhance their stability and institutionalisation (Zucker, 1991). Going beyond Weber and religious values, in a traditional environment, religious ideas have been shown to be a powerful resource towards social change (Ter Haar, 2001) – enabling a new 'narrative' on women – particularly if used by progressive and charismatic leaders, or credible outsiders in 'receptive' local conditions.

Looking at the nature of emerging institutions, in more progressive contexts with public-spirited and pioneering entrepreneurs, *purdah* rules were shown to be open, flexible and evolving, and collaboratively shaped by entrepreneurs and her allies with light oversight by authorities. In contrast, in stricter and closed contexts, with individually oriented entrepreneurs, new *purdah* rules were tightly controlled, leading to exclusive and constrained practices. In all cases, the initially negotiated norms reflected an obvious change in *purdah* norms demonstrated in the target women's permitted mobility, yet there were similar degrees of difference across the women (i.e. heterogeneity across the (target) women's norms remained the same). Going beyond Horne (2001), evolving norms have tended to manifest growing degrees of differences between the lead women and worker women in the emergence of a new order, particularly where control mechanisms were strict within the group and within the community with individually-orientated entrepreneurs. But where there was more flexibility and trust with progressive actors, and public-spirited entrepreneurs, new norms and ideas have evolved both within the group, and have started to diffuse into the wider community, with broad knock-on effects to local attitudes and practices. In these environments, new ideas on women's roles, and relations have been facilitated, positively shaping evolving community values and preferences.

Notes

1 'The separation of women and men in everyday life applied even to their religious practice. Women not only worked, ate, socialized and often slept apart from men; they also prayed and worshipped separately, and in rather different ways. Whereas the spiritual life of men emphasized formal, communal observances, women were excluded from joining them for prayer in mosques, and had no public gathering-place . . .' (Doubleday, 2006: 45).
2 For example, the Koran instructs women to guard their private parts, and cover their bosoms (Sura 24:31–32).
3 According to the NGO, villages were selected that were considered marginalised in local city districts (without aid projects), where fruit and vegetables were available, and where security was deemed acceptable.
4 Women were selected that were interested to join an enterprise group, had their family's approval, and were from similar low wealth backgrounds.
5 Criteria for the leader selection included those that were respected, honest and responsible (religious, active); and those that had more mobility due to age and marital status (older and/or widows).
6 In traditional middle-class families, there was still much pride attached to being able to keep their women in strict *purdah*.
7 As indicated in Chapter 3, there is a great distrust of foreign 'modern' ideas regarding women, driven by the fear that Afghan traditions and Islamic values will be jeopardised.
8 The criteria for participating farmers included women from poorer families with small available plots of available land, and a willingness to work in vegetable production.
9 The criteria for lead farmer selection included 'capable' women (preferably widows with more mobility) that were good Muslims with 500 metres squared of land, able to give training, and critically, representing a different *qawn* or family clan in the community. Some of the lead farmers were already part of the women's village council (women's CDC subcommittee).
10 The use of local 'champions' was strategically employed by the facilitating NGOs in Cases 2 and 3. These were male elders that were identified by the NGO at the start of the project as project supporters. They were both charismatic and persuasive, and progressive in their views. They were motivated by a belief in the project and women's empowerment. In some circumstances, they received small financial tokens by the NGO for community work (e.g. in helping resolve family conflicts around women's participation).
11 During the Russian times, comprehensive efforts were made to push through social change into the rural areas, particularly with regard to women. Strategies included employing people as 'secret agents' to infiltrate villages in order to spy on the local community (and report back to central authorities).
12 In one particularly unstable project village (beyond the research), this in fact led to the ultimate collapse of the project.
13 This NGO was involved with participatory community infrastructure development.
14 Yet the Parwan governor, a bureaucrat from Kabul, was adamant that 'human universal values' were more appropriate. This highlighted the typical disconnect between the Afghan urban middle class and the common (rural) majority, underscoring the former's poor appreciation of the latter's reality/world view.
15 Poor families were identified as those without land or, in extreme cases, without homes. Families were prioritised that were female-headed, and had disabled members.
16 It is worth noting that the women's ministry in Kabul recounted similar stories of other emerging women's enterprises in Kabul, with families becoming doubtful and nervous as new boundaries were pushed, particularly when the security situation appeared to be uncertain. An independent business organisation in Kabul further expanded upon this 'problem', and emphasised the importance of creating an early solid (cognitive)

'foundation' with both the families and the women in fostering a 'strong belief' in the women's emerging work.

17   In one village related to Case 2 (outside of the research), the NGO was forced to abandon all efforts due to 'persisting (intra) village conflict', and notably cited a 'lack of charismatic champions'. And without strong power holder support, broader security became a key concern for NGO staff. Unfortunately, due to the high instability of the area, the village could not be visited in person.

References

Ahmed, L. (1992) *Women and Gender in Islam: Historical Roots of a Modern Debate*, New Haven, CT and London: Yale University Press.

Aoki, M. (2001) *Toward a Comparative Institutional Analysis*, Cambridge, MA: MIT Press.

Appiah, K.A. (2010) *The Honor Code: How Moral Revolutions Happen*, New York and London: W.W. Norton & Company.

Arrow, K. (1971) 'Political and economic evaluation of social effects and externalities', in M. Intriligator (ed.), *Frontiers of Quantitative Economics*, Amsterdam, The Netherlands: North-Holland.

Axelrod, R. (2006) 'Robert Axelrod, 1986, "An Evolutionary Approach to Norms", "American Political Science Review" 80 (December): 1095–1111', *The American Political Science Review*, 100(4): 682–3.

Battilana, J., Leca, B. and Boxenbaum, E. (2009) 'How actors change institutions: towards a theory of institutional entrepreneurship', *The Academy of Management Annals: A Journal of the Academy of Management*, 3(1): 65–107.

Beckert, J. (1999) 'Agency, entrepreneurs, and institutional change: the role of strategic choice and institutionalized practices in organizations', *Organisation Studies*, 20(5): 777–99.

Beckert, J. (2003) 'Economic sociology and embeddedness: how shall we conceptualize economic action?', *Journal of Economic Issues*, 37(3): 769–87.

Berger, P. and Luckmann, T. (1966) *The Social Construction of Reality*, New York: Doubleday.

Bicchieri, C. (2006) *The Grammar of Society: The Nature and Dynamics of Social Norms*, New York: Cambridge University Press.

Biccheri, C. (2010) 'Norms, preferences and conditional behavior', *Politics, Philosophy and Economics*, 9(3): 297–313.

Boettke, P.J., Coyne, C.J., and Leeson, P. (2008) 'Institutional stickiness and the new development economics', *The American Journal of Economics and Sociology*, 67(2): 331–58.

Bourdieu, P. (1977) *Outline of a Theory of Practice*, Cambridge: Cambridge University Press.

Boyd, R. and Richerson, P.J. (1985) *Culture and the Evolutionary Process*, Chicago, IL: University of Chicago Press.

Camic, C. (1986) 'The matter of habit', *American Journal of Sociology*, 91(5): 1039–87.

Chang, H.-J. (2005) 'Understanding the relationship between institutions and economic development: some key theoretical issues', paper presented at the *WIDER Jubilee Conference*, WIDER, Helsinki, Finland 17–18 June.

Crandall, C. (1988) 'Social contagion of binge eating', *Journal of Personality and Social Psychology*, 55: 588–98.

Darley, J.M. and Latane, B. (1970) *The Unresponsive Bystander: Why Doesn't He Help?*, New York: Appleton Century Crofts.

De Jong, E. (2011) 'Religious values and economic growth: a review and assessment of recent studies', in G. Ter Haar (ed.), *Religion and Development*, London: C. Hurst & Co.

Dewey, J. (1922) *Human Nature and Conduct: An Introduction to Social Psychology* (1st edn), New York: Holt.

DiMaggio, P.J. (1988) 'Interest and agency in institutional theory', in L.G. Zucker (ed.), *Institutional Patterns and Organizations*, Cambridge, MA: Ballinger.

Doubleday, V. (2006) *Three Women of Herat*, New York: Tauris Parke Paperbacks.

Durkheim, E. (1895/1950) *The Rules of Sociological Method* (S.A. Solovay and J. Mueller, trans.), New York: The Free Press.

Durkheim, E. (1912/1961) *The Elementary Forms of the Religious Life*, New York: Collier.

Elster, J. (1989) 'Social norms and economic theory', *Journal of Economic Perspectives*, 3(4): 99–117.

Fligstein, N. (2001) 'Social skill and the theory of fields', *Sociological Theory*, 19(2): 105–25.

Gaventa, J. (2006) 'Finding the spaces for change: a power analysis', *IDS Bulletin*, 37(6).

Geertz, C. (1973) *The Interpretation of Cultures*, New York: Basic Books.

Gomez, G. (2008) *Making Markets: The Institutional Rise and Decline of the Argentine Red de Trueque*, Maastricht, Netherlands: Shaker Publishing BV (PhD Thesis).

Guiso, L., Sapienza, P. and Zingales, L. (2003) 'People's opium? Religion and economic attitudes', *Journal of Monetary Economics*, 50(1): 225–82.

Hayami, Y. (2001) *Development Economics: From the Poverty to the Wealth of Nations*, Oxford and New York: Oxford University Press.

Hechter, M. and Opp, K. (2001) *Social Norms*, New York: Russell Sage Foundation.

Hirschman, A.O. (1958) *The Strategy of Economic Development*, New Haven, CT: Yale University Press.

Hodgson, G. (1997) 'The ubiquity of habits and rules', *Cambridge Journal of Economics*, 21: 663–84.

Hodgson, G. (2003) 'The hidden persuaders, institutions and individuals in economic theory', *Cambridge Journal of Economics*, 27: 159–75.

Hodgson, G. (2004) *The Evolution of Institutional Economics: Agency, Structure and Darwinism in American Institutionalism*, London: Routledge.

Hofstede, G.H. (1980) *Culture's Consequences: International Differences in Work-Related Values*, Beverly Hills, CA: Sage.

Hofstede, G.H., Hofstede, G.J. and Minkov, M. (2010) *Cultures and Organizations: Software of the Mind: Intercultural Cooperation and its Importance for Survival*, New York: McGraw-Hill.

Horne, C. (2001) 'Sociological perspectives on the emergence of norms', in M. Hechter and K. Opp (eds), *Social Norms*, New York: Russell Sage Foundation.

Jacoby, W. (2001) 'Tutors and pupils: international organizations, Central European elites, and Western models', *Governance*, 14(2): 169–200.

Kakar, P. (2005) 'Tribal law of pashtunwali and women's legislative authority', *Harvard Islamic Legal Studies Program*, 3.

Kandori, M. (1992) 'Social norms and community enforcement', *The Review Economic Studies*, 59: 63–80.

Kim, J.Y. and Nam, S.H. (1998) 'The concept and dynamics of face: implications for organizational behaviour in Asia', *Organisation Science*, 9(4): 522–34.

Knight, J. (1992) *Institutions and Social Conflict*, Cambridge: Cambridge University Press.

Koford, K.J. and Miller, J.B. (1991) *Social Norms and Economic Institutions*, Ann Arbor, MI: University of Michigan Press.

Kuznets, S. (1968) *Toward a Theory of Economic Growth*, New York: W.W. Norton.

Lewis, W.A. (1955) *The Theory of Economic Growth*, London: George Allen & Unwin.

Li, D., Feng, J. and Jiang, H. (2006) 'Institutional entrepreneurs', *The American Economic Review*, 96(2): 358–62.

Meyer, J.W. (1970) 'Institutionalization', unpublished paper, Department of Sociology, Stanford University, CA.

Mills, M.A. (2011) 'Between covered and covert: traditions, stereotypes, and Afghan women's Agency', in J. Heath and A. Zahedi (eds), *Land of the Unconquerable: The Lives of Contemporary Afghan Women*, Berkeley, CA and London: University of California Press.

Parsons, T. (1937) *The Structure of Social Action*, New York: McGraw-Hill.

Parsons, T. (1951) *The Social System*, New York: Free Press.

Peyton Young, H. (1998) *Individual Strategy and Social Structure*, Princeton NJ: Princeton University Press.

Peyton Young, H. (2007) 'Social norms', *Oxford Department of Economics Discussion Paper Series No 307*, Oxford: University of Oxford.

Pickthall, M.M. (1938) *The Meaning Of The Glorious Quran*, Hyderabad-Deccan, India: Government Central Press.

Pitt-Rivers, J. (1965) 'Honour and social status', in J.G. Peristiany (ed.), *Honour and Shame*, London: Weidenfeld & Nicolson.

Platteau, J.P. (1994) 'Behind the market stage where real societies exist (part I and II): the role of moral norms', *Journal of Development Studies*, 30(4): 753–815.

Platteau, J.P. (2000) *Institutions, Social Norms, and Economic Development*, Amsterdam, The Netherlands: Harwood Academic Publishers.

Rzehak, L. (2011) *Doing Pashto: Pashtunwali as the Ideal of Honourable Behaviour and Tribal Life among the Pashtuns*, Kabul: Afghanistan Analysts Network.

Schultz, N., Nolan, J.M., Cialdini, G., Griskevicius, V. and Goldstein, N. (2007) 'The constructive, destructive, and reconstructive power of social norms', *Psychological Science*, 18(5): 429–34.

Scott, A. (2004) 'Institutional theory: contributing to a theoretical research program', in G. Smith and M.A. Hitt (eds), *Great Minds in Management: The Process of Theory Development*, Oxford: Oxford University Press.

Seabright, P. (2010) *The Company of Strangers: A Natural History of Economic Life*, Princeton, NJ: Princeton University Press.

Shepsle, K.A. (1986) 'Institutional equilibrium and equilibrium institutions', in H. Weisberg (ed.), *Political Science: the Science of Politics*, New York: Agathon.

Shepsle, K.A. (1989) 'Studying institutions: some lessons from the rational choice approach', *Journal of Theoretical Politics*, 1: 131–47.

Sperber, D. (1996) *Explaining Culture: A Naturalistic Approach*, Oxford and Cambridge, MA: Blackwell.

Sunstein, C.R. (1996) 'Social norms and social roles', *Columbia Law Review*, 96(4): 903–68.

Ter Haar, G. (ed.) (2011) *Religion and Development*, London: C. Hurst & Co.

Weber, K. and Dacin, M.T. (2011) 'The cultural construction of organizational life: introduction to the special issue', *Organisation Science*, 22(2): 287–98.

Weber, M. (1904/1930) *The Protestant Ethic and the Spirit of Capitalism* (translated by T. Parson), New York: Charles Scribner's Sons.

Weber, M. (1924/1968) *Economy and Society: An Interpretive Sociology* (G. Roth and C. Wittich, eds), New York: Bedminister Press.

Wikan, U. (1984) 'Shame and honour: a contestable pair', *Man (New Series)*, 19(4): 635–52.

Zucker, L. (1991) 'The role of institutionalization in cultural persistence', in W.W. Powell and P.J. DiMaggio (eds), *The New Institutionalism in Organizational Analysis*, Chicago, IL: University of Chicago Press.

5 Constructing institutions in enterprise

> Before wealth can be created, human beings have to learn to work together, and if there is to be subsequent progress, new forms of organisation have to be developed. While we typically associate economic growth with technological development, organisational innovation has played an equal if not more important role since the beginning of the industrial revolution.
>
> (Fukuyama, 1995: 47)

Building on the previous chapter, and the transformation of norms, this chapter looks onwards to the construction of new institutions in the three women's businesses in Afghanistan. The discussion initially elaborates on relevant discourse on specific economic institutions for group enterprise, going beyond general institutional discussions in Chapter 2. These include routines within the firm, institutional arrangements (and value chain links), and institutions for collective action. Further interrogating the research cases, I then examine the gradual development of these three types of economics institutions in the women's enterprises. In vein with Chapter 4, the roles of key actors in the process of institutional development are highlighted, and the varying influence of the context. Looking across the cases, the discussion draws attention to dominant aspects of the construction process and the evolving nature of rules. Finally, the discussion explores further outcomes in terms of broader social, economic and political institutions.

5.1 Socially embedded institutions in economic activity

Adam Smith postulated that economies themselves could not be divorced from the 'customs, morals and habits of the society' (Muller, 1992). Indeed, while norms such as *purdah* present critical boundary institutions, sociocultural institutions also shape and influence the scope of emerging economic institutions. In particular, prevailing institutions determine levels of trust, 'the expectation that arises within a community, of regular, honest, and cooperative behaviour, based on commonly shared norms, on the part of other members of that community' (Fukuyama, 1995: 26), crucial in the development of institutions. Where there is little trust between agents, people may tend to require more codified rules and regulations to cooperate. And where there is little trust within environments, people may only cooperate within their own social groups. In unwrapping the nature of enterprise development, it is instructive to examine key institutions in economic activity. At the level of the enterprise, internal 'routines' provide a framework for group production and management. Beyond the firm, institutional arrangements or 'chain rules' facilitate vertical inter-firm coordination (chain governance). Meanwhile, 'institutions for collective action' and exchange permit collaboration between groups or firms.

5.1.1 Building blocks: routines shaping organisations and firms

At the foundation of organisations and firms, the discussion initially look at basic internal 'routines' to examine their emergence, effects and change in organisations. As described in Chapter 2, evolutionary work by Nelson and Winter (1982) applied Darwinian concepts of variation, replication and selection to the evolution of the firm. This has stimulated lively cross-discipline debate on routines within organisations. Considered the 'building blocks of organizational capabilities' (Winter, 2003), Becker (2004) highlights pertinent insights from the different streams of the literature. First, Becker broadly describes routines as referring to 'recurrent activity' or 'interaction patterns' (e.g. Winter, 1990), or to 'cognitive regularities' (e.g. March and Simon, 1958). Second, Becker draws attention to typical characteristics of routines both in their collective nature (Nelson and Winter, 1982), and in their potential for distribution across space or organisation (e.g. Winter, 1994). Yet Becker highlights that the collective nature of routines may be threatened when people act in an individualistic way (e.g. Weick, 1990). Third, Becker cites different communities that may be involved in routine development, including 'functional' communities (which are 'hierarchical, are homogonous and share a disciplinary specialization'), horizontally defined 'epistemic' communities (involved in the production of new knowledge), and 'communities of practice' (those with a shared interest in a given practice) (Cohendet and Llerena, 2003). These communities influence the context in which routines emerge, learning processes, and routine outcomes in terms of the power of replication, degree of inertia and 'search potential' (ibid.). Fourth, Becker describes routines as encompassing in part 'mindlessness' and in part as being 'effortful' (Feldman and Pentland, 2003), permitting 'adaptive and creative behaviour' in routine change. Fifth, he draws attention to the 'processual' nature of routines, providing 'a "window" on the drivers underlying change', including their development, stability and change. And sixth, Becker highlights both the context dependence of routines, embeddedness in an organisation, and their specificity to the context (e.g. Cohendet and Llerena, 2003).

Becker (2004) summarises four key organisational effects of these (intra) enterprise rules. Primarily, routines permit coordination and control (e.g. March and Olsen, 1989) through providing a cognitive and governance framework (Nelson and Winter, 1982: 107). Routines further reduce uncertainty and provide relative stability with potential change endogenous to routines (as a result of the agency of participants; Feldman and Pentland, 2003). Routines also allow savings in the use of cognitive resources (e.g. Hodgson, 1997). And finally, routines store knowledge (Nelson and Winter, 1982). Towards a more nuanced conception of routines, Hodgson (2007: 110) defines routines as 'organizational dispositions' that may generate 'conditional patterns of behaviour within an organised group of individuals, involving sequential responses to cues'. Further considering the influence on actors, Cohendet and Llerena (2003: 274) also highlight the crucial capacity of routines to facilitate collective action (Cohen *et al.*, 1996). This may enable both the development of new routines and the formulation of other enterprise rules.

Evolutionary insights

Yet in terms of the original evolutionary-oriented discussions (championed by Nelson and Winter, 1982), the progress on understanding routines has been 'slow' (Becker, 2004: 663). Taking up the Darwinian agenda, Hodgson and Knudsen (2004) distinguish between the level of routines and habits as 'replicators', and the level of the firm and 'cohesive' organisations as 'interactors' or vehicles for routines. Habits may be 'replicated' when individuals follow the behaviour of other people, which may be driven by incentives and constraints; or through conscious or less-conscious imitation (Hodgson and Knudsen, 2004: 288). Once imitation has been triggered and established, the motivation for imitation may be related to reputation and status, or social conformity (as described by Henrich and Boyd, 2001). There may also be degrees of variations and innovation. With routines belonging to groups and habits to individuals, routines are indicated to depend on individuals within a particular group (Hodgson and Knudsen, 2004: 295), with their own individual habits, and related 'procedural memories' (Hodgson and Knudsen, 2004: 290). Advancing this, Hodgson suggests that routines are the 'organizational analogue of habits . . . [but] are irreducible to habits alone: they are organizational meta-habits, existing on a substrate of habituated individuals in a social structure. Routines are one ontological layer above habits themselves' (Hodgson, 2007: 111). The replication of routines is considered to be more difficult than habits, especially through imitation, due to limitations of organisations (compared to individuals) to appreciate the 'tacit rules and meanings associated with that behaviour' (Hodgson and Knudsen, 2004: 291). In terms of 'selection', this may occur both through interactions within the organisational environment, including between individuals and groups of individuals (as a result of the behaviour of managers); and at the firm level, driven by factors related to its organisational health (Hodgson and Knudsen, 2004: 293). Routines may then be spread through the active and deliberate sharing of information/instructions and guidance, through rules that stem from a third party, through a cloning strategy by a receiving organisation, or by lower-level interaction between several individuals (ibid.). Hodgson and Knudsen describe hierarchies of groups or firms as 'interactors', and a hierarchy of replicators or 'routines'. Hodgson (2007: 111) suggests that the actual structure of organisations may be significant in that they provide the required social and physical environment to 'enable specific activities, cue individual habits and deploy individual memories'.

Levinthal (1991) underscored the interrelated processes of change in organisational adaptation and environmental selection and indicated that organisational phenomena such as routines need to be viewed together to understand organisations. Yet Hodgson (2007) argues that organisations are like the human body, and thus more than just the collection of cells that they contain, but with a life of their own. Meanwhile, exploring insights by Schumpeter (1934, 2005) and theories by Winter (2006), Becker *et al.* (2006) elaborate on routines and system 'novelties' as emerging in the 'combinatorics' of routines (the mix of routines) and in the 'unreliability' of routine imitation, drawing on ideas from chemistry, linguistics and the diffusion of fashion.

Whilst the discourse has shed light on routines and their dynamics, Becker (2004) highlighted gaps in understanding the nature of collective versus individual routines, and the role of agency in engaging in interaction patterns (Becker, 2004: 664). In terms of the latter, Hodgson (2007) suggests better understanding agency in the implementation and evolution of rules, and their persistence, combining insights from both evolutionary economics (e.g. Winter, 1982) and organisation science (Aldrich, 1999).

5.1.2 Economic coordination through multiple institutional arrangements

I next consider institutions related to 'economic coordination'. According to Hollingsworth (2002: 7), literature on so-called 'institutional arrangements' (e.g. forms of economic coordination) remains largely 'fragmented and unintegrated'. In Chapter 2, Hollingsworth and Boyer (1997, 2002) defined institutional arrangements as the (multi) coordination of various economic actors ('governance' mechanisms) by markets, hierarchies and networks, associations, the state, communities and clans. Hollingsworth distinguishes between two dimensions influencing coordination: that of economist's self-interest and a more sociological perspective of obligation and compliance with social rules. Drawing this together, Hollingsworth and Boyer (1997: 14) considers both the actor 'action motive' and the distribution of power 'coordination' within different institutional arrangements, each with its 'own logic – its own rules, its own procedures for enforcing compliance, and its own norms and ideologies', which can help lower the costs of enforcement (see Figure 5.1).

At one end of this conceived spectrum of economic coordination, Hollingsworth and Boyer (1997) positions 'hierarchies' (e.g. of firms) as driven by self-interest with vertical forms of power. Individual compliance may be more motivated by rewards to individuals or a threat of sanctions (through asymmetric power). Collective compliance may be motivated by rules, use of sanctions and a firm culture. Networks of actors of groups are more situated midway between both self-interest and obligation, and horizontal and vertical power, with individual compliance motivated by contractual bonds and resource dependence, and collective compliance motivated by personal relations and trust. Meanwhile, at the other end of the spectrum, Hollingsworth describes communities that are motivated more by common interests, with horizontal distributions of power that are based on

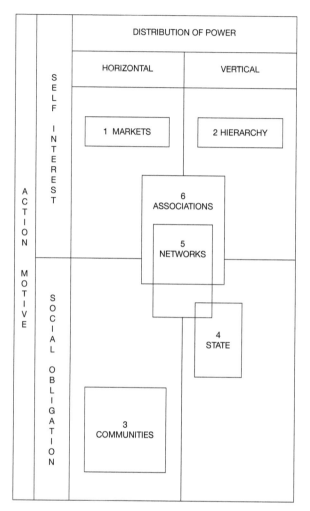

Figure 5.1 A general taxonomy of institutional arrangements
Source: Hollingsworth and Boyer (1997: 7)

trust, reciprocity or obligation, in vein with the discourse of anthropologists, political scientists and sociologists (e.g. Polanyi, 1944; Streeck and Schmitter, 1985; Gambetta, 1988; Sabel, 1992; Putnam, 1993, 2000; Fukuyama, 1995). Hollingsworth argues that the more perfect a market, the greater the need for codified rules. In less perfect markets, Hollingsworth and Boyer (1997) draws attention to the framework of social context and the nature of embeddedness influencing collective forms of governance, and the extent that actors participate in markets, networks or hierarchy. Going beyond the assumed sovereignty of the firm, Hollingsworth (2002) suggests that the dominant type of institutional

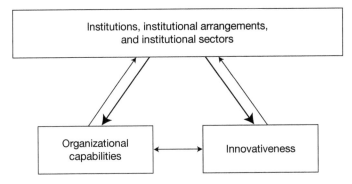

Figure 5.2 Institutional environments, organisations and innovativeness
Source: Hollingsworth (2000: 598)

arrangements in a given societal context may tend to place 'severe constraints on the definition of needs, preferences and choices of economic actors'. He emphasises the links between institutions, institutional arrangements and institutional sectors; organisational capabilities; and innovativeness (Figure 5.2). Yet theories on prevailing institutions, and their potential upward effects on institutional arrangements (i.e. institutional interaction) remain largely unexplored.

Governance in value chains: power dynamics and relations

Economic coordination has been particularly discussed in the value chain literature towards understanding the links between firms. This discourse evolved predominantly from three primary sources: the *filiere* (literal meaning 'thread') approach in the 1960s (Centre Internationale en Research Agronomic pour le Developpement), Porter's work (1980, 1985, 1990) on upgrading of national capabilities and the 'value system', and most recently Gereffi's studies (1994) on global commodity chains (GCCs). A popular tool for deconstructing and understanding global market chains, a value chain is defined as the entire range of activities through which a product or service passes from initial production to final delivery to the consumer (Kaplinsky and Morris, 2000: 4). Essentially, value chains are the same as supply chains but the point of analysis differs, with a focus on integration, rather than on the efficiency of large companies, and on power structures in the broader economy (Meyer-Stamer and Waltring, 2007). From the perspective of development policy and practice, value chains are crucial tools for working toward poverty reduction, supporting entrepreneurship and realising adequate labour conditions (Helmsing and Vellema, 2011: 1). The approach takes a special focus on the participation and competitiveness of poor producers and market barriers (Meyer-Stamer and Waltring, 2007). From a scientific perspective, value chains are also an important concept as a 'heuristic device' for unravelling the complexities of economic development (Helmsing and Vellema, 2011: 1).

The influence of non-economic dimensions (e.g. relationships and power) has been identified as critical to the functioning and efficiency of value chains. Gereffi (1994) highlighted the importance of inter-firm coordination and global buyers as drivers of 'spatially dispersed' production and distribution networks. 'Governance' is defined as the 'non-market coordination of economic activity' and includes the various types of hierarchies, or systems of coordination that exist in global production networks through parties internal and external to the chain (Humphrey and Schmitz, 2000; Kaplinsky and Morris, 2000; Gereffi and Memodovic, 2003). Yet while a great deal of attention has been paid to the nature of governance in value chains, particularly inter-firm relations, there has been a gap in understanding how these various dynamics determine evolving institutions in market activity, and the inclusion and participation of different groups. Indeed, the construction of appropriate market-oriented institutions is imperative to efficient market structures and integration. Powerful groups in more fragile and undeveloped societies may constrain the development of equitable informal or formal institutions in value chains (e.g. trade laws, ethical codes and local policies), limiting recognition or participation of certain groups. Social regulation and pervasive prejudice may also inhibit the inclusivity of new horizontal institutions such as associations and cooperatives, and the establishment of vertical linkages. Such sociocultural dynamics and power asymmetries may generate and sustain less efficient institutions and (continued) suboptimal chain functioning.

Towards unwrapping institutional processes, Helmsing and Vellema (2011) point to the importance of further considering the broader influence of *non-chain* actors within different contexts. Non-chain actors are those actors that are outside of the production network, including public or private agents. These actors may influence the participation of other actors in networks through mechanisms such as regulation, skills development or facilitating access to resources. They may also influence engagement in 'partnerships', described as 'voluntary and collaborative arrangements between actors from two or more societal domains' (Helmsing and Vellema, 2011: 3), which can influence inclusion in value chains through facilitating access to information, and market connections. In addition, Helmsing and Velema (2011: 13) argue that it is critical to appreciate prevailing sociocultural institutions and experience in cooperation or exclusion, and existing political structures, influencing chain and non-chain actors and their role in institutional development (and the related distribution of benefits). Thus, while Coe *et al.* (2008) drew attention to power distribution within value chains, there is a further need to examine power dynamics embedded in informal institutions (in the local environment) that affect the nature and functioning of the chain. Knorringa *et al.* (2011) examined the emergence of new institutions and norms in value chains and highlighted variables such as institutional legitimacy, and institutional life cycle and evolution, as related to the strategies of different actors. Going beyond 'value chain' governance, it is clear that a broader approach is needed to unravel coordination dynamics – such as the global production network approach – to incorporate networks and relations, and to better appreciate the embeddedness of value chains in social contexts (Helmsing and Vellema, 2011: 11).

5.1.3 Institutions for collective action: diverse outcomes in different settings

> All effort to organize collective action, whether by an external ruler, an entrepreneur, or a set of principals who wish to gain collective benefits, must address a common set of problems. These have to do with coping with free riding, solving commitment problems, arranging for the supply of new institutions, and monitoring individual compliance with sets of rules.
>
> (Ostrom, 1990: 27)

In a third set of key economic institutions for group enterprise, the paper draws attention to institutions for collective action. In a highly influential and much criticised book, Olson theorised that group size was critical in actor cooperation, and that large 'latent' groups with rational self-interested individuals would prevent collective action (Olson, 1965). He further highlighted the negative impact of 'free riding' on levels of trust. In vein with the theory of rational choice, Olson argued that collective action problems could only be solved by coercion or by activities with individual rewards. Hardin (1982) contended, however, that Olson conflated typologies with the assumption that all small groups were privileged and large groups were latent. Taking a different approach, Elster (1985) drew on themes of rationality and morality to discuss diverse motivations in collective action. For example, 'unconditional cooperators' may act out of duty or for the 'pleasure of participation'. These actors may encourage the participation of 'conditional cooperators', and then eventually nudge others that may be 'ashamed of being free riders' (Elster, 1985: 154). In vein with these arguments and further disputing Olson, Udehn (1993) looks further at motivations for cooperation (beyond 'self-interest'), and the extent of such cooperation. Building on Elster (1985), he suggests that there may be 'mixed motivations', and that it may be more pertinent to ask: how much cooperation and under what conditions? Meanwhile, Douglas (1986: 23) criticised Olson for exempting religious organisation from his analysis, which was 'clearly a mistake', since the history of religion may best corroborate his theory of diverse motivations for collective action, for more complex reasons, possibly bound up with beliefs in (spiritual) rewards and related prosocial behaviour.

Going beyond Olson's (1965) challenge to the notion of collective benefits in group theory and the 'tragedy of the commons' (Hardin, 1968),[1] Ostrom (1990) drew attention to how local people can self-organise to co-manage common pool resources and reduce free riding through developing diverse institutional arrangements with broad practical examples such as inshore fisheries and ground water basins. In a widely acclaimed work, she highlighted a number of crucial insights useful across the institutional spectrum. First, Ostrom emphasised the importance of a common set of values, increasing the probability of developing adequate rules (Taylor, 1987), and developing 'shared mental models', for good communication (Denzau and North, 1994). Ostrom also described the significance of certain social norms, particularly those of reciprocity. Second, Ostrom underscored the importance of developing fair, effective and legitimate rules for 'sustaining self-governing institutions over time' (Ostrom, 2005: 288). In social dilemmas, she contrasted rational egoists and those who value trust, reciprocity and equity (Ostrom, 2005: 131). In vein with Commons (1957), Ostrom emphasised rules in particular that contained all three of the 'deontic operators' (i.e. rules that forbid, require and permit some action or outcome; Ostrom, 1990: 139). Third, she drew attention to the attributes of the biophysical world that shapes and is shaped by individual interactions and those of a community, with the same set of rules generating different outcomes in different settings (Ostrom, 2005: 23). Fourth, Ostrom looked at participation in, and levels of, authority. For example, if individuals are given more authority in rule design, it may permit individuals to resolve their collective action problems (Ostrom, 2005: 287). Ostrom highlighted the negative effect of external rules and monitoring on cooperation (e.g. Fehr and Rockenbach, 2003). Ostrom described 'polycentric' governing systems as those that involve multiple authorities at different levels, and their (potentially) positive effect in reducing the 'tragedy of the commons' (Ostrom, 2005: 283). Finally, Ostrom also highlighted the interrelatedness of rules, and conceived of multiple levels of 'nested' rules, including rules that affect operational situations, rules that affect collective-choice situations, and rules that affect constitutional situations. The implications of this 'nestedness' were cited as twofold: higher-level rules may be considered as exogenous, and changes to lower-level rules may necessitate changes to higher-level rules. In terms of further theory and research, she highlighted the need to understand how different contexts influence the types of individuals in collective action situations (and those that leave).

These different discourses on economic institutions – routines, economic coordination and collective action – have shed light on both the particular institutions (and their dynamics), as well as generating further insights into institutional interaction and development, emphasising actor and structural influences. Yet the potential links between these institutions have not been elaborated, or how they may co-emerge in firms and business.

5.1.4 Creating institutions: actors, collaboration and strategies

Looking closer at sociological insights, creating institutions essentially requires interaction between actors (Fligstein, 1996). In Chapter 2, I drew attention to crucial insights into actors in institutional development including power struggles between actors (e.g. Chang, 2002), institutional entrepreneurs (DiMaggio, 1988) and the role of strategic agency (Beckert, 1999), and the importance of relations and networks (e.g. Granovetter, 1992). In Chapter 4, I looked at the empirical transformation of existing social institutions, and emerging insights into the collaboration between actors in different situations. Further reflecting on theories on actor interaction and influence here, I expand on the notion of 'social skill' and actor collaboration in the creation of new institutions. Fukuyama (1995: 10) argues that the ability of people to collaborate depends 'on the degree to which communities share norms and values, and are able to subordinate individual interests to those of larger groups'. Contrasting to rational choice theory, sociologists have drawn attention to social structure and connections between agents (e.g. Giddens, 1984). In vein with new institutionalism, Fligstein (2001) argues that much of the debate has been abstract and does not sufficiently account for agency. Furthering discussions in Chapter 2, Fligstein proposes a conception of agency that he terms 'social skill', drawing on the 'skilled reproduction of social life' (Giddens, 1984), the 'creativity of social action' (Joas, 1996), and other work by Emirbayer and Goodwin (1994), and Hays and Wincott (1994) (Fligstein, 2001: 105–6). With the broad view that institutions both enable and constrain social actors, the perspective looks at actor cooperation in groups: those within a group, and those who exist outside of the group (or in other organisations). Under situations of instability or uncertainty, social skill may be critical in securing 'local orders' in such groups, or alternatively, social skill may be imperative in the founding of new local orders and institutions. Fligstein (2001: 107) describes these skilled actors as having a 'vision to create new things'. Fligstein suggests that social skills may be more effective under some social conditions than others (ibid.). As seen in Chapter 4, tactics such as framing 'stories' can help induce cooperation, link frames to existing interests (and present ideas as also in the common interest), gain authority (Weber, 1921), and set agendas to demarcate boundaries of the discussion. Yet in order to be successful in the creation of new institutions, Fligstein cites the importance of obtaining collective support, often through creating a 'collective identity' (Ansell, 1998).

5.2 Constructing 'nested' institutions in enterprise

> With these new women's habits [of *purdah*], it was our duty to harness the 'rivers of change' in social and economic development.
>
> (NGO staff member)

To further examine institutional phenomena in the research, the paper returns to relevant findings from the case studies: the construction of (economic) institutions in the three women's enterprises in Afghanistan. Following the initial transformation of *purdah* (as described in Chapter 4), I look here at the development of key market-oriented institutions, permitting the commencement of the enterprise activities and scope of individual and group participation. In each case, significant effort was channelled into the formulation of these enterprise rules, led by the NGO in negotiation with local power holders, and shaped by the entrepreneurs. The first set of rules pertained to the enterprise 'routines' and related to group production and management. The second set of rules concerned business linkages 'chain rules', and related to physical marketing and procurement. Finally, the third set of rules outlined cross-firm coordination or 'collective action' with other similar groups. These three different sets of rules tended to be created sequentially as the women started producing, marketing and forming alliances, although there was considerable variation in the scope and implementation of the rules in each case. As with the transformation of *purdah*, for each level of rules, three stages were broadly observed in rule development. First, there was an initial phase in which the new enterprise institutions were conceptualised and introduced. After the approval of these tentative new rules, there was a secondary phase of practical experimentation in the reshaping of the proposed rules. Finally, with approval of new respective rules, there was a third phase, marked by the stabilisation and 'operationalisation' of the reformed institution with approval for replication within agreed groups.

5.2.1 Case 1: simple institutions with organic innovation and guided evolution

Business overview: rural women's food processing network

I return to the first case study, the women's food processing enterprise in West Afghanistan. In this case, the main business was organised at the village level in designated food processing centres. Products included tomato paste, jams, chutney and dried produce. The produce was sold by weight (unpackaged) locally by individual groups (80 per cent), and the rest (20 per cent) was co-marketed in the network as 'premium' packaged produce in the city (through shops and exhibitions, under a common label). In order for the women to engage in group enterprise, the local NGO led the initial development of internal rules, guiding production and group administration (enterprise routines). As the women started marketing, there was a secondary set of rules formulated related to their market interaction, including links with buyers and input providers (chain institutions). Finally, across the food processing groups, there was a third layer of rules created pertaining to their collective activity for higher-level marketing and technical exchange (collective action institutions). Enterprise institutions were characterised by their relative initial simplicity, with gradual localised innovations as the business matured, supported by the NGO.

Enterprise routines: introduction, reshaping and operationalisation

The first set of institutions, the enterprise 'routines', aimed to clarify women's roles and tasks in food processing work, and were delimited by both the women's capacity and permitted mobility. These internal rules tended to be enforced by transparency and trust fostered through close working conditions and group meetings in the research villages, guided and supported by the NGO. New practices were also reinforced by (progressive) proverbs, and religious *hadiths* (particularly important in some more conservative villages). Rules were first introduced and discussed in their monthly meetings.

In the initial stage, a basic set of preliminary rules was introduced by the NGO, following the trigger of the 'unlocking' of, or negotiated revision to *purdah*. Simple internal routines expanded upon the earlier SHG rules,[2] and were formulated with the approval of the entrepreneurs and power holders, and with the consensus of the other producer women. For example, all women were to be equally involved in group-level production in the village, according to agreed schedules. And the location of the production was decided to be inside a designated 'food processing' centre in the village. This would be situated in one room of a woman's house from the group. Yet difficulties were faced with gaining initial participation and even finding a spare room, due to the women's fear of what people might say:

> Many people refused to have their house used for training and production for fear of gossip from the village . . .
>
> (NGO female staff member)

Management-wise, selected women were elected by the group into key positions of responsibility, according to their capacity and levels of mobility, with an assigned group head (entrepreneur), deputy and sales agent. Initial profits were agreed to be equally divided between the group members. Meanwhile, assets would be group-owned. Due to the relative transparency of this preliminary rule-making (verbally in group meetings), there was a good (initial) sense of inclusion and trust between members.

In the subsequent reshaping stage, internal routines were trialled and elaborated. This included specifying the overall business structure and individual roles, clarifying labour commitments, and articulating rules over profit distribution with guidance by the women's *shura* and NGO:

> There was intensive discussion within the groups at this stage as new timetables were organised and agreed, and some advice was given by the women's *shura* . . . New routines built on the existing self-help group rules [specific to each group] which were democratic, and very transparent . . . and respected through group trust and further enforced by the group leader . . .
>
> (NGO male staff)

Yet as these new routines were tentatively tested, major bottlenecks were faced with husbands that were difficult and unsupportive (many of the men were still nervous with these new roles). This was aggravated by general local distrust and intimidation by local households. For example, the women were taunted with disparaging proverbs about women's capacities. Yet the women encouraged one another with more progressive proverbs:

> We faced so many pressures in the village in this new work, and there was much negativity and ridicule. For example, people would joke using local proverbs '*if a woman makes a knot, it will be washed away*' (i.e. all women's efforts are useless) . . . or '*the mind of a woman is near to the heel*' (i.e. women are stupid) . . . Yet the strong women in the group encouraged our participation and were patient, supporting the gradual development and growth of our business. They used common [morale-boosting] proverbs such as '*Drop by drop it becomes a river*' (i.e. the small contributions and teamwork of ordinary individuals can produce a big result) . . .[3]
>
> (Women producers, Cases 1a and b)

While the *shura*, NGO and entrepreneur were indicated to be the critical figures in the development of the routines, the producer women also mentioned the influence of other community groups. For example, even the mullah's wife was described to play a part in 'spying' on their new routines, and reporting back to the mullah!

In the final (dynamic) stage, group routines were agreed by all food processing group members in their monthly meetings, and the new rules were instituted. This stage was precipitated by the approval of the trialled institutions by both the female and male *shura*. With this go-ahead, all of the women participated in the group production in the village according to agreed schedules, carried out agreed respective responsibilities, and were remunerated according to days worked by agreed amounts within the group. At this point, the women described the new 'authorised' routines finally receiving some sort of 'respect' from the men:

> With transparency in our work, it obligates men to respect to you: they can see what you are doing, and they say '*You can work as well as us, and we accept you!*'
>
> (Women workers, Case 1b)

As expected, however, new situations soon arose, precipitating the necessary clarification or reformulation of existing routines. For example, the exit of a group member presented a new challenge when her husband demanded a share of both the physical assets of the group, in addition to the (agreed) invested cash portion (Case 1b). This was quickly resolved by the NGO in coordination with the *shura* and the entrepreneur, and they jointly (re)clarified the group rules with the group itself (ensuring that it was written clearly in their enterprise book) and the *shura*. Meanwhile, group heads began to be offered part-time employment as trainers by the NGO in other emerging centres. This necessitated some shifts in worker production responsi-bilities and an increased need for attendance sheets (instituted in Case 1b). In addition, with expansion, the increasing responsibilities of the entrepreneurs and senior women influenced the group decision to apportion a greater share of profits to emerging 'higher-level' members.

Internal routines began as equitable arrangements across workers. With production expansion, and visible higher-level responsibilities, there has been a need to adapt the worker routines to permit the further division of labour and specialisation in tasks. This has included the entrepreneur delegating new work to senior women to support administrative work. Power dynamics have changed within the groups accordingly. The entrepreneur largely led in the monitoring and enforcing of routines, and spearheading changes (with the support of the NGO), but the context notably affected her decision-making (especially in Case 1a), impacting the emerging roles of other women.

Chain rules: introduction, reshaping and operationalisation

Following the development of internal routines, rules were then formulated to clarify selected women's external responsibilities in the marketplace (i.e. public-facing duties beyond the production centre). These 'chain rules' were arguably more difficult to negotiate, since they required selected women to extend the agreed boundaries of *purdah*.

In the initial stage, a basic set of 'chain rules' was again introduced by the NGO to the group, and formulated in agreement with the entrepreneur and power holders. The rules conceived were related to physical marketing and the sourcing of vegetable inputs, and involved designated, more mobile and respected women (initially only the entrepreneur). Since this activity was tied up with a 'secondary' transformation of *purdah*, there was some delay in the initial negotiation of these rules. Once more, setbacks included stubborn elders and mullahs, nervous entrepreneurs and local intimidation. The NGO described the introduction of these marketing rules as particularly difficult in the first villages that they mobilised, due in part to their own inexperience:

> We faced enormous challenges in the first communities that we worked, but with time and experience, we learnt ways to persuade the communities and to quell their fears . . . We drew on the stories from other communities to explain how marketing could work and how women could still respect Islamic customs . . . And we used our own local ways, and these were the most effective and acceptable . . .
>
> (NGO male staff)

Meanwhile, the entrepreneurs described the need to be both determined and patient at this stage, since there was so much 'sensitivity' with women engaging in this public-facing activity:

> Every woman who does a job in Afghanistan must be really committed to get involved in this as she will face many challenges . . . As we struggled with marketing, I looked to the future and thought about potential prospects . . . We really had to keep pushing to support the marketing . . . Because of my strong belief in our work, I kept pushing it forward . . .
>
> (Entrepreneur, Case 1a)

In the following 'reshaping' stage, agreements were made on the marketing and the women's roles, with most of the produce to be sold locally, but as the business matured, a portion (30 per cent) would be sold at a joint (city) marketing level. At the local level, there was more flexibility on women's involvement, but travelling to the city was (initially) strictly restricted to the entrepreneurs. In this phase, continued village resistance was experienced, particularly in Case 1a, with women forced to carry out city-bound activities surreptitiously. With the continued support of the NGO, however, women drew on group solidarity, religious *hadiths* and particularly local proverbs to motivate one another to be strong in the face of such opposition:

We faced difficulties again in our families and within the community. Yet we supported one another with local proverbs: *'Don't hit someone else's door with a finger, because your door might be hit by a fist'* (i.e. be careful not to antagonise people, because they might take revenge on you in an even bigger way). These sayings were important to us in keeping calm and focusing on our work.

(Women producers, Case 1a)

The entrepreneurs further elaborated on the battle to carry out the marketing, initially alone – as the other women were forbidden – and the personal stress that this brought. They described complaining to the group that 'it was not fair' that they (alone) were wholly responsible for this work, and that they needed their help too. Eventually, they managed to persuade other older women to assist with this activity. Yet this tended to generate renewed community nervousness, as indicated in Chapter 4 in the pressure towards a 'further transformation of *purdah*'. The NGO female staff recalled a particular incident in one of the villages:

Suddenly, there was tension in the community again, as the mullah started to create trouble regarding the women's business during the prayers at the Friday mosque. A meeting was promptly called with the women's sub-committee and women workers. A letter was then drafted to the male *shura* from the women's subcommittee explaining how women had learnt new skills and how to make new products, and that they now needed to sell these in the market. The letter specifically pleaded: *'Please allow the older women to do this [marketing] activity otherwise it will be a great setback for our work'.* A *shura* meeting was then held and our boss joined. He again explained the stories of Prophet Mohammed's wife, Khadija who was a businesswoman, and other personal stories from his experience in Pakistan.

(NGO female staff member)

Finally, a set of chain rules were agreed by the group members in their monthly meetings, and approved by the power holders. Designated women became active in their marketing and input supply roles according to agreed terms (e.g. frequency of market visits and specified locations), with the support of the group members. The new rules were reinforced by transparency and trust fostered through 'good communication and openness', in close coordination with power holders. During the research, the NGO elaborated on the new and growing business networks of the entrepreneurs (although these were still tightly controlled in Case 1a):

From only knowing close family and having no business relations, now the entrepreneurs are independent with connections to multiple actors including shopkeepers, offices, exhibition halls, women's associations, banks and packaging agents . . .

(NGO female staff)

The entrepreneurs further expanded on their new business and social relations:

> Before we only each knew about 20 people in the village and these people were mostly family related ... Now we know almost everyone in the community, people in the nearby shops and villages, and even in the city. We have links to businessmen, and offices! It has completely changed our lives ... and the perception of us in our communities.
>
> (Entrepreneur, Case 1b)

Similar to the evolving routines, as the groups matured, new situations emerged, requiring some renegotiation of the prevailing rules. For example, with increased sales, there was a need to permit other women workers to join the marketing outside of the village. Meanwhile, other women also had begun to assist in sourcing supplies (vegetables) within the village. Both of these extended chain activities necessitated a renegotiation of rules with village leaders. In Case 1a, where the context was stricter, this led to the controversial decision to bring in male family members to support the marketing.

Overall, in both Cases 1a and 1b, the extension of evolving rules influenced power dynamics within the groups, with three emerging tiers of workers: lead women, close women supporters (and men), and basic workers. The entrepreneur has largely led the change in these routines. A conservative context – and entrepreneur motivations – has affected the possibility to delegate work to other women.

Collective action rules: introduction, reshaping and operationalisation

In the final tertiary set of enterprise institutions, 'collective action' rules were formulated between the food processing groups, including joint marketing and technical troubleshooting. These rules were led by the NGO, and in part implemented by the NGO through the facilitation of monthly meetings in their office. Initially, a basic set of rules was introduced by the NGO, following the development of earlier basic marketing (chain) rules. These new rules related to higher-level collaborative city marketing (quality control, branding, exhibitions, sharing of market demand), and technical troubleshooting (in production and group administration). With regard to the city marketing, there was an agreement to use common labels and to share basic market information. This was supported by the NGO that facilitated the monthly meetings of group heads (entrepreneurs).

Yet initial constraints faced related to the entrepreneur's capacity and her 'allowances' to travel to the city. Following further negotiations with local community leaders, coordination arrangements were then trialled and elaborated. This entailed mapping out specific rules related to monthly exchange, including administrative/technical exchange, applications from new groups, spot-checking on city sales produce, and sharing market information (from shopkeepers and exhibitions), as well as rules related to collaboration in city exhibitions. At this stage, bottlenecks faced included the willingness of heads to cooperate (equally) and reciprocate support to other groups, the reliability of heads (and scope of trust between them), and the capacity of group heads to maintain group standards. Besides the entrepreneurs, power holders also controlled the nature and frequency of interaction (in the office and at exhibitions):

> At the beginning, coordination was difficult because we were meeting in the city in the [NGO] office, and the community leaders were not happy with this. While the heads could go, it was difficult for other senior women to join since their husbands threatened to throw them out of the house! Over time, we have gained their trust, however.
>
> (Senior women workers, Cases 1a and 1b)

But interestingly, village culture tended to reinforce the overall collective nature of these tasks:

> In the village, it is common for all men to be involved in obligatory community work such as cleaning the canals, and so it is in our culture . . . In Islam, a fundamental value is helping one another! 'We are like one big family!'
>
> (Women producers, Cases 1a and 1b)

Finally, the 'collective action' rules were agreed by the respective group heads (the entrepreneurs), and the new rules were instituted. The entrepreneurs were involved with technical exchange (with the NGO support), troubleshooting and joint marketing (labels, exhibitions marketing according to agreed terms). And occasional disagreements that flared up between group heads were mostly resolved by the NGO! Yet with the further growth of the business, new situations have challenged existing rules. First, the nature of engagement between heads of each group was called into question, as some entrepreneurs were believed to 'work harder' than others. Second, as the village centres matured, several groups began to form their own sub-associations, and to receive money to carry out their own projects. This created power/wealth disparities between the centres, necessitating a reconsideration of the links between the groups. Compounding this, the reputation of the more mature centres was growing quickly with high-quality goods, particularly for specialised products. Yet new emerging (immature) groups were joining the network and producing substandard products. As a result of this perceived 'free riding' and perceptions of their own independent power, more mature groups had begun to break away from the common marketing label, and started to use their own village identity instead. Finally, group coordination was further complicated by technology-sharing agreements. With higher levels of demand, a new processing machine had been introduced by the NGO, yet sharing arrangements between the groups remained informal (and imbalanced). Across the groups, discussions were eventually triggered on exploring the formalisation of their coordination agreements, with new potential rules for association 'membership' (including quality control of goods, collaboration in exhibitions and asset-sharing arrangements). And membership was decided to initially be between the higher-standard centres only (with other centres applying with maturity).

Once more, coordination routines began as simple arrangements, involving lead women across centres sharing basic technical tips, market information and participating in joint exhibitions (as far as they were permitted to do so). Yet with increased business and a growing network, the rules have needed appropriate revisions, and this has been aided by the NGO.

In summary, Case 1 has demonstrated the development of fairly transparent, decentralised enterprise institutions – including routines, chain rules and collective action rules – that have evolved with support of the NGO and led by the entrepreneur. Yet in Case 1a, institutions have been notably more stifled by the village power holders, affecting the women's participation, and the (natural) growth and development of the business. (*Ongoing dynamics of the business are expanded in Appendix 3.*)

5.2.2 Case 2: innovative elaborate institutions with guided/own evolution

Business overview: rural women's vegetable collective

Moving to the second case study, I now revisit the women's vegetable business, situated across nine villages in central Afghanistan. More intensive than Case 1, 10 women's farmers groups were established in each village (with 15–20 women per group). These were led by designated lead farmers and overseen by village facilitators (the 'entrepreneurs'). Where possible, sales agents were later elected to assist with farmer marketing in the city (on commission). Organised at the village level, priority vegetable products included onions, potatoes, tomatoes, carrots and cucumbers.[4] Produce was sold locally by individual women farmers, and jointly co-marketed at a village or cross-village level (in village contracts or city exhibitions). Similar to Case 1, for the women to participate in productive enterprise, the local NGO led the early development of rules guiding individual production, joint exchange and group administration (enterprise routines). In later phases, there was a secondary level of rules instituted related to market interaction, including developing links with buyers and input providers (chain institutions). Finally, between similar groups (at a village and cross village level), there was a third layer of rules created related to their collective activity for higher-level marketing and technical exchange (collective action institutions). In this case, enterprise institutions were notable in their initial elaborate formulation, with guided development by the NGO team.

Enterprise routines: introduction, reshaping and operationalisation

As in Case 1, the first set of enterprise institutions pertained to the internal 'routines'. These outlined different women's roles and routines in vegetable production (farmers, lead farmers and entrepreneurs), and were shaped by both the women's capacity and permitted mobility. These rules were enforced by the lead farmers in farmer group meetings, and reinforced by the entrepreneurs.

As in the previous case, new practices were also guided by (progressive) proverbs and religious *hadiths* (particularly important in some more conservative villages).

In the early stages, internal routines were tentatively introduced by the NGO after the initial *purdah* negotiations. These were then further formulated in agreement with the entrepreneurs and power holders, and with the consensus of lead farmers. For example, all women were to be equally involved in priority vegetable production in their home compounds, and all women belonged to specific farmer groups. Management-wise, selected women were put forward for key positions of responsibility according to their capacity and levels of mobility, including an assigned village entrepreneur and lead farmers (approved by the *shura*). Routines were given further weight with the NGO requesting the signature of the village leader to formalise the general participation of the women, and to ensure that nervous families did not drop out (i.e. there was clear approval by local authorities):

> The office [NGO] proposed new farming routines, and the village authorities signed an agreement so that all participating women farmers would work. The women were then organised into farming groups, which built on the SHG formula with an elected leader and rules jointly agreed by the group.
>
> (NGO staff)

The women farmers described this transition and the introduction of new work rules (intertwined in evolving *purdah* allowances):

> Before this project, we were 'jobless' at home and just involved in household chores. We did not have access to information on other skills and alternatives. Our lives were generally confined to the house and we were not permitted to go outside. In this new gardening project, we started following a whole new 'life' system where we agreed to work outside on our plots from 8 a.m. until 4 p.m., and to attend weekly farmer meetings . . .
>
> (Women farmers, Case 2b)

In the second trialling phase, routines were then elaborated. This included articulating respective farmer, lead farmer and entrepreneur responsibilities, and clarifying labour commitments. At this stage, there was intensive discussion within the groups led by the entrepreneur and lead farmers – with some advice by the women's *shura* and NGO – as training, home production and village meetings were agreed. Constraints faced included obstructive husbands, conservative members of the *shura* and local distrust. Where there was a lack of household support, women's meeting attendance was low, necessitating further negotiation by lead farmers, the entrepreneur and the NGO with the families (with the support of local community leaders). Religious messages were drawn on to support this new work, particularly in Case 2b where conservative elders, husbands and common people continued to gossip and cause problems:

We faced many difficulties [in Case 2b], since in rural Afghanistan there is often little tolerance for outsiders, trust is low and cooperation with non-village people is limited . . . The mullahs can also be strong but I can convince them, as I am able to describe Islamic values and principles of humanity . . .

(NGO female staff)

To strengthen the new routines, lead farmers were given literacy training with an Islamic component. And a religious village woman (*kaaria*) was specifically selected by the *shura* to help with this activity:

Learning more about Islam was so important to us. The [village] *kaaria* told us many stories from the Koran about strong women, and also how to be better Muslims. For example, we learnt how to properly perform our ablutions.[5] This knowledge helped us to gain respect from our families, particularly as we took on these new [work] responsibilities.

(Women lead farmers, Case 2a)

In Case 2a, progressive *shura* members also facilitated new routines. This was further boosted by the leadership of the strong, well-respected and educated entrepreneur. Finally, in both Cases 2a and 2b, group routines were eventually agreed by the entrepreneur, and lead farmers and their respective group members, and approved by the village *shuras*. Routines were then instituted: selected women farmers were involved with home-based vegetable production, and lead farmers held weekly farmers' group meetings (submitting reports as required to the village entrepreneur):

With this farming business, our lives completely changed and we work like men now! All of us work on our plots from Saturday to Thursday. I then organise weekly meetings where we discuss any problems that we are facing, and I provide some training and advice.

(Woman lead farmer, Case 2a)

Yet persisting challenges were faced in conservative Case 2b, since the entrepreneur deliberately restricted the lead farmers, and kept tight control of their activities. Underestimating the power of the entrepreneur, the NGO described this village 'as generally the same as other villages, but with some particularly strong characters [such as the entrepreneur] that makes the project more difficult!' Indeed, the entrepreneur was observed to dominate the entire village project, and controlled all aspects of the emerging business. While the lead farmers were excited about their new routines – 'our lives have been transformed with this work' – they felt both suffocated by the entrepreneur and intimidated.[6] Another NGO that had been periodically working in the village over many years elaborated more frankly on the behaviour of the entrepreneur:

She rejects the customs and norms of her village in not consulting with anybody, and dominating women's forums. Local people have asked us to stop all projects in the village if this woman continues to be head of any group. Yet this is difficult for us, since she is supported by local commanders [strongmen] in the village . . . and we are afraid to cross her . . .

(Non-project NGO, Case 2b)

Over time, as in Case 1, new situations precipitated some reformulation of existing routines and tasks. Internal routines began as a three-tiered arrangement. With high levels of production, and increased city responsibilities of the entrepreneur, there was a need to improve administration and further divide up emerging routines. This included the entrepreneur delegating tasks to some other women to support record-keeping, creating a secondary layer of senior management (Case 2a). Meanwhile, in Case 2b, the entrepreneur clung tightly to all aspects of responsibility (constraining internal development). While the NGO endeavoured to guide the reformulation of rules, the entrepreneur ultimately determined any changes in the village routines, influencing the emerging roles of other women and internal organisational development.

Chain rules: introduction, reshaping and operationalisation

The next stage saw the formulation of enterprise 'chain rules'. As previous, a basic set of rules was initially proposed by the INGO, with subsequent consultation with the entrepreneurs and power holders. The rules conceived were specifically related to the more public-facing activity of city marketing (and the sourcing of agricultural inputs), and involved only selected, more mobile and respected women (entrepreneurs and sales agents). Since this activity necessitated a secondary transformation of *purdah*, there was a need for significant renegotiation at the village level. In more tolerant contexts (Case 2a), the evolving rules were secured and enforced by transparency and trust fostered through good communication and openness, particularly with power holders. Meanwhile, in more distrustful communities (such as Case 2b), rules tended to be strictly controlled by the entrepreneur, with restrained external roles for any women beyond the entrepreneur herself (sales agents were nominated but prevented from becoming operational). Further setbacks included conservative elders and mullahs, and local destabilising events related to village politics and perceptions on the women's work. Yet women leaders in each village drew on relevant religious beliefs to support their work:

We reminded people of Prophet Mohammed's emphasis on women, his wife's Khadija's participation in business and the Koran's focus on learning.

(Entrepreneur, Case 2a)

We are Muslims and trust in God and the Koran. As such, we should trust in God in our work and observe the *hijab* to work safely.

(Lead farmers, Case 2b)

As indicated, such messages were critical in permitting the women's participation in marketing and procurement activities. Yet in contrast to Case 2a, the entrepreneur in Case 2b was not keen for other women to participate in these tasks, and did not widely promote such messages in the village.

In terms of the nature of marketing arrangements, most of the produce was still sold locally by individuals, but a growing portion (20 per cent) was proposed to be sold in Kabul, at joint (urban) marketing level on commission. At the local level, there was some flexibility on women's marketing (with *maharams*), but at the city level this activity was strictly restricted to the entrepreneurs (and if existing, nominated women's sales agents). In the trialling phase, village resistance was again experienced with limited women permitted to engage in these external-facing tasks, particularly in Case 2b (with control by the entrepreneur). The NGO put extensive effort into facilitating links to suppliers, and new open markets and exhibitions, introducing the women and supporting their gradual interaction. And over time, the women gained both the trust of these new traders and their families:

> At the beginning, the village women were shy and unsure of themselves and me, now they trust me and greet me like a family member.
>
> (Supplier in Kabul)

> Before the project, men did not believe women could be skilful and could support the family like this but experience [and business profits] has been visible proof of our capacity . . .
>
> (Entrepreneur, Case 2a)

Finally, designated women in Case 2a became active in their marketing and input supply roles with the approval of power holders and most village members. Yet with an increase in city sales in later phases, the sales agents needed to travel to Kabul more frequently. This necessitated a renegotiation with village leaders. Meanwhile, in Case 2b, the entrepreneur tended to continue to control most of the external work, much to the frustration of the NGO, and the women themselves:

> After being nominated as sales agents [with the approval of the *shura*], the office [INGO] taught us about marketing. Yet it has been difficult to begin this work officially [i.e. with the support of the entrepreneur]. Sometimes our husbands are now helping us.
>
> (Women sales agents, Case 2b)

As in Case 1, with increasing business maturity, and growing sales and contracts, there was ultimately a need to further broaden the initial marketing rules (in both Cases 2a and 2b). This has included the entrepreneur taking on village contracts (from city-based offices), and dividing commissions on farmer sales with the sales agents (only in Case 2a) and lead farmers. Power dynamics have evolved within and between the groups accordingly, with an emerging three to four tiers of women: the entrepreneur (and her assistants in Case 2a), sales agents (in Case 2a), lead farmers and producers. The entrepreneur once again led the change in these rules. The local context (in particular, trust levels), and the entrepreneur motivations have both affected the women's emerging roles, and distribution of benefits (e.g. on village-based contracts).

Collective action rules: introduction, reshaping and operationalisation

Much less developed than in Case 1, in the tertiary level of enterprise institutions, 'collective action' rules were introduced between the villages for joint basic marketing (at city exhibitions), and technical troubleshooting. These rules were led by the NGO with approval of the power holders, and were initially supported through the facilitation of weekly meetings in the NGO city office. Rules included guidelines on marketing for exhibitions (quality control, labels) and representation, and agreements on troubleshooting regarding technical/non-technical aspects of the business. Challenges included obtaining the permission of power holders for selected lead women to attend weekly meetings.

In the second reshaping phase, rules were then elaborated on the women's participation, the quality of produce on display, and packaging. Constraints here included the willingness/interest of entrepreneurs to cooperate and reciprocate support to other groups, and the reliability of entrepreneurs and levels of trust between them. Standing in deep contrast to one another, while the entrepreneur in Case 2a was extremely amenable and keen to exchange, and delegate tasks if needed to other lead women (in the village), the entrepreneur in Case 2b was less interested to share information and in fact, actively prevented other women from joining these activities:

> The situation of the village [Case 2b] is very difficult because of the entrepreneur. She has blocked other women's participation in activities beyond the village. She has become so powerful and acts like a man with short hair, wearing a watch and a large ring, driving a car and threatening people . . . She is even involved in local security activities now, providing information. We are quite afraid of her . . .
>
> (NGO staff)

Finally, while different arrangements existed across the villages (and levels of agreed women's participation), a set of basic collective action rules was approved (by the authorities and the entrepreneurs), with the entrepreneurs collaborating according to agreed terms. Notably, during the major NGO support phase, occasional disagreements that emerged between the group heads (particularly arising with the entrepreneur from Case 2b) tended to be resolved by the NGO team staff.

Over time, new situations prompted changes in the nature of the arrangements. As in Case 1, the entrepreneurs started to form their own sub-associations, and to receive their own money and projects. This created power/wealth disparities between the villages, and reduced some of the entrepreneur's willingness to share information and collaborate. Yet even with the establishment of their own associations, and in the absence of NGO support, they still appeared to value periodic cooperation for higher-level exhibitions in the city.

In summary, Case 2 has demonstrated the development of more elaborate institutions in enterprise (due to a greater density of village production groups) – including routines, chain rules and collective action rules – that have been designed and supported by the NGO, and led by the entrepreneur. Yet in Case 2b, institutions have been notably hindered by both the entrepreneur, and the conservatism of village power holders. (*Ongoing dynamics of the business are expanded in Appendix 3.*)

5.2.3 Case 3: underdeveloped institutions with little innovation/ evolution

Turning to the third case study, I now examine enterprise institutions in the small women's electronics business in Kabul City. Originally comprising 13 women workers, at the time of the research, the business was struggling and only four women remained due to 'limited' work contracts. The company was involved with assembling basic electrical devices including solar lights and repairing domestic appliances, and was based in a women's only leisure/commercial area in the city (known as the women's sanctuary). Similar to Cases 1 and 2, in order for the women to engage in group enterprise, the international NGO led the initial development of internal rules guiding production and group administration (enterprise routines). As the women started seeking contracts, there was a secondary level of rules designed related to market interaction, including links with buyers and input providers (chain institutions). Finally, as with the other two businesses, a third layer of rules was emerging at the end of the research, related to their collaborative activity with similar firms, for potential marketing, training and technical exchange (collective action institutions). Enterprise institutions in this case were characterised by their lack of development and imagination (contrasting to Cases 1 and 2), and subsequently constrained evolution.

Enterprise routines: introduction, reshaping and operationalisation

As in the previous cases, the enterprise 'routines' aimed to clarify the women's roles and routines in the business, appreciating individual capacities and permitted mobility. Basic internal routines were initially proposed by the NGO, and formulated in agreement with the entrepreneurs and local leaders, and with the consensus of other worker women. For example, all women were initially equally involved in group-level production assemblage, according to agreed schedules with equal remuneration (salaries were distributed by the NGO). And the location of the production was initially in the community. Management-wise, selected women were elected into key positions of responsibility according to their capacity and levels of mobility, with an assigned head and deputy. In the subsequent reshaping phase, this led to the further specifying of the business structure, clarifying labour commitments, and articulating rules over profit distribution. There was intensive discussion within the group at this point regarding different responsibilities and salaries with general 'guidance' provided by the NGO. The entrepreneur took on the bulk of non-production responsibilities but was still heavily supported by the NGO:

> We have assisted with the development of roles and positions but the women are greatly hindered by their low capacities [illiteracy], even the business head cannot read or write very well. She maintains the logbook (expenses, sales) and submits this to us to check and finalise each month. The other women are just involved in assemblage activities.
>
> (NGO male staff)

Other constraints faced at this stage were jibes by neighbours and conservative-leaning husbands, particularly as little 'benefits' were perceived in their involvement, and as local security incidents occurred in the city. The use of religious messages and *hadiths* was once again employed by the NGO male staff – to boost earlier efforts in the initial *purdah* transformation, described in Chapter 4 – alongside providing extensive reassurance to the women's husbands:

> [The NGO male staff member] . . . has helped enormously and has been a bridge between our work and our families . . . He has secured their trust, and our husbands are now happy with his behaviour and approach. Step by step, he has helped push boundaries for us to engage in this work. He knows our culture, and is sensitive and respectful.
>
> (Women worker)

The more supportive husbands elaborated on this coordination, emphasising that the staff member 'solved all of our wives' problems!' through their close liaison. For example, the staff member would approach them if a change in routines was required, or if there were training opportunities outside of Kabul (to gain their permission). A second key supporter of the women was the (independent) technical trainer that encouraged both the women and their families as they started productive work:

> [The trainer] . . . was like a mentor to us, and encouraged us to carry out this work and to become a good company. He encouraged my husband so much by telling him that I was strong and that I would bring in a good income with this new work.
>
> (Entrepreneur)

The entrepreneur herself further endeavoured to encourage her staff through her confidence and adherence to religious customs, and through taking pride in being the first women electrical 'mechanics' in Kabul:

Our participation [in productive activities] has been greatly supported by the behaviour of our boss . . . her achievements and strength, her dress that looks like a director, and good Muslim behaviour have persuaded our families to let us do this work . . .

(Women workers)

Finally, the initial group routines were agreed by the women, and instituted. All of the women were involved in the group assemblage in the workshop as required, and were remunerated at agreed levels (according to completed 'work days'). Yet there was still a great deal of control by the NGO of basic administrative tasks such as record keeping and group management, in addition to salary distribution! As the business obtained more experience, increasing responsibility was handed over to the entrepreneur by the NGO. However, the entrepreneur struggled to delegate tasks to other women, both due to the women's 'limited capacity', and because of their highly restricted *purdah* norms, inhibiting their participation in the enterprise and leading to their frequent absences. To support her administrative work, she tended instead to bring in male family members (her husband and son).

Chain rules: introduction, reshaping and operationalisation

'Chain rules' were then tentatively proposed by the NGO to prompt external business links to buyers and resource providers. With tighter restrictions imposed on the rest of the workers (by their husbands), these tasks were predominantly managed by the entrepreneur. The rules were initially heavily supported by the NGO. To gain further local trust in the arrangements, the entrepreneur endeavoured to show strong leadership and transparency, particularly in keeping local leaders informed of their new market links (as there was significant sensitivity related to the overall business embarking on such public-facing tasks).

Preliminary rules conceived were related to contract development and procuring raw materials for the business (e.g. electronic boards, cables). While these were challenging for the entrepreneur (in breaking new *purdah* ground), it emerged to be a bridge too far for the other (Pashtun) women, due to the pressures of *Pashtunwali* by conservative elders and families, as described by the local *wakil*:

Kabul people are usually open but Pashtun people are closed, and they see it as a great shame for their women to be out of the house working [let alone marketing!] . . .

(Community *wakil*)

Other constraining factors included the protective and controlling nature of the NGO, and local destabilising events related to security (with women further discouraged from working outside the home). With the support of the NGO, however, the entrepreneur finally managed to gradually forge new links with other firms and clients:

> At the beginning, we knew nobody outside of our families . . . Now we [the business] have several connections, from established electronics companies to some international offices. Our boss [the entrepreneur] made these links with help from the NGO. She manages these outside connections as our husbands forbid us to get involved in these activities particularly in speaking with foreign men. Our boss has become a real director, and together we do not even represent 50 per cent of her capacity . . . She is now stronger than her husband!
>
> (Deputy head of the business)

As these chain rules were finalised, the entrepreneur began to engage in these new marketing tasks. The entrepreneur took on the bulk of responsibility, although she was still heavily micromanaged by the NGO. And as the business matured, she still found it difficult to delegate even basic tasks to other women, due to their 'weakness' and 'family opposition'. During the research, however, the deputy endeavoured to start to engage in small tasks (surreptitiously), but was constantly challenged by a conservative family. Other women remained in the 'safety' of the workshop in the women's sanctuary (considered acceptable by their husbands since it was a women-only zone, and out of the main city hub). Beyond the physical marketing, the entrepreneur was also frustrated with the location of their business, as they could not receive male customers. In addition to this, gender issues further complicated participating in off-site work:[7]

> We wanted to employ the women for a short-term contract in our compound but it is both difficult for them to come here, and for them to work alongside our male staff.
>
> (Director of a Kabul electronics company)

In contrast to Cases 1 and 2, chain rules began and remained as simple arrangements related to basic contract development and procurement, involving just the entrepreneur with extensive support by the NGO. Power dynamics have evolved within the group accordingly, with only two resulting tiers of women: the entrepreneur, and basic workers. The entrepreneur has led the further development of chain-related rules but a conservative context, and possibly her own motivations, has affected the delegation of tasks to other worker women.

Collective action rules: introduction, reshaping and operationalisation

While the business endeavoured to remain afloat (with women dropping out due to family pressures), towards the end of the research, as in Cases 1 and 2, a third set of enterprise institutions, 'collective action rules', was proposed by the NGO. These rules were in the form of company 'alliances', with a vision that these would strengthen the women's flagging business. These included forging partnerships with other like firms for cross-training, and potential contract work outside of their workshop (in the city women's area). Rules were initially articulated by the NGO with regard to the potential location and scope of work, in order that the autonomy of the business could be respected and the boundaries of the (worker) women's *purdah*. However, the workers' husbands strongly objected to the external nature of this work, and the location in a male environment. Rules were then refined to specify particular companies for contract work and training (within certain city domains). With a new partnership eventually facilitated by the NGO, rules were then negotiated and elaborated on the type of work (e.g. assembling tasks), physical conditions (e.g. private room for women), and duration (e.g. work hours). Rules were also extended to improve internal quality control, with the addition of more systematised spot-checking on assembled products by the head worker, thus enhancing their productive practices. Finally, with the extensive support of the NGO, the new rules were operationalised with the (tentative) approval of the worker women's husbands. However, these appeared to be fragile agreements:

> Our boss has helped make links to two companies as partnerships for training and mentoring, and we do some basic work for them inside their company. Yet our participation has created many problems with our families . . . particularly as the security situation remains uncertain . . .
>
> (Women workers)

Overall, in summary, Case 3 has indicated the underdevelopment of enterprise institutions – including routines, chain rules and collective action rules – introduced by an NGO, and then handed over to the entrepreneur. Evolving institutions have been further hindered by the entrepreneur herself and strict power holders, in addition to structural factors, including local uncertainty and complex sociocultural dynamics (related to *purdah* and industry preferences). (*Ongoing dynamics of the business are expanded in Appendix 3.*)

5.2.4 Evolving dynamics of language and power in rule development

Going beyond Chapter 4 (and the introduction of a new narrative regarding women), renewed pressures on *purdah* in the development of emerging enterprise rules have shown to be negotiated through both religious messages (and verses), and more subtle, but deliberate changes to the common household/community vernacular. In particular, this included proverbs and Islamic sayings that were typically used to guide and regulate local behaviour (to mixed effect). It is pertinent to further examine the changing use of certain proverbs. Afghans tend to draw on proverbs as a form of explanation or to highlight morals in society. Proverbs may also be used to open up a dialogue: '*Az gap, gap mey-khezad*' (from talk comes talk), which can mean 'good conversations lead to more good conversations' (Zellem, 2012). Yet too much talk may be ill perceived, *poor khoree wa poor goyee aabru raa mey-barad* (eating too much and talking too much removes your reputation) or being a 'glutton' or chatterbox causes people to lose respect for you (ibid.).

In the process of enterprise rule development, there were notably tangible degrees of change in the types of proverbs (and sayings) used by the enterprise women, both to encourage one another in the business, and to assert themselves within their families and in the community. These proverbs tended to relate to women's capacity and trustworthiness. In addition to those described earlier, other proverbs employed included:

> *Elm taaj-e sar ast* (literal meaning: Knowledge is a crown on the head): The more you know and learn, the more successful and respected you will be.

> *Ta jaan batan ast, jaan bekan ast* (literal meaning: While we live, we strive): Life is full of challenges. People must work hard to overcome them.

Meanwhile, conservative elements tended to cite less positive or cautious proverbs related to either women's (lack of) abilities, or the dangers of risk-taking behaviour:

> *Charaa kari kunad aaqil ke baar aarad peshaimanee* (literal meaning: Why would a wise person do something that brings regret): Wise people think before they act, so they do not have regrets later.

In Cases 1a, 1b and 2a, the women described deliberately drawing on more positive sayings, and using these to move away from 'typical', more negative, derogatory and close-minded expressions. Meanwhile, going beyond the use of proverbs, the entrepreneurs in Cases 2b and 3 tended to prefer an assertion of their own power. For example, the entrepreneur in Case 2b was said to behave 'like a woman-man' (as described by the NGO staff), and in Case 3 the entrepreneur tended to use 'male-like speech and behaviour' (as described by the women workers):

> Our boss is like a man . . . And men should know that she is active and strong like a man . . . and that she can work like one too. People now come to her for advice on women's business. She has become stronger than her husband.
> (Women workers, Case 3)

And as the entrepreneur in Case 3 strove for further power, the worker women were left in her wake, battling with prevailing traditional attitudes and sayings entrenched in *Pashtunwali*, as indicated by the women at the end of the research:

> Some of our family members [still] tell us that our work is inside the house, and that we are rich enough for women not to work, that is our culture . . .
> (Women workers, Case 3)

In Chapter 4, a new basic narrative of women was introduced, fostering change in *purdah* – promoted by the NGOs, progressive leaders and the entrepreneurs –

with women emphasised as equal, worthy and responsible (with varying degrees of success). While these themes were continually championed, as the women went on to embrace their new work roles in the enterprise activities, somewhat more radically, the core language of the household was shown to be deliberately moderated by the women. This reinforced and consolidated new attitudes and perceptions within the heart of families and cultural life. Meanwhile, some less socially oriented entrepreneurs (Cases 2b and 3) chose to instead assert their (own) roles and positions, through increasing and emphasising their own personal power.

5.3 Discussion

Corroborating findings from Chapter 4, and building off Fligstein (2001) and Gomez (2008), the process of institutional construction in enterprise has involved the interaction of a multitude of actors, including NGOs, entrepreneurs and power holders, further shaped by the local context. In examining this process, I will discuss the nested nature of evolving institutions in enterprise, the uncertain process of construction (and varied actor strategies), and emerging rule dynamics and outcomes, both within and beyond the enterprise.

5.3.1 Complex institutional construction: nested institutions in enterprise

Ostrom (1990) used the innovative concept of 'nested' rules to describe the linkages between rules, and their capacity for change. Similarly, the research has pointed to the embedded and nested nature of institutions (or rules) within enterprise, and further anchored in dynamic sociocultural institutions. Following the transformation of the boundary institution of *purdah*, the research has highlighted the development of associated enterprise institutions. Initially, internal 'routines' were formulated related to the basic division of labour in production (primary level). External 'chain rules' (institutional arrangements) were then agreed with regard to local supply and marketing (secondary level). Finally, across similar groups, 'collective action institutions' were facilitated for joint marketing and exchange (tertiary level). The motivation for the development of 'nested' layers of enterprise institutions lay partly in the logical development of the business, but also in the social requirements of the required business activities, including the physical domains of operation, and the need for interaction with different players. These rules tended to be created sequentially, although remained dynamic and continuously evolving. Within each level, early rules were initially proposed by the NGO, and jointly formulated in agreement with the entrepreneurs and power holders. The reshaping of group rules was then predominantly led by the entrepreneur (and active workers), in negotiation with power holders. Initial enterprise rules tended to be enforced by a culture of transparency and trust, supported by the NGO. In later stages, rules (and the associated organisational culture) were fostered by the entrepreneur, influenced by local conditions and (evolving) dynamics of language and power.

Nested institutions embedded in social institutions, trust and power

Taking a closer look at the embeddedness of institutions, at the primary level, internal enterprise rules were initially developed by the NGO to clarify women's roles and routines in production and management. These were delimited by both the women's capacity and permitted mobility. As indicated by Becker (2004), these routines permitted coordination and control, a reduction in uncertainty, and cooperative action. Yet their regularity also facilitated 'professionalism', reinforcing the women's credibility as enterprise workers (with their families and in the community). Meanwhile, the entrepreneur has largely led later revisions in the routines – tempered by the context/power holders – influencing the evolving roles of other women, and strategies in expansion/growth. In low-trust environments, strict control was maintained by the entrepreneurs, particularly by less public-spirited entrepreneurs, affecting their natural potential development (e.g. Case 3). The secondary level of enterprise 'chain' rules aimed to next clarify selected women's external responsibilities. These rules were related to physical marketing and procurement of inputs, and involved designating more mobile and respected women (and thus new boundaries of *purdah*). In vein with Hollingsworth (2002), these rules facilitated economic coordination, and were embedded in *purdah* (obligation) and local power dynamics (Coe *et al.*, 2008). Going beyond the theory, their initial innovativeness was also influenced by the external NGO. As sales and volumes increased, there was a need to revise these original rules. In higher-trust contexts, with socially minded entrepreneurs, this has permitted other women to support the marketing and input supplies. In such cases, power dynamics have evolved within the groups accordingly, with three possible tiers of women: lead women, assistants and basic workers (Case 1); or four possible tiers of women: entrepreneur, sales agents, lead women and basic producers (Case 2). However, a conservative context, coupled with the entrepreneur's desire for control has affected the possibility to delegate to other women at all, with just two emerging tiers of women in such scenarios (particularly Case 3). Meanwhile, in one low-trust, whilst the entrepreneur has been willing to share responsibilities, the context has led to the necessary part-involvement of male family members of the entrepreneur, creating challenging dynamics in an all-women's enterprise (Case 1a). Finally, at the tertiary level, networking and collective action rules were formulated between similar producer groups or firms. These rules were related to joint marketing (quality control, branding, exhibitions, sharing of demand) and technical troubleshooting in Cases 1 and 2. In Case 3, coordination related to collaborating for training and subcontracting, necessitating frequent interaction with similar firms. As indicated by Ostrom (1990), these rules have enabled cooperation across groups. And as these rules were then reshaped and adapted in later phases, they were shown to be stronger if led and owned by the groups themselves, with similar 'mental models' (ibid.), particularly once groups had reached maturity (e.g. Case 1). In the latter case, the rules not only facilitated 'economies of scale', but also permitted an emerging 'community of entrepreneurs', empowering enterprise groups in the face of existing and future challenges.

Towards better understanding the nature of emerging rules and their dynamics, it is pertinent to examine the influence of different actors and power. The scope of each layer of rules was predominantly led by the entrepreneur (and her assistants), and this has determined the level of participation of worker women, coordination across groups and interaction with market actors. As the businesses have grown, shifting roles have led to changes in work responsibilities and profit shares. This has created power differences between the women, and potential conflict within and between groups, without transparency and agreement on 'fair' rules. For example, in terms of cross-group coordination, arrangements have permitted crucial economies of scale and improved profits, but with expansion there has been a risk of negative association, with some groups performing poorly or heads not equally cooperating, threatening the reputation and market share of older groups, and motivation for collaboration (as in Case 1). Mature entrepreneurs in Case 1 opted out of full coordination due to the free riding of newer groups producing sub-quality goods (particularly as mature groups specialise and produce higher-quality items). Imbalanced power dynamics across entrepreneurs (with different interests) has also led to dissatisfaction with arrangements. Yet the supportive NGO made concerted efforts to assist the groups to find a new common solution. Meanwhile, in Case 2, distrust and competiveness has limited collaborative work following the end of the NGO project, and in the context of available donor funds for women's groups. In Case 3, coordination has been compromised by worker restrictions in mobility and interaction, and a volatile context. In addition, the entrepreneur capacity and motivations and the nature of power holders have strongly influenced the degree of sharing and collaboration. Across the cases, there tended to be stronger links between firms with strong charismatic entrepreneurs that had gained local trust with supportive NGOs.

The women's businesses have clearly highlighted the layered development of institutions in enterprise – with lower-level rules (initially) influencing the design of higher-level rules (later, the reverse is also possible) – and the role of a multitude of actors in shaping these arrangements. Figure 5.3 illustrates this process. External actors (such as NGOs) have shown that they can aid with the initial design of institutions, and can also guide entrepreneurs (and local supporters) in navigating local conditions to (re)shape the resulting design towards the development of fair and appropriate routines in enterprise, although controlling entrepreneurs may block their efforts. At the outset, initial cooperation between women was facilitated through mutual trust from shared Islamic norms/values. The decentralised decision-making and profit distribution seems to have further increased accountability and transparency in rules, enhancing the motivation of members and levels of trust. This has bolstered social cohesion, and support for primary-, secondary- and tertiary-level institutions (particularly in Cases 1 and 2).

Uncertain thresholds of change: shaped by power, interests and conditions

In line with Gomez (2008), three phases were identified in institutional construction in enterprise. Expanding on similar findings from Chapter 4, these phases were

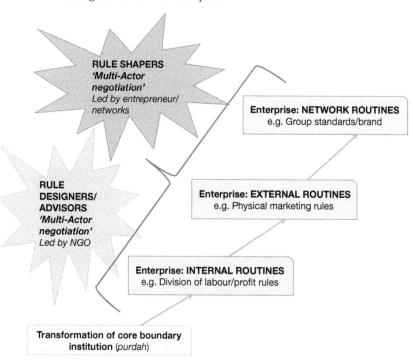

Figure 5.3 Nested institutional development led by NGO and shaped by the entrepreneur
Source: Author's own illustration

shaped by power, agent interests and local conditions. New rules were initially proposed by the NGO, and jointly formulated in agreement with the entrepreneurs and power holders. The reshaping of group rules then took place, predominantly led by the entrepreneur (and active workers) in negotiation with power holders. Finally, if successful, institutions were then stabilised, and 'operational' with potential for 'replication'. The latter two phases were dynamic.

Further examining these phases, in the first stage, early rules were introduced by the NGO. This phase was characterised by extensive discussions between the NGO, local power holders and the women's families (particularly in lower-level rules), to reach agreements on participating women and initial conditions. Difficulties in this phase included obstructions by powerful and difficult individuals (non-acceptance of new proposed routines), unrelated instability due to local politics, or a weak NGO that struggled to gain local trust. In higher-level rules (e.g. collective action rules), this phase was less extensive due to the greater 'distance' from the root of the social norm, and application only for selected women. The second experimental stage was triggered by the introduction of the new (tentatively approved) institutions to the enterprise women. This phase included a period of trialling, shaping and fleshing out of the designed institutional arrangements through experimentation (e.g. elaborating routine timetables/locations, and roles of women). Promotional strategies were used to garner support for the institutions, and selected producers were involved with trialling them. Yet strict local authorities affected the nature of the institutional design and who had access (e.g. production work hours or the frequency of market trips, and permitted women). This period was characterised by intensive discussion between community leaders, ongoing gossiping and threats from local people, and NGOs active in promoting and solving problems (alongside the entrepreneur and active women). Blockages or setbacks here once again included difficult individuals (continuing to resist rules), local politics, and weak NGOs that were unable to resolve problems. Setbacks also included the 'unacceptable' behaviour of women workers (e.g. prematurely pushing boundaries beyond agreed terms), fighting within the group, and weak or difficult entrepreneurs. A failure to overcome these problems, and particularly the persistence of multiple blockages, caused delays or constrained the progression to Stage 3. This forced a significant reformulation of rules and narrowing down their applicability. This was particularly evident both in Case 2b and in Case 3 in the attempted development of marketing and coordination routines (with the entrepreneur only participating in these tasks). With the end of the trialling phase, Stage 3 was characterised by the formal operationalisation and approval of the institutional arrangements with potential for 'replication'. The final design and enforcement mechanisms were generally facilitated through the women's networks (both within and outside of the business; this is discussed further in Chapter 6), with continued negotiation with power holders towards final 'diffusion'. Relevant women then engaged in the newly created rules, with general acceptance on design, scope and access. Typical indicators of this phase included the subsiding of gossiping, power holders supporting the new rules, and rules instituted with designated women active in their agreed roles.

With the advent of new situations, the last two phases were in reality dynamic. For example, changing situations have prompted necessary shifts in routines such as the increased scale in business and complexity, new private responsibilities (e.g. the new additional roles of entrepreneurs as part-time trainers in Case 1), or local politics. Such situations required rule reformulation towards changing the scope of rules (or their formalisation), or creating new internal hierarchies of women with rule variation. As rules evolved, both key actors (e.g. entrepreneurs, NGO or power holders) and local stability have been critical in their development. In most of the cases, new rules tended to be enforced by a culture of transparency and trust supported by the NGO, and fostered through close working conditions, openness and group meetings. In low-trust environments, however, tight control over rules was maintained by entrepreneurs with little flexibility, particularly by self-oriented entrepreneurs (Cases 2b and 3), affecting institutional development. New practices and appropriate behaviour were supported by proverbs, and religious *hadiths* (sayings) (particularly important in some more conservative villages). As the business developed, further rules were formulated as required. The entrepreneur has largely led these revisions in the routines – tempered by the context/ power holders – influencing the evolving roles of other women, and strategies in expansion/growth.

Figure 5.4 summarises the three key phases in institutional construction.

Who is involved	Power issues	Micro-context	Who has access
Stage 1: Newly introduced basic institutional arrangements			
Trigger: (Environmental) Social institution unlocked (purdah), or 'higher' level layer			
External agent Entrepreneur Power holders	NGO guides design with women in negotiation with local leaders	Stability/trust in context influences design and support	Lead women
Stage 2: Shaping institutional arrangements: trialed/elaborated through experimentation (dynamic)			
Trigger: Institutional arrangements introduced to enterprise women			
Entrepreneur **Power holders** External agent	Entrepreneur guides reshaping in coordination with local leaders and advice of NGO	Stability/trust of context influences reshaping (scope and participation)	Lead women Permitted other women *Controlled by entrepreneur*
Stage 3: 'Operational' institutional arrangements with potential for 'replication' (dynamic)			
Trigger: Institutional arrangements trialed and approved			
Entrepreneur **Power holders** External agent	Entrepreneur leads arrangements and local leaders control boundaries in further evolution	Stability/trust of context affects boundaries for change	Women in enterprise *Controlled by entrepreneur*

Figure 5.4 Phases in institutional construction: shaped by actors and context

Source: Author's own illustration

Diverse and dynamic actors influencing nature of institutions

In Chapter 4, I discussed the broad interaction of a variety of actors in the transformation of the social institution of *purdah*. As indicated in the first part of this chapter, the discourse on economic institutions has presented important insights into the influence of actors in institutional development, drawing attention to their physical domain and the role of local communities (Cohendet and Llerena, 2003); the influence of different actor strategies (Knorringa *et al.*, 2011); and the effect of individual habits and experience (Hodgson and Knudsen, 2004), and varying values, motivations and skills (Ostrom, 1990, 2005). From sociology, Fligstein (2001) looked specifically at institutional creation, highlighting the roles of 'skilled' actors in navigating existing rules with a vision to 'create new things', and the use of varying strategies to induce cooperation. In the course of enterprise, the research findings have painted a more nuanced picture of skilled (and less skilled) dynamic actors in institutional development, deploying diverse strategies, shaped by local shifting conditions. This process has been further affected by the entrepreneur's own interests, influencing the flexibility, stability and ultimate nature of evolving enterprise institutions. In Case 1, the NGO has provided strong support to evolving equitable institutions, often 'learning by doing', predominantly within a religious framework. And the entrepreneurs have proved to be tough and charismatic, with a growing public vision beyond their work with the support of enterprise allies. Yet while the local authorities grew to be more progressive in Case 1b, they remained strict in the distrustful context of Case 1a. In the latter case, this constrained the flexibility, stability and nature of evolving institutions, and collective processes. Meanwhile, in Case 2, the NGO provided significant support to the early development of equitable institutions but was weaker in providing guidance with shorter-term support. In Case 2a, the open-minded entrepreneur flourished with increasingly progressive authorities. Yet in Case 2b, the controlling entrepreneur grew more self-oriented, and profited from strict local authorities. Emerging institutions were highly contrasting in this case: with flexible, open and evolving institutions in Case 2a against inflexible, controlled, and closed institutions in Case 2b. Finally, in Case 3, the NGO struggled with institutional design and guidance, particularly in a difficult context, preferring a protective paternalistic strategy. In part as a defensive reaction to hostile conditions (including a highly male-dominated industry), the controlling entrepreneur nurtured more closed institutions. Table 5.1 summarises these environmental and actor influences on evolving enterprise institutions.

These research findings indicate the important (and unexpected) influence of external actors in institutional creation in fragile environments, particularly in the introduction of new ideas, going beyond actors in the community (Cohendet and Llerena, 2003) and local habits/experience (Hodgson and Knudsen, 2004). And, adding deeper insights to Ostrom (1990, 2005) and Fligstein (2001), and expanding upon findings in Chapter 4, diverse internal and external actors have been shown to be involved in both early and broader institutional processes, and they may have both varied skills and evolving objectives; and these actors may be further influenced by the context (and other actors).

5.3.2 Examining evolving routines across cases as a 'window' on enterprise

It is instructive to take a closer look at the nature of evolving routines in enterprise, as an indicator of broader institutional stability, change and flexibility. In the research, the emerging 'layered' enterprise routines have significantly influenced

Table 5.1 Evolving institutions influenced by dynamic actor strategies and shifting conditions

Case number	Environment/ power holders	Core NGO strategy	Entrepreneur strategy in institutions	Flexibility in evolving institutions	Nature of evolving institutions and stability
1a	Strict, closed	Strong support for transparent evolving institutions Strong religious framework in long-term approach	Determined but restricted	Limited flexibility in participation in higher level institutions	Open but constrained Mediocre stability
1b	Becoming more progressive and open	Strong support for transparent evolving institutions Strong religious framework in long-term approach	Determined, open	Negotiable flexibility in participation in higher-level institutions	Open Good stability
2a	Progressive and open	Strong support for elaborate institutions Short-term support in semi-socio-religious framework	Determined, open	Negotiable flexibility in participation in higher-level institutions	Open Good stability
2b	Strict, closed	Strong support for elaborate institutions Short-term support in semi-socio-religious framework	Self-oriented, tight power	Participation in routines but limited power of workers Exclusive participation in higher-level institutions	Closed, inflexible Stability for entrepreneur
3	Strict, closed, uncertain	Weak support for new institutions and their development Protective, long-term support in semi-socio-religious framework	Self-oriented, protective	Participation in routines but limited power of workers Exclusive participation in higher-level institutions	Closed, inflexible Stability for entrepreneur

the scope of women's participation, the nature of enterprise operations, and enterprise growth. Where there was more transparency in rule-making, and participative rule changing and enforcement, routines remained open and flexible. Where there was more control in rule-making, and constraints in rule changing and enforcement, routines were closed with limited flexibility. Going beyond Pentland and Feldman (2005), routines provide an interesting window on environmental social constraints, actors and the emerging nature of the firm (and power dynamics therein).[8] In situations where routines were flexible for the entrepreneur to delegate tasks and to develop the business, and for the workers to take on new tasks (e.g. Cases 1b and 2a), power holders were more liberal, social norms were more open and evolving, and there were socially oriented entrepreneurs. In these scenarios, the business was growing in an equitable manner. Yet where routines were semi-flexible for the entrepreneurs (i.e. flexibility in their own work, but little possibility to delegate tasks) and even less flexible for the workers, strict power holders were observed that maintained conservative social norms, and the business was shown to be constrained (forcing the entrepreneur to grow the business in other ways; e.g. Case 1a). Meanwhile, where routines were flexible only for the entrepreneur but strictly controlled for the workers, power holders were shown to be highly traditional, entrepreneurs were both powerful and self-oriented, and social norms remained conservative for the workers. In this scenario, the business was indicated to be growing but in a less equitable manner (entrepreneur receives the bulk of the benefits; e.g. Cases 2b and 3). *Appendix 4 expands on the nature of 'layered' routines across the cases, and their dynamics in each of the scenarios.*

Advancing the evolutionary discourse (e.g. Hodgson and Knudsen, 2004), these insights on the flexibility and openness of routines indicate that the 'spread of routines' (or their diffusion) in enterprise may be influenced both by the agency of different actors (in particular the entrepreneurs), as well as by local structural dynamics. In terms of 'routine selection', the research points to the additional influence of entrepreneur interests (social and political), going beyond just internal interactions or organisational health motivations (as indicated by Hodgson and Knudsen, 2004). The nature of emerging routines and their flexibility also provide indicators on their capacity for 'replication'. In the case of open and flexible routines (for all the participants), new routines are generated organically as needs arise. In the contrasting case, where routines are controlled and inflexible, the development of new routines is hindered.

5.3.3 Outcomes of bundles of enterprise institutions: new evolving sociopolitical norms, and economic institutions

Evolutionary insights by Hodgson (1997) theorised the potential capacity of institutions to 'mould the dispositions and behaviours of agents' (described in Chapter 2). Hodgson's theory was revisited in Chapter 4, with new community preferences and attitudes emerging from the transformation of *purdah*. Meanwhile, Becker *et al.* (2006) describe the effects of 'combinatorics of routines' (i.e. the interaction of routines) in generating 'system novelties', and new potential institutions. In this chapter, going beyond initial *purdah* gains, new enterprise institutions seem to have both permitted business and generated widespread effects on community life. The bundles of enterprise institutions have had a powerful effect on both individual and group dispositions, and further stimulated the development of new community social, political and economic institutions. Yet the inclusivity of enterprise institutions, actor interests and local conditions have influenced the scope of new institutional development. In this section, I discuss the effect of enterprise institutions on evolving social and political norms (within and outside of the group), and the emergence of broader economic institutions.

Further reshaping purdah and influencing sociopolitical institutions

Enterprise institutions have had a significant impact on evolving *purdah*, as well as triggering new sociopolitical institutions. In terms of *purdah*, routines have precipitated new respect for women as professionals, enhancing family and community credibility in these new *purdah* norms. Further to this, in Case 1, the location of production (outside of the women's homes) has given the women a new sense of independence and mobility, crucially away from home chores and childcare. And in Case 2, while the location of production remained within the women's own family domain, it departed from their usual indoor work, thus liberating the women into newer work roles. These activities have reinforced new ideas on the women's evolving roles, and triggered changes in attitudes. Yet in Case 3, while the development of internal routines greatly affected the *purdah* norms of the entrepreneur, these remained fragile for worker women (particularly in a 'man's business', with increasing insecurity in the city, and social pressures to stay at home). Meanwhile, marketing and coordination rules have necessitated the further direct expansion of *purdah* norms, for both the entrepreneurs and selected women in the case studies. Worker women (and beyond) have also been encouraged by their roles. And with the respective entrepreneur's permission, some women have increased their participation in production (including increased hours or levels of responsibility), or have even begun to get involved in external tasks such as marketing, with positive effects for the business.

Going beyond *purdah* influences, enterprise institutions have also influenced broader sociopolitical institutions. Tangible indicators of typical social change observed across the case studies are highlighted in Table 5.2[9] (these were especially notable in Cases 1 and 2a). In the development of these institutions, the influence of the entrepreneur has been particularly significant, as she has become a visible role model in the enterprise and beyond, in further pushing forward the boundaries of *purdah*, participating in village politics, and changing attitudes towards women in general (and their 'rights' to education and health). In addition to new degrees of women's mobility, communities described increasing levels of girls attending school, and the rising age of women entering into marriage. Perceptions of women as responsible and capable had also changed: with enterprise women now involved in skilled production work as well as marketing, purchasing household equipment, family decision-making, and even advising their own husbands on culture! In the case of 'public-spirited' entrepreneurs that championed more equitable enterprise institutions (particularly Cases 1b and 2a), the emergence of new sociopolitical institutions has had far-reaching effects, with the enterprise women using a revolutionary language of change, and a new strength and power observed in the women's *shura*. In these cases, the entrepreneurs fostered a strong enterprise group identity, enhancing further collective processes (Ansell, 1998). For example, in Case 1, the communities now celebrate 'Women's Day' on an annual basis, organised by the food processing enterprise in collaboration with the community women's *shura*. And in Case 1b in particular, the food processing group had influenced the development of new democratic rules on voting in the women's *shura*, permitting non-elite women to join the local council. Meanwhile, in the case of less public-spirited entrepreneurs that fostered more exclusive institutions, the entrepreneurs were more focused on personal power. In Case 2b, the controlling and self-oriented entrepreneur had used her new-found power for less positive personal political gain, in both dominating local women's groups and organising private forces (local militias). And in Case 3, the entrepreneur described similar power-oriented political ambitions to return to her province of origin and lead a regional women's *shura*.

Generating further economic institutions (property rights, assets, training and banking)

In addition to sociopolitical institutions, enterprise institutions have further stimulated the generation of new economic institutions (once again, in contrast to neighbouring communities). For example, the visible benefits of women working has highlighted the dividends of women receiving training, and encouraged families to let more women attend capacity building activities (see also Appendix 5). Yet for the entrepreneurs in particular, enterprise institutions have both empowered them and pushed them into more public spheres, raising their awareness of local actors, services and resources, as well as their own rights and assets. This has set in motion new financial norms for example, all of the entre-preneurs in the cases had opened up bank accounts (for the business), encouraging other village women to set up bank accounts too (and consider participation in other banking options, such as taking out micro-loans). Further to this, some entrepreneurs had hence been able to secure independent funds to expand their businesses or engage in community development. For example, in Case 1a, the entrepreneur had further managed to obtain funding from a donor and purchased land in a neighbouring community for the expansion of the business (since strict power holders in her own community prohibited expansion there). In Case 2, the entrepreneurs had similarly obtained funding for their women's community work (although in Case 2b this appears to have been more motivated by personal power). Meanwhile, others were empowered to retrieve inherited assets. For example, in Case 1b, the entrepreneur had finally claimed her rightful property as a widow

Table 5.2 Embedded enterprise institutions shaping new women's institutions

Case number	Environment/ power holders	Entrepreneur interests in business	Enterprise institutions	Sociopolitical institutions (e.g. girls education)	Economic institutions (e.g. propery rights)
1a	Strict	Public-spirited	Open but constrained	Changing for all but slow	Changing for elite and middle class but slow
1b	Open/progressive	Public-spirited	Open	Tangible change in all social groups	Changing for elite and middle class
2a	Open/progressive	Public-spirited	Open	Tangible change in all social groups	Changing for elite and middle class
2b	Strict	Selfish, controlling	Closed, inflexible	Changing for elite but slow	Changing but limited to elite
3	Strict, uncertain	Selfish, controlling	Closed, inflexible	Changing for elite but slow	Changing but limited to elite

(30 years after her husband's death). And this had stimulated discussions across the entire enterprise network, leading to a new interest in Islamic law, and presenting a challenge to the village tradition of widows being forced to marry their brothers-in-law (thus losing their rightful property). Other non-enterprise women have observed these developments, and have been quietly influenced by their gains.

Consolidating these findings across the cases, Table 5.2 draws together the overall character of the local environment/power holders, the inclination of the entrepreneur and the resulting nature of enterprise institutions, and emerging sociopolitical and economic institutions. Adding insights to evolutionary thinking and the interaction between agents and institutions (Hodgson, 1997), where enterprise institutions are open with supportive actors, new liberal sociopolitical institutions and economic institutions have been generated (Cases 1b and 2a, but less for Case 1a). Where enterprise institutions are more closed and constrained/ inflexible, emerging sociopolitical and economic institutions remain exclusive and predominantly serving the elite (Cases 2b and 3).

5.4 Concluding remarks

Looking through the lens of the initial transformation of *purdah* (discussed in Chapter 4), this chapter has highlighted the 'nested' nature of institutional construction in enterprise (Ostrom, 2005), embedded in social institutions. Reflecting on findings against the prevailing institutional discourse (described in Chapter 2 and here), emerging 'nested' economic in the case studies are indicated to be a combined result of initial top down design (Beckert, 1999), with the intervention of NGOs, and bottom-up (grass-roots) evolutionary processes (Hodgson, 1997, 2003, 2007) in the reshaping of institutions and stabilisation by entrepreneurs and their networks. Kaplinsky and Morris (2000) describe institutions that govern the value chain within and between firms, and they emphasise the role of 'rule-makers' (internal and external to the chain). Meanwhile, recent value chain literature highlights the importance of looking closer at the influence of non-chain actors in economic institutions (Helmsing and Velema, 2011). Indeed, the research shows a broad range of local and external actors that play key roles in the institutional process, from initiating tentative institutions (NGOs), reshaping institutions (entrepreneurs and their networks), to articulating their boundaries and determining access (local power holders). This expands upon the concept of 'rule-making' to include rule designers, shapers, boundary makers and enforcers. The research also takes the focus beyond the community (Cohendet and Llerena, 2003) and local habits/experience (Hodgson and Knudsen, 2004), and illustrates broader mechanisms to overcome sociocultural barriers in a societal setting (Hollingsworth, 2002). Advancing Hodgson and Knudsen (2004) and Ostrom (2005), the existing habits, skills and interests of actors are both nuanced and dynamic, and these may be influenced by the context as well as other actors. Actor capabilities and motivations are also influenced by their ongoing experience within the business and participation in institutions. Related actor strategies are indicated to have a broad effect on emerging institutions – influencing institutional scope and participation, domains of applicability, diffusion and replication, and evolution – with significant ramifications for broader enterprise development. Actor inclination also affects the nature of collective processes (Fligstein, 2001), and intra-group culture and firm dynamics (Cohendet and Llerena, 2003). NGOs have played a notable role in endeavouring to design equitable institutions and guiding their development in Cases 1 and 2 – initially through fostering solidarity organisations – although they have struggled both with conservative power holders and controlling entrepreneurs. In Case 3, however, the NGO has been less effective, both as a result of their limited skill, but also due to local pressures such as *Pashtunwali* and poor security, adding empirical insights to Fligstein's theory of social skill in less stable environments (Fligstein, 2001).

Research findings indicate the emergence of dominant entrepreneur types, with critical implications for the nature and scope of institutional development. In more progressive contexts with 'public-spirited' entrepreneurs, institutions were able to evolve more naturally, with replication among confident women. Emerging institutions have tended to be more open, egalitarian and flexible, with a balance of power in horizontal coordination and an evolving network of buyers. In contrast, in stricter and closed contexts, with 'controlling' entrepreneurs, institutional construction was more exclusive, leaning towards a reinforcement of the status quo (and arguably institutional failure in Case 3), with less interest in balanced horizontal coordination and links to buyers that may offer political as well as economic benefits. As indicated by Pentland and Feldman (2005), the basic level of routines was shown to be a useful window on the enterprise and environmental constraints. Flexible and open routines reflect more supportive local conditions permitting more equitable and balanced enterprise growth and development (with participation by women). This contrasts with inflexible and closed routines that reflect more difficult conditions, with restricted or top-down controlled enterprise growth and development. Advancing Cohendet and Llerena (2003) and their contention that routines can facilitate collective action, or that 'combinatorics' of routines can generate further routines (Becker *et al.*, 2006), the research demonstrates that this may depend on the nature of institutions with more exclusive institutions prohibiting collective action and new routines. Going beyond the business itself, broader effects of enterprise institutions are indicated, with the generation of new social, political and economic institutions, in vein with evolutionary insights of the influence of institutions on preferences (Hodgson, 1997), and these are further boosted by local collective action. Open enterprise institutions, championed by public-spirited entrepreneurs with supportive actors, have generated more equitable sociopolitical and economic institutions with positive effects for the enterprise and beyond. These community processes have been actively supported by the cooperation of enterprise women, boosted by a strong collective identity (Ansell, 1998) and open institutions. Meanwhile, closed institutions, with less amenable actors, has stifled the development of further institutions and cooperation, and confined their access to the elite.

Notes

1   Hardin (1968) famously coined the expression the 'tragedy of the commons', where a common resource would eventually become exploited by each man acting in his 'own best interest'.
2   SHG rules are group-led, and identify responsibilities of members and heads, meetings times, savings amounts, rules on loans, and book-keeping.
3   This interpretation was given by Zellem (2012). The proverb can also mean 'don't give up – good things take time and patience'.
4   These vegetables were preselected by the INGO as a result of an initial market assessment.
5   This refers to the Islamic ritual of washing oneself before engaging in prayer.
6   In the research, they implored 'Please tell our story too'.
7   It is interesting to note that in the 1970s, there were in fact mixed-sex factories in Kabul. Yet the prevailing cultural norms of Kabul at that time were significantly more open, as the city looked towards the West as a model for urban living. As such, the city was distinctly removed from the common Afghan (rural) reality. With the onset of war, however, at the end of the 1970s, many Kabuli families (particularly from the elite) fled to Europe and beyond. Kabul was then repopulated with more conservative rural groups.
8   It is worth noting that the research cases have generated a certain set of scenarios, but there may indeed be more 'combinations' across a greater number of cases.
9   These broad case study indicators stand in stark contrast to neighbouring (non-participating) communities over the same time period (as indicated by the communities themselves and NGO workers).

References

Aldrich, H.E. (1999) *Organizations Evolving*, London: Sage.

Ansell, C. (1998) 'Symbolic networks', *American Journal of Sociology*, 103: 359–90.

Becker, M.C. (2004) 'Organizational routines: a review of the literature', *Industrial and Corporate Change*, 13(4): 643–77.

Becker, M.C., Knudsen, T. and March, J.G. (2006) 'Schumpeter, Winter and the sources of novelty', *Industrial and Corporate Change*, 15: 353–71.

Beckert, J. (1999) 'Agency, entrepreneurs, and institutional change: the role of strategic choice and institutionalized practices in organizations', *Organisation Studies*, 20(5): 777–99.

Chang, H.-J. (2002) 'Breaking the mould: an institutionalist political economy alternative to the neo-liberal theory of the market and the state', *Cambridge Journal of Economics*, 26(5): 539–59.

Coe, N.M., Dicken, P. and Hess, M. (2008) 'Global production networks: realizing the potential', *Journal of Economic Geography*, 8: 271–95.

Cohen, M.F., Burkhart, R., Dosi, G., Egidi, M., Marengo, L., Warglien, M. and Winter, S. (1996) 'Routines and other recurring action patterns of organisations: contemporary research issues', *Industrial and Corporate Change*, 5: 653–98.

Cohendet, P. and Llerena, P. (2003) 'Routines and incentives: the role of communities in the firm', *Industrial and Corporate Change*, 12: 271–97.

Commons, J.R. (1957) *Legal Foundations of Capitalism*, Madison, WI: University of Wisconsin Press.

Denzau, A.T. and North, D.C. (1994) 'Shared mental models: ideologies and institutions', *Kyklos*, 47(1): 3–31.

DiMaggio, P.J. (1988) 'Interest and agency in institutional theory', in L.G. Zucker (ed.), *Institutional Patterns and Organisations*, Cambridge, MA: Ballinger.

Douglas, M. (1986) *How Institutions Think*, Syracuse, NY: Syracuse University Press.

Elster, J. (1985) 'Weakness of will and the free rider problem', *Economics and Philosophy*, 1(2): 231–65.

Emirbayer, M. and Goodwin, J. (1994) 'Network analysis, culture, and the problem of agency', *American Journal of Sociology*, 99(6): 1411–54.

Fehr, E. and Rockenbach, B. (2003) 'Detrimental effects of sanctions on human altruism', *Nature*, 422(March): 137–40.

Feldman, M.S. and Pentland, B. (2003) 'Re-theorising organizational routines as a source of flexibility and change', *Administrative Science Quarterly*, 48: 94–118.

Fligstein, N. (1996) 'Markets as politics: a political-cultural approach to market institutions', *American Sociological Review*, 61: 656–73.

Fligstein, N. (2001) 'Social skill and the theory of fields', *Sociological Theory*, 19(2): 105–25.

Fukuyama, F. (1995) *Trust: The Social Virtues and Creation of Prosperity*, New York: Free Press Paperbacks.

Gambetta, D. (1988) (ed.) *Trust: Making and Breaking Cooperative Relations*, New York: Basil Blackwell.

Gereffi, G. (1994) 'Capitalism, development and global commodity chains', in L. Skylair (ed.), *Capitalism and Development*, London: Routledge.

Gereffi, G. and Memodovic, O. (2003) 'The global apparel value chain: what prospects for upgrading by developing countries?', *United Nations Industrial Development Organization Sectoral Studies Series*, available at: www.unido.org/doc/12218, accessed 1 December 2012.

Giddens, A. (1984) *The Constitution of Society: Outline of the Theory of Structuration*, Cambridge: Polity Press.

Gomez, G. (2008) *Making Markets: The Institutional Rise and Decline of the Argentine Red de Trueque*, Maastricht, Netherlands: Shaker Publishing BV (PhD Thesis).

Granovetter, M. (1992) 'Economic institutions as social constructions: a framework for analysis', *Acta Sociologica*, 35(1): 3–11.

Hardin, G. (1968) 'The tragedy of the commons', *Science*, 162: 1243–8.

Hardin, R. (1982) 'Exchange theory on strategic bases', *Social Science Information*, 21(2): 251–72.

Hays, S. and Wincott, D. (1994) 'Structure and agency and the sticky problem of culture', *Sociological Theory*, 12(1): 951–7.

Helmsing, B. and Vellema, S. (2011) *Value Chains, Social Inclusion and Economic Development: Contrasting Theories and Realities*, Oxford: Routledge Studies in Development Economics.

Henrich, J. and Boyd, R. (2001) 'Why people punish defectors: conformist transmission stabilizes costly enforcement of norms in cooperative dilemmas', *Journal of Theoretical Biology*, 208: 79–89.

Hodgson, G. (1997) 'The ubiquity of habits and rules', *Cambridge Journal of Economics*, 21: 663–84.

Hodgson, G. (2003) 'The hidden persuaders, institutions and individuals in economic theory', *Cambridge Journal of Economics*, 27: 159–75.

Hodgson, G. (2007) 'Institutions and individuals: interaction and evolution', *Organisation Studies*, 28(1): 95–111.

Hodgson, G. and Knudsen, T. (2004) 'The firm as an interactor: firms as vehicles for habits and routines', *Journal of Evolutionary Economics*, 14(3): 281–307.

Hollingsworth, J.R. (2000) 'Doing institutional analysis: implications for the study of innovation', *Review of International Political Economy*, 7(4): 595–644.

Hollingsworth, J.R. (2002) 'Some reflections on how institutions influence styles of innovation', paper for Swedish Collegium for Advanced Study of the Social Sciences, 26 September, available at: http://history.wisc.edu/hollingsworth/documents/Some_Reflections_on_How_Institutions_Influence_Styles_of_Innovation.htm, accessed 1 December 2012.

Hollingsworth, J.R. and Boyer, R. (1997) 'Coordination of economic actors and social systems of production', in J.R. Hollingsworth and R. Boyer (eds), *Contemporary Capitalism*, Cambridge: Cambridge University Press.

Humphrey, J. and Schmitz, H. (2000) *Governance in Global Value Chains*, Institute of Development Studies, University of Sussex, UK.

Joas, H. (1996) *The Creativity of Action*, Chicago, IL: University of Chicago Press.

Kaplinsky, R. and Morris, M. (2000) *A Handbook for Value Chain Research*, London: IDRC.

Knorringa, P., Meijerink, G. and Schouten, G. (2011) 'Voluntary governance initiatives and the challenges of inclusion and upscaling', in B. Helmsing and S. Vellema (eds), *Value Chains, Social Inclusion and Economic Development: Contrasting Theories and Realities*, Oxford: Routledge Studies in Development Economics.

Levinthal, D.A. (1991) 'Organizational adaptation and environmental selection: interrelated processes of change', *Organizational Science*, 2: 140–5.

March, J.G. and Olsen, J.P. (1989) *Rediscovering Institutions: The Organizational Basis of Politics*, New York: Free Press.

March, J.G. and Simon, H.A. (1958/1993) *Organizations*, Cambridge, MA: Blackwell.

Meyer-Stamer, J. and Waltring, F. (2007) *Linking Value Chain Analysis and Making Markets Work Better for the Poor Concept*, Duisberg, Germany: GTZ.

Muller, J.Z. (1992) *Adam Smith in His Time and Ours: Designing the Decent Society*, New York: Free Press.

Nelson, R.R. and Winter, S.G. (1982) *An Evolutionary Theory of Economic Change*, Cambridge, MA: Harvard University Press.

Olson, M. (1965) *The Logic of Collective Action: Public Goods and the Theory of Groups*, Cambridge, MA: Harvard University Press.

Ostrom, E. (1990) *Governing the Commons: The Evolution of Institutions for Collective Action*, Cambridge: Cambridge University Press.

Ostrom, E. (2005) *Understanding Institutional Diversity*, Princeton, NJ and Oxford: Princeton University Press.

Pentland, B. and Feldman, M.S. (2005) 'Organizational routines as a unit of analysis', *Industrial and Corporate Change*, 14(5): 793–815.

Polanyi, K. (1944/2001) *The Great Transformation: The Political and Economic Origins of Our Time*, Boston, MA: Beacon Press.

Porter, M. (1980) *Competitive Strategy: Techniques for Analyzing Industries and Competitors*, New York: Free Press.

Porter, M. (1985) *Competitive Advantage: Creating and Sustaining Superior Performance*, New York: Free Press.

Porter, M. (1990) *The Competitive Advantage of Nations*, New York: Free Press.

Putnam, R.D. (1993) *Making Democracy Work: Civic Traditions in Modern Italy*, Princeton, NJ: Princeton University Press.

Putnam, R.D. (2000) *Bowling Alone: The Collapse and Revival of American Community*, New York: Simon & Schuster.

Sabel, C.F. (1992) 'Studied trust: building new forms of cooperation in a volatile economy', in F. Pyke and W. Sengenberger (eds), *Industrial Districts and Local Economic Regeneration*, Geneva: International Institute for Labour Studies.

Schumpeter, J.A. (1934) *The Theory of Economic Development*, Cambridge, MA: Harvard University Press.

Schumpeter, J.A. (2005) 'Development', *Journal of Economic Literature*, XLIII: 104–16 (Entwicklung) (translated by M.C. Becker and T. Knudsen).

Streeck, W. and Schmitter, P.C. (1985) 'Community, market, state and associations? The prospective contribution of interest governance to social order', in W. Streeck and P.C. Schmitter (eds), *Private Interest Government: Beyond Market and State*, Beverly Hills, CA: Sage.

Taylor, M. (1987) *The Possibility of Cooperation*, Cambridge: Cambridge University Press.

Udehn, L. (1993) 'Twenty-five years with "The Logic of Collective Action"', *Acta Sociologica*, 36(3): 239–61.

Weber, M. (1921/1978) *Economy and Society: An Outline of Interpretive Sociology*, Berkeley, CA: University of California Press.

Weick, K.E. (1990) 'The vulnerable system: an analysis of the Tenerife air disaster', *Journal of Management*, 16: 571–93.

Winter, S.G. (1982) 'Schumpeterian competition in alternative technological regimes', *Journal of Economic Behaviour and Organisation*, 5: 137–58.

Winter, S.G. (1990) 'Survival, selection and inheritance in evolutionary theories of organisation', in J.V. Singh (ed.), *Organizational Evolution: New Directions*, Newbury Park, CA: Sage.

Winter, S.G. (1994) 'Organising for continuous improvement: evolutionary theory meets the quality revolution', in J. Baum and J. Singh (eds), *Evolutionary Dynamics of Organisations*, Oxford: Oxford University Press.

Winter, S.G. (2003) 'Understanding dynamic capabilities', *Strategic Management Journal*, 24: 991–5.

Winter, S.G. (2006) 'Toward a neo-Schumpeterian theory of the firm', *Industrial and Corporate Change*, 15(1): 125–41.

Zellem, E. (2012) *Zarbul Masalha: 151 Afghan Dari Proverbs*, US: CreateSpace Independent Publishing Platform.

6 Unwrapping agency

Interests, power and networks

This chapter looks more closely at 'agency' across the three women's businesses to unravel the influence of interests, power and networks in institutional development, building off Chapters 3, 4 and 5. In Chapter 2, Hodgson described agency as the capacity of agents to 'reflect and deliberate upon the context, options, purpose and possible outcomes of action', while structure referred to a 'set of significant relations between individuals that can lead to causal interactions' (Hodgson, 2004). For this research, I conceptualised actors as influenced by their own dynamic motivations and interest, skills/capacity and networks, with these in turn continually influenced by structure (existing institutions, relations, and endogenous politics). Initially, the discussion re-examines and expands upon the literature on entrepreneurs, networks and agency. Turning to the cases, the discussion considers the underlying motivations and interests of key actors, and identifies core dimensions of the local context (environmental particularities) and structure towards unwrapping actor strategies in institutional processes. Finally, it draws attention to dominant entrepreneurs, and the role of networks and collective power in institutional diffusion and adoption.

6.1 Entrepreneurs, networks and agency

Some economists – particularly in the developing context – have drawn on the notion of 'institutional entrepreneurs' (as described in Chapter 2) to characterise entrepreneurs that are also involved in institutional innovations (e.g. Li *et al.*, 2006). Such entrepreneurs may possess additional skills that enable them to coordinate with authority and navigate public opinion. They describe these entrepreneurs as facing more risk than traditional entrepreneurs, but suggest that such entrepreneurs may generate certain 'positive externalities' for the economy and 'constitute a force of economic development and reform'. In the absence of state institutional frameworks – where the 'state is weak, absent or neglectful' – typical in developing country contexts, Boettke and Leeson (2009) described a situation of 'institutional entrepreneurialism' where entrepreneurs have developed both 'productive-tier' technology (for the business), alongside non-productive 'protective-tier' techno-logy (for property security). Yet they cite the paradox of such 'environmental' innovations in that they can both enable commercial activity, but equally inhibit commercial expansion due to their limited sphere of influence (particularly in a greater context of uncertainty).

6.1.1 Towards a broader perspective of institutional 'entrepreneurs'

Towards examining the role of actors in institutional processes, much can be learned from organisational studies. Battilana describes institutional entrepreneurs as organisations or groups of organisations (e.g. Greenwood *et al.*, 2002), or individuals or groups of individuals (Fligstein, 1997; Maguire *et al.*, 2004) who introduce 'divergent changes' (e.g. Amis *et al.*, 2004), engage in active participation in change efforts, and mobilise resources to implement change (Battilana *et al.*, 2009: 69). Looking at the 'paradox of embedded agency', she highlights how actors can become institutional entrepreneurs, despite institutional pressures, with the help of enabling conditions (Strang and Sine, 2002), from drawing on the actor's own characteristics to characteristics of the environments in which they are embedded (Battilana *et al.*, 2009: 74). She also draws attention to the harnessing of formal authority, which can help institutional entrepreneurs legitimize divergent ideas (Maguire *et al.*, 2004), frame stories (Fligstein, 2001), and promote acknowledgment and 'consumption' of their discourse by other actors (Phillips *et al.*, 2004). Yet it is still not fully understood how and why 'institutional entrepreneurs' pursue certain strategies, or obtain the necessary resources, formal authority and social capital. In looking at change agents and the spread of ideas, Ford *et al.* (2008) presented a more nuanced picture of such actors, and degrees of resistance. They propose that change agents may in fact contribute to resistance through their own 'actions and inactions' such as through, for example, broken agreements and a violation of trust, communication breakdowns, and misrepresentation. Yet, this resistance may in fact have positive effects in generating attention through discourse, ensuring engagement in issues, and possibly necessary conflict.

6.1.2 Networks and entrepreneurial outcomes

In Chapter 2, Davern (1997: 288) defined a social network as a series of formal and informal ties or relations between a central actor (or group), and other actors. Comprised of fluid relations, social networks are not fixed or necessarily in constant use, and may be 'activated' for different needs (e.g. Granovetter, 1985), and governed by rules of exchange, codes of conduct, and hierarchies of deference and power (Nordstrom, 2000). Granovetter (1992) posited that 'stable' economic institutions emerge as growing clusters of activity around existing personal networks. Granovetter described the level of network fragmentation and cohesion, or 'coupling and decoupling', as a significant indicator of potential outcomes, with actors whose networks straddle the largest number of institutional spheres having the most advantage. Summarising sociologist contributions, Granovetter (2005) highlighted four principles of social networks and economic outcomes. The first principle relates to norms and network density, and posits that in dense networks norms are more easily enforced. With this perspective, overcoming free rider problems in collective action may be facilitated in groups with dense and cohesive networks due to higher levels of trust. The second relates to the 'strength of weak ties', which suggests that novel ideas/information tend to flow more easily through weak rather than strong ties. The third principle draws attention to 'structural holes', as theorised by Burt (1992). Here, the emphasis is on different networks and the way that they are bridged. The fourth principle underscores the social embeddedness of the economy affecting 'costs and available techniques' in economic activity. Meanwhile, Uzzi (1996) looked at embedded ties, and suggested that in stable situations these may offer advantages, but in more dynamic situations, they may constrain relationship flexibility and adaptation. Yet while network discussions and analysis has provided a powerful conceptualisation of social structure in looking at relationships between actors, Emirbayer and Goodwin (1994) suggest that it has neglected culture, agency and process.

In the field of entrepreneurship, Greve (2003) highlights a number of recent studies that elaborate on the embeddness of enterprise in social structures, and the role of networks and actors (e.g. Borch, 1994; Hansen, 1995). Earlier papers had also indicated the embeddedness of entrepreneurs in social context and local relations. For example, Baumol (1990) emphasises the social sanctioning of entrepreneurs (i.e. sociocultural influences) affecting entrepreneurial behaviour. With increasing recognition of the further importance of social relations and ties, there has in fact been a great deal of research on social networks in enterprise since the 1980s, after a series of more individual-oriented studies of entrepreneurs (particularly psychological). These network studies led to the so-called resource perspective (Wernerfelt, 1984), positing that entrepreneurs can gain useful resources from their networks boosting their performance. Two crucial arguments have been presented in this regard (Klyver and Schott, 2011: 5). In vein with Coleman (1988, 1990), the first is known as the 'closure' argument, and contends that a tight or closed network around an entrepreneur generates trust within the network and enhances the exchange of information and support, and can further enhance more substantial collective action (e.g. Aldrich and Zimmer, 1986). The second is the 'structural holes' argument (as described above), and contends that those entrepreneurs with gaps in their network or disconnects can gain access to more broad and useful information (e.g. Burt, 1992). Drawing on both, others have further suggested that the most efficient network type may also depend on the stage of the entrepreneurial process (i.e. in the early phases, business needs may differ from more mature phases; e.g. Larson and Starr, 1993). Meanwhile, Greve (2003) elaborated on a number of properties of networks that entrepreneurs can exploit for access to resources, including size, positioning within a social network and relationship structure.

As discussed in Chapters 2 and 5, Fligstein (1996) theorised that new paths of action could be opened up and institutionalised by 'skilful actors' by repeated learning within networks. Building off this, Maguire *et al.* (2004) suggest that institutional entrepreneurs may draw on social capital to influence others and gather allies, and their social capital may enable institutional entrepreneurs to engage in collective action among diverse stakeholders. The notion of a third party (described as 'gatekeepers', not to be confused with gatekeepers described later in this study) has been used to describe a group that mediates between two groups of actors within a system (Gould and Fernandez, 1989). Graf describes these groups as either internal or external to the system (Graf, 2011: 176). With sufficient internal and external ties, the broker serves two functions for the system: external knowledge sourcing and diffusion within the local system (Allen, 1977; Giuliani, 2005; Malipiero *et al.*, 2005). Exploring the influence of networks on actors, Klyver and Schott (2011) have innovatively looked at how the structure of networks shapes the development of entrepreneurial intentions. Intentionality is defined as 'a state of mind directing a person's attention (and therefore experience and action) towards a specific objective (goal) or path in order to achieve something' (Bird, 1988: 442). Models of entrepreneurial intention have previously explored entrepreneurial events (e.g. Shapero, 1982), and 'planned' behaviour with (entrepreneurial or otherwise) intention depending on individual attitudes, norms and perception of feasibility (e.g. Ajzen, 1991). Klyver and Schott (2011) have shown that the type of social network that entrepreneurs are embedded in influences entrepreneurial intentions, with those embedded in networks with structural holes more likely to engage in entrepreneurship. Yet network size, diversity and age appeared not to affect entrepreneurial intentions. This study assumes that the network precedes the intention. There remains a gap in looking at intentions related to existing enterprise phenomena, and evolving network structures.

6.1.3 Collective agency in learning, adoption and diffusion

From an institutionalist perspective (Battilana *et al.*, 2009: 90), most existing research looks at institutional entrepreneurs in the initial stages but does not look ahead to the 'stabilization and possible diffusion of divergent change', and how actors can individually or collectively 'ensure the maintenance of the novel practices they promote' (Hwang and Powell, 2005; Jain and George, 2007; Wijen and Ansari, 2007). Expanding the theory from Chapter 5, new routines may be spread through learning in contagion (e.g. March and Olsen, 1989) or diffusion in social networks. Huber (1991) highlights four different 'constructs' crucial to organisational learning: knowledge acquisition (related to different types of learning), information distribution, information interpretation and organisational memory. Organisations are viewed as systems of distributed knowledge within which knowledge is exchanged through the sharing of capabilities (March, 1999). Powell and DiMaggio (1991) describe the evolution of shared mental models in organisations, and the occurrence of collective learning. Becker *et al.* (2006) discuss routine evolution, which may be explained through the incremental change of routines in experiential learning (Levitt and March, 1988; Greve, 2003).

Becker *et al.* (2006) draw attention to diffusion research, which provides insights into the incremental spread of routines, which can lead to 'wide adoption' and 'notable persistence in routines' (Fischer, 1989; Vincenti, 1994; Nelson *et al.*, 2004). In line with Veblen (1919), Redmond (2003) distinguished between more abrupt change and a 'gradual drift' in traditions or norms. Moving away from a 'supply-side' of institutional innovation and change, and a focus on 'inventors', Redmond looked at the 'demand' perspective, drawing attention to dimensions of acceptance in response to the novelty and adopters (ibid.). In this regard, Redmond draws on diffusion theory with an institutional perspective, and integrates the role of actors in broader uptake processes. Redmond explores the diffusion of innovation in connection with informal 'mid-level' institutional change, particularly cultural change. Building off Everett Rogers' rich and influential work on the diffusion of innovation (Rogers, 1962), he elaborates on diffusion in institutional change (Bush, 1987; Witt, 1989). In particular, in diffusion theory, the overall spread of technology and techniques is argued to generate considerable social change in society, since innovations are triggered and prevailing social institutions are changed. Yet beyond technology, and pertinent to broader diffusion research, new 'ideas' may equally precipitate social innovations and change, with arguably more complex roles for actors (due to embedded beliefs).

Towards a more nuanced understanding of diffusion

Looking closer at the influence of actors, Redmond (2003: 667) highlights two particular problems with diffusion theory: the implicit assumption of bounded rationality, and the explained time gap between introduction and adoption justified solely in terms of actor communication (Gatignon and Robertson, 1985). The latter fails to incorporate broader influences such as values and tradition, habits and routines (Hodgson, 1988), and social relations, as highlighted in institutional theory. Redmond further discusses self-interest in preferences and plans in cognitive responses to innovation. Departing from diffusion theory, Redmond differentiates between 'innovators', and two main adoption categories: 'innovative adopters' (minority) and 'followers' (majority). 'Innovators' are the original inventors. Early adopters are then described as 'innovative adopters', and are characterised by 'venturesomeness, intelligence, ability to cope with uncertainty and willingness to accept risk' (Rogers, 1962) and 'planning without emulation', underscoring motives of self-interest and potential status enhancement. Finally, once the innovation has been perceived as 'socially desirable', Redmond describes later adopters as 'followers'. This second set of adopters are characterised by planning 'with emulation' and a 'drive to keep up with others' (in vein with Veblen and Bourdieu), with late followers driven by peer pressure to conform (Granovetter, 1978). Individuals thus respond in view of their own perceived risk/reward. The end of diffusion is then signified once the 'novel' becomes a 'routine' (Redmond, 2003: 672).

Redmond indicates three core areas in which institutional (and actor) insights may add value to diffusion theory. First, he cites a need to appreciate the 'prestige value of newness', the pace of diffusion, and the social context (with variations on acceptance of the new depending on economic history and actual alternatives). Second, he highlights 'creative destruction', highlighting the downside of the loss of tradition and customs – rather than the novelty – in the emergence of new practices with adopters focused on individual outcomes rather than social outcomes. And third, he draws attention to the less-discussed but critical area of non-adoption, which may be voluntary (due to perceived loss of values or tradition such as the Amish), or involuntary due to inadequate funds or education. Looking beyond the innovation itself and characteristics of the adopters in diffusion, Ford *et al.* (2008: 366) highlights the importance of the 'discursive practices' of change agents in understanding adoption in organisational innovation and change (as described by Green, 2004), and 'conversations, discourses, and texts' drawing attention to several studies (e.g. Fairclough, 1992; Barrett *et al.*, 1995; Boje, 1995; Czarniawska and Sevon, 1996; Ford, 1999).

Bringing in relevant discussions on social networks, Granovetter (2005) emphasises studies in Rogers (1962) that highlight the impact of social structure and networks on innovation and diffusion. He cited an interesting paper by Zelizer (1978), which showed the insurance industry drawing on religious language to spread an innovation in life insurance in the 1800s through the clergy (urging their congregation to provide for their family members after death, thus making it a 'sacred duty'). Meanwhile, Day (1994) adds a further dimension and suggests that the distance of actors from power structures can influence the nature of innovations, with greater distances permitting more radical innovations (although, there is still a gap in understanding power in broader uptake processes). Offering insights for uptake, Acemoglu *et al.* (2011) looked at how the structure of social networks affects learning dynamics in sequential settings. The latter draw attention to gaps in the discourse and areas for future research including shedding light on equilibrium learning when there are heterogeneous preferences, and the influence of a subset of a social network (e.g. the media or interested parties) in influencing the views of the rest as a function of the network structure. Yet in exploring institutional innovation and diffusion in networks, it appears crucial to also look at dynamic, as well as heterogeneous, preferences within networks, and environmental influences.

6.2 A closer look at case study actors and context

In the process of institutional construction and development, the research points to the interaction of three key sets of actors that play varying roles as 'institutional entrepreneurs' in individual and collective processes. These included the NGO as an 'external' player, the entrepreneur (and 'active workers'), and local power holders. These actors were driven by a mixture of (both private and public) social, economic and political incentives. Towards examining evolving motivations and interests, it is imperative to look closer at actor backgrounds and their involvement in the respective businesses to appreciate their shifting drives and interaction.

6.2.1 NGOs driven by women's socio-economic development

As described in Chapter 1, the NGOs were organisations that were involved with facilitating and supporting the evolving women's businesses, and played a key role in institutional design and development. They included both local and international

NGOs. Yet with different backgrounds and goals, they varied in their evolving motivations and interests, influencing the nature of their approaches and outcomes.

Case 1: a local NGO

In Case 1, whilst from the region (Herat), the local NGO was new to development work at the start of their activities with the women entrepreneurs. Yet under the auspices of a well-known international NGO, through the course of their work, they have succeeded in securing an excellent local reputation in facilitating culturally sensitive community-based development. All of the male staff had lived in Afghan diaspora communities in Peshawar, Pakistan, where women's projects were prevalent and attitudes less conservative. The staff were very religious but progressive (they believed strongly in women's right to work). At the time of the research, the NGO had been active for five years. In terms of their motivations and interests, the overall goal of their original intervention was to economically empower poor village-based women through market development to reduce household poverty. Specifically, they aimed to organise women into village food processing groups and to facilitate market links to promote broader community development. Their main focus was thus to support these (poorer) women in market activities, and to ensure a culturally sensitive and sustainable approach (with 'progressive' religious norms).

Adopting this locally oriented approach, the NGO has carefully facilitated the women's enterprise activities from community mobilisation, technical training to marketing and business development. In the beginning, they utilised a deliberate religious strategy to gain the confidence of the communities, particularly in villages that were fragile, distrustful and resistant to change. Using these strategies, the NGO was able to begin the negotiation of a reformulation of *purdah* for the women (as described in Chapter 4). The NGO then introduced (initial) enterprise institutions – routines, institutional arrangements and (cross-firm) institutions – designing these intuitively and reactively, as needs arose for group cooperation, interaction and coordination (as described in Chapter 5). The strategy to link the groups for higher-level marketing was thus conceived at a later stage in the course of the work. The NGO has been instrumental in both designing institutions and guiding their reformulation as necessary, while endeavouring to ensure continued cooperation and coordination, and maintain local peace with communities!

Notably, despite confronting challenging situations (e.g. extensive resistance from the elite, weak entrepreneurs, community conflict), the NGO had not suffered ultimate 'failure' in any of the villages that they had supported (i.e. no villages had 'dropped out'). Instead, lead women may have shifted positions (or been replaced), and early phases may have been prolonged. As the business evolved across a network of villages, the NGO tried to support the organic growth of the business through the development of equitable institutions that were both transparent and agreed by the group. This included ensuring fair remuneration that reflected responsibility levels and workloads. With group maturity, the NGO then moved from intensive group work to supporting the network of groups as a mentor.

Their motivations and interests thus evolved from the simple goal of establishing a few enterprise groups of village women to facilitating a much more ambitious network of village-based women's groups that were independent and successful, selling foodstuffs at a city level with community approval and support. They viewed their work as a good model for women's economic development, and had long-term interest in their growth and sustainability. During the research, they further diversified their general portfolio of activities in the region to include rights training, and other vocational skills.

Case 2: an international NGO and local NGO/business association

In the second case, the facilitating 'NGO' comprised a joint team of NGOs. The main NGO was an international organisation with globally renowned expertise in market development but with limited local experience or networks. As such, the INGO immediately teamed up with a local NGO/women's business association from Kabul in order to support their work in community development. At the time of the research, the NGO team had been active for three years. In terms of their motivations and interests, the overall goal of the INGO's original intervention was to empower poorer women through value chain development to reduce household poverty. Specifically, they aimed to organise village-based women into vegetable farmer groups and to facilitate market links (to services, resources and buyers) to promote local economic development. With ideals of 'accelerating markets'[1] and women's empowerment, however, they initially stumbled on cultural issues related to community interaction and women's participation, particularly in under-estimating norms of *purdah*, and local expectations of close consultation with community power holders (with male staff). From the outset, their core interests were geared towards introducing new techniques and technology, ensuring efficient marketing systems, and creating scale across several villages within the designated project time frame.

With the local NGO assistance, the INGO has provided intensive support to the target communities, notably in the form of technical skills development in vegetable production (land preparation, harvesting and post-harvest), introduction to new technology (greenhouses, storage units, solar driers and drip irrigation) and training in marketing (including price, timing, place and packaging). Through these strategies, the INGO has brought in both new skills and technology – visibly increasing productivity – and a systemised production and marketing system. To streamline the business and as needs arose, they have also introduced elaborate and innovative enterprise institutions within the village, linking the village to market players and creating loose ties across villages. These institutions were adapted from projects in regional contexts (such as Pakistan). Together, these new technologies and institutions have appeared to generate a thriving business. Yet with little appreciation of village-level conservatism, at the beginning, the INGO approach suffered without male staff on board to foster the necessary relationships with local power holders. In response to this, the INGO eventually hired an experienced male worker to support the community mobilisation and coordination.

Meanwhile, the female staff were heavily involved with technical training, marketing, and holding monthly office meetings with the representatives. Similar to Case 1, staff and village leaders (designated in this case as 'champions') initially employed the use of subtle religious messages to convince traditional community village members that new social and economic practices were indeed acceptable, and within the framework of their religion and culture.

This combined NGO approach has generally proved successful in gaining local participation in most of their target villages (with the exception of one village, which emerged to be too unstable, as mentioned earlier). The elaborate and sophisticated village structure of the vegetable business – with designated roles for the women, and the facilitation of links to suppliers and buyers – has reinforced new beliefs in women's work and given it a strong and credible framework. And the visibility of new skills/technology and clear financial benefits have arguably accelerated acceptance of the evolving social and market-oriented institutions. These strategies in institutional development – facilitating an enterprise structure, market networks and new skills/technology – have been strong persuasive forces in permitting the evolving habits and practices of the women, particularly in Case 2a. The INGO was instrumental in designing these initial enterprise-related institutions, and guiding the further development of these institutions, while simultaneously trying to ensure that the overall village business remained operational and active in the marketplace. However in Case 2b, they have struggled with the controlling entrepreneur, and even tried to have her replaced (but this was blocked by the local *shura*). During the research phase, the INGO project came to a close with responsibilities, and informal continued support was passed on to the local women's association.[2]

Case 3: an international NGO

In the third case, the NGO was an international organisation, although the project had a strong Afghan 'face', and was predominantly led and managed by a charismatic and open local man (an Afghan Tajik). With little experience in business development, though (in contrast to Case 2), the NGO was forced to learn by doing over their several years of support to the women's enterprise, and this has often led to them taking on a paternalistic role and propping up the business financially. In terms of motivations and interests, the initial goal of the organisation was to facilitate poor women's enterprise development to support destitute households in deprived areas of Kabul. Specifically, they aimed to train a group of women in basic electronics-related skills, organise them into a business, and then link them to the market. Their main focus was to enable target women to work and to generate an income for their families. However, with little appreciation of local fragility and conservatism, the approach stumbled on extensive cultural issues around Pashtun women participating in projects outside of the house (as a result of *Pashtunwali*).

To facilitate women's mobilisation and entry into business, the NGO initially adopted a highly culturally sensitive strategy in terms of their presentation (clothes, language) and behaviour. They also utilised extensive religious messages to gain the further confidence of the neighbourhood, since the area was conservative, distrustful and strongly resistant to women's development. The senior male employee tried to exhibit a strong Muslim but progressive faith, and this was described to have brought him much respect, securing him an excellent reputation with local elders and husbands, and enhancing the women's sense of protection, trust in foreigners and belief in the project. He further visited the women's families to encourage the women and protect them from premature public interaction (including from other project staff!).

At the project outset, the NGO focused their attentions on negotiating new *purdah* arrangements for the participating women. As indicated earlier, in the strictly Pashtun community, these were still conservative formulations. The NGO then began carefully facilitating the extensive year-long technical training in electronics alongside literacy support. As the business operations tentatively started, the charismatic male staff member led the initiation of joint production, while endeavouring to keep the husbands and power holders on board with the work. Other staff included 'modern' and 'influential' young female employees as literacy trainers, notably acting as role models for the women (and impressing them significantly with their 'city ways'). At the time of the research, the NGO had provided intensive support to the electronics enterprise for a period of six years, in the form of extensive social outreach (coordinating with local leaders and husbands), technical training and business development. Involved with the project from the outset, the NGO head had been instrumental in persuading conservative husbands, fathers and elders of the acceptability of the women's work and value for the family economy. He was described to be like a 'father' to the women, and had often 'gone beyond the call of duty'. Yet as the business developed, he still largely micromanaged the operations, and controlled their finances, administration and strategy. Towards the end of the research, the business was struggling, both due to the male-centric and fickle nature of the electronics sector, persisting issues of *purdah* (due to *Pashtunwali*), and arguably the inadequate and weak business institutions. Due to little visible profits, families were also growing impatient with the women's enterprise work, and pressuring the women to drop out. Despite little success, the motivations and interests of the NGO had evolved from basic women's empowerment to endeavouring to promote a viable women's enterprise, but they remained constrained by limited ideas on how to realise this, and how to cope with ongoing cultural and situational dynamics.

6.2.2 Entrepreneurs driven by economic and sociopolitical interests

As described in Chapter 1, the 'entrepreneurs' were the designated heads of the women's enterprise groups at the community level. While not theoretically initiating the businesses, they led and championed the enterprise and organisational innovations, and were either selected by their peers or by the local leaders. Across the cases, entrepreneurs were involved with shaping institutions and determining their adoption and diffusion. Expanding on the earlier profiles, here

I further explore the characters of the entrepreneurs, and their evolving motivations and interests.

Case 1: group-selected leaders

In Case 1, entrepreneurs were selected from the middle of the community, were respected women (religious, active), and had more mobility due to age and marital status (older and/or widows). The entrepreneurs and their supporters (active women) were shown to be instrumental in reformulating rules and routines, troubleshooting and determining the overall direction of the business, including their links to suppliers and buyers, and to other food processing groups.

The entrepreneur from Case 1a was naturally cautious in character with strong religious beliefs, but was determined with a keen sense of belief in the work and new women's practices. Approximately 38 years old, she was married with children, including one son who worked in the enterprise-own shop in the city. Stemming from a strict family (her father and grandfather were both mullahs), she was known as religious (a 'good Muslim') and wary of cultural boundaries, but was equally described as active and intelligent within her household despite being illiterate. Her family was considered to be relatively 'ordinary', with little resources, and the family men worked as sharecroppers on less than two *jeribs* of land (one acre). Despite this humble background, she proved to be progressive and quietly influential. She liked to remind the women that Khadija (the wife of Prophet Mohammed) was a businesswoman, and that the daughter of Mohammed was also strong! She hinted that with patience and openness to change, economic dividends were possible. The entrepreneur's husband and son were key supporters of her work, and (in later phases) jointly facilitated logistics (transporting goods to market) and procurement as required (under her authority).

Her motivations and interests to join the group were initially (in part) financial, in addition to social interests (to collaborate with other women). With her reputation of level-headedness and reliability, and strong faith, she was elected the group head. With experience, she has proved to be entrepreneurial, courageous, resilient and adaptive to community pressures. She has led the navigation and subtle confrontation with strict local power holders. As the business matured, she further managed to expand the business beyond the community to neighbouring villages, through the receipt of donor funds, following the establishment of her own association. At the time of the research, her motivations and interests were firmly twofold: growing the business to increase profits (business-oriented), while keeping difficult power holders 'on side' (and thus looking beyond the community for business expansion); and quietly improving women's rights to work, be educated and be respected (socially oriented).

The entrepreneur from Case 1b was an older widow (55 years old) with one son that has emerged to be a tough, bold and active entrepreneur. According to NGO staff, the entrepreneur appeared 'ordinary' at first but later demonstrated a rare determination and business acumen. She was seen as clever, thoughtful and open-minded. Her family was considered to be fairly prominent (they were employed in the government), and she was (unusually) educated until she was 12 years old. She married young, however, and was already widowed by her early twenties (both her husband and father were killed by the Russians). As a widow in her husband's village, she was described as having been poor and powerless. However, participation in the project has visibly empowered her and raised her standing on many levels, leading her to rightfully eventually reclaim her husband's property from her brother-in-law. Since her son travelled frequently, she was often in sole charge of the family property, and had significant control over other family resources. When home, her son was a key supporter of her work, and jointly assisted with finances and logistics (transporting goods to market).

Her initial motivations to join the group were similarly (part) financial in addition to social interests (to collaborate with other women). With seniority and an open mind, she was voted as head of the business after an earlier choice proved incapable of leading the group. With experience, she has also proved to be notably entrepreneurial and able to rise well to the challenge of managing the group and navigating authorities. Putting her own resources into the business, she has used her newly claimed inherited land to expand the production centre, and has also set up her own shop for the products of the business network in the city. At the time of the research, her motivations and interests were also twofold: growing the business to increase profits (business-oriented), while keeping power holders 'on side'; and perhaps more so than Case 1a, actively championing women's rights to work, be educated and be respected (socially oriented).

Case 2: elite-selected leaders

In Case 2, the 'entrepreneurs' (known in the project as village facilitators) were selected by the *shura* to manage the business, and oversee the farmers' groups. The entrepreneurs and senior women (lead farmers and sales agents) have been instrumental in reformulating and guiding rules and routines, troubleshooting and determining the overall direction of the business, including their links to supplies and buyers, and to other villages.

In Case 2a, the *shura* selected the most educated woman in the village, since she was the most respected and crucially, the most mobile (i.e. lower *purdah* restrictions). At the time of the research, she was approximately 40 years old and lived between the village and a wealthy district in the city. She was known locally to be very bright with 'good habits' (i.e. respecting religious norms), and persuasive. Previously, she was a teacher at a local girls' school (and thus one of few educated women). She described her family possessing 'respectable' amounts of land (and thus perhaps influential). The entrepreneur was considered to be an open, educated and well-respected woman. She was also visibly determined, with a keen sense of belief in the work and new women's practices. Her initial motivation for participation in the business was a sense of obligation (as the village's most capable and mobile woman) and social interest, but there was also a sense of pride to be head of this new initiative. Her interests would have been also part monetary (salary). As the business has evolved, she has been both motivated by the business prospects (financial), but also emerging social objectives, in championing new girls and women's roles. She has proved adept at navigating the authorities, and propelling the business forward with evolving structures (and delegating responsibilities to sales agents and lead farmers where possible).

In the more conservative village of Case 2b, the *shura* selected the most dominant, well known, and arguably the most extraordinary village woman. As such, she was also the most mobile woman in the village, and would face fewer difficulties in potential work obligations. Daughter of the village head (the *arbab*), at the time of the research, she was one of the most powerful women in the region (and had recently been assigned head of the new cluster of women's groups in the district). The entrepreneur was 35 years old, unmarried and, uniquely, the sole supporter of her mother and sister. Shedding light on her unconventional behaviour, the entrepreneur had an unusual upbringing in being brought up as a boy (a *bacha posh*)[3] until her teenage years. *Bacha posh* remains a largely under-researched phenomenon, but is deemed to be significant in influencing the resulting woman's habits and practices. It can also be psychologically damaging, particularly if left until late to switch the 'boy girl' back to a normal girl. This can leave women struggling to adapt to women's behavioural and social norms, including communication with other women, gender roles in the household, and strict rules on dress and mobility. In the entrepreneur's situation, this has indeed had a complicated effect on her behaviour and identity, and left her unable to relate to other women. As a result, she saw herself as a 'woman-man'. In the business, she emerged to be controlling, power-hungry and self-centred. In deep contrast to Case 2a, the entrepreneur here was motivated by both power and control from the outset, and lured by the salary. Unsuccessful attempts by the NGO to remove her, and fear by other actors, meant that despite her lack of popularity among the women, she remained head of the village enterprise. As the business evolved, opportunities for her to increase her power have been sought and gained. She had few obvious social objectives, and instead seemed explicitly driven to gain more power through status, accumulation of assets (business and private) and profits.

Case 3: group-selected leader

In Case 3, the charismatic 'entrepreneur' was elected by the other women at the end of the initial training course. She was fairly young, in her early thirties, but commanded respect from the other women for her strength of character and her natural leadership ability. She also was from a more open-minded Tajik family, permitting her more mobility. At the time of the research, she was 40 years old with six children (four boys and two girls, including one handicapped child). With an illiterate mother and the death of her father when she was young, she was fortunate to be educated until she was 17 years old, and then was married. During the war years, her family was displaced from the neighbouring province of Parwan to different parts of Kabul, and then finally to Pakistan for a year. At the time of the research, her husband struggled with temporary employment in Kabul. Initially, they were living in a poor city neighbourhood (where the business was initiated), but with her (NGO paid) salary, her family later moved to a more central, progressive and affluent area of Kabul ('all of the families here have TVs!').

Before the project, the entrepreneur was mostly confined to the house, looking after her children. While having little experience in any type of economic activities, she was semi-literate and bold, and the other women perceived her as stronger than the rest of the women, and thus voted for her to be the head of the group. She was described to have notably grown in her role in the business, and during the research was described to be acting and dressing 'like a proper director'! She was considered to be stronger than her husband, and emerging to be the main family decision-maker (and breadwinner). The entrepreneur has led in shaping emerging rules and routines (mostly in taking over INGO-controlled tasks), troubleshooting and determining the overall direction of the business, including their links to other firms. Her initial motivations to participate in the project were once again (in part) financial but she also had a social interest to join the group. With experience and power, she has secured a strong position in the company as head, and has become both mobile and confident. Yet in so doing, she has distanced herself from the other women. During the research, her motivations lay with making profits and achieving company success, and becoming powerful. While recognising her fellow business colleagues, she appeared to feel less association with them as the business evolved, particularly as they had different ethnic backgrounds, with their strict Pashtun families and remained more conservative (and she made little effort to change this). Her social objectives beyond the business were fairly limited. Meanwhile, she had strong emerging political aspirations to be head of a women's council in her native province of Parwan.

6.2.3 Power holders driven by control (and community development)

In this research, the power holders pertained to the community leaders in the business locale. They included the local neighbourhood council (city), the Community Development Council (CDC) (village), and arguably, most important, the traditional *shura*. These bodies tended to comprise the overall community head (the government-elected *arbab* or *wakil)*, senior elders and the mullah(s). The village *shura* tended to be further supported by local regional commanders (strongmen). Underneath the CDC (only in the rural areas) was the female CDC/*shura* (new CDC women's subcommittee), comprising mostly elders' wives. Across the cases, power holders were motivated to support the emerging institutions by a mix of personal and public interests. These included maintaining social control and order, and community development. In their role of rule 'authorisation' (agreeing rule scope and applicability, and providing their consent), power holders endeavoured to create boundaries around women's evolving new institutions, and, where approved, ensure wider support in the community for these new habits and practices through educational or intimidation strategies. In progressive cases, some power holders had leveraged the women's work to promote more equitable and participative community development.

Case 1: village shura

In Case 1a, there was both a strict male *shura* with a women's *shura* subcommittee, and a strong local commander that held sway over the village. Key powerful figures in the *shura* included the *shura* head and the mullah, 'the second head of the village'. The latter was seen as moderately powerful, but his support was viewed as crucial for gaining consent on new practices. The local commander appeared to be able to rule over village members, and to resolve problems quickly. The women coordinated their activities initially through the women's *shura*. Motivations for the elite interest and coordination in this village lay predominantly in the need to maintain control. In Case 1b, there was a strict but increasingly flexible and progressive male community *shura*. Key powerful figures in this group included the *shura* head (main project focal point), the village *arbab*, and the village mullah. Once again, the women coordinated their activities through the women's *shura*. Motivations for the elite coordination in the second village lay in the need to maintain control, but later they were also motivated to actively promote women's economic development. This was in part due to a powerful and respected influential commander that was openly supportive of the women's work. The power holders from Case 1a tended to be less flexible than in Case 1b, perhaps due to the more conservative environment and less charismatic champions (see section 6.2.4).

Case 2: village shura with identified volunteer champion

In Case 2a, there was an open and fairly educated male *shura*. Key powerful figures in the community included the head of the *shura* and the village *arbab*. The former was a previous local commander, and was well respected and an influential member of the community ('even against the mullah!'). He was known for his progressive ways and was more educated. He acted as the designated 'champion' in the farming enterprise project. The village leader, the *arbab*, was more conservative and illiterate. The INGO staff described him as requiring more time to 'open up to new ideas and systems', particularly those introduced by 'outsiders'. Meanwhile, the female (secondary) *shura* was deemed useful for their coordination with the male *shura*. Other 'power holders' included religious authorities and advisors: the main mullah, and local *kaari* and *kaaria* (village holy men and women). The main motivations for the elite engagement in this first village lay in the need to keep social control, as in the previous case. But for more progressive members of the *shura*, their motivation has evolved to also include an interest in women's socio-economic development. In the less receptive village of Case 2b, there was a less amendable *shura*, however, with more difficult religious clerics. Key powerful figures in this community included the *shura* head (one of the husbands of the lead farmers), and again the village *arbab* and the main village mullah. Whilst the rest of the *shura* members were conservative, the actual *shura* leader was progressive and the key village 'champion' of this project with unusual libertarian views. Yet at the end of the research, his efforts appeared to have been halted with his abrupt removal from the village, in what appeared to be a bizarre and suspicious turn of events.[4] Meanwhile, the village *arbab* was very traditional, and the village mullah was highly distrustful of outsiders. The latter was particularly well known for 'spying' on the women's activities in the early part of the project (through his wife!), although he was described to be more supportive during later phases. In terms of coordination with the women's *shura*, since the entrepreneur was already head of both the village and cluster village women's (secondary) *shura*, she dominated this forum and controlled any potential feedback to the (male) *shura*. The main motivations for the elite coordination in this second case lay in both social control and a strong desire to ensure that the village culture and local order were not disrupted (i.e. there was a notable fear of change).

Case 3: Neighbourhood shura with paid local coordinator

In Case 3, the local male *shura* was headed up by a city representative known as a *wakil*. Situated in a poor ethnically Pashtun neighbourhood, the *shura* was known to be strict, traditional and mistrustful of outsiders. While appearing conservative, the *wakil* has emerged to be instrumental in supporting the women's work, facilitating elder/mullah meetings with the NGO staff and otherwise, reassuring and troubleshooting with husbands and quelling local rumours and gossip. Yet he was (in part) financially motivated, in receiving a monthly stipend from the NGO. Nonetheless, he has acted as a vital bridge between the women (with NGO support) and the male *shura*, since there was no female *shura* (as was common in the urban areas at the time). Other 'power holders' included the local mullah and the community elders. The main motivations for elite coordination in this case lay in the need to maintain control, and in monitoring the new evolving practices of the women, within careful agreed Pashtun boundaries.

Looking across each of the cases, it is clear that actors have had varying motivations and interests in supporting and interacting in institutional processes related to the women's work. In terms of the NGOs, there was a strong common desire for women's socio-economic development – particularly in roles beyond the household – although they differed in their capacity and determination for equitable outcomes. Notably, many of the female NGO staff have also faced their own struggles for empowerment, and their community work has become a greater part of a personal crusade for change. In the case of the entrepreneurs, their general initial motivations lay (mostly) in increasing their household incomes and social interaction (although in one case, power was the initial motivation, and in another there was a strong sense of obligation). Later, in addition to business objectives, entrepreneurs were motivated to different degrees by either social outcomes or in gaining personal power. Finally, the power holders were primarily motivated by preserving social order and control; although, in two cases, more progressive elements were later (equally) interested in equitable community development.

6.2.4 Appreciating local conditions within greater Afghan context

Towards understanding actor strategies, it is necessary to further unravel the particularities of the micro-context in each case. While residing within the greater

Afghan context (Chapter 3), it is pertinent to briefly assess and identify the key attributes of the local situation for each case/sub-case, expanding upon initial overviews in Chapter 1. In appreciating these dimensions – including ethnicity, local cultural norms, levels of wealth and typical livelihoods – alongside the character of the power holders, critical insights may be generated into the relative nature of the context, particularly levels of openness and trust (regarding outsiders and new ideas), and stability. It is worth noting that over the course of the business lifespan, the broader country context has changed significantly, with new ideas slowly percolating from nearby countries to the cities, and even to sub-urban communities, through TV and new media. For wealthier urban households, this has brought in new perspectives on family life, and the roles of women. As a consequence, in these households, attitudes and practices had begun to slowly change, influencing women's work, education and marriage. Yet for the majority of rural and poorer households, with little access to such media, and where attitudes remain traditional, there had been very little change in local practices. Below, I expand upon the environmental attributes particular to each case, and levels of relative trust, stability and openness, as indicated by the nature of local power holders, local observed fragility and receptivity to outside ideas.

Case 1: village realities differentiated by nature of elites

In Case 1, Case 1a was situated in a large conservative Tajik village that was still fragile after many years of war, with medium levels of wealth and land (on average, two *jeribs* of land per family). At the start of the project, typical livelihoods prevailed, with men involved in agriculture and women largely confined to domestic spheres (handicrafts and gardening). Power holders were conservative and religious. These factors led to a lower-trust context that was less receptive to new ideas, particularly vis-à-vis women's development. Meanwhile, Case 1b was situated in a smaller (slightly less) conservative Tajik village, but with similar levels of wealth and land. Typical livelihoods also prevailed, with women largely confined to domestic spheres. Power holders were conservative, but there were progressive and respected elements that championed new ideas (e.g. the local commander). This led to a higher-trust context that was more open to change.

Case 2: village realities differentiated by wealth, culture and elites

Meanwhile in Case 2, Case 2a was located in a Tajik village close to the provincial centre with limited land (and where house renting was the norm), and medium to low levels of wealth. Traditionally male livelihoods have been in shop keeping in addition to agriculture (share-cropping), and low-skilled Kabul city daily labour. At the start of the project, most women were involved in traditional homebound activities, although there was one woman working as a teacher (who subsequently became the entrepreneur). The village was known to be receptive to outsiders and 'city' ways with progressive power holders. The facilitating NGO attributed this partly due to their displacement during the war years, mostly to Iran (with more progressive educational systems, and attitudes regarding women), the location of their village (close to the main road) and limited resources (forcing the men to find work in the city). This has led the village to be fairly open, with medium levels of trust. Meanwhile, in the contrasting land-rich and wealthier but more remote Tajik/Pashtun village of Case 2b (on average, five *jeribs* of land per family), traditional agricultural livelihoods dominated, with men involved in cereal farming and horticulture, and women working within the confines of the home with limited mobility. Power holders in this community were known to be strictly conservative with strong religious clerics. While households in this village were also displaced during the war, most went to the refugee camps on the border areas of Pakistan/Afghanistan (these camps were heavily Pashtun-dominated and conservative). This village was known to be both traditional and highly mistrustful of outsiders with closed attitudes.

Case 3: urban reality characterised by fragility and conservatism

Finally, in Case 3, the urban-based community was located in a poor, war-scarred *Pashtun* neighbourhood of Kabul. Preselected for its marginalisation, many families in this area had migrated from the conservative south of Afghanistan, and were internally displaced people (IDPs) during the 1980s and 1990s. The neighbourhood was both strict and fragile. Typical work for the men included shopkeeping or daily labour. As is common with poor urban-based Pashtun communities (see Chapter 3), women remained strictly housebound with sporadic home-based work in handicrafts. Very few educated women worked as teachers, and only a handful of women (widows) had other jobs (such as domestic helpers). The area was notably unstable, with low levels of trust and limited receptivity to new ideas.

Table 6.1 summarises these varying environmental characteristics across the cases, and highlights the implications for the context.

6.3 Examining actor strategies in institutional processes

Going beyond a single set of creative actors or 'institutional entrepreneurs', the case studies have drawn attention to the combined involvement of various key actors in transforming, designing, shaping and setting boundaries in institutional development with both positive and negative effects for resulting institutions (Chapters 4 and 5). The NGO has shown that outsiders can indeed be institutional change catalysts through the introduction of new institutions. Yet it is clear that the subsequent phases of institutional shaping, operationalisation and adoption require strong leadership and inclination from within the business itself. The entrepreneur – and her active supporters (close assistants) – have led this reformulation of the enterprise rules (routines, chain rules and collective action institutions) in negotiation with the local power holders and guided by the NGO (where capable and interested). This has been further tempered by the local context, in particular levels of stability, openness and trust. Looking more closely at key actor strategies across the cases, it is imperative to appreciate their diverse and subtle roles in institutional design and development.

Table 6.1 Summary of context variations across cases

Case number	Key characteristics of local environment	Power holders	Implications for context
1a	Highly conservative Medium levels of wealth/land Typical rural livelihoods for men and women Majority Tajik	Conservative	Stable Low trust Semi-open
1b	Medium conservative Medium levels of wealth/land Typical rural livelihoods for men and women Majority Tajik	Conservative then progressive	Stable Trust Open
2a	Limited resources/land Men involved in city work One woman teacher Majority Tajik Open village culture (receptive to new ideas)	Progressive	Stable Trust Open
2b	Land-rich village Highly traditional/religious/wary of outsiders Women limited mobility Majority Tajik/some Pashtuns	Conservative	Stable Low trust Less open
3	Fragile with limited resources War-stricken urban neighbourhood, displaced families Near to progressive areas but men mostly shopkeepers in area Pashtun	Conservative	Less stable Low trust Less open

6.3.1 NGOs as designers and advisors

As crucial institutional drivers, the NGOs were the 'principal designer and advisor' of emerging and innovative enterprise routines, towards permitting the start of women's enterprise while ensuring a supportive village environment in the development of fair rules. In the early trialling of institutions, the NGO coordinated with the male and female power holders, and the female staff problem-solved with producer women, resolving problems directly with their families (where possible). The NGO then supported the (re)shaping of the emerging institutions in coordination with the other women, and the power holders. Various tactics that were employed by the NGOs included *sociocultural/religious strategies* such as religious messages, proverbs and storytelling; *physical strategies*, including pious Muslim behaviour, dress and reciting prayers (particularly critical in low-trust and fragile environments); and *economic strategies*, including highlighting to women and their families the financial profits gained (as questions were raised over necessity of work). These were directed at reassuring and guiding participating women in both the early phases of the business, and as new boundaries were broached; and garnering the support of the power holders, immediate families and the wider public. As layers of market institutions were created, tactics have been refocused to ensuring proportionate and fair rules (if possible) within the groups (particularly in Cases 1 and 2, where stronger routines were fostered), or simply maintaining the business operations (as in Case 3, where routines were weaker). Tactics also sought to keep peace with the power holders and broader community to permit the development of gradual and productive market activity. The capacity of the NGO in both rule design, and in supporting the gradual development of rules has greatly affected the resulting nature of institutions. The INGOs/NGOs were also under varying pressures from the donors to meet targets influencing their strategies and choices. This was particularly evident in Cases 2 and 3, leading to the acceptance in Case 2b of the controlling entrepreneur (and exclusive institutions), and a micromanaging approach in Case 3. Where there were poor initial designs by the NGO, or weak support and excessive control over the business (e.g. Case 3), enterprises institutions have been underdeveloped and stifled in their potential evolution.

6.3.2 Entrepreneurs as shapers and diffusers

Meanwhile, the entrepreneurs (together with active workers) were the 'lead shapers and diffusers' of new enterprise routines, and were involved in (re)formulating and promoting the final rules to ensure agreed participation of various enterprise women in designated roles. In the early trialling of institutions, the entrepreneurs were specifically involved with deciding which women may have access to new revised institutions, and under which conditions. The entrepreneurs coordinated with both male and female power holders, problem-solved with producer women and their families, quelled rumours at wedding parties, and liaised with the NGOs. Similar to the NGO approach, tactics employed included *sociocultural/religious strategies* such as religious messages, proverbs and storytelling; *physical strategies*, including exhibiting 'model' behaviour, attending prayers, ensuring care on dress and warning women on boundaries (particularly in very low-trust environments with much resistance); and *economic strategies*, including highlighting salaries (where they received them), new technology and financial gains, and quickly distributing visible profits. In higher-trust villages, the women described 'everyone playing their part' in convincing the men. Women reported the men being 'afraid' of the new practices, and then later jealous (this caused some problems in lower-trust contexts such as Case 1a). In Case 2b, the controlling entrepreneur drew on coercive measures to keep women in check through threats and intimidation, and simply blocked other women's further development outright (e.g. she prohibited the activation of sales agents). In Case 3, the entrepreneur was such a dominant and powerful figure that her 'habits' progressed to a level that was almost unattainable for the other women, ironically inhibiting the other women's (socio-economic) development (and the entrepreneur did not really endeavour to delegate tasks to the worker women, or find ways to change the status quo). In stricter and low-trust contexts (e.g. Case 1a), the entrepreneur tended to place a high emphasis on physical persuasion in terms of pursuing model behaviour. In such conditions, there was also an observed tendency for close male family members to be brought in as assistants (since worker women were unable to carry out more public roles). Similarly, this was observed if entrepreneurs were controlling in nature (e.g. Case 3). In this situation, male family members have been brought in to do work that the other worker women cannot.

As layers of market institutions were created, going beyond initial routines, and overcoming marketing challenges (with *purdah* renegotiated for particular women), the trialling and reshaping processes led by the entrepreneurs appeared to become increasingly private, with less elaborate strategies needed or employed as their sphere of applicability was less (only selected women were participating), particularly where trust had been developed within the community. Tactics became directed at controlling and maintaining the order created within the groups with 'fair' payback (particularly in the case of progressive entrepreneurs), keeping peace with the power holders and broader community, and permitting the development of gradual market relations. Where there were more controlling entrepreneurs, as in Cases 2b and 3, higher-level rules (such as marketing) were strictly controlled, inhibiting the participation of other workers.

6.3.3 Power holders as authorisers and boundary makers

Finally, the power holders were the 'key authorisers' of new enterprise routines in their role of upholding order and peace within the broader community, and delimiting boundaries. Their main focus was ensuring that the public accepted their authorised rules, and that these were respected by the designated women. The power holders thus provided legitimacy for new rules. In the early trialling of institutions, the power holders observed the revised institution, upheld boundaries and problem-solved in coordination with the NGO. In the (re)shaping of the final 'product', power holders approved or disapproved proposals towards agreeing which women could have access to the various revised institutions (of *purdah* or enterprise rules), and under which conditions. Meanwhile, the female power holders (only present in Cases 1 and 2) observed the revised institution and reported back to male power holders, upheld boundaries and problem-solved/quelled rumours in coordination with the NGO. As described in the previous section, as higher market institutions were created, power holders tended to be less involved in the details (particularly if there was less required change in the underlying social institution of *purdah* for multiple women), although they remained informed. Where power holders were more controlling, in a low-trust environment, there has been less flexibility with regard to women's participation and business expansion. Reflecting these differences in motivations and behaviour, tactics of progressive power holders included *sociocultural strategies* (as above) and *economic strategies*, including highlighting to the women's families the (Islam-approved) financial benefits. For more conservative power holders, however, these extended to *physical strategies*, including threats and intimidation. These various tactics were aimed at keeping participating women 'in check' or secure, and ensuring support

Table 6.2 Exploring key actor strategies and their typical usage

Actor	Motivation/interest	Strategy	Under which conditions	Desired outcome
NGO Principal initiator and advisor	Functioning women's enterprise with women's participation	(i) *Sociocultural strategies* such as religious messages, proverbs and storytelling	Early participation	Routine rules exist with family and public support
	Supportive and conducive village environment		Community/family uncertainty	Market and cross-firm rules exist for selected women with support
	Proportionate and fair rules (later)		Emerging new roles of selected women	Rules are respected
			Free riding of women	
		(ii) *Physical strategies*, including pious Muslim behaviour and dress, reciting prayers at start of meetings	Fragile/low-trust environment with strong resistance	Power holders and public have trust in NGO and rules
		(iii) *Economic strategies*, including providing 'salaries', highlighting financial profits gained, and additional work/responsibilities of some members	Families are nervous and question continued work Creating fair rules with differing roles and responsibilities	Rules are culturally acceptable and bring dividends Rules are fair and respected
		(iv) *Technological strategies* such as the introduction of new productive equipment and methodologies	Used to accelerate returns in business	(Unintended) Rules gain reinforcement
Entrepreneur Lead advocates and shapers	Women's participation	(i) *Sociocultural/religious strategies* such as religious messages, proverbs and storytelling	Early participation Community/family uncertainty	Routine rules exist with family and public support
	Support of power holders and families		Pushing new boundaries	Market and cross-firm rules exist
	Successful enterprise with links to market and services		Free riding of women	Rules are respected

Actor (goal)	Strategy	Community response	Rules / outcome
	(ii) *Physical strategies*, including exhibiting 'model' behaviour, attending prayers, care on dress and warning women on boundaries, inviting *shura*/mullah's wives to check work	Fragile/low-trust environment; Strong initial resistance; Pushing new boundaries	Routine rules have family and public support
	(iii) *Economic strategies*, including new technology, financial salaries or gains and quickly distributing visible profits; and highlighting different levels of responsibilities of some members	Families question continued work; Supporting continued enterprise work with emerging hierarchies of women	Rules are culturally acceptable and bring fair dividends; 'Fair' payback for different roles
Power holders — Social order and culture maintained	(i) *Sociocultural strategies*, including religious messages, proverbs and storytelling	Early participation; Community uncertainty	Routine rules exist with family and public support under agreed terms
Key authorisers and legitimacy makers — Community peace; Participating women remain within agreed boundaries	(ii) *Physical/coercive strategies*, including threats and intimidation	New boundaries; Gossiping; Strong resistance; Women push boundaries too far	Market and cross-firm rules exist for selected women with support under agreed terms; Public have trust in new work and power holders; Rules remain within agreed boundaries
Community development	(iii) *Economic strategies*, including highlighting to the women's families the salaries and (Islam-approved) economic benefits	Families are nervous; Supporting continued enterprise work	Rules are culturally acceptable and bring dividends

from their immediate families and the wider public within the agreed reformulated cultural boundaries. Yet power holders were also shown to change during the course of the business influencing their desire for control, driven by their own evolving power interests, beliefs in new practices or as a result of the changing context. In the case of controlling or nervous power holders, institutions were shown to be constrained with little growth, (part) perpetuating the traditional market order and relying on (or requiring) men to carry out more public facing roles (e.g. Case 1a).

Adding new insights to the discourse, Table 6.2 draws together the diverse motivations of these three sets of actors, the different strategies deployed under different conditions, and for which desired outcomes. The NGO was shown to be predominantly motivated to create viable and sustainable enterprises with women's participation, and (if possible) equitable rules in a supportive and conducive environment. To this end, strategies aimed to ensure the establishment of basic rules for business functioning, broad community support for these emerging rules, and equitable rules as the business evolves. Meanwhile, the entrepreneurs tended to be motivated to secure women's collaboration (with power holders' and family support), and ensure the development of businesses with the necessary market links. Strategies thus aimed at instituting rules that were both supported, and that women could follow (and respect). Later, strategies aimed at garnering support for diverging roles and dividends, or alternatively boosting personal power. Finally, the power holders were mainly motivated to keep community order and control (with the local culture undisturbed as far as possible), and thus aimed to ensure that participating women remained within agreed boundaries. As such, strategies focused on overseeing and authorising rule development (scope and applicability), and obtaining public support and trust in these new arrangements. In progressive cases, motivations were shown to extend to an interest in women's community development (going beyond the business). Across these actors, key strategies were identified, including *sociocultural strategies* (e.g. religious messages) used during the early phases and in situations of uncertainty, or as new boundaries are pushed in *purdah*; *physical strategies* (e.g. appearance/dress) used to gain respect in the conservative environment, or more intimidating physical strategies used to keep women in check (if they go beyond boundaries); and *economic tactics* used to gain general support for ongoing rules, particularly with diverging responsibilities of women. A fourth set of *technological-oriented strategies* was used unintentionally by the NGO (particularly in Case 2), in the introduction of new equipment and methodologies. Yet these have had the significant effect of reinforcing the new and emerging rules.

It is worth mentioning that inherent tensions existed between these three sets of actors with their differing objectives and capacities, influencing the deployment of strategies and institutional outcomes. Reflecting more generally upon such tensions, this appears to be particularly critical for NGOs that are often process-oriented with a focus on community capacity building and achieving targets, but require the participation of the entrepreneur (and the other women), and the support of the power holders to carry out their 'uncertain' work. And, as indicated, entrepreneurs may have varying capacities and interests to deliver (as shown in Cases 2b and 3), or allow other women to join. And the research shows that power holders can pose further unexpected challenges to the NGO agenda, particularly if they are conservative or reactive to destabilising external events (such as insecurity in Case 3), affecting their willingness to allow participation and enterprise activities.

6.4 Dominant entrepreneurs and collective power

Advancing the literature on 'institutional entrepreneurs' (e.g. Li *et al.*, 2006; Battilana *et al.*, 2009), the research indicates the emergence of dominant entrepreneurs in enterprise, as indicated in Chapters 4 and 5 (although manifesting shades of variation within each type). Towards understanding this phenomenon, it is instructive to look initially at the agency of the NGO and power holders within the context, and their role in fostering local institutions and conditions. In terms of the NGO, in Case 1, the NGO was highly motivated to ensure cultural/religious sensitivity and fostered equitable well-thought-out institutions gradually over time. In Case 2, the NGO was keen to institute functioning institutions that were socially acceptable, but was less concerned with achieving equitable arrangements (and was particularly weak in Case 2b). In Case 3, the NGO was primarily motivated to ensure the culturally sensitive participation of women in the business, but lacked creativity in actual institutional development and had difficulty in relinquishing control. In terms of the power holders, in the less stable environments of Cases 1a, 2b and 3, the elite were acutely conservative, controlling the introduction and development of new ideas and practices, contrasting to more progressive power holders in Cases 1b and 2a. Reflecting upon these findings, the NGO and local power holders seem to display certain tendencies in institutional development. NGOs may be capable of fostering strong and equitable institutions, particularly in more stable (and higher-trust) conditions (e.g. Cases 1 and 2a); or they may be controlling or weak in less stable (and low-trust) conditions (e.g. Cases 2b and 3), and constrain evolving institutions. Meanwhile, power holders may be either progressive, and open to new ideas and supportive of evolving equitable institutions, or conservative and less trusting, and keen to maintain the status quo.

6.4.1 Emerging entrepreneur types and institutional characteristics

As a result of these broader actors' agency and contextual dynamics, two dominant types of entrepreneurs have tended to emerge, with crucial implications for broader institutional development. Looking across cases in Table 6.3, these two 'ideal' types of entrepreneurs appear to generate characteristic patterns of routines, chain rules and collective action institutions in enterprise. This is illustrated in the various rules emerging from the cases. Under conditions of higher stability with supportive NGOs and power holders, socially minded entrepreneurs have generated open institutions that are transparent and collectively agreed (Cases 1b and 2a). In terms of internal routines, these institutions were characterised by more flexibility and participation in rules for production, including work hours and related tasks. For example, in Case 1, women could swap workdays or make up missed days later. In terms of marketing and collective action, there was more collaborative agreement on tasks, and less rigidity in market responsibilities and in agreed women's movement. Yet such 'prosocial' entrepreneurs may be stifled in less conducive and conservative environments with strict power holders, generating more constrained institutions (Case 1a). Meanwhile, under conditions of low stability and mistrust where NGOs were weak, more selfish entrepreneurs have tended to generate more top-down, exclusive and controlled institutions with little

Table 6.3 Looking across cases: emerging entrepreneurs and institutions

Case number	Local conditions	NGO	Sector	Entrepreneur	Emerging institutions
1a	Stable	Fostering	Open	Quiet, ambitious	Open but constrained
	Low trust			Trailblazer (constrained)	
	Semi-open Conservative power holders				
1b	Stable	Fostering	Open	Strong, determined	Democratic and open
	Trust Open Progressive power holders			Trailblazer	
2a	Stable	Fostering	Open	Open, determined	Democratic and open
	Trust Open Progressive power holders			Trailblazer	
2b	Stable	Fostering but weak	Open	Controlling and power-hungry	Controlled, non-transparent, no flexibility
	Low trust Less open Conservative power holders			Gatekeeper	
3	Less stable	Constraining	Closed	Insecure, controlling	Controlled, non-transparent, little flexibility
	Low trust Less open Highly conservative power holders			Gatekeeper	

possibility for change. In these cases, the participation in rule development was minimal, the entrepreneur responsibilities and activities were less transparent, and the delegation of higher-level tasks was limited, with few opportunities for lower-level workers.

It is useful to elaborate on these emerging ideal entrepreneurs. The first type may be described as charismatic entrepreneurs that engender open, flexible institutions within the business. These entrepreneurs are public-spirited with a view to inclusiveness in enterprise, and an interest in promoting women's economic and social empowerment both within and outside of the business. As pioneering actors, these entrepreneurs can be described as 'trailblazers' in fostering new open institutions, and setting in motion new trends that go beyond the realm of the business. This type may flourish in higher-trust and stable micro-environments, with progressive power holders and the support of strong external actors. And their agency is indeed boosted by the support of these other actors. The second entrepreneur type relates to more controlling entrepreneurs that are motivated by power (and may be defensive and insecure), generating closed, tightly controlled and exclusive institutions. Driven by maintaining the broader status quo, these entrepreneurs can be described as 'gatekeepers' in keeping new practices to themselves or within a tight-knit group, and not permitting their diffusion or allowing new broader orders to emerge. These types tend to flourish in less stable, low-trust environments with controlling power holders, and where NGO actors may be weak or absent (e.g. Cases 2b and 3). Notably, in Case 3, the triple combination of conservative power holders (and low trust), engagement in a male-dominated sector together with a 'weak' NGO has generated an insecure controlling entrepreneur that acts partly out of self-protection.

Disentangling the various factors underlying the emergence of these two contrasting entrepreneurs, it is crucial to highlight key driving forces related to both actors and local conditions. In the more positive scenario, the influence of a strong external actor (i.e. the NGO), the presence of open power holders in a trusting and stable context, in addition to the active participation of enterprise women, have permitted the generation of capable trailblazer entrepreneurs. And where necessary, initial less capable and public-spirited entrepreneurs have been replaced (as described for Case 1b in Chapter 4). Interestingly, trailblazers may also emerge if some of the conditions do not exist (i.e. less supportive power holders) but are constrained in their efforts (Case 1a). Yet where NGOs are weak, power holders are conservative and the context is fragile (and the workers have little voice), gatekeepers have been more likely to emerge (and persist). And arguably, in such conditions without local support and trust, entrepreneurs may also become more defensive and self-oriented (e.g. Case 3). Overall, it is thus indicated that the dual influence of structure (the prevailing environmental conditions including levels of trust and stability) and agency (strength of the external actor; the participation of women in selection; and the openness of power holders) may together tend to generate specific types of entrepreneurs or allow them to persist. These dominant entrepreneurs shape the evolving nature of the enterprise institutions.

Dominant entrepreneurs and emerging incentives

As highlighted by Adam Smith (1759) in *The Theory of Moral Sentiments*, the motivation for engagement in enterprise may not be merely rational or economically driven. Further, while entrepreneurial abilities may be randomly distributed throughout populations and situations, entrepreneurial opportunity and its social sanctioning may affect economic participation (Baumol, 1990). It is pertinent to examine the diverse incentives influencing entrepreneurs to engage in enterprise that have emerged in the course of enterprise, beyond just financial gain. In the case of trailblazer entrepreneurs, there is a strong social incentive to cultivate new norms for women within and outside of the group, to improve the lives of women and their families, and to create new opportunities for girls and women in the future. And notably, to promote this goal, the entrepreneur had tried to garner the support of women workers. In the case of gatekeeper entrepreneurs, incentives may be more political in maintaining or expanding her own power in the business and community. Often in her case, she may rely on existing power holders to meet her objectives. In some cases, gatekeepers may be forced to keep tight control as a 'protective' strategy to maintain her strong role in the business in a hostile environment (as in Case 3). Table 6.4 illustrates dominant types of entrepreneurs, the conditions under which they thrive, their various characteristics, and emerging personal motivations/interests.

6.4.2 Drawing on collective power for group or self-interest

In corroboration with the theory (particularly in this chapter and Chapters 2 and 5), the research suggests that creating and shaping institutions, and facilitating their diffusion and further development tends to involve interactions between people (Fligstein, 2001). Social networks have contributed to the scope of rules and their

Table 6.4 Dominant entrepreneurs and motivations/interests

Entrepreneur	Ideal conditions emerging	External actor	Characteristics	Core personal motivation/ interests
Trailblazer	Stable Medium-high trust Open culture Progressive power holders	Strong	Public-spirited	Social incentive
Gatekeeper	Unstable Low trust Exclusive industry Protected culture Conservative power holders	Weak or absent	Controlling/ self-interest Insecure/ defensive	Power incentive

reshaping, rule learning and enforcement, and rule adoption and broader diffusion. They have also contributed to the initial emergence of rules, rule credibility, and rule evolution. From a limited circle of family connections, the entrepreneurs have tended to develop four tangible networks at a group, community, market and cross-firm level. The first immediate network includes the active workers in the group (the entrepreneur's direct allies). This network contributes to the shaping of rules, and their diffusion and adoption. The second network includes key ties with power holders, including the elders' and mullahs' wives. This network influences rule type used, boundaries and flexibility for change. They also determine the extent of rule adoption. The third network includes the local buyers (e.g. shopkeepers), and support services for example, for packaging, agricultural resources and training. This network determines the scope of rules for the market in terms of interaction and frequency. The fourth network includes links to other similar groups or firms for market collaboration. These ties may influence existing rule credibility, and lead to imitation and learning (particularly routines and institutional arrangements). The network also influences the scope of rules, rule evolution and development, and the emergence of new rules. Yet the scope/nature of these four networks are influenced by both actors and local conditions, and differ in diversity and size across the cases. Networks are also interrelated with implications for their development.

Intertwined influence of actors and structure in network scope and development

Building off Bird (1988), Klyver and Schott (2011) argued that pre-existing networks shape entrepreneurial intentions. Yet the research suggests that entrepreneurial intention combined with broader actor agency, in addition to structural influences, also shapes (emerging) enterprise networks. Within the enterprise, entrepreneurs can draw on worker allies to boost their agency and support further network development. But gatekeeper entrepreneurs may view these workers as threats to their position and power, and thus not engage in this immediate network or value it as a resource. Or workers may also choose not to cooperate for cultural reasons (e.g. Case 3). Meanwhile, it is the agency of local power holders (i.e. the second network) that can most determine the extent and development of external market and cross-firm networks (in terms of both size and diversity). But a third party in the form of the external NGO can play an important intermediary role in facilitating entrepreneur network development through their links to power holders, and through facilitating new enterprise connections (e.g. through physically introducing the enterprise women to suppliers and buyers). It is instructive to look at the emerging scope of market and cross-firm links across the cases. In Case 1, the enterprise networks to buyers and service providers were extensive. And since they were linked to other villages, their horizontal links were also significant. It appears that links in Case 1a were more strictly controlled by the power holders than in Case 1b, however, particularly in terms of which women could participate and the frequency of interaction. Meanwhile, in Case 2, in terms of the diversity of local buyer links, this was measurably less than in Case 1, although the buyers themselves were bigger market actors. Links to support services were similar in both Case 1 and 2, however. Notably, in Case 2b, more value was placed by the entrepreneur on ties to potentially useful higher-level power holders (e.g. government ministries, for obtaining funds) than on market ties. Finally, in Case 3, links to buyers were almost non-existent, partly as a result of the exclusive sector, although they had relatively good links to services, with a few ties to technical support firms for potential collaboration through subcontracting.

These findings indicate a contrast between emerging dominant entrepreneur networks. With the support of the NGOs and power holders, the networks of public-spirited trailblazers (especially Cases 1b and 2a) are indicated to be diverse across social and economic realms, and evolving in vein with group interests. Yet these are constrained in the economic realm where power holders are more conservative (e.g. in Case 1a). Meanwhile, in the case of self-oriented gatekeepers (Cases 2b and 3) where NGOs are weak, networks are directed more towards powerful players within the environment for the personal gain of the entrepreneur. In these cases, there is less interest in achieving network diversity within the general marketplace and across similar firms (cooperative relations). Yet it is worth considering that networks may be particularly challenging where there are additional industry barriers, insecurity or complex social pressures (*Pashtunwali*) (such as in Case 3). In summary, building off Graf (2011), the NGOs have been shown to be able to broker or mediate between the entrepreneurs/active workers in the negotiation and development of new networks, initially with the power holders in the community, and later as permitted, in formulating market and firm networks (see Figure 6.1). Yet in vein with Helmsing and Vellema (2011) and barriers to entry in institutional construction, strict industry preferences can also inhibit market networks, limiting NGO efforts.

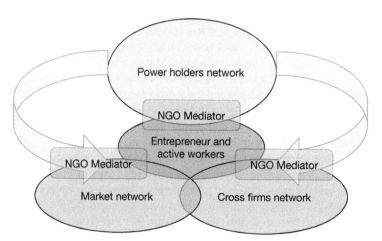

Figure 6.1 Emerging networks and their interrelations

Source: Author's own illustration

6.4.3 Entrepreneurial networks in institutional diffusion and adoption

As indicated in the literature, enterprise is firmly embedded in social structures (Greve, 2003), facilitating potential access to resources, boosting performance (Wernerfelt, 1984) and aiding collective action (Maguire *et al.*, 2004). These evolving networks are shown to be rooted in local codes of conduct, relations and power (Nordstrom, 2000), shaped by individual attitudes and norms (Ajzen, 1991), and affected by local stability (Uzzi, 1996). Looking across the cases, emerging networks crucially influence both rule development, and broader diffusion and adoption through actor agency (Redmond, 2003; Granovetter, 2005; Becker *et al.*, 2006). In particular, it is the agency of entrepreneurs and her active workers that is critical in permitting and facilitating the diffusion and adoption of lower-level institutions, with the approval of power holders. In low-trust contexts (Cases 1a, 2b and 3), the existence of tightly controlled networks can lead to increased exclusivity of certain women in the business, and constrain broader uptake. While power holders can issue their approval, and articulate boundaries, final levels of adoption may ultimately be determined by the entrepreneur, and family power holders (influenced by the character and reputation of the entrepreneur and the enterprise networks). In a highly conservative context, the personal credibility of the entrepreneur and her allies was critical in this regard through adherence to religious institutions, as in Case 1a (e.g. pious behaviour). In contrast, some controlling entrepreneurs may draw on their individual networks – particularly power holders – to secure their own self-interest, deliberately blocking other (potential) adopters (e.g. Case 2b). Where trust is improved and power asymmetries are lower, access may be more open, allowing unregulated diffusion of new institutions by trailblazer entrepreneurs and their networks (Case 2a in particular). Yet the strength of the entrepreneur's power holder networks – and endogenous politics (determining public motivations and interests) – can also influence the potential extent of engagement in, and receptivity towards, institutional innovations, influencing the overall uptake of institutions and affecting the scope of diffusion.

In addition to facilitating network development, the influence of 'external' agency – through the NGO – has been also notable in institutional diffusion and adoption. Returning to Graf (2011), a third-party 'broker' is described as serving two functions for the system: external knowledge sourcing in generating novelty, and enabling diffusion within the local system. In the research, the NGO has proved that they can be instrumental in both generating novelty through institutional innovation, and aiding institutional diffusion. Diffusion can be supported through fostering enabling conditions such as local stability and trust, encouraging more open-minded and supportive power holders, facilitating new power holder links, and enhancing the credibility of entrepreneurs to allow diffusion through networks. For example, in Cases 1b and 2a, power holders have become more progressive in part due to the NGO influence. Meanwhile, in Cases 1a, 1b and 2a, the entrepreneurs describe the NGO supporting new links to the female *shura* to coordinate with the male *shura*.

Table 6.5 summarises evolving networks and levels of diffusion and adoption in institutions across cases. In the case of strong trailblazer public-spirited

Table 6.5 Character of emerging networks across cases, and nature of diffusion/adoption

Case number	Entrepreneur	Network				Nature of diffusion/ adoption
		Active workers	Power holders	Market	Cross-firm	
1a	Trailblazer	Tight	Controlling	Dynamic/ restricted	Open/ restricted	Semi-inclusive
1b	Trailblazer	Open	Becoming more open	Dynamic/ open	Dynamic/ open	Inclusive
2a	Trailblazer	Open	Becoming more open	Dynamic/ open	Dynamic/ open	Inclusive
2b	Gatekeeper	Limited	Controlling	Static	Controlled	Exclusive
3	Gatekeeper	Limited	Controlling	Limited	Limited	Limited

entrepreneurs (Cases 1b and 2a), there are more open and dynamic networks, and there is fairly unregulated diffusion and adoption of institutions. Yet where power holders remain controlling in less trusting contexts (Case 1a), trailblazer networks are inhibited, and diffusion and adoption are more restricted. In the case of gatekeeper power-motivated entrepreneurs (Cases 2b and 3), networks are more controlled or limited with exclusive levels of diffusion and adoption.

6.5 Concluding remarks

This chapter has endeavoured to unravel the complexity of 'agency' within institutional processes in the research, situating this in the prevailing micro-contexts. Initial discussions expanded on theories of 'institutional entrepreneurs' and their diverse strategies, the role of networks and collective agency, building off Chapters 2, 4 and 5. Looking across the cases, the interaction of three sets of actors has been shown to contribute in different degrees to institutional development. And reflecting on later outcomes, beyond just distance from power structures (Day, 1994), it is the agents' negotiation of cultural norms and local conditions that can influence the scope and stability of innovations in institutional processes. In exploring actor involvement, the chapter examined evolving agent interests and motivations, and the characteristics of the local context, to deconstruct subtle actor strategies in the process of rule-making, shaping and enforcement. Catalysing institutional processes, NGOs played an innovative role in initiating new and revised institutions – drawing on social/religious strategies – and were an important mediator between power holders and entrepreneurs. Meanwhile, local power holders played a significant role in new rule authorisation, creating legitimacy and articulating boundaries. Finally, entrepreneurs led in reshaping the institutions and facilitating their uptake, and were characterised by charisma and power. Two dominant entrepreneurs were highlighted: trailblazers, emerging under more stable conditions and generating more participative institutions, and gatekeepers, emerging under less stable conditions and generating more exclusive institutions.

Going beyond individualism, the chapter has elaborated on the development of actor networks in enterprise and institutional processes. Rather than looking at networks shaping entrepreneurial intentions (Klyver and Schott, 2011), the empirical research has looked at intentions and actor agency – moderated by structure – influencing the scope and diversity of emerging networks. Boosted by the agency of NGOs and progressive power holders, public-spirited trailblazer entrepreneurs were shown to foster diverse networks across multiple realms. Meanwhile, gatekeeper entrepreneurs, in a situation of weaker NGOs and strict power holders, were more self-motivated to nurture restricted and homogenous networks of powerful people. In revisiting Granovetter's (2005) core principles of social networks and economic outcomes, insights from this research contribute to better appreciating the influence of culture, agency and process (Emirbayer and Goodwin, 1994), and interaction with structure. First, in terms of network density in facilitating norm enforcement, the tight-knit groups have indeed aided new norm enforcement, although these norms have been heterogeneous. And the entrepreneur, as head of the network, has controlled the development of these norms and norm enforcement, drawing attention to additional power dimensions. Second, in terms of the importance of 'structural holes' (Burt, 1992), nuances of power, agency and structure have provided further depth to this notion. Through bridging structural holes, the (varying) agency of NGOs has been notable in playing a brokering role (Graf, 2011) towards facilitating the women's different network development, with the approval of local power holders. And as the women transgress social norms in forming new controversial market relations beyond the household, the NGO has endeavoured to reinforce the women's credibility and increase levels of trust. Finally, considering the principle of the 'social embeddedness' of the economy, this lies at the very heart of the research cases. Social structure indeed presents environmental barriers in business, and delimits options. Yet norms can be transformed, although there are social 'costs' (loss of tradition), although these 'costs' may also lead to new opportunities.

In further examining the influence of allies and networks, I drew attention to collective power in broader institutional processes of learning, adoption and diffusion. Going beyond the four constructs of organisational learning (Huber, 1991), Acemoglu *et al.* (2011) highlighted the need to look closer at heterogeneous preferences, and the influence of particular actors in learning processes. Similarly, Redmond (2003) described the importance of considering individual agency and social structure in the diffusion of innovations. In the research, actors, trust and prevailing social norms have influenced both the pace and scope of diffusion of new enterprise practices, with different rules assigned for different enterprise members. Using Redmond's terminology, the entrepreneurs play a lead role in the remoulding and establishment of innovations, and may be described as 'innovators' (even if the initial innovation is presented by the NGOs). Meanwhile, their close allies may be regarded as 'adopters' and the rest of the group as 'followers'. Where there is more trust and stability, public-spirited trailblazer entrepreneurs and their allies tend to foster more open networks with dynamic diffusion and adoption of democratic practices. This contrasts with self-oriented gatekeepers in less certain contexts, with more controlled and exclusive networks, constraining the scope of diffusion and adoption of broader institutions. Yet from a demand perspective, and highlighting individual preferences, the women as 'adopters or followers' have also asserted their own preferences in choosing whether to follow new practices (voluntary) in view of the social outcomes.

Drawing this chapter together, the research has shown (multiple) agency in institutional processes to be influenced by skills, knowledge and capacity (critical in institutional design), and shifting motivations and interests (critical in institution reformulation, articulating boundaries and facilitating their diffusion), leading to diverse strategies of actors in enterprise. The individual and collective agency of entrepreneurs in particular may also be boosted or thwarted by others' agency. Further to this, agency has been shown to be both affected by structure (local trust, stability), and to affect structure, through transforming existing norms and creating new degrees of trust and stability. Yet agency and institutional processes remain fragile in a greater context of political and economic uncertainty.

Notes

1 The INGO was a keen promoter of the '*Making Markets Work for the Poor*' approach to value chain development, with notions that poor people can simply be trained and organised, and then connected to markets.

2 It is worth noting that the overall interests of the INGO were in the sustainability of the work in general, and less attention was paid to dominant entrepreneurs or fair institutions (particularly towards the end of the project). Meanwhile, the motivations of the local NGO were predominantly financial – with the women's project potentially leading to further donor funds – and hence, there was little future interest in promoting equitable arrangements.

3 *Bacha posh* is a rural phenomenon in Afghanistan where girls are brought up as boys. This is elaborated in the following description:
'Afghan families have many reasons for pretending their girls are boys, including economic need, social pressure to have sons, and in some cases, a superstition that doing so can lead to the birth of a real boy. Lacking a son, the parents decide to make one up, usually by cutting the hair of a daughter and dressing her in typical Afghan men's clothing. There are no specific legal or religious proscriptions against the practice. In most cases, a return to womanhood takes place when the child enters puberty. The parents almost always make that decision. In a land where sons are more highly valued, since in the tribal culture usually only they can inherit the father's wealth and pass down a name, families without boys are the objects of pity and contempt. Even a made-up son increases the family's standing, at least for a few years. A *bacha posh* can also more easily receive an education, work outside the home, even escort her sisters in public, allowing freedoms that are unheard of for girls in a society that strictly segregates men and women. But for some, the change can be disorienting as well as liberating, stranding the women in a limbo between the sexes . . .' (Nordberg, 2010).

4 Towards the end of the research, news came of the *shura* member's arrest for apparent 'collaboration' with the Taliban.

References

Acemoglu, D., Dahleh, M.A., Ozdaglar, A. and Lobel, I. (2011) 'Bayesian learning in social networks', *Review of Economic Studies*, 78: 1201–1236.

Ajzen, I. (1991) 'The theory of planned behavior', *Organisational Behaviour and Human Decision Processes*, 50: 179–211.

Aldrich, H.E. and Zimmer, C. (1986) 'Entrepreneurship through social networks', in D.L. Sexton and R.W. Smilor (eds), *The Art and Science of Entrepreneurship*, New York: Ballinger.

Allen, T.J. (1977) *Managing the Flow of Technology: Technology Transfer and the Dissemination of Technological Information within the R&D Organization*, Cambridge, MA: MIT Press.

Amis, J., Slack, T. and Hinings, C.R. (2004) 'The pace, sequence, and linearity of radical change', *Academy of Management Journal*, 47(1): 15–39.

Barrett, F., Thomas, G. and Hocevar, S. (1995) 'The central role of discourse in large-scale change: A social construction perspective', *Journal of Applied Behavioural Science*, 31: 352–72.

Battilana, J., Leca, B. and Boxenbaum, E. (2009) 'How actors change institutions: towards a theory of institutional entrepreneurship', *The Academy of Management Annals: A Journal of the Academy of Management*, 3(1): 65–107.

Baumol, W. (1990) 'Entrepreneurship: productive, unproductive and destructive', *The Journal of Political Economy*, 98(5): 893–921.

Becker, M.C., Knudsen, T. and March, J.G. (2006) 'Schumpeter, Winter and the sources of novelty', *Industrial and Corporate Change*, 15: 353–71.

Bird, B.J. (1988) 'Implementing entrepreneurial ideas: the case for intention', *Academy of Management Review*, 13: 442–53.

Boettke, P. and Leeson, P. (2009) 'Two-tiered entrepreneurship and economic development', *International Review of Law and Economics*, 29(3): 252–9.

Boje, D. (1995) 'Stories of the storytelling organization: a post- modern analysis of Disney as "Tamara-land"', *Academy of Management Journal*, 38: 997–1035.

Borch, O.J. (1994) 'The process of relational contracting: developing trust-based strategic alliances among small business enterprises', in P. Shrivastava, A. Huff and J. Dutton (eds), *Advances in Strategic Management*, 10B: 113–35.

Burt, R.S. (1992) *Structural Holes: The Social Structure of Competition*, Cambridge, MA: Harvard University Press.

Bush, P. (1987) 'The theory of institutional change', *Journal of Economics Issues*, 21: 1075–1116.

Coleman, J.S. (1988) 'Social capital in the creation of human capital', *American Journal of Sociology*, 94: 95–120.

Coleman, J.S. (1990) *Foundation of Social Theory*, Cambridge, MA: Harvard University Press.

Czarniawska, B. and Sevon, G. (eds) (1996) *Translating Organizational Change*, Berlin: de Gruyter.

Davern, M. (1997) 'Social networks and economic sociology: a proposed research agenda for a more complete social science', *American Journal of Economics and Sociology*, 56(3): 287–302.

Day, D. (1994) 'Raising radicals: different processes for championing innovative corporate ventures', *Organisation Science*, 5(2): 148–72.

Emirbayer, M. and Goodwin, J. (1994) 'Network analysis, culture, and the problem of agency', *American Journal of Sociology*, 99(6): 1411–1454.

Fairclough, N. (1992) *Discourse and Social Change*, Cambridge: Polity Press.

Fischer, D.H. (1989) *Albinos Seed: Four Brittan Folkways in America*, Oxford and New York: Oxford University Press.

Fligstein, N. (1996) 'Markets as politics: A political-cultural approach to market institutions', *American Sociological Review*, 61: 656–73.

Fligstein, N. (1997) 'Social skill and institutional theory', *American Behavioural Scientist*, 40(4): 397–405.

Fligstein, N. (2001) 'Social skill and the theory of fields', *Sociological Theory*, 19(2): 105–25.

Ford, J.D. (1999) 'Organizational change as shifting conversations', *Journal of Organisational Change Management*, 12(6): 1–39.

Ford, J.D., Ford, L.W. and D'Amelio, A. (2008) 'Resistance to change: the rest of the story', *The Academy of Management Review*, 33(2): 362–77.

Gatignon, H. and Robertson, T.S. (1985) 'A propositional inventory for new diffusion research', *Journal of Consumer Research*, 11: 849–67.

Giuliani, E. (2005) 'Cluster absorptive capacity: why do some clusters forge ahead and others lag', *European Urban and Regional Studies*, 12(3): 269–88.

Gould, R.V. and Fernandez, R.M. (1989) 'Structures of mediation: a formal approach to brokerage in transaction networks', *Sociological Methodology*, 19: 89–126.

Graf, H. (2011) 'Gatekeepers in regional networks of innovators', *Cambridge Journal of Economics*, 35: 173–98.

Granovetter, M. (1978) 'Threshold models of collective behavior', *American Journal of Sociology*, 83: 1420–43.

Granovetter, M. (1985) 'Economic action and social structure: The problem of embeddedness', *American Journal of Sociology*, 91(3): 481–510.

Granovetter, M. (1992) 'Economic institutions as social constructions: A framework for analysis', *Acta Sociologica*, 35(1): 3–11.

Granovetter, M. (2005) 'The impact of social structure on economic outcomes', *Journal of Economic Perspectives*, 19: 33–50.

Green, S.E. (2004) 'A rhetorical theory of diffusion', *Academy of Management Review*, 29: 653–69.

Greenwood, R., Suddaby, R. and Hinings, C.R. (2002) 'Theorizing change: the role of professional associations in the transformation of institutionalized fields', *Academy of Management Journal*, 45(1): 58–80.

Greve, H.R. (2003) *Organizational Learning from Performance Feedback*, Cambridge: Cambridge University Press.

Hansen, E.L. (1995) 'Entrepreneurial networks and new organization growth', *Entrepreneurship, Theory and Practice*, 19(4): 7–19.

Helmsing, B. and Vellema, S. (2011) *Value Chains, Social Inclusion and Economic Development: Contrasting Theories and Realities*, Oxford: Routledge Studies in Development Economics.

Hodgson, G. (1988) *Economics and Institutions: A Manifesto for a Modern Institutional Economics*, Cambridge: Polity.

Hodgson, G. (2004) *The Evolution of Institutional Economics: Agency, Structure and Darwinism in American Institutionalism*, London: Routledge.

Huber, G.P. (1991) 'Organizational learning: the contributing processes and the literatures', *Organisation Science*, 2: 88–115.

Hwang, H. and Powell, W.W. (2005) 'Institutions and entrepreneurship', in S.A. Alvarez, R. Agarwal and O. Sorenson (eds), *Handbook of Entrepreneurship Research*, Dordrecht, The Netherlands: Kluwer Academic Publishers.

Jain, S. and George, G. (2007) 'Technology transfer offices as institutional entrepreneurs: the case of Wisconsin Alumni Research Foundation and human embryonic stem cells', *Industrial and Corporate Change*, 16(4): 535–67.

Klyver, K. and Schott, T. (2011) 'How social network structure shapes entrepreneurial intentions?', *Journal of Global Entrepreneurship Research*, 1(1): 3–19.

Larson, A. and Starr, J.A. (1993) 'A network model of organization formation', *Entrepreneurship Theory and Practice*, 17: 5–15.

Levitt, B. and March, J.G. (1988) 'Organizational learning', *Annual Review of Sociology*, 14: 319–40.

Li, D., Feng, J. and Jiang, H. (2006) 'Institutional entrepreneurs', *The American Economic Review*, 96(2): 358–62.

Maguire, S., Hardy, C. and Lawrence, T.B. (2004) 'Institutional entrepreneurship in emerging fields: HIV/AIDS treatment advocacy in Canada', *Academy of Management Journal*, 47(5): 657–79.

Malipiero, A., Munari, F. and Sobrero, M. (2005) 'Focal firms as technological gatekeepers within industrial districts: evidence from the packaging machinery industry', *SSRN eLibrary*, No. 717702.

March, J.G. (1999) 'A learning perspective on some dynamics of institutional integration', in M. Egeberg and P. Lægreid (eds), *Organising Political Institutions: Essays for Johan P. Olsen*, Oslo: Scandinavian University Press.

March, J.G. and Olsen, J.P. (1989) *Rediscovering Institutions: The Organizational Basis of Politics*, New York: Free Press.

Nelson, R.R., Peterhansl, A. and Sampat, B. (2004) 'Why and how innovations get adopted: a tale of four models', *Industrial and Corporate Change*, 13: 679–99.

Nordberg, J. (2010) 'Afghan boys are prized, so girls live the part', *New York Times*, 20 September.

Nordstrom, C. (2000) 'Shadows and sovereigns', *Theory, Culture and Society*, 17(4): 35–54.

Phillips, N., Lawrence, T.B. and Hardy, C. (2004) 'Discourse and institutions', *Academy of Management Review*, 29(4): 635–52.

Powell, W.W. and DiMaggio, P.J. (1991) *The New Institutionalism in Organizational Analysis*, Chicago, IL: University of Chicago Press.

Redmond, W.H. (2003) 'Innovation, diffusion, and institutional change', *Journal of Economic Issues*, 37(3): 665–79.

Rogers, E. (1962/1995) *Diffusion of Innovation*, New York: Free Press.

Shapero, A. (1982) 'Social dimension of entrepreneurship', in C.A. Kent, D.L. Sexton and K.H. Vesper (eds), *Encyclopedia of Entrepreneurship*, Englewood Cliffs, NJ: Prentice Hall.

Smith, A. (1759/2000) *The Theory of Moral Sentiments*, Amherst, NY: Prometheus Books.

Strang, D. and Sine, W.D. (2002) 'Inter-organizational institutions', in J. Baum (ed.), *Companion to Organizations*, Oxford: Blackwell.

Uzzi, B. (1996) 'The sources and consequences of embeddedness for the economic performance of organisations: the network effect', *American Sociological Review*, 61: 674–98.

Veblen, T. (1919/1998) 'Why is economics not an evolutionary science?', *Cambridge Journal of Economics*, 22: 403–14.

Vincenti, W.G. (1994) 'The retractable airplane landing gear and the Northrop "anomaly": variation-selection and the shaping of technology', *Technology and Culture*, 35: 1–34.

Wernerfelt, B. (1984) 'A resource-based view of the firm', *Strategic Management Journal*, 5: 171–80.

Wijen, F. and Ansari, S. (2007) 'Overcoming inaction through collective institutional entrepreneurship: insights from regime theory', *Organization Studies*, 28(7): 1079–1100.

Witt, U. (1989) 'The evolution of economic institutions as a propagation process', *Public Choice*, 62: 155–72.

Zelizer, V. (1978) 'Human values and the market: the case of life insurance and death in 19th-century America', *American Journal of Sociology*, 84: 591–610.

7   Towards a dynamic and interdisciplinary theory of institutional change

After all, the ways economic activities are organized, and the ways they link up with other institutions provide crucial ingredients of the setup of the whole social fabric. I do not think one is exaggerating by suggesting that understanding them better will give us also a better understanding of how contemporary democratic systems work, and also better ways to preserve and defend them.

(Dosi, 1995: 15)

The outcome of any serious research can only be to make two questions grow where only one grew before . . .

(Veblen, 1899)

This book has explored the fundamental question of how institutions change in fragile environments, going beyond the assumed 'tabula rasa' in neo-institutional theory towards appreciating more nuanced outcomes, and their influence on economic development. In the market arena, there are powerful institutions that define who participates, and the scope of that participation. Drawing off Chang (2002), this study has sought to appreciate the causal relationships within firms and in the local environment, departing from the conventional focus on the power between firms and profit distribution. Using an innovative approach, the empirical research has specifically examined the development of institutions in women's enterprise in Afghanistan through the transformation of a critical social institution, *purdah*. The case studies indicate the interaction of diverse actors (from both within and outside of the value chain) in the transformation of *purdah* and the formulation of enterprise institutions. This influences the nature of emerging rules – including degrees of equity and flexibility – shedding new light on the institutional change process.

In this final chapter, I draw together and endeavour to advance key arguments on institutional change, considering in particular core drivers of institutional processes, actors and networks, and institutional outcomes. I further reflect on the research cases and specific theories, and discuss new empirical insights supporting and challenging existing propositions. I consider why we are interested in the role of institutions in value chain creation, and the influence of dominant entrepreneurs (e.g. trailblazers and gatekeepers). Finally, and more generally, I also reflect on the research for the field of *development studies*, and highlight the critical value of interdisciplinary work straddling anthropology to economics in generating pertinent insights into institutional development, and broader processes of change in human society.

7.1 Multilevel drivers in institutional emergence

Towards integrating relevant insights from institutional political economy, evolutionary discussions and economic sociology, the overall study has endeavoured to go beyond the notion of 'efficiency' driving institutional processes, to explore the interaction of *diverse drivers* in institutional emergence, particularly in a fragile and informal setting. The research has examined the emergence of institutions in enterprise through the lens of women's *purdah*, a critical boundary social institution within the context of Afghanistan, which I argue influences entry, participation and the functioning of the value chain. At the core of traditional Afghan society – as in many Middle Eastern and Asian cultures – this social institution defines all aspects of women's lives influencing local norms, attitudes and practices, and delimiting the potential development of new institutions. In the research cases, this institution is transformed using progressive interpretations of religious/cultural codes and references by local actors. This process of transformation provides a subsequent anchor and opening for developing enterprise, and for the gradual formulation of enterprise institutions. Yet due to both shifting environmental and actor influences, outcomes vary with knock-on effects for the development of enterprise institutions. Expanding on earlier discussions, this section draws attention to notable aspects of institutional emergence: the nested nature of emerging institutions and their interconnectedness; socio-economic triggers and motivations; and the influence of trust.

7.1.1 Nested institutions in enterprise

In vein with Heckathorn (1984) and his description of 'nested' games, Ostrom (1990: 52) used the innovative concept of 'nested' rules to describe the linkages between rules, and their capacity for change. With such layers of rules, change was conceived to be more difficult for deeper level rules, with some rules considered fixed or exogenous. This concept was later used by Holm (1995) to describe nested organisational systems. Gomez (2008) further hinted at notions of nestedness in her study of exchange clubs, with local business groups linked to evolving higher-level organisations, and the issue of related – and potentially conflicting – rules and enforcements. Meanwhile, advancing related discussions of institutions and scale by Philo and Parr (2000), Parto (2008: 1014) suggested that institutions may further 'manifest at different levels of inter-relation, scales of governance, and in different spheres of the political economy'. This adds insights to institutional interaction and power. He identifies institutions as residing at the individual, organisational and societal level. Categorising institutions further according to their different roles and levels of formality, he distinguished between *informal behavioural* institutions as social habits, manifested as norms; *cognitive* institutions as mental models; *associative* institutions as facilitating mechanisms of social interaction; *regulative* institutions as 'prescriptions and proscriptions', denoting the boundaries of individuals and groups; and finally more formal *constitutive* institutions, as setting the frame of social relations and delimiting the boundaries of action.

Corroborating concepts of nestedness, the research cases have indicated the embedded nature of institutions within enterprise, and their ultimate anchoring in sociocultural institutions (and power relations). In rule generation, lower-level rules such as *purdah* (initially) influence the emergence and design of higher-level enterprise rules. And thus further desired innovations at higher levels may then require more fundamental changes and negotiations to lower-level evolving norms of *purdah*. Initially, tentative change in the sociocultural institution of *purdah* was deliberately introduced through changing ideas and perceptions (cognitive institutions). This enabled the development of internal routines related to the basic division of labour in production (primary enterprise level). Pushing boundaries further, chain routines were then agreed with regard to local supply and marketing (secondary enterprise level). Finally, the groups instituted collective action rules for cross-group marketing and exchange (tertiary enterprise level). These sets of enterprise rules tended to be created sequentially, and depended on lower-level rule formulation. The scope of each layer of enterprise rules seemed to be shaped by the core sociocultural institution (i.e. *purdah*) influencing both the nature and spheres of emerging business activities, and determining gradual rule formulation.

In the institutional development process, the research has highlighted the involvement of a multitude of actors in transforming, designing and shaping social institutions, and institutions in enterprise. External actors (such as NGOs) have shown that they can aid with the initial transformation and design of new institutions, in coordination with community power holders. They can also guide willing and capable entrepreneurs (and local supporters) in navigating local conditions and actors, to necessarily (re)shape the resulting design of institutions, towards the development of fair and appropriate rules in enterprise. And the process of reformulation cannot in fact be done without the involvement and support of these entrepreneurs (as the key implementers). Yet NGOs can equally play a less effective role through the poor design of institutions and/or later through constraining their evolution. Enterprise rules have proved dynamic and evolving within the respective context, but the scope of their evolution has remained grounded in the dynamism of the core sociocultural institution, largely determined by the entrepreneurs, and the broader influence of local conditions and key actors.

The 'institutional ripple effect' controlled by powerful actors

Adding insights to Ostrom (1990), the nature of the interdependence of 'nested' rules has been elaborated empirically in the research, to indicate spheres of applicability, scope of variation, and enforcement with overall control firmly resting with powerful actors (entrepreneurs and power holders). Specifically, the development of higher-level enterprise institutions has been conceived as being nested in lower-level enterprise routines, and finally embedded in the tightly regulated evolving social institution of *purdah*, entrenched in deeper cognitive institutions. With their proximity to social institutions, lower-level enterprise rules (such as routines) are indicated to require significant negotiation, and their sphere of applicability is shown to be larger since they extend to all enterprise participants. Lower-level rules may also manifest more variations than higher-level rules (i.e. within agreed internal routines), and there may be layers of rules for different enterprise members. There may also be stronger levels of enforcement of lower-level rules by the group members (due to their wider applicability). Higher-level enterprise rules (e.g. chain rules and collective action rules) build on existing rules for selected women but still require renegotiation of core rules in their formulation, with potential 'ripple effects' for lower-level rules as layers of institutions are established. For example, new chain rules will necessitate new agreements on *purdah* for selected women, and this may in turn influence their participation in internal routines. Higher-level rules may tend to apply to fewer women, and can be less transparent (if the entrepreneur wishes), with looser levels of enforcement by the group members, and enforcement instead through market actors or by similar-firms. This can create both suspicion and conflict within the group if poorly managed. These higher-level rules may be more quickly negotiated with local power holders, due to their limited sphere of applicability (less women involved).

In summary, it can be useful to view institutions as a series of overlying 'webs' or 'layers' with rules for different players, and different levels of enforcements and related power dynamics (see Figure 7.1). The use of concentric circles

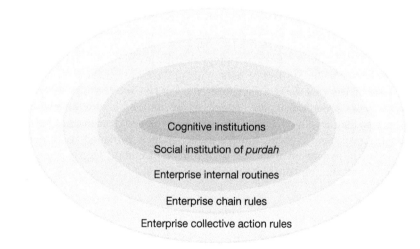

Cognitive institutions

Social institution of *purdah*

Enterprise internal routines

Enterprise chain rules

Enterprise collective action rules

Figure 7.1 Nested institutional development rooted in social and cognitive institutions
Source: Author's own illustration

illustrates the relationship between institutions, with the social institution and cognitive institutions at the core of the conceived 'onion' scheme, and emerging outer layers of enterprise institutions each with associative (describing mechanisms of social interaction), regulative (describing boundaries of social behaviour), and constitutive (describing physical and social (relations) bounds) dimensions. Negotiated changes to the core 'driver institution' can thus ripple out, and generate change in the broader overlying layers. Yet, beyond the research, it is perhaps important to emphasise that the nestedness of institutions in social institutions (and power relations) may not apply equally in every environment. Rather, it may be a particularly dominant phenomenon in more fragile developing country environments: where the state is weak and exclusive (informal) institutions persist (in terms of gender, caste, ethnicity), and where there are strong power asymmetries in society. As such, the phenomenon of the nestedness of enterprise institutions in social institutions may be considered 'context-dependent'.

7.1.2 Dual motivations in emergence of new embedded market institutions

While having established the nested nature of emerging rules, it is necessary to further explore the initial mechanisms precipitating change. Neoclassical economists draw attention to efficiency objectives and reducing uncertainty in institutional change and development. Taking a broader approach, scholars such as Lanzara (1998) and Johnson (1992) add further social dimensions and highlight the importance of 'societal inertia' (the durability of norms, rules and values) as providing the basic stability necessary for (path-dependent) institutional change (Hollingsworth, 2002: 7). Yet in critical points in history, there may be shifts in the equilibrium (Somit and Peterson, 1992). Battilana *et al.* (2009: 74) describes the enabling role of dramatic events such as social upheaval, technological disruption, competitive discontinuity, and regulatory changes that might upset the status quo and allow the generation of new ideas (Holm, 1995; Fligstein, 1997, 2001; Greenwood *et al.*, 2002; Child *et al.*, 2007). In more intentional institutional change, the role of change agents is particularly emphasised (Battilana *et al.*, 2009) and those that may be external to the system (Appiah, 2010; Helmsing and Vellema, 2011).

It is interesting to reflect on both triggers and motivations of institutional emergence in the study. Institutions have been shown to be interdependent and crucially anchored in a core social institution. At the outset, the deliberate introduction of a revised sociocultural idea/belief by an outside actor was crucial in setting institutional transformation and development in motion. While not viewed as a radical single event, the results were quietly revolutionary in permitting the initiation of new economic routines and establishing a new institutional path. Triggers for the subsequent development of enterprise institutions were then tied to the initiation of lower institutional layers (as discussed), and motivated by social and economic dimensions, with reasonable levels of trust/stability within the community, group and across groups. For example, in the initial transformation of the social institution, the trigger was the introduction of the new social idea and belief permitting the new concept of women's involvement in business. In the subsequent development of internal routines (necessary for group productive work), the trigger was the transformation of the social institutional barrier permitting rule formulation on women's physical place of work, technology and productive tasks and participation levels. In the secondary development of chain rules (necessary for market interaction), the trigger was the establishment of internal routines. In the final development of networking arrangements (notably, boosting potential economies of scale), the trigger was the establishment of external routines. Drawing this together, as a result of the socially embedded nature of rules, the motivations for the development of different tiers of institutions has been situated both in the evolving nature and needs of the business (and efficiency objectives) ('economic' motivation), and in the negotiation of social requirements ('social' motivation), including the scope of actor participation, the sphere of operation and the need for interaction with different players. This is captured in Table 7.1.

Table 7.1 Motivation and triggers of layers of nested institutional arrangements

Institutional layer	Primary 'economic' motivation	Secondary 'social' motivation	Trigger/conditions
Transformation of boundary social institution	Need for initiation of business, and engagement in production/technology	Conceptual Women's involvement in business	New sociocultural idea/belief introduced Community stability and trust
Internal routines	Need for collaborative production	Practical Sphere of operation Extent of participation	Environmental institution transformed Community/group stability and trust
External chain rules	Need for market transactions	Practical Sphere of operation Extent of participation Interaction with market players	Internal routines established Community/group stability and trust
Networking institutions (similar firms)	Need for economies of scale	Practical Sphere of operation Extent of participation Interaction with market players (other firms)	External chain rules established Community/group/ cross-group stability and trust

7.1.3 Nuanced group cooperation and coordination

In the emergence of institutions, it is also critical to understand how actors have managed to come together and cooperate, permitting the development of layers of institutions in enterprise. Under neoclassical economics, economic actors engage with one another due to self-interest. Going beyond this standpoint, institutional arrangements have been extensively discussed in 'collective action' theory exploring actor interaction, and how and why different arrangements can work (Ostrom, 1990, 2005). Further to this, Udehn (1993) suggests that it may be more pertinent to ask 'how much [cooperation]?' and 'under what conditions?'. In looking at cooperation within the cases, it is essential to appreciate the research context. As discussed in Chapter 3, Afghanistan is a complex environment, dominated by informality with persisting conflict and instability, and a limited rule of law. This has impacted upon the nature of society and markets with behaviour shaped by strong traditions, and societal-based networks and relations (and lower levels of trust outside of networks). Yet the common bond of religion (Islam) has permitted people to 'maintain a "shared language of good and evil"', crucial to the development of trust, social capital and the economic benefits that can proceed from this (Fukuyama, 1995: 270). Within Afghan communities, this has created a moral framework of common beliefs, values and norms that facilitates social and economic interaction, even without formal or codified institutions. Yet there remains a profound distrust of outsiders that may disrupt community order. In the research, this has necessitated NGOs that centrally were involved in institutional change and development to deliberately adopt local norms and rituals (of dress, prayers) to boost trust and credibility.

Tackling the free rider problem through values, trust and new institutions

Ostrom (1990) indicated that appropriate institutional arrangements could reduce the occurrence of free riding. Indeed, in the research, new enterprise institutions seemed to function particularly well at the decentralised level of the group (i.e. members respecting and adhering to rules), where the group made its own rules and felt ownership of those rules. And these set of institutions appeared to be suitable in a less certain context. Bringing in the role of culture and beliefs, the Durkheimian (sociological) view has highlighted the role that religion can play in binding groups together towards effective actor cooperation (Coser, 1977; Haidt, 2012). Religion is conceived to unite people through their 'common symbols and objects of worship', with physical activities such as ceremonies bringing people together and serving 'to reaffirm their common bonds and to reinforce social solidarity' (Coser, 1977: 136–9). Closely linked to this, Weber (1904) highlighted the power of religion in promoting certain values, and strengthening economic development (through famously fostering the 'Protestant' work ethic). In the research, Islamic prayer rituals at the start of meetings have indeed reinforced cooperation and good behaviour in the groups, nurturing 'moral capital', facilitating collective action and constraining individualism. And religious values of hard work and honesty embedded in Islamic sayings boosted this collaborative work. However, while the moral imperative to behave honestly and work hard in accordance with Islam was strong, and reinforced by the NGOs and the entrepreneurs, the *free rider* problem still arose in productive and collective work. Yet evolving institutional rules have been shown to further bolster cooperation, and created a structure for collective action, with later adjustments and some formalisation brought in where possible, facilitated particularly by more reflective and able NGOs (e.g. Cases 1 and 2).

It is instructive to look across the cases to further examine the free rider problem, and how it has risen and been overcome. At the outset, as indicated, initial cooperation between women has been facilitated through mutual trust from shared Islamic norms/values. The free rider problem was then shown to emerge later, and be resolved partly through institutional development. For example, in Case 1, the free rider problem has surfaced at both the group and inter-group level. At the group level, due to members taking extended time off for family functions (perhaps as family obligations), there was a need to bring in a new rule for calculating profit distribution based on the number of days worked in the month with the introduction of formal records (in Case 1a only). At the inter-group level, 'free riding' – in terms of inconsistent product quality by groups using the common label – has resulted in the breakdown of common marketing. This has proved to be a significant problem as the number of food processing groups has grown. Such factors have been perceived to threaten the reputation and market share of older groups, and have reduced the motivation for collaboration. This has led to mature groups (with strong leaders) demanding new conditions on the association membership (i.e. institutional elaboration). Meanwhile, in Case 2, production was individual, and villages engaged in joint marketing at exhibitions only (for premium produce). Free riding appeared to be less of a problem at the individual farmer level. Yet at the cross-group level within the village, this was indicated to remain a threat and could even be perverted by the entrepreneur. Lead farmers (group heads) participated in regular meetings with the entrepreneur to troubleshoot, report production and individual sales, and to discuss village contracts. It was clear that some group heads were more active than others. In Case 2a, there appeared to be a democratic system for groups to participate in village-level contracts, in which active lead farmers with good produce were rewarded. Yet in Case 2b, the entrepreneur could deliberately distort these group arrangements to condone free riding, particularly by favourable lead farmer connections (from her own clan). Finally, in Case 3, there was significant free riding of workers (days absent) at the beginning. This led to the development of a formal daily register for the fair calculation of monthly salaries (i.e. institutional formalisation).

Cooperation boosted by culture and solidarity structure

Taking a closer look at the culture and existing structures in cooperation, Lyon and Porter (2009) drew attention to local cooperative norms of behaviour (e.g. reciprocity and obligation) that can assist in spurring economic life in addition to social life after conflict. In Afghan communities, there is a strong tradition of collective voluntary work, with each household engaging in annual tasks such as canal cleaning. Yet such collective activities have been strained over the war years. In vein with this tradition, and creating an early platform for cooperation in Cases 1 and 2, women (of similar wealth) were initially deliberately organised into self-help groups (and in Case 2, women were even gathered from the same clan). Self-help groups aimed to provide a solidarity structure for common work, notably building off the culture of local self-help and ensuring a strong transparent structure for subsequent institutional arrangements. With a strong common cultural framework, these structures have indeed created initial trust, group cohesion and cooperation, and facilitated the development of enterprise routines. And where there is little organisation of women outside of families, this has created an initial social base, and enabled enterprise rules to be instituted on top of this structure. The structure has also encouraged members to partake in more voluntary activities for the collective good, without financial remuneration (such as supporting village festivals and events). The decentralised decision-making and profit distribution seems to have further increased accountability and transparency in rules, enhancing the motivation of members and levels of trust. These findings indicate the value of (indigenous) collective action institutions together with solidarity group structures (such as SHGs) as providing a strong foundation for further cooperation (and institutional development).

In this way, the SHG structure (i.e. the set of informal institutions concerning local collective/public goods) seems to have bolstered initial social cohesion and cooperation, facilitated group work, and enabled support for primary, secondary and tertiary level institutions in enterprise. With engagement in enterprise, the close-knit equitable SHG structure was shown to particularly boost both trust and confidence, and arguably eased the further transformation of *purdah* with family and power holder authorisation. In Cases 1 and 2, the group structure has both permitted cooperation within groups, and links between groups in and outside of the village, although there was more top-down decision-making in Case 2 with the entrepreneur positioned outside of the groups (and this was notably exploited in Case 2b). Yet as the businesses have grown, shifting roles has necessitated changes in work responsibilities and profit shares. This led to power differences between the women, and potential conflict without transparency and agreement on 'fair' rules. Meanwhile, in Case 3, women were gathered without common bonds or the framework of the self-help group, and had less structured enterprise routines. This has affected group cohesion, the possible delegation of tasks and the scope of cooperation.

Cooperation boosted by pleasure and struggle for women's freedom and value

Beyond institutional structures and a cooperative culture, women were also motivated to participate in the enterprise groups by a simple sense of enjoyment. In Afghanistan, women have limited opportunities for social exchange outside of the family. Bowles and Gintis (2011: 3) described the pleasure gained from cooperation with like-minded people, terming these feelings 'social preferences'. All of the participating women in the cases spoke with passion about their interest in collaboration to break free from their own confinement, highlighting their 'pleasure' in working together (even though financial gains were low). However, in some progressive cases, the group's motivation went beyond pleasure to embrace a greater purpose in the work, in the belief that this work represented their emancipation and the achievement of greater women's rights (greater social struggle) towards a new order in the community. Social psychologists describe this phenomenon as groups 'sacralising' goals of justice and freedom (Haidt, 2012). This higher 'women's struggle' was particularly harnessed by the entrepreneurs in Case 1 to further galvanise the women, creating a type of supra-religious fervour to their work and cooperation, and new group identity (Ansell, 1998). In their view, the work that they undertook was both a model for other women, and contributed to a greater crusade for change, towards new thinking regarding women's involvement in social, economic and political activities, and women's value as both capable and responsible citizens. Meanwhile, in Case 3, while the women were initially strongly motivated to join the group, for the worker women – with little results and a sense of frustration with the business, feelings of powerlessness and a growing gulf between them and the entrepreneur – they have grown bored, and the social incentive has diminished. This was further exacerbated by family pressures to reduce their level of participation or drop out.

7.1.4 Role of trust and authority in institutional development/ formalisation

Institutional emergence and formalisation was also influenced by trust and perceived degrees of authority. As discussed in Chapter 2, trust reduces the opportunity for purely self-driven behaviour and facilitates emerging economic activity. Cultural, social and historical contexts and prevailing social relations are described to influence trust levels and arrangements (Hollingsworth and Boyer, 1997; Lyon and Porter, 2009). In particular, Fukuyama (1995) highlighted shared values and norms as providing a basis for trust, in the development of loose, less codified and flexible rules at the (small) group production and marketing levels. In the research, while previous (market-oriented) orders were dominated by informal institutions (home-based production), in the transformation of *purdah* and development of institutions in enterprise, new forms of less personal trust and relations in the marketplace have generated both formal (e.g. written contracts with buyers), as well as informal institutions (e.g. internal routines). And thus in this new socioeconomic order, the traditional dichotomy has disappeared (i.e. formal state versus informal market). In Case 1, formal institutions have now become more important in business transactions, and originate from this new evolving business environment. The NGO plays an initial and notable role in these contracts as an unofficial guarantor (in the short-term before trust is established).

Towards examining levels of authority, Ostrom (2005) described the benefits of 'polycentrism', where multiple layers of governing authorities at different levels assist with coping with the tragedy of the commons, and strengthen abidance and trust in institutional rules. At the firm/group level, the formalisation of rules was determined by local levels of trust (before efficiency objectives set in), in addition to levels of authority. Evolving rules have tended to remain informal where trust is high both in the enterprise group and within the community, with oversight by power holders and a secondary perceived level of authority by the NGO. This was particularly typical in early to mid stages of the enterprise, where roles remained more similar within the group and power relations homogenous, with strong oversight by power holders and the NGO. This arrangement led to significant efficiency, and savings on costs related to explicit worker contracts and enforcement. It also increased trust between members and bolstered voluntary group activities. However, as roles matured and diversified with a necessary division of labour and responsibilities, this affected trust levels within the group. In Case 1b, this has led to the introduction of formal attendance registers for production-level routines. Yet, even if trust between women was high, in low-trust community environments, power holders have enforced strict and more codified rules related to task participation (for example, requiring the submission of names of marketing women) and brought in more rule rigidity (e.g. Cases 1a and 2b). Essentially, where there may be strong trust at both the group and community level, rules have remained informal until the business complexity has necessitated the formalisation of rules. This has likewise been shown at the coordination level, particularly in the more developed Case 1. As the number of groups have increased, the codification of roles and responsibilities has been deemed necessary to manage more diverse relations between many groups.

7.2 Muddling through or strategic design: multiple-actor negotiation in institutional development[1]

> Institutions do not as a rule fit with each other because they were designed for the purpose . . . More often than not actors have no way of knowing exactly what institution best 'fits' the other institutions on which it might depend for positive complementarity . . . Institutional coherence and complementarity is as much discovered and improvised as it is intended. Both rationalism and functionalism grossly exaggerate the capacity of actors to know what they are doing before they have done it.
>
> (Streeck, 2002, cited in Hollingsworth, 2002: 15)

Looking more closely at the process of institutional change, it is necessary to re-examine arguments from Chapters 4 and 5 on institutional transformation and construction in the research cases. In particular, research findings aimed to build off Fligstein (1997), Hodgson (2000, 2003, 2007), Chang (2002), Beckert (2003) and Gomez (2008) in looking at the influence of existing institutions in institutional development and the role of different actors (and their motivations, interests and power). In this section, I draw together and elaborate on critical insights in the institutional process, including the nature of institutional phases, and the interaction of key actors to further analyse dynamic interests and the myriad of strategies deployed (building on Chapter 6).

7.2.1 Institutional design process: devils in the detail

Rational actor theory holds that actors are perfectly informed of costs and benefits in choice, and that choices are made independent of other influences. Looking beyond neoclassical economics, Chapter 2 drew attention to the influence of power and history in institutional development (e.g. Bardhan, 1989; Chang and Evans, 2000; Chang, 2002; Greif, 2006), existing institutions and organisational structures (e.g. DiMaggio and Powell, 1991; Hollingsworth and Boyer, 1997; Platteau, 2000), and habit (e.g. Hodgson, 1997). Others have highlighted the role of agents and collective action (e.g. Lawson, 1997; Beckert, 1999, 2003; Fligstein, 2001), with more radical change precipitated by clashes between agents with differing interests (Campbell, 1997). Ostrom (2005) emphasised the importance of locally led ownership, in agents devising and shaping their own (appropriate) rules, permitting social norms to evolve and enhancing the strength of cooperation. Meanwhile, anthropologists highlight links to religious or cultural traditions with comfort derived from familiarity of language, art and ritual (Geertz, 1973), and suggest that new innovations usually fail unless the culture is prepared for it (and innovations are suitably adapted), or if the environment is changing radically (Everett, 2012).

Uncertain 'creative' design and guided reformulation

Gomez (2008) identified three stages in institutional evolution, namely experimentation, design and replication. Gomez conceived that agents experiment with new institutions in 'reflective action', and that actors embedded in networks play a key role in interpretation and decision-making. In vein with Gomez, three institutional phases were also observed in this research, although actor involvement was indicated to be more complex, influencing the scope of each phase, duration and outcomes. Institutional phases thus included the initial introduction of the 'innovation' (the reformed or early rule), proposed by the NGO, and jointly formulated in agreement with the entrepreneurs and power holders. The second phase then saw the reshaping and trialling of new rules, predominantly led by the entrepreneur in negotiation with power holders. And notably even if the original NGO designs were appropriate, there was a need for local adaptation and elaboration. Finally, if successful, the last phase included the 'operationalisation' and 'stabilisation' of new rules, with potential for 'replication'. In higher-level rules, the three phases were observed to be less extensive with shorter durations, due to more 'distance' from the root of the social norm, and a reduced sphere of application (only for selected women).

Reflecting further on this three-step process, the first stage, early rules were introduced by the NGO. These 'external' actors have demonstrated varying capacity in design, drawing on their own experience and expertise where available, and endeavouring to ensure that rules were appropriate with the prevailing culture and boundaries imposed by power holders. Trust has played a part in the acceptance of initial institutional innovations (and their ability to gain local trust). NGOs described this phase as crucial, with less credible, staff delaying the introduction of new institutions in addition to local destabilising events (such as local conflicts). The second experimental stage was triggered by the introduction of these new institutions to the enterprise women. This phase included a period of trialling, shaping and fleshing out of the designed institutional arrangements through experimentation. Rules tended to be promoted by highlighting their link to their existing religion/culture (progressive aspects), and fostered through close working conditions, openness and group meetings. Failures to overcome local resistance and conflict were shown to either delay or prohibit the progression to Stage 3. This led to the significant reformulation of rules and narrowing down their applicability (as evident both in Cases 2b and 3, in the development of marketing routines). In most of the cases, the final Stage 3 was characterised by the formal operationalisation and stabilisation of the institutional arrangements with potential for 'replication'. Stages 2 and 3 were observed to be dynamic as shifting roles and conditions necessitated rule reformulation and rule variation with business development. The entrepreneur largely led revisions in the routines, navigating the context and power holders, and influencing the evolving roles of other women, and strategies in expansion/growth. In low-trust environments, however, strict control over rules was maintained by entrepreneurs, with little flexibility, particularly by less public-spirited (or insecure) entrepreneurs, affecting institutional development. Power holders could also equally micromanage the rules, leading to high restrictions on their applicability. Likewise, NGOs could micromanage rules too (or retain too much control), constraining local ownership and their ongoing development.

Overall, the duration, negotiation and ease of phases were influenced by three specific factors. First, this included the *level of the rule* and *its relation to the root social institution*, with lower-level institutions (e.g. routines) and those requiring significant change to the social institution proving most difficult. Second, this included the *nature of local conditions* with more unstable, lower-trust environments creating setbacks and delaying rule development. Third, the phases were influenced by the *capacity and interaction of local actors*. This included the credibility and capacity of NGO staff (particularly in phase 1) in introducing new ideas and gaining early support within the community. Meanwhile, the charisma, capacity and interests of entrepreneurs were instrumental in the mid to final stages of institutional development (stages 2 and 3), in encouraging the other women, and shaping and championing their new rules, and negotiating with female and male power holders. Finally, the attitudes and support of power holders was shown to be critical across all phases in actor coordination and institutional approval. Power holders played a strong role in both the introduction and renegotiation of rules – particularly lower-level rules and where rules touched upon social institutions – and in the designation of physical and social boundaries.

7.2.2 Interaction of dynamic and diverse actors

In reviewing the process of institutional construction above, the integral role of several actors has been identified. Building off Chapter 6, it is critical to further examine the interaction of actors, and agency. Revisiting the discourse, discussions have emphasised the entrepreneur as a key 'agent of change' and 'innovation'. Baron (2004) highlighted the cognitive role that entrepreneurs play in the careful analysis of situations, events and making strategic plans. Going beyond entrepreneurs themselves, organisation studies drew attention to 'institutional entrepreneurs' as broad agents involved in the creation of new institutions (e.g. Battilana *et al.*, 2009). Most of the literature emphasises their positive force, while a few more nuanced studies have indicated that change agents may also employ mixed strategies with varied outcomes (e.g. Ford *et al*, 2008). Streeck (2002) suggests that actors may be less strategic in the design of institutions, but highlights 'entrepreneurial creativity' in the shaping phase to ensure that they fit with existing institutions. Several authors have elaborated on the emerging design of institutions as influenced by individual intentions and interests (Joas, 1996; Lawson, 1997; Beckert, 2003). Beckert (2003: 774) highlights that most action is based on 'unreflected routines' (Joas, 1996) in line with previous theories on 'habits' (Dewey), 'practical consciousness' (Giddens), 'routines' (Schutz), 'knowing-in-action' (Schon) and the 'tacit knowledge' of actors (Polyani). And it is when these routines fail or are inadequate that actors engage in creative action through a 'process of innovation by experimentation' (Gomez, 2008). Gomez suggests that there is still a gap in the theory when the conditions of the environment change and the rules of action become redundant, and new rules need to be created.

Pushing the discussion forward, Gomez (2008) cited three necessary conditions to facilitate the bottom-up design of institution: the initial presence of collective action skilled/resourceful entrepreneurs, the participation of agents interested in new rules, and pre-existent institutions that delimit experimentation and aid the search for 'new solutions'. In the research case studies, these conditions have proved important, although not entirely sufficient for the bottom-up design of institutions. An extreme social environment has necessitated the outside support of an NGO to assist with the initial transformation of the boundary institution of *purdah* and the related development of enterprise rules in negotiation with power holders. Meanwhile, resourceful (and less resourceful) entrepreneurs together with 'active workers' were intricately involved with shaping evolving institutions with the approval of local power holders. This phase of trial and error was critical in creating participation in the formulation of rules and local ownership (as described by Ostrom, 2005). The research has indicated that easier resolutions were possible in more stable environments with progressive actors (where gradual deviation was more acceptable), and more challenging in low trust situations, with the need to employ more extensive strategies, and some entrepreneurs exploiting the situation for their own benefits. Eventual outcomes have proved to be nuanced. Entrepreneurs are both influenced and activated by their own motivations/interests in addition to their 'power'. These factors affect the resulting nature of the revised institutions, and levels of access by others. Yet, in addition to institutional design affecting access, the character and reputation of the entrepreneur and their networks themselves can also influence the extent of uptake by others and scope of replication (i.e. these individuals are 'role models', affecting the broader adoption of new routines). Hence, in vein with bounded rationality theory, it is not just the qualities of the institutions that matter, but who the originators and promoters may be that are associated with those particular institutions.

7.2.3 Agents of uncertain change: diverse interests and power

Case studies indicate that actors involved with transforming, designing, shaping and setting boundaries in institutional development may have both positive and negative influences on emerging institutions, due to their diverse interests. Three groups of actors have been identified as particularly significant. First, these include the NGOs as 'external' agents. The NGOs were involved with catalysing institutional processes through introducing new designed institutions, and then guiding their development. NGOs may be motivated by diverse social goals and monetary funds, determining the nature of their strategies, and duration and scope of their engagement. The capacity of NGOs to design appropriate institutions, negotiate with different actors and build trust, and their ability to provide plausible advice in their reformulation (and thus be perceived as credible 'Islamic' actors) were critical factors in their performance. Further to this, the perception of these external actors was equally important. To be accepted, they needed to show respect, and be trusted and credible as outsiders yet perceived to speak the same 'language' as the community (e.g. dress, rituals). These 'capacities' may be influenced by prior experience and expertise, the nature of their understanding of the local cultural context, their ability to design locally adapted institutions, and their strategic choices (in sector, institutions introduced, advisory approach). The local environment and other actors were shown to further influence their capacity to act. The second group of actors included the *entrepreneurs*. Entrepreneurs (and their allies) have been predominantly involved with remoulding institutions in negotiation with power holders, garnering trust and facilitating their adoption and diffusion within the group. Entrepreneurs may be initially motivated by economic benefits and simple social interaction, but motivations may later broaden to include social goals, or more selfish desires for personal power (particularly if NGO support is weak or if the context is low-trust). Significantly, dominant types of entrepreneurs were observed to thrive under different conditions. These included public-spirited 'trailblazers' in more stable contexts, generating more open institutions; and power-oriented 'gatekeepers' in less stable contexts, interested in self-aggrandisement generating closed institutions. Yet it is worth noting that trailblazers may also emerge in less favourable situations, if supported by NGOs and enterprise allies. Meanwhile, gatekeepers may equally emerge in more favourable contexts, but would ultimately be removed (by power holders, enterprise women or the NGO). The entrepreneur's capacity to act may be influenced by previous leadership experience and personal qualities (including interest in risk-taking), and the perception of entrepreneurs as upstanding members of the community and charismatic (particularly respectable and religious). Finally, the third group of actors included the involvement of *power holders* (such as community leaders), as institutional authorisers and boundary makers. Power holders have been influenced by their experience of culture in foreign countries, trust of outsiders and interest in change. Power holders may be initially motivated by control, but motivations may later broaden to include community social goals (particularly where progressive members of the elite are influential, and the NGOs are successful in opening up new ideas), or more personal power incentives. The capacity of power holders to jointly agree (finding a common position) and negotiate, and to garner local trust have been essential to institutional outcomes.

Mixed strategies dominated by sociocultural themes

As discussed in Chapter 6, there is limited understanding of how and why 'institutional entrepreneurs' behave in the ways that they do, and how they mobilise resources, formal authority, and social capital across contexts (Battilana *et al.*, 2009: 86). Looking more closely at key actor strategies across the cases, it is imperative to appreciate their practical influence in institutional design and development to better understand respective actor behaviour (and its impact). The effects of these strategies has been further tempered by the local context, in particular levels of stability and trust. Chapter 6 outlined various tactics – positive and negative – that have been deployed to persuade, intimidate or block actors to accept, adopt and control the new values, norms and practices. Promotional strategies tended to flourish in stable, high-trust and progressive contexts while resistance strategies tended to be more successful in less stable, low-trust and traditional contexts. Strategies have been both purposeful and intended, or unconscious and unintended. These tactics can be grouped into four major themes. These have included *sociocultural* and *religious strategies* that included proverbs, storytelling and use of progressive religious texts and sayings (and even the reinterpretation of texts). Of critical importance in traditional and conservative environments, these strategies have tended to be deployed initially, and then during setbacks prompted by personalities and unsettling local events, and aimed to persuade and convince women and community members that new practices were supported by progressive local/religious norms. And the perception of the NGO as well as the entrepreneur and group members – as Islam-abiding, capable and charismatic – was critical in gaining credibility, and the support of the power holders (and later in formulating links with buyers). Yet if these messages were not credible, conservative elements could also use the same type of strategies to argue the reverse, going against the new practices. A second set of strategies has included *physical tactics* such as charismatic and religious behaviour (including participation in local rituals, and pursuing dress norms), and less positively, threats and intimidation. The former would be deployed continuously and aimed to demonstrate that new practices had respectable advocates. The latter strategies would be deployed when boundaries were crossed, or if power holders felt a loss of control and aimed to ensure that new practices remained within boundaries and social order was maintained. The third set of strategies may be described as *economic tactics*, including the highlighting of profits and success of the work, and have been deployed when confidence was low. The final set of strategies included the introduction of *new technologies* used to accelerate returns in the business, yet with the unintended positive consequence of reinforcing the 'professional' nature of practices and their association with village 'progress', if technologies were successfully adopted. This has helped new enterprise institutions gain more traction.

The paradox of socio-religious strategies in institutional change

Plato maintained that storytellers 'rule society', drawing attention to the power of narrative. The research has explored the varied use of local religious and cultural messages in institutional change for both positive and negative effect. Promotional sociocultural strategies assume particular importance in conservative areas, or communities that are fragile after years of war with high levels of distrust. Introducing ideas that were perceived to come from their own society and religion was critical, as high levels of suspicion typically surround foreign ideas, even international law. New ideas have been most effectively introduced through reviewing existing codes (e.g. religious texts). The research showed that the use of relevant sociocultural/religious ideas and rituals has been particularly effective in gaining trust and cooperation in the early phases, or during later setbacks. Yet narrow-minded power holders and religious authorities can equally draw on more conservative texts and proverbs as a form of resistance and intimidation. Sociocultural strategies have included religious texts, proverbs, and powerful storytelling of other local communities or foreign experiences. Cultural sociology draws strong attention to the power of narrativity, since traditional societies are organised through stories and they draw inspiration and power. Cognitive science echoes this, highlighting storytelling as instrumental, emphasising that most information that humans process is through induction, 'reasoning by pattern recognition' (Beinhocker, 2007: 126). Indeed, Afghan society is rich in poetry and in storytelling (Mills, 1991), often even predating religious traditions. Adopting local behavioural norms has also been important. Anthropologists have drawn attention to adherence to rituals and symbols within communities (Geertz, 1973). Further to this, in the Afghan setting, actors that are charismatic (usually religious) are given tremendous authority (Entezar, 2007). In the research, successful promoters have drawn on extensive sociocultural strategies, and adopted local dress and norms, and were described as 'good Muslims' (particularly apparent in Case 1). Yet, where they have failed to fully address cultural issues (e.g. the honour code of *Pashtunwali*), particularly in a more uncertain context, they have been less successful (as in Case 3). Overall, socio-religious strategies have thus been used for double effect: to both resist change, and to promote new ideas; and the effectiveness of their strategies was shown to depend on the capacity of the champions and credibility of the message, other actors and local context.

Shifting actor motivations, interests, and power

It is interesting to further examine the shifting nature of the motivations and interests of actors making, shaping and enforcing the rules, and how this has affected rule-making and development in the research cases. Hodgson (2003) discussed the changing nature of habits as precipitating new preferences. In Chapter 4, it was shown that new practices and habits triggered new values and preferences among both the related women (directly) and more broadly among the power holders (indirectly), with significant implications for rule evolution and development. This was indicated to be particularly noteworthy where *purdah* practices were less restrained with more open power holders and public-spirited entrepreneurs, with increasing levels of interest in women's empowerment. Yet among some sets of power holders, there were diverging opinions leading to protracted conflict and unrest, constraining the realisation of new joint preferences (e.g. Case 1). In a fragile environment, capable NGOs have been instrumental in boosting the confidence of women, and opening up attitudes of power holders, resolving conflicts, and creating vital conditions to allow support for open and evolving practices.

With a strong influence on outcomes, the dynamic motivations and interests of dominant entrepreneurs were shown to be particularly critical. This impacted the nature of evolving institutions, and levels of access and adoption by others. In higher-trust environments with progressive power holders, public-spirited trailblazers may foster inclusiveness in enterprise, and have an interest in women's social and economic empowerment both within and outside of the business. Meanwhile, in less stable, low-trust, conservative environments with controlling power holders – and where NGO actors may be weak or absent – controlling gate-keepers may be more motivated by personal power. Often entrepreneurs have grown into these roles realising new strengths and motivations (trailblazers), or alternatively becoming corrupted by their own power and greediness (gatekeepers). Trailblazers and gatekeepers have also endeavoured to influence structure through their agency, to create favourable conditions. For example, in Case 2b, the gatekeeper entrepreneur has ensured that the community remains conservative and blocked other women's development. Meanwhile, in Case 1a, the trailblazer entrepreneur remained stifled by conservative elements, but continued to find subtle ways to bring in progressive ideas to promote change in her community.

7.3 Innovation, learning, adoption and diffusion in networks

Beyond individual actors, there is strong support for the role of collectivism and the interdependence of agents in institutional development. As discussed in Chapter 6, the creation of institutions tends to arise from the interactions between people, as opposed to individual activity. Going beyond Hodgson's framework (i.e. actions Y, outcomes Z in response to new situations X), Gomez (2008) incorporated institutional learning and innovation among agents through adding a lower 'innovation' loop as agents encounter 'new, uncertain, complex situations' to fill institutional gaps (i.e. actions Y^1, outcomes Z^1 and situations X^1). The evolved institutions experiment in 'reflective action' and 'skilful actors' begin innovating and learning. Such activity is indicated to be embedded in networks that play a key role in interpretation and decision-making. If a positive response is received, the action is repeated until such activity produces a new 'rule' or 'institution' for the respective situation. In this section, I reflect on actor collaboration in institutional development towards re-conceptualising a multi-actor institutional construction scheme.

7.3.1 Harnessing power of allies in creating support and critical mass

Social networks can influence resource availability, collective action and entrepreneurial intentions. Fligstein (1996) theorised that new paths of action could be facilitated by 'skilful actors' within networks, while Maguire *et al.* (2004) suggested that institutional entrepreneurs could draw on social capital to gather allies for collective action. In the research, it is the group effort of entrepreneurs and their close workers that is indeed critical in contributing to shaping institutions, and facilitating their broader adoption and diffusion through group learning processes as new practices are taken up. The gathering of allies and their agency is affected by the charisma and agency of the entrepreneur, existing cultural norms, and local stability and trust. Beyond the entrepreneur allies, three further (interrelated) networks (or sets of relations) have also been identified that affect institutional development in enterprise. These include the group links to the power holders, permitting institutional legitimacy; and if permitted by power holders, market networks facilitating interaction in the value chain, and cross-firm connections, permitting collective action and exchange.

The research has tentatively explored the development of these four networks in enterprise (diversity and size), and the influence of actor agency and intentions, and structure (e.g. trust, social norms). The research shows that network development is determined by agency from both within, and outside of the networks. In particular, NGOs appear to play an uncertain brokering or mediating role between the power holders, and the entrepreneurs and active workers in the negotiation of new networks (in vein with insights from Graf, 2011). If capable, the external NGO can also have a powerful influence on both agency and local relations in boosting the credibility of the entrepreneur and workers (such as in market links), and gaining the support of power holders in network establishment and development. This is particularly important in the early stages of network development, and in less trusting environments. Market networks can be especially vulnerable in these early phases (as women go beyond traditional relations), and may be manipulated, threatened and disrupted by power holders, or destabilised by local events. Yet the capacity, perceptions and interests of NGOs can affect network establishment and development (i.e. not all NGOs are able, or view such activities as a priority). Alternatively, where NGOs are viewed with suspicion or uncertainty, this can also create barriers to network establishment, or slow down the development of networks, particularly in the context of instability. Where there is the mix of the active support of NGOs, local trust and progressive power holders, public-spirited trailblazer entrepreneurs have been shown to create diverse networks across multiple realms. Yet, in a situation of weak NGOs, mistrust and strict power holders, gatekeeper entrepreneurs may nurture more restricted and homogenous networks of powerful people.

Insights gained from this research contribute to better appreciating the influence of culture, agency and process in networks (Emirbayer and Goodwin, 1994) adding depth to Granovetter's principles (Granovetter, 2005) and institutional diffusion (Redmond, 2003). First, there is a need to integrate the role of agents, power dimensions, and heterogeneous norms in understanding how 'dense networks' can facilitate norm enforcement. Even within close-knit networks, powerful actors can lead on these processes, and determine 'layers' of norms and enforcement measures. Second, in terms of the structural holes argument, intermediary actors such as NGOs may enable entrepreneurs to bridge holes to create multiple networks. Yet local power holders may block or inhibit the NGO efforts, or prohibit the entrepreneur's activation of those links. The new ties themselves (such as buyer links) may also shun the new links to the entrepreneur, due to low trust of these newcomers, or even their own traditional principles. Third, evolving norms, stability and agency can influence the scope of adoption and diffusion within networks. Where there is trust and stability, and more progressive norms, public-spirited trailblazers encourage unregulated diffusion and adoption of new institutions in open and dynamic networks. Such entrepreneurs may also be motivated to extend new practices beyond the group leading to more widespread diffusion, drawing on progressive broader community members as allies. This contrasts with gatekeepers in less uncertain and closed contexts that control levels of diffusion and adoption in more exclusive networks. These entrepreneurs may interact less with their own peer group, and instead try to gain support from conservative power holders to secure their own self-interest, deliberately barring other (potential) adopters. Yet equally, 'adopters or followers' (Redmond, 2003) may also assert their own preferences in deciding whether to follow new practices (voluntary non-adoption).

7.3.2 How institutions affect networks, and how networks affect institutions

I have discussed how social institutions and emerging enterprise institutions can influence network establishment, development, access and usage. Where institutions were open, the development of networks has been more extensive, with a greater degree of participation and distribution of power. In contrast, where institutions were closed, the development of networks has been constrained, exclusive and power skewed. Yet, there are also emerging indicators to show that networks themselves influence the development of institutions. In this regard, it is pertinent to revisit Hodgson (1997, 2003) on habits and preferences, and their congruence in groups; Chang (2002) on power dynamics; and Klyver and Schott (2011) on networks and entrepreneur intentions. Participation in networks can influence group habits and routines, and trigger new preferences. This is illustrated in the research with women creating new work rules, and new congruent preferences being born with regard to women's roles (in progressive cases). Networks may thus foster new shared values, preferences and trust, and facilitate the collaborative exploration of new rules and their reformulation as the business expands. Yet if power dynamics are skewed with tight networks, and network leaders are self-oriented (e.g. Cases 2b and 3), new preferences will not be congruent, and new rule formulation will not be mutually formulated and agreed.

7.3.3 Towards re-conceptualising a multi-actor institutional construction scheme

In the construction and development of new institutions, the research advances Gomez's (2008) theory of the development of 'new rules' through trial and error by entrepreneurs (resourceful 'skilful' agents of institutional adjustment) in the additional incorporation of the support of external agents (NGOs), and negotiation with power holders, in vein with Chang (2002). Going beyond individuals or a single set of actors, the scheme incorporates the presence of multiple actors that influence institutional innovation, design and their final shaping. Figure 7.2 attempts to go beyond Gomez's 'institutional-action-information double loop'. In this revised version, external actors play a role in navigating existing institutions towards generating an innovation design concept, I. This is presented to power holders generating boundary information, W. External actors feed this in to the revised innovation concept I^1. The entrepreneurs trial this in reflective action Y^1 and a new concept is presented to the power holders, I^2. Further boundary information is generated in W^1 towards new information X^1.

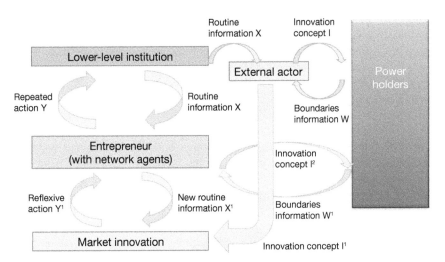

Figure 7.2 Interaction of multi-actors in institutional-action-information double loop

Source: Author's own illustration

7.4 Institutional outcomes: robust or fragile? Evolving or stagnated?

As highlighted by Parto (2008: 1013), there have been extensive efforts over the last 30 years to better understand economic collaboration, cooperation and coordination of actors in markets, networks and firms. In institutional development, the discourse suggests that institutional outcomes reflect a balance of self-interest, social obligation and social relations (Hollingsworth and Boyer, 1997). Others have indicated that institutions tend to reflect existing orders and hierarchies (unless forces have been revolutionary, as described by Marx), and that institutions may generate higher-order and lower-order institutions. Institutional legitimacy has also been discussed by DiMaggio and Powell (1991), Beckert (1999) and Gomez (2008), in addition to notions of sustainability through 'institutional stickiness' (Boettke *et al.*, 2008). Expanding earlier arguments in Chapters 4, 5 and 6, it is instructive to further examine the emerging institutional outcomes in the research. The cases exhibit different sets of institutions as a result of initial designs, reshaping and boundary setting influencing the nature of collaboration, cooperation and coordination. Here, I discuss the nature of emerging institutions and hierarchies, indications of path dependence, and institutional effects towards broader reflections on rule making.

7.4.1 Social stratification: heterogeneous purdah norms towards a new order?

Chapter 4 highlighted critical features of norms. For example, norms may differ across groups (Peyton Young, 2007), and variations in those norms may be rooted in different roles in society and social order (Marx, 1986), with communities playing a role in norm development and enforcement (Kandori, 1992). There may also be a hierarchy of power in the making and shaping of norms in visible and less visible forms. From the cases investigated, it is evident that there have been 'quiet women's revolutions' at the local level, precipitated by the motivation to get involved in enterprise. This process has involved external NGOs, entrepreneurs and local power holders, permitting significant social change to prevailing sociocultural practices for selected women. From the research, it is indicated that a reinterpretation or reclarification of the Koran has largely facilitated a transformation of *purdah* norms, permitting broader economic engagement (although this varies across women). If reassured that this was not out of step with the culture and religion, the broader local community has – in different degrees – accepted these new practices. In some cases, acceptance has been aided by observing these practices first-hand, and through viewing the gradual economic returns that such practices have generated. This type of institutional change may be considered 'radical' in forcing substantive change in beliefs assumed to be encoded in the Koran 'rule book', and generating new norms for women both within and outside of the enterprise groups.

A number of pertinent observations can be made from these changes in norms. First, the transformation of local norms does not lead to either homogenous outcomes (if original norms were the same across the group), or reflect initial diversified outcomes (if original norms were varied across the group). Advancing Horne (2001), while there may have been existing differences in the original norms practiced (or not), in the transformation, these differences can be reduced or overturned with new orders created (e.g. Case 1); reproduced, generating the same existing order; or made more extreme and exacerbated (e.g. Case 2b). This may be affected by the motivations of the entrepreneur, local norms and conditions, or the interests of power holders. In ethically Pashtun communities (Case 3), additional cultural aspects of *purdah* – namely the honour code of *pashtunwali* – have complicated the transformation of *purdah* for the worker women. Second, there may be a period of uncertainty in the transformation process (lengthening the trial-and-error phase), particularly where there is more abrupt change. In the readjustment stage, women may face resistance from power holders and be forced to engage in extensive renegotiation. Third, there may also be unintended consequences of empowerment, in terms of both the women themselves (particularly the entrepreneur), and broader societal reverberations (at the household and community level). New forms of power may also lead to the emergence of both charismatic as well as more selfish leader women. New roles can also lead to disruptions to household and community relations, and a potential backlash against the women. Fourth, evolving *purdah* norms (as core social institutions) can affect various aspects of the emerging organisation and structure of the business. For example, this can determine the scope of women's involvement in production and management, and their participation in external activities such as marketing.

Figure 7.3 illustrates the diverse shades of *purdah* observed in enterprise, influencing women's mobility, participation in the business, and scope of networks. For women to join collective enterprise, it is imperative that women at least surpass the limits of 'strict *purdah*'. Yet it is not necessary for all women in enterprise to advance to the most progressive form of *purdah*. As indicated, the women with the most mobility (to leave the house and to meet with non-family men) have the most potential within the enterprise (to lead the company and make decisions). Such women may be engaged in both production and marketing with broad external relations and networks. These women tend to manage and drive the enterprise, and are responsible for negotiating and interacting with local and market actors. They also play a strong part in the potential *purdah* evolution of worker women. *Purdah* trajectories (individual and group) influence women's participation in the business, firm performance, and value chain linkages.

7.4.2 Enterprise institutions: healthy hierarchies or arrested development?

As described in Chapter 2, Douglas (1986: 124) describes the creation of new institutions often reproducing old orders. It is useful to further examine institutions in enterprise, the nature of emerging orders and institutional hierarchies. Towards assessing such intra-organisational hierarchies in the research, and variations within enterprise institutions, it is useful to re-examine emerging institutional

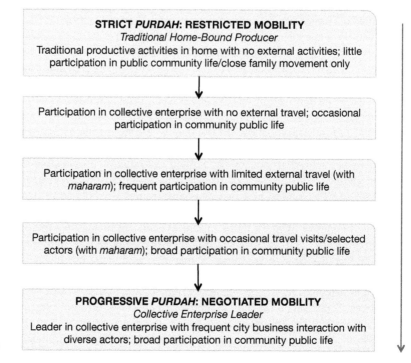

STRICT *PURDAH*: RESTRICTED MOBILITY
Traditional Home-Bound Producer
Traditional productive activities in home with no external activities; little participation in public community life/close family movement only

Participation in collective enterprise with no external travel; occasional participation in community public life

Participation in collective enterprise with limited external travel (with *maharam*); frequent participation in community public life

Participation in collective enterprise with occasional travel visits/selected actors (with *maharam*); broad participation in community public life

PROGRESSIVE *PURDAH*: NEGOTIATED MOBILITY
Collective Enterprise Leader
Leader in collective enterprise with frequent city business interaction with diverse actors; broad participation in community public life

Increasing mobility and power in household, enterprise, community and beyond

Increasing business networks with non-family men and more independence

Figure 7.3 Shades of diverse *purdah* observed through economic empowerment
Source: Author's own illustration

structures across the cases. In the first case, women were organised into small village groups of approximately 20 women headed by a group 'entrepreneur', with higher marketing links to other village groups. This enterprise may be characterised as a decentralised group structure, with strong ties at the group network level. In the second case, women were organised into similarly sized groups, although at a density of 10 women's groups per community (each with their own leaders). Above the farmers' groups, village sales agents were designated, with the overall structure then overseen by a village head (the 'entrepreneur'). This case may be described as an elaborate institutional set-up, with three to four tiers of participating women at the village level, depending on the entrepreneur, and with loose and undeveloped cross-village links. In the final case, the business comprised of just one small group of women (originally 15 ladies but shrinking) with an appointed head, the 'entrepreneur'. Case 3 may be characterised as a top-down business with largely undeveloped rules at all levels, and persisting micromanagement by the external NGO.

Institutional openness reflected in local evolving hierarchies

In Case 1, initial hierarchies that were created by the NGO included the entrepreneur and the worker women, but all were considered equal in terms of work efforts and remuneration. In the evolving hierarchy, in Case 1a, three tiers then emerged: the entrepreneur, male assistants and female assistants, and the workers, with agreed variations in remuneration. Yet due to the strict and low trust context, there appeared to be limited flexibility of the women's roles. In Case 1b, three tiers also emerged: the entrepreneur, one male assistant and female assistants, and then the workers, and again with agreed variations in remuneration. However, in this more stable context, there was more mobility within the women's roles if needed (e.g. worker women helped out with village supplies and local sales). Meanwhile, in Case 2, initial hierarchies that were created by the NGO included the entrepreneur, the lead farmers, and finally the producer women, with designated work roles and differentiated remuneration. In the evolving hierarchy, in Case 2a, four tiers emerged: the entrepreneur, the sales agents, the lead farmers, and the producers. The structure was perceived as strong but open, with power decentralised and evolving roles and remuneration. In Case 2b, however, three tiers remained fixed: the entrepreneur, the lead farmers and the producers, and there was notably limited mobility or remuneration change. There were even indications of a reduction of farmer group power, and the further centralisation of control by the entrepreneur. Finally, in Case 3, initial hierarchies created by the NGO just included the entrepreneur and the worker women, with equal work efforts and only marginal differences in remuneration. In the emerging structure, however, power was largely centred further with the entrepreneur, and an increasing gap was wedged between her and the workers. Across the cases, the NGOs initially designed the institutions and early hierarchies, in negotiation with the power holders, and in coordination with the participating women. This design was conceived as a starting point for enterprise work. The further development of institutions and hierarchies was then largely led by the entrepreneur (and her allies), in negotiation with power holders and guided by the NGO. As a result, it is the entrepreneur that is heavily responsible for the emerging levels of rigidity within the enterprise (and power dynamics), and the scope of flexibility in tasks of worker women and degrees of remuneration.

7.4.3 Critical junctures and emerging pathways

In developing a scheme for institutional analysis, it is important to reconsider the relations between actors and institutions, the nature of rules (and incentives, sanctions, and enforcement), and actor values and power. Abrupt change in the development of new institutions may be precipitated by 'critical junctures' (Collier and Collier, 1991), and this may be followed by renewed stabilisation and path dependence (DiMaggio and Powell, 1991). According to neoclassical economists, institutional (often undesirable) path dependence exists because of the 'network externalities, economies of scope, and complementarities that exist within a given institutional matrix' (North, 1995: 3) (i.e. economic agents with bargaining power have strong interests in maintaining the status quo). Institutional development may involve 'path dependent' processes due to the different groups' relative power and by their own subjective analysis of alternative paths. From the perspective of institutional political economy, pre-existing institutions – resulting from the power of a particular group – can be resistant to change, leading to path dependency. Agents may appreciate the inefficiencies but be unable to change them due to the 'enormity of the collective action' (Bardhan, 1989). Meanwhile, North *et al.* (2009) identified and contrasted emerging institutional 'orders' and their degrees of openness. They described the 'natural state' of society as a self-reproducing social formation, with personal relations among members of the elites, and more progressive 'open access' orders with impersonal institutional relations that depend more on meritocracy, market competition and political democracy. Towards exploring indicators driving the nature of emerging institutions, Ostrom (1990) emphasised examining the compatibility of the interests of the entrepreneurs versus members, and the degree of participation in the rules in terms of who makes and shapes rules, who enforces the rules, and who may propose change rules.

As discussed, two dominant entrepreneurs have produced characteristic patterns of institutions in enterprise, creating either 'open' inclusive institutions, thriving under stable conditions (trailblazers), or fostering more 'closed' exclusive institutions, under more disruptive conditions (gatekeepers). Institutions appear to be clearly linked to levels of compatibility between the entrepreneurs and enterprise members, influencing the latter's participation in the emerging rules. In the case of trailblazers, there are high levels of compatibility of interests between the entrepreneurs and workers, and a greater participation of workers in rule-making/shaping, enforcement and change. Trust levels are also higher, and there are savings in transaction costs inside the business. In the case of gatekeepers, there is limited compatibility of interests between the entrepreneurs and workers, and less participation of workers in rule-making/shaping, enforcement and change. In these situations, trust levels may be lower, and transaction costs higher (e.g. in Case 2b, there is much distrust of the entrepreneur, and village sales may require cross-checking of profits released). Overall, under stable conditions, trailblazer entrepreneurs have therefore produced more democratic and participative institutions in their motivation towards inclusiveness (e.g. Cases 1b and 2a). Yet arguably more interesting, trailblazer entrepreneurs may also emerge under less favourable conditions (where there are conservative power holders and low levels of trust), but this appears to significantly constrain their institutional endeavours (or lead to compromised solutions; e.g. Case 1a). Meanwhile, under these difficult conditions, gatekeepers have flourished and produced more top-down and self-oriented institutions (e.g. Cases 2b and 3). In these situations, the development of institutions may thus be heavily biased towards their own strategic interests and purposes, and power asymmetries may sustain less efficient institutions. It is pertinent to reflect on the fact that there were no examples of gatekeepers emerging under favourable conditions in the research. Yet findings suggest that if indeed they had emerged (due to initial selection or otherwise), progressive local actors

Table 7.2 Emerging institutional pathways and influence on value chain development

Institutional pathway	Productive	Unproductive	Destructive
Enterprise institutions	Equitable/fair evolving institutions	Constrained institutions	Unfair institutions
	Participation in rule-making, shaping and enforcement	Some participation in rule-making, shaping and enforcement	Entrepreneur only involved in rule-making, shaping and enforcement
	Flexibility in evolving design	Limited flexibility in evolving design	No flexibility in evolving design
Value chain effect	Increasing returns to workers with increasing participation in diversified enterprise activities	Fixed returns to workers with participation in rigid enterprise activities	Limited returns to workers with controlled participation in productive enterprise activities only
	Good intra-firm growth and development	Mediocre intra-firm growth and development	Limited intra-firm growth and development
	Evolving new economies with new democratic emerging orders	Stilted economies tending towards reproduction of existing orders	Skewed economies and extreme emerging orders

in these contexts would have eventually removed them (either the worker women, local power holders or the NGO). Overall, the research indicates that dominant entrepreneurs tend to persist in certain conditions due to a mixture between their own agency and local structural-actor dynamics.

Advancing understandings of path dependence, the research indicates that entrepreneurs play a critical role in generating patterns of institutions. Going beyond productive, unproductive and destructive enterprise activities (Baumol, 1990; Desai and Acs, 2007), this research has looked at enterprise institutions and emerging productive, unproductive and destructive institutional pathways influencing firm performance, value chain development and broader trends of economic development. 'Productive institutional pathways' are indicated to be championed by trailblazer entrepreneurs (e.g. Cases 1b and 2), generating more equitable, open and flexible institutions. For example, these entrepreneurs may permit worker mobility, and promote fair remuneration based on responsibility level and work hours of workers. This can boost worker participation in business, with evolving roles and returns, positively affecting firm development. Ultimately, this can generate evolving new economies, towards evermore open and democratic orders. Meanwhile, 'unproductive institutional pathways' are characteristic of more stilted trailblazers (as in Case 1a), generating enterprise institutions that are more constrained with limited levels of flexibility. In these cases, returns to workers may be more fixed with participation in rigid activities (i.e. less flexibility in productive (or other) tasks). This can constrain the development and growth of the firm. This can then lead to stilted economies, and tend towards the reproduction of emerging orders. Finally, 'destructive institutional pathways' are observed in situations with gatekeeper entrepreneurs (e.g. Cases 2b and 3). These entrepreneurs generate enterprise institutions that are inequitable with controlled participation and observable rigidity. The returns to workers are fixed by the entrepreneurs, and worker tasks are confined to low-level work, limiting intra-firm growth and development. This can lead to skewed economies, power imbalances and more extreme emerging orders. Table 7.2 summarises these trends of institutional pathways.

7.4.4 New attitudes and preferences with broad institutional spin-off effects

Engagement in economic activity can often lead to potential new relations and cooperation, with the market constituting 'a school for sociability, by providing the opportunity and incentive for people to cooperate with one another for the sake of mutual enrichment' (Fukuyama, 1995: 356). Historically, participation in trade has also prompted an increasing interest in local governance and institutional development to 'lower communication costs and trust ceilings' (Wright, 2010: 121). Towards deeper insights into the effects of enterprise institutions, Hodgson (1997) describes the potential of institutions to subtly influence individual habits of thought and action, and to have the capacity to generate new preferences.

Building on Hodgson's (1997, 2003) insights, this research has shown how transforming social norms and constructing new enterprise institutions have indeed precipitated new attitudes and preferences (as indicated in Chapter 4), or 'cognitive' institutions, and further triggered the development of broader institutions beyond the business (as indicated in Chapter 5), creating new (potential) opportunities for social and economic development. In vein with Ostrom (1990), I have termed these 'lower-level' (sociopolitical norms and practices) and 'higher-level' institutional effects (economic institutions related to enterprise and beyond). The generation and scope of these institutional effects, and levels of openness (i.e. democratic nature), are indicated to depend on the motivations and interests of the entrepreneur, power holders and the stability of the context. Worker agency and the group subculture were also shown to be significant. The latter has affected group levels of trust, and their motivation and interest to realise greater social goals (as earlier described in section 4.1). In progressive cases, there was a concerted effort to champion new attitudes, with enterprise women organising women's rights events such as Women's Day for the first time in the village (Case 1).

Fragile new social, political and economic institutions with diverse effects

Further reflecting on these effects, in terms of the lower-level institutional effects, new perspectives (or ideas) on women's *purdah* have precipitated new broader 'beliefs' related to other prevailing social norms. In the case of public-spirited entrepreneurs, where the context is stable, this has encouraged local women into more active roles; and inspired them to learn from the enterprise group and to be active in the community. This has particularly influenced both women's and girls' norms (e.g. girls school participation and marriage age). Evolving norms (or 'habits') and enterprise institutions have also generated new broader beliefs regarding women's economic roles, and triggered higher-level institutional effects. This includes the development of critical economic institutions, further influencing enterprise development, such as women's property rights, access to training and banking. It has also encouraged women to participate in community governance, increasing their interaction in women's community councils, and creating a new voice outside of the elite. Yet in less stable contexts, these new norms may remain exclusive and fragile, or bring backlashes from conservative elements. In particularly extreme situations (e.g. Case 2b), new (exclusive) norms have led to the generation of more detrimental institutions. In this case, exclusive political institutions have been developed, with the entrepreneur assuming lead (and intimidating) roles in local and regional women's groups (against the wishes of the people), and setting up local militia groups.

7.4.5 What makes rule-making more or less successful?

Drawing insights together, it is useful to reflect on what this study tells us about rule-making. Douglas (1986) drew attention to the key role of cognition in the creation of institutions through the combined 'squeezing' of ideas. Meanwhile, North *et al.* (2003, 2004) emphasised the 'interplay among cognition, belief systems, and institutions' in institutional development. Others have highlighted the process of socialisation (Hodgson, 2007), power struggles between actors (Chang, 2002), and the importance of local participation and ownership in rules and 'shared mental models' (Ostrom, 1990, 2005). Gomez (2008) described four factors that aid in the final sustainability of rules, including 'input legitimacy', mechanisms for 'enforcement of rules', 'resource synergies' in which material benefits of pursuing rules are shared, and clarity on 'transaction and organisational costs'. From this research, successful rules are rules that are efficient, equitable, open and dynamic with participation of agents and support of power holders. To this end, the research indicates that rule-making requires five crucial elements, particularly in more fragile contexts. First, this includes 'contextual stability and receptivity'. This relates to a local environment that is steady with power holders that are open and progressive. External agents (such as NGOs) can play a crucial role in enabling these conditions and creating 'islands of institutional experimentation'. Second, in the early phases, rule-making requires the introduction of institutions with 'innovative, culturally embedded design'. This refers to the formulation of progressive rules that are led by creative experts, and emphasises the importance of appropriate design, with rules that fit with existing sociocultural institutions. Third, rule-making needs 'collaborative and skilled reformulation legitimacy', with the reshaping of rules led by charismatic and capable entrepreneurs with group-oriented interests embedded in networks. This emphasises the importance of a participative process that promotes the local ownership of rules in addition to permitting (necessary) local adaptations. And notably, NGOs can be instrumental in giving credibility to these new evolving institutions, and garnering local trust in the women's work. Fourth, this includes 'authoritative legitimacy', with rule boundaries negotiated and agreed with local authorities. And fifth, in the final stabilisation phase, the achievement of 'cognitive synergies' between the community and enterprise leaders is vital. Failures in rule-making include underdeveloped rules (Case 3), the remoulding of rules that are hijacked or skewed towards the entrepreneur (Case 2b), and institutional fragility (Case 3), where there is cognitive dissonance between the women and power holders, with contrasting values and beliefs, leading to a lack of local support. It is worth noting that institutional sustainability (or the steady evolution of prevailing institutions) appears to be heavily shaped by both ongoing community dynamics and wider contextual political and social influences (beyond the community). The latter may be of particular relevance in a situation of uncertainty such as Afghanistan.

Socio-economic institutional trade-offs

Game theorists highlight the generation of trade-offs in new institutional arrangements. To this end, it seems important to look closer at the question of 'legitimacy' and 'cost' (social, economic) related to emerging institutions, and how this plays out in varying environments and evolving control mechanisms. The research shows that (conscious or unconscious) institutional trade-offs may arise both in terms of the business, in the functioning and future development of the enterprise, as well as in generating broader effects within the local social sphere. With regard to the business, the nature of enterprise institutions can have immediate and far-reaching economic implications. The level of 'openness' of the institution, and extent of legitimacy (by power holders), can have impacts on business efficiency, participation, flexibility, and intra-organisational hierarchies. Early choices on institutions can also set institutional pathways (described in section 7.4.3). Beyond the business, new institutions may also have unpredictable social ramifications (in the household and community), particularly in less stable environments. These new practices may generate short-term and long-term impacts on women's familial and community relations, and subsequently trigger change to household roles and expectations. New roles may be perceived to threaten the traditional order and control in the community (particularly if brought in too quickly), and resistance may persist with women ostracised and excluded from social events such as weddings (and their families intimidated). This can also disrupt the women's routines and hinder enterprise development. Further to this, new habits and practices may have knock-on effects within the community, as other interested and confident women try to mimic new roles and push social boundaries, creating further potential trouble for the enterprise women. Yet progressive (i.e. liberal) power holders can help the community to manage the new, evolving roles of women, and potential power shifts towards a new evolving order, particularly if supported by capable NGOs.

7.5 Concluding remarks and reflections on inclusive development

Pulling all of the various threads of this book together, in this study, I have endeavoured to carefully open up the 'institutional black box' to better understand the role of structure and agency in institutional change. This notably pushes forward the frontier of institutional theory, particularly where the discourse meets sociology and development studies. To date, key institutional contributions have been made by North (1989, 1990, 2004) (in the development of institutions); Hodgson (1997, 2004, 2007) and Gomez (2008) (in the effects of upward causation); Chang (2000, 2002) (in the role of power dynamics); and Ostrom (1990, 2005) (in understanding cooperation and institutional arrangements). Combining these theories with broader insights from the social sciences (e.g. Beckert, 1999; Fligstein, 2001), the research has unravelled the process of institutional change and development in enterprise, shaped by evolving norms, interests and local conditions. The study draws attention to the nested nature of institutions, non-economic motivations in institutional emergence, complex cooperation, and the role of trust and power. In an unusual approach, the study specifically looked at the transformation of a social institution (*purdah*) in precipitating the subsequent development of institutions in women's enterprise in Afghanistan, and the role of actors and local conditions in the institutional process. The research indicates that in fragile and conservative environments, external actors such as NGOs can both initiate and guide institutional development, alongside local actors. Yet there may be limitations to the NGOs' endeavours, with strong resistance from local power holders, unpredictable local entrepreneurs and disruptive events. Towards overcoming local opposition, the use of sociocultural (and religious) strategies has proved particularly notable. Progressive aspects of local culture (e.g. proverbs) and more favourable interpretations of religious texts have enabled the introduction of new ideas on women's roles, and have opened up attitudes regarding their mobility, permitting their culturally acceptable engagement in enterprise.

Drawing on expanded notions of agency, and the interaction with structure (Hodgson, 2004), agents are influenced by evolving skills, knowledge and capacity, and shifting motivations and interests, leading to diverse strategies. Agents may be further boosted by others' agency, reinforcing their own agency or garnering collective agency; or they can equally be thwarted by others' agency. Agents may also be affected by structure (e.g. norms, levels of trust and stability in the environment), or they can affect structure through transforming existing norms, and creating new degrees of trust and stability within environments. With significant implications for institutional path development, the research has indicated the emergence of dominant entrepreneurs in enterprise in fragile contexts. Thriving under more stable and conducive conditions, trailblazer entrepreneurs were shown to draw on their allies and be boosted by others' agency to facilitate open, democratic and 'inclusive' institutions with equitable participation, and diverse networks with less regulated levels of adoption and diffusion. This can positively influence value chain development towards 'productive' institutional path development. Yet if such entrepreneurs are constrained, this may lead to 'unproductive' institutional path development. Going beyond the enterprise, these new open institutions may further precipitate new attitudes and preferences among women and within the community, generating broader positive social, economic and political institutions. Meanwhile, flourishing under less stable conditions, gatekeeper entrepreneurs may foster more destructive pathways, in the generation of closed and 'exclusive' institutions and tight networks with highly regulated levels of adoption and diffusion. This can lead to more skewed economic development and 'destructive' institutional path development. Lessons for successful rule development include the critical role that NGOs can play as institutional innovators and guides; the need for legitimacy in reshaping and ongoing institutional development, led by the entrepreneurs; and the importance of gaining the support of local authorities. Ultimately, the research underscores the value of attaining cognitive synergies between these major players, in a receptive and stable context, towards more sustainable institutional development.

In these closing arguments, it is also necessary to reflect more broadly on women's economic development and such processes of facilitation and institutional evolution, transcending the research context of Afghanistan (and research cases). Sen (1999) described five instrumental types of freedom, including political freedoms (e.g. free speech and elections), economic engagement (e.g. participation in trade and production), social opportunities (e.g. access to education and health facilities), transparency guarantees and protective security. He describes how different freedoms can strengthen one another, and draws attention to the underlying nature of social values and norms, which can influence these freedoms. Finally, he underscores the importance of individual and collective agency in bringing about change. Recently, the particular influence of social institutions has been re-emphasised in the development of the Organisation for Economic Co-operation and Development's Social Institutions and Gender Index (SIGI) (Jones *et al.*, 2010). The SIGI highlights the relationship between discriminatory social institutions – defined as laws, norms, traditions and codes of conduct – and the scope of women's engagement in economic activities. The research has touched directly upon such issues, exploring the promotion of equitable social institutions in precipitating women's economic development, and the development of broader inclusive and democratic institutions. The original roots of debates on social inclusion and exclusion are in fact found in social policy discourse within the European Union (Hospes and Clancy, 2011: 23). Wider discussions have generated a more nuanced understanding of inclusion (ibid.). First, these indicate that inclusion may not always be desired by the excluded. For example, studies show how some groups preferred their outside status, and were keen to retain their own values and priorities (Kabeer, 2000). Second, these highlight the limitations of top-down policies and programmes in reducing discrimination, which ignore the role of 'privileged insiders' who influence and determine local norms and rules (ibid.). Third, these show that social inclusion or exclusion is neither a permanent status nor a dichotomy; instead, there may be more of 'continuum' between the positions (Berkel *et al.*, 2002). The research notably adds further nuanced insights into these observations. It highlights the role that capable outsiders can play in initiating change – on a continuum – in a fragile and conservative context, and the role that powerful insiders can also play, either in supporting such change or in intimidating the excluded into accepting prevailing (discriminatory) beliefs and practices.

Meanwhile, rights campaigners view formal laws as the ultimate mechanism to overcome discriminatory practices and promote broader social, economic and political roles for women. Yet new formal institutions need to resonate with the prevailing culture to enable a sustainable change in behaviour (World Bank, 2002). While constraints on women's mobility pervade the Third World poor,[2] in traditional Muslim communities conservative interpretations of Islam can lead to an exacerbation of this 'global norm', in further restricting women's mobility. Yet in such communities, there may also be opportunities for measured change, if scriptures can be reinterpreted. Religion thus may be a resource, as well as a barrier for development. Ter Haar (2011) argues that development through religion can indeed be transformative, particularly if progressive religious leaders can be involved. Reinforcing this perspective, the study has shown that facilitating careful change to fundamental social institutions such as *purdah* through progressive religious messages can be both transformative, and act as an anchor for stability in subsequent enterprise development, particularly in supportive contexts (where there is trust with progressive actors). In similar contexts such as the Yemen, the raising of awareness of egalitarian Islamic codes has also been shown to enable activities related to women's empowerment (Zahedi, 2011: 302). However, the research has shown that where strong local honour codes prevail, this can limit the effectiveness of religious strategies to development.

In examining institutional processes and diverse actors in a fragile context, the study provides further critical insights for value chain and enterprise work, and local economic development. Kaplinsky and Morris (2000) describe how value chain analysis has tended to look at power between actors in the chain but not within the different segments of the chain. The role of non-chain actors has also been overlooked in chain governance (Helmsing and Vellema, 2011). In traditional and volatile contexts such as Afghanistan, value chains are heavily influenced by informal structures, relations and norms, and often exacerbated by the situation of risk. Yet the main emphasis of market development projects has been simply in 'accelerating small and medium-sized enterprise', with an implicit assumption that this will gradually resolve all other 'market failures'. Projects with (non-elite) women thus stumble upon sociocultural barriers to both entry and participation in enterprise initiatives. Market development programmes tend to overlook the fundamental importance of these (dynamic) social institutions and the nature of local contexts, and their influence on social relations, trust and cooperation. Over the long term, this risks being counterproductive. As indicated by this study, pursuing a strictly economics-based strategy may indeed perpetuate and exacerbate the nature of existing social exclusion (Christoplos and Hilhorst, 2009), particularly in an informal and unstable context. Meanwhile, the entrepreneurship literature has typically classified (poor) entrepreneurs as either 'survival' or 'growth-oriented', with these factors influencing the scope of enterprise development (e.g. Berner *et al.*, 2009). Yet arguably as crucial, the research indicates that entrepreneur motivations may be further rooted in more deep-seated social and political inclinations, with significant implications for broader socio-economic development.

This book has advanced discussions on the importance of multi-actor, structural and evolutionary thinking in institutional change, going beyond either pure individualism or structuralism, towards appreciating institutional processes and their outcomes. In particular, the nature of institutional development may have important implications for local economic development, with patterns of (nested) institutions generated by dominant entrepreneurs. The research has indicated that *trailblazer entrepreneurs* can generate both open and democratic institutions, and promote inclusive opportunities for (new) power and wealth, even in fragile contexts, particularly if supported by enlightened actors. Yet *gatekeeper entrepreneurs* can equally foster distorted economies through the reproduction of more exclusive institutions. To incorporate crucial non-economic influences, the role of agency and the interconnectedness of institutions, this book argues for a more collaborative and interdisciplinary approach to the critical study of institutions (Hollingsworth, 2002; Hodgson, 2007), towards the potential development of a common framework (Ostrom, 1986). This may enable the further development of theory, with a greater appreciation of culture, religion and fragility. For the field of *development*, this may also permit both deeper and more nuanced understandings of fundamental processes of change in human societies.

Notes

1   Charles Lindblom (1959) used the term 'muddling through' in his famous paper, *The Science of Muddling Through*, to describe non-linear processes of decision-making in public policy, emphasising instead a process of negotiation.
2   For example, physical insecurity or occupational hazards often restrict poor women's movement and choices (e.g. Moser *et al.*, 2005).

References

Ansell, C. (1998) 'Symbolic networks', *American Journal of Sociology*, 103: 359–90.
Appiah, K.A. (2010) *The Honor Code: How Moral Revolutions Happen*, New York and London: W.W. Norton & Company.
Bardhan, P. (1989) 'The new institutional economics and development theory: A brief critical assessment', *World Development*, 17(9): 1389–1395.
Baron, R.A. (2004) 'Potential benefits of the cognitive perspective: Expanding entrepreneurship's array of conceptual tools', *Journal of Business Venturing*, 19: 169–72.
Battilana, J., Leca, B. and Boxenbaum, E. (2009) 'How actors change institutions: towards a theory of institutional entrepreneurship', *The Academy of Management Annals: A Journal of the Academy of Management*, 3(1): 65–107.
Baumol, W. (1990) 'Entrepreneurship: productive, unproductive and destructive', *The Journal of Political Economy*, 98(5): 893–921.
Beckert, J. (1999) 'Agency, entrepreneurs, and institutional change: the role of strategic choice and institutionalized practices in organizations', *Organisation Studies*, 20(5): 777–99.

Beckert, J. (2003) 'Economic sociology and embeddedness: how shall we conceptualize economic action?', *Journal of Economic Issues*, 37(3): 769–87.

Beinhocker, E. (2007) *The Origin of Wealth: Evolution, Complexity and the Radical Remaking of Economics*, London: Random House Business Books.

Berkel, R., van Moller, I.H. and Williams, C.C. (2002) 'The concept of inclusion/exclusion and the concept of work', in R. van Berkel and I.H. Moller (eds), *Active Social Policies in the EU: Inclusion through Participation*, Bristol, UK: Policy Press.

Berner, E., Gomez, G. and Knorringa, P. (2009) *Helping a Large Number of People Become a Little Less Poor*, The Hague: ISS.

Boettke, P.J., Coyne, C.J. and Leeson, P. (2008) 'Institutional stickiness and the new development economics', *The American Journal of Economics and Sociology*, 67(2): 331–58.

Bowles, S. and Gintis, H. (2011) *A Cooperative Species: Human Reciprocity and its Evolution*, Princeton, NJ: Princeton University Press.

Campbell, J.L. (1997) 'Mechanisms of evolutionary change in economics governance: interaction, interpretation and bricolage', in L. Magnusson and J. Ottosson (eds), *Evolutionary Economics and Path Dependence*, Cheltenham, UK: Edward Elgar.

Chang, H.-J. (2002) 'Breaking the mould: an institutionalist political economy alternative to the neo-liberal theory of the market and the state', *Cambridge Journal of Economics*, 26(5): 539–59.

Chang, H.-J. and Evans, P. (2000) 'The role of institutions in economic change', *Proceedings of the 'Other Canon' Group*, Venice, Italy, 13–14 January.

Child, J., Lua, Y. and Tsai, T. (2007) 'Institutional entrepreneurship in building an environmental protection system for the People's Republic of China', *Organisation Studies*, 28(7): 1013–34.

Christoplos, I. and Hilhorst, D. (2009) *Human Security and Capacity in Fragile States*, Netherlands: Wageningen University.

Collier, R.B. and Collier, D. (1991) *Shaping the Political Arena: Critical Junctures, the Labor Movement and Regime Dynamics in Latin America*, Princeton, NJ: Princeton University Press.

Coser, L.A. (1977) *Masters of Sociological Thought: Ideas in Historical and Social Context* (2nd edn), Fort Worth, TX: Harcourt Brace Jovanovich.

Desai, S. and Acs, Z.J. (2007) 'A theory of destructive entrepreneurship', *Jena Economic Research Papers 2007*, 085, Max-Planck-Institut fur Okonomik.

DiMaggio, P.J. and Powell, W. (1991) 'Introduction' in W. Powell and P.J. DiMaggio (eds) *The New Institutionalism in Organizational Analysis*, Chicago, IL: University of Chicago Press.

Dosi, G. (1995) 'Hierarchies, markets and power: some foundational issues on the nature of contemporary economic organisations', *Industrial and Corporate Change*, 4(1): 1–19.

Douglas, M. (1986) *How Institutions Think*, Syracuse, NY: Syracuse University Press.

Emirbayer, M. and Goodwin, J. (1994) 'Network analysis, culture, and the problem of agency', *American Journal of Sociology*, 99(6): 1411–1454.

Entezar, E. (2007) *Afghanistan 101: Understanding Afghan Culture*, Bloomington, IN: Xlibris Corporation.

Everett, D. (2012) *Language: The Cultural Tool*, New York: Pantheon Books.

Fligstein, N. (1996) 'Markets as politics: a political-cultural approach to market institutions', *American Sociological Review*, 61: 656–73.

Fligstein, N. (1997) 'Social skill and institutional theory', *American Behavioural Scientist*, 40(4): 397–405.

Fligstein, N. (2001) 'Social skill and the theory of fields', *Sociological Theory*, 19(2): 105–25.

Ford, J.D., Ford, L.W. and D'Amelio, A. (2008) 'Resistance to change: the rest of the story', *The Academy of Management Review*, 33(2): 362–77.

Fukuyama, F. (1995) *Trust: The Social Virtues and Creation of Prosperity*, New York: Free Press Paperbacks.

Geertz, C. (1973) *The Interpretation of Cultures*, New York: Basic Books.

Gomez, G. (2008) *Making Markets: The Institutional Rise and Decline of the Argentine Red de Trueque*, Netherlands: Shaker Publishing BV (PhD Thesis).

Graf, H. (2011) 'Gatekeepers in regional networks of innovators', *Cambridge Journal of Economics*, 35: 173–98.

Granovetter, M. (2005) 'The impact of social structure on economic outcomes', *Journal of Economic Perspectives*, 19: 33–50.

Greenwood, R., Suddaby, R. and Hinings, C.R. (2002) 'Theorizing change: the role of professional associations in the transformation of institutionalized fields', *Academy of Management Journal*, 45(1): 58–80.

Greif, A. (2006) 'The birth of impersonal exchange: the community responsibility system and impartial justice', *Journal of Economic Perspectives*, 20(2): 221–36.

Haidt, J. (2012) *The Righteous Mind*, London: Allen Lane.

Heckathorn, D.D. (1984) 'A formal theory of social exchange: process and outcome', *Current Perspectives in Social Theory*, 5: 145–80.

Helmsing, B. and Vellema, S. (2011) *Value Chains, Social Inclusion and Economic Development: Contrasting Theories and Realities*, Oxford: Routledge Studies in Development Economics.

Hodgson, G. (1997) 'The ubiquity of habits and rules', *Cambridge Journal of Economics*, 21: 663–84.

Hodgson, G. (2000) 'What is the essence of institutional economics?', *Journal of Economic Issues*, 34(2): 317–29.

Hodgson, G. (2003) 'The hidden persuaders, institutions and individuals in economic theory', *Cambridge Journal of Economics*, 27: 159–75.

Hodgson, G. (2004) *The Evolution of Instituional Economics: Agency, Structure and Darwinism in American Institutionalism*, London: Routledge.

Hodgson, G. (2007) 'Institutions and individuals: interaction and evolution', *Organisation Studies*, 28(1): 95–111.

Hollingsworth, J.R. (2002) 'Some reflections on how institutions influence styles of innovation', paper for Swedish Collegium for Advanced Study of the Social Sciences, 26 September, available at: http://history.wisc.edu/hollingsworth/documents/Some_Reflections_on_How_Institutions_Influence_Styles_of_Innovation.htm, accessed 1 December 2012.

Hollingsworth, J.R. and Boyer, R. (1997) (eds) *Contemporary Capitalism*, Cambridge: Cambridge University Press.

Holm, P. (1995) 'The dynamics of institutionalization: transformation processes in Norwegian fisheries', *Administrative Science Quarterly*, 40(3): 398–422.

Horne, C. (2001) 'Sociological perspectives on the emergence of norms', in M. Hechter and K. Opp (eds), *Social Norms*, New York: Russell Sage Foundation.

Hospes, O. and Clancy, J. (2011) 'Unpacking the discourse on social inclusion in value chains', in B. Helmsing and S. Vellema (eds), *Value Chains, Social Inclusion and Economic Development: Contrasting Theories and Realities*, London: Routledge.

Joas, H. (1996) *The Creativity of Action*, Chicago, IL: University of Chicago Press.

Johnson, B. (1992) 'Institutional learning', in B. Lundvall (ed.), *National Systems of Innovation: Towards a Theory of Innovation and Interactive Learning*, London: Pinter.

Jones, N., Harper, C. and Watson, C. (2010) *Stemming Girls' Chronic Poverty: Catalysing Development Change by Building Just Social Institutions*, Northampton, UK: Chronic Poverty Research Centre.

Kabeer, N. (2000) 'Social exclusion, poverty and discrimination: Towards an analytical framework', *IDS Bulletin*, 31: 83–97.

Kandori, M. (1992) 'Social norms and community enforcement', *The Review Economic Studies*, 59: 63–80.

Kaplinsky, R. and Morris, M. (2000) *A Handbook for Value Chain Research*, Rugby, UK: IDRC.

Klyver, K. and Schott, T. (2011) 'How social network structure shapes entrepreneurial intentions?', *Journal of Global Entrepreneurship Research*, 1(1): 3–19.

Lanzara, G.F. (1998) 'Self-destructive processes in institution building and some modest countervailing mechanisms', *European Journal of Political Research*, 33: 1–39.

Lawson, T. (1997) 'Realism, explanation and science', in T. Lawson (ed.), *Economics and Reality*, London: Routledge.

Lindblom, C. (1959) 'The science of "muddling through"', *Public Administration Review*, 19(2): 79–88.

Lyon, F. and Porter, G. (2009) 'Market institutions, trust and norms: exploring moral economies in Nigerian food systems', *Cambridge Journal of Economics*, 33: 903–20.

Maguire, S., Hardy, C. and Lawrence, T.B. (2004) 'Institutional entrepreneurship in emerging fields: HIV/AIDS treatment advocacy in Canada', *Academy of Management Journal*, 47(5): 657–79.

Marx, K. (1986) 'Outlines of the critique of political economy', in *The Collected Works of Karl Marx and Frederick Engels: Volume 28*, New York: International Publishers.

Mills, M.A. (1991) *Rhetorics and Politics in Afghan Traditional Storytelling*, Philadelphia, PA: University of Pennsylvania.

Moser, C., Winton, A. and Moser, A. (2005) 'Violence, fear and insecurity among the urban poor in Latin America', in M. Fay (ed.), *The Urban Poor in Latin America*, Washington, DC: World Bank.

North, D. (1989) 'Institutions and economic growth: A historical introduction', *World Development*, 17(9): 1319–1332.

North, D. (1990) *Institutions, Institutional Change and Economic Performance*, Cambridge, Cambridge University Press.

North, D. (1995) 'The new institutional economics and development', *Economics Working Paper Archive 9309002*, St. Louis, MO: Washington University, available at: www.nju.edu.cn/cps/siteNJU/njuc/dep/shangyuan/2.doc, accessed 1 December 2012.

North, D. (2003) 'The role of institutions in economic development', *ECE Discussion Papers Series*, 2003(2).

North, D., Mantzavinos, C. and Shariq, S. (2004) 'Learning, institutions and economic performance', *Perspectives on Politics*, 2(1): 75–84.

North, D., Wallis, J.J. and Weingast, B.R. (2009) *Violence and Social Orders: A Conceptual Framework for Interpreting Recorded Human History*, Cambridge: Cambridge University Press.

Ostrom, E. (1986) 'An agenda for the study of institutions', *Public Choice*, 48: 3–25.

Ostrom, E. (1990) *Governing the Commons: The Evolution of Institutions for Collective Action*, Cambridge: Cambridge University Press.

Ostrom, E. (2005) *Understanding Institutional Diversity*, Princeton, NJ and Oxford: Princeton University Press.

Parto, S. (2008) 'Economic activity and institutions: taking stock', *Journal of Economic Issues*, 39(1): 1005–1030.

Peyton Young, H. (2007) 'Social norms', *Oxford Department of Economics Discussion Paper Series No 307*, Oxford: University of Oxford.

Philo, C. and Parr, H. (2000) 'Institutional geographies: introductory remarks', *Geoforum*, 31(4): 513–21.

Platteau, J.P. (2000) *Institutions, Social Norms, and Economic Development*, Amsterdam: Harwood Academic Publishers.

Redmond, W.H. (2003) 'Innovation, diffusion, and institutional change', *Journal of Economic Issues*, 37(3): 665–79.

Sen, A. (1999) *Development as Freedom*, Oxford: Oxford University Press.

Somit, A. and Peterson, S.A. (eds) (1992) *The Dynamics of Evolution: The Punctuated Equilibrium Debate in the Natural and Social Sciences*, Ithaca, NY: Cornell University Press.

Streeck, W. (2002) 'Institutional complementarity and dynamics of economic systems', *Notes for International Seminar Organized by CEPREMAP*, 5–6 April, Paris.

Ter Haar, G. (ed.) (2011) *Religion and Development*, London: C. Hurst & Co.

Udehn, L. (1993) 'Twenty-five years with "The Logic of Collective Action"', *Acta Sociologica*, 36(3): 239–61.

Veblen, T. (1899) *The Theory of the Leisure Class: An Economic Study in the Evolution of Institutions*, New York: Macmillan.

Weber, M. (1904/1930) *The Protestant Ethic and the Spirit of Capitalism* (translated by T. Parson), New York: Charles Scribner's Sons.

World Bank (2002) *World Development Report: Building Institutions for Markets*, Oxford: Oxford University Press.

Wright, R. (2010) *NonZero: History, Evolution and Human Cooperation*, London: Abacus.

Zahedi, A. (2011) 'When the picture does not fit the frame: engaging Afghan men in women's empowerment', in J. Heath and A. Zahedi (eds), *Land of the Unconquerable: The Lives of Contemporary Afghan Women*, Berkeley, CA and London: University of California Press.

Appendix 1

Reflections on research methods and process

This appendix adds further reflections on the research methods and process.

A1.1 Use of ethnographic techniques in exploring institutional change

Of the research techniques employed, it is particularly pertinent to elaborate on the ethnographic methods used to explore the perspectives of the women at the community level and those participating in the business. Complementing interviews with NGO staff and entrepreneurs, and researcher observation, these innovative techniques proved critical in further unravelling the intricacies of institutional transformation and construction processes and the role of key actors, and delving into sensitive topics around culture, religion and local power. A crucial participatory exercise sought in particular to prompt and unwrap key events, actor stories and the different strategies employed, and change dynamics, in the course of institutional transformation and development. Sets of flash cards depicted illustrations of various groups from within and outside of the community, and were used to open up discussions on dominant actors.[1] Coloured cards were then used to denote different types of strategies employed,[2] and handfuls of beans represented the respective actor's power and influence. From early interviews and discussions, several community and non-community groups had been pre-identified as playing a crucial role in institutional change processes, including local male leaders and religious clerics, the NGO and the enterprise women themselves. Conducted at the community level, women from within and outside of the enterprise groups (including women leaders) were invited to participate in these discussion sessions. With the aid of the cards, women elaborated on the roles that respective groups had played, and their strategies, background and key events. This interactive session endeavoured to ensure that different women spoke, and were able to share their perspectives. Across the cases, this proved to be a powerful research tool that generated new insights into opaque institutional processes, and permitted the women to openly discuss the change process, both in a non-threatening way and in greater depth and detail.

Meanwhile, a second exercise looked at indications of change in local practices as a result of these institutional processes. In this session, flash cards depicted illustrations of women's social practices (such as their mobility (to move beyond the house) and local relations (beyond the family)), as well as (new) economic practices (such as engagement in banking, property and training). This exercise sought to prompt discussions on behaviours both before the business was initiated, and new emerging norms during the time of the research. Finally, in the latter stages of the research, a third exercise finally explored women's emerging business relations and networks. This session aimed to better understand the new relationships forged in the course of the business. The entrepreneur (and in some cases senior workers) was tasked with labelling blank cards with different specific actor descriptions (places, names, etc.). These included buyers, service providers (e.g. packaging agents, banks), suppliers, offices and other villages. The cards were then physically attached by string to a core card representing the enterprise group. Finally, the women were asked to assign handfuls of beans to the most 'important connections' for their business. Initially approached with some confusion, as this exercise unfolded, the women became animated as they described all of their various 'new relations'. This prompted an open discussion on their businesses, including persisting challenges, as well as new ideas. This final exercise provided broader insights into the nature of their growing businesses and the diversity (and quality value) of their connections, and the evolving goals of the entrepreneurs.

Overall, these participatory-oriented sessions permitted both relaxed, and strikingly rich discussions, in a style that was arguably more suitable for less educated women in low-trust contexts (that were unaccustomed to interview style questions and/or afraid to speak out). While varied in their effectiveness (across the exercises and cases), the sessions generated deeper levels of understanding of the attitudes, perceptions and relations at the local level in the course of institutional change. It is worth noting, however, that in more conservative communities (e.g. Cases 2b and 3), these participative sessions proved to be more challenging (particularly the first two exercises). This was in large part due to the dominance of the entrepreneur, leading to significantly less openness by the other enterprise women. In these communities and groups, it was more difficult to fully discuss the various community actors in institutional development, and the ways that life had changed (beyond the entrepreneur).

A1.2 'Conscious' bias shaping research

Three potential levels of bias are said to typically influence the research process and outcomes, including the researcher, the research respondents, and the research process (Sumner and Tribe, 2004: 12). In this research, it is important to highlight how such biases have indeed shaped the investigation in different ways. First, I endeavoured to be aware of my own influence on the research process, and how my experience, values and interests shaped the design/approach of the research. The overall investigation built on several years of work in the research context, and businesses were purposively selected from previous field experiences to allow for deeper analysis. This broad exposure had greatly informed me and enabled me to dip beneath the complex surface of Afghanistan and learn (culturally) appropriate ways of interacting and communicating. During this time, I had also gained a significant understanding of agent behaviour within the environment, and this permitted greater sensitivity to the layered dynamics of reality in the research. These experiences and insights influenced the direction of the research, the tools used and interpretation. Conscious of this, I tried to remain open to broader ideas, and to keep the research process flexible, reshaping the investigation as necessary. I also tried to remain aware of the researcher tendency to reject non-hypothesis supporting evidence during the course of the research. To this end, the research investigation was divided over three research phases, allowing time to reflect on intermediary findings and biases.

Second, I recognised the potential bias by the researched in the course of the investigation: in possibly under-reporting, giving inaccurate accounts, and in responding for (less powerful) others. Being a non-Afghan may have influenced tendencies for people to be suspicious and to distort stories. To reduce this, I adopted modest Afghan dress, and endeavoured to ensure culturally appropriate behaviour in both verbal and non-verbal communication, respecting key rituals of greetings, listening, and maintaining suitable levels of eye contact and bodily movements. In the male community forums, it was also critical to speak with purpose and strength. Afghanistan is a traditional oral culture where the ability to speak well in public is highly regarded, and this equally applies in a community group setting. Yet as a foreign woman, I was privileged to be able to enter both the female and the male spheres of the community as a token 'third sex' (unlike Afghan men and women, or even the foreign male). As Centlivres and Centlivres-Demont (2010: 54) described: 'in men's eyes, the foreign woman before being a woman is a person whose female character is neutralized by the quality of being a European guest, and by her independent, manlike status and behaviour. Thus her presence can be accepted in places where their own wives, daughters and sisters are not allowed'. To further gain local trust and confidence, I also adopted a gradual and sensitive approach. And to ensure that I gained clear information, I revisited similar themes over time with different research techniques and a diverse set of respondents.

Third, I remained conscious of the bias of the research process itself: the scope of the research cases, the research methodologies employed, the level of interpretation, as well as the potential influence of the actual research on the cases. While the exploratory, sensitive and gradual research phase was fruitful in terms of the breadth of data collected, field visits completed and the use of some innovative techniques, the process was significantly more challenging and constrained than anticipated. In terms of access to respondents, enhanced security concerns during the research period greatly disrupted the schedule of research activities and influenced the possible time spent in the field (with increased pressure to complete activities quickly). Further to this, some of the NGO staff in the case studies proved to be uncooperative, creating barriers to village visits without their necessary accompaniment. To overcome these difficulties, it was sometimes necessary to arrange meetings outside of the village. In terms of specific research methodologies, the investigation drew on diverse techniques,

Figure A1.1 Visual technique with cards and beans exploring local actor strategies

Note: Cards depict different common strategies (e.g. white = use of Islamic messages/sayings, green = coordination, yellow = troubleshooting, red = causing problems, e.g. gossiping, threats, etc.). Beans indicate level of actor influence.

Source: Author's own picture

Figure A1.2 Visual techniques with (a) cards exploring scope of change in
attitudes/practices at the village level and (b) cards, string and beans
exploring type/importance of links between the enterprise and other actors

Source: Author's own picture

including a mix of ethnographic methods to better understand situational/actor nuances. The latter elicited fascinating insights, although the design of these techniques and choice of respondents naturally influenced the type of research results (narratives and themes). In terms of interpretation, I was constrained by a less than full mastery of the language (Persian) at the field level, necessitating the part use of a translator. Where possible, however, I tried to ensure that I partially communicated in the local language throughout the process. Nonetheless, the translation of key discussions, and more subtle expressions and social behaviours was crucial. This proved difficult at times (due to the varying capacities of the translators), constraining a more careful and in-depth discussion of new attitudes and practices. To keep original language remarks, I tried to ensure literal translations. Touching upon the extremely sensitive and delicate topic of Islam and changes related to *Koran/hadith* interpretation/practices was also particularly challenging as a foreigner, a non-Muslim and a woman. Yet, in some cases, upon settling into conversations with the male elders, being a woman transpired to be oddly less threatening, and discussions were (surprisingly) broad and open. Finally, I was also fully cognisant of my own impact on the research cases, influencing the nature of the cases and their business direction during the course of the research (Hawthorne effect).

Notes

1   These illustrations were drawn from a BBC comic strip depicting Afghan village life (from the radio programme *New Home New Life*).
2   Coloured cards represented different actor tactics, including religious strategies (e.g. using messages from religious texts); cultural strategies (e.g. using stories from other villages, proverbs); coordination/mediation strategies (e.g. brokering between groups); and resistant-oriented strategies (e.g. blocking new ideas, causing conflict).

References

Centlivres, P. and Centlivres-Demont, M. (2010) *Afghanistan on the Threshold of the 21st Century. Three Essays on Culture and Society,* Princeton, NJ: Markus Wiener Publishers.
Mills, M.A. (1991) *Rhetorics and Politics in Afghan Traditional Storytelling*, Philadelphia, PA: University of Pennsylvania.
Sumner, A. and Tribe, M. (2004) 'The nature of epistemology and methodology in development studies: what do we mean by rigour?', Paper prepared for The Nature of Development Studies DSA Annual Conference, 'Bridging Research and Policy', Church House, London, 6 November.

Appendix 2
Case study business backgrounds

This appendix presents brief and consolidated business backgrounds of the three research cases, elaborating upon the respective enterprise status and operations. It specifically outlines aspects of their production and supply, marketing, management and technology.

A2.1 Case study 1: women's food processing business

Supported by a local NGO, the rural women's food processing business was located across three districts close to Herat City in West Afghanistan. With initial groups established in 2004, towards the end of the research, the business association comprised 36 women's food processing centres (15–20 women per centre) across 36 villages (with a total of approximately 700 workers). The business had notably doubled in size during the course of the study. Participating women tended to be between 25 and 55 years old, with most stemming from medium-wealth groups within the community. Food processing (FP) groups were linked for trouble-shooting and higher-level marketing (using a common market label in the city). While 70 per cent of the produce was still sold by weight locally, there were growing levels of city sales through the association. Yet in the final phases of the research, some of the more mature groups were intending to break away from the network, due to dissatisfaction with the product quality of other groups and collaborative exchange.

(i) Production and supply

Each of the FP groups had their own designated 'food processing centre' in the village that was usually a spare room (6 m²) in a traditional local mud house usually belonging to one of the women's relatives. The room tended to be very basic with bare walls, no running water and simple electricity (bulb and one power socket). Vegetable and fruit resources were gathered from the village (and surrounding villages) by the entrepreneurs, with the support of their families. Production was then organised in shifts, with women assigned either to morning or afternoon work times (with Fridays and national holidays considered legitimate days off). Goods produced by the groups were described to incorporate over 20 varieties of food-processed products! The main products, however, included tomato paste, chutney, pickle, carrot and apple jams, and dried okra and eggplant. In the high season, the groups reported producing 200 jars (i.e. 500 g of produce) per week each (for city sales), in addition to more than 240 kg of unpackaged goods (village service). In the absence of food standards agencies, the local NGO had helped the business seek approval of the Ministry of Health (MOH) to certify product quality and production hygiene. In-house, the groups also used a refractometer to occasionally measure the water and sugar content of jarred products, and the local NGO conducted additional spot checks.

(ii) Marketing and demand

The food processing groups sold their products both at the local level (most), and increasingly at a joint city level. Within the village, the processed produce was sold by weight, with orders also received from neighbouring villages (often raw produce was brought directly to the centre, and a fee paid for processing only). At first, these products and services were promoted through wedding parties and in family settings (since these forums were the most accessible to the women). As their centres became well known, and both the village and neighbouring villages became aware of their existence, people came directly to them. At the city level, the groups sold their 'premium quality' packaged products in their own shop (Herat), at exhibitions, and to local bulk buyers (shopkeepers, offices and hotels) (with initial support by the NGO). Cheap packaging (jars, plastic sealed bags and plastic sandwich boxes) was still mostly sourced from Pakistan (organised by the local NGO), although adequate packaging was beginning to be available locally through emerging distributors. During the research, the groups had trouble keeping up with the high city demand for tomato paste and carrot jam. Their main market competitors included large Iranian companies (especially for tomato paste and jams). Yet while the packaging was more sophisticated, the quality was indicated to be lower for these imports and the price steeper. Small national food processing companies were also starting to emerge in Kabul – producing a range of jams and chutneys – but these companies were not yet supplying to the Herat market.

(iii) Management/operations

The 36 village-based 'food processing centres' were innovatively networked into one FP business. While the groups' representatives (group entrepreneurs) met at a collective level to coordinate on higher-level (city) business activities, the overall business strategy was still guided by the local NGO. Notably, new groups (initiated by the NGO) were not permitted to join the business (and thus market with the common label) until a 'good standard' had been reached, as decided by the existing heads. Management-wise, the FP enterprise was largely decentralised to the village level, with production (including quality control), local marketing and profit distribution organised by each group. This appeared to facilitate transparency, accountability and local decision-making.

Running costs of each centre were estimated at $100 per month (low season) to $500 per month (high season), with typical expenses including raw produce, gas, bottles, labels and packaging. Each group covered their own costs through their profits and savings. Further to this, each centre had rented (or planned to rent) a garden for growing produce (two *jeribs*) to make savings in the purchase of raw produce (from village farmers). There were no 'worker salaries' per se, but rather profit was divided up at the end of each month within the group, with the group head taking a slightly higher agreed share. On average, workers received $40 per month in the high season, with 15 per cent of profits retained for savings. Workers described each centre functioning almost autonomously (except for city marketing).

(iv) Technology and assets

Initial group assets were purchased by the NGO, and included a basic set of equipment such as buckets, metal saucepans, packaging/sealing machine, protective clothing, manual pulveriser, juicers, generator and stove, with total costs of approximately $4,000 per centre. In terms of larger business assets and technology (e.g. pulping machine), this was predominantly organised at a collective group level, and sharing arrangements were agreed between the entrepreneurs. At the end of the research, some of the more mature groups (including the research villages) were upgrading their own group technology and purchasing new assets through externally sourced funds. These included electrical processing machines and solar driers.

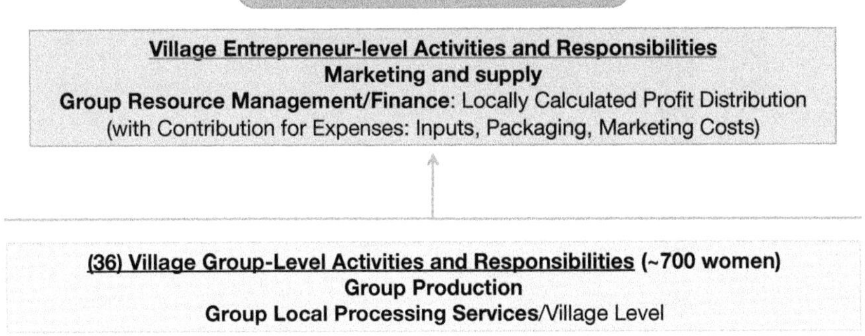

Business Network-level Activities and Responsibilities
Marketing for Sale of Group Agreed Produce in Herat
Link to Packaging Agents

Network of 36 FPC Entrepreneurs

Village Entrepreneur-level Activities and Responsibilities
Marketing and supply
Group Resource Management/Finance: Locally Calculated Profit Distribution
(with Contribution for Expenses: Inputs, Packaging, Marketing Costs)

(36) Village Group-Level Activities and Responsibilities (~700 women)
Group Production
Group Local Processing Services/Village Level

Figure A2.1 Women's food processing business management and operations
Source: Author's own illustration

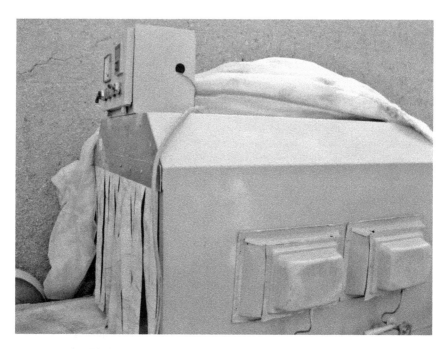

Figure A2.2 Upgrading food processing technology in the village: electric processors
and drying machine

Source: Author's own picture

A2.2 Case study 2: women's vegetable production business

Supported by an international NGO (in collaboration with a local NGO), the second (rural) enterprise was a series of women's vegetable production groups in the central province of Parwan. With the first village groups mobilised in 2007, at the start of the research, he business was straddled across nine villages with a total of 90 women's farmer groups (with approximately 20 women per group), and approximately 2,250 farmers. In each village, the NGO employed one woman as the lead coordinator or village facilitator (the '*entrepreneur*' for this research), to oversee the established farmers' groups. The NGO paid her a generous monthly salary, although this was phased out at the end of the research (with the INGO's exit). At the head of each of the farmers' groups, one woman was then selected as a *lead farmer*, receiving a small stipend for basic supplies for her farmers' groups (again, this was phased out with the INGO's exit). Lead farmers supported their group members in individual production and local marketing. At a later stage in the project, village *sales agents* (two per village) were nominated to support joint city marketing of produce (on commission).

(i) Production and supply

Essentially, the participating women farmers agreed to work independently on their own private land (at least 0.25 *jeribs* or 500 m^2), sharing their progress and yields in their respective farmers' groups. Priority vegetables and fruits included carrots, cucumbers, onions, potatoes, tomatoes, and grapes (as preselected by the NGO). In the middle of the research, new techniques and facilities had also been introduced to make processed foods such as tomato paste, chutney and dried products. After three years in the business, average women farmers described typically producing between 750 kg and 1,000 kg of vegetables per year, with annual profits of approximately $300–$400 (with lead farmers described to produce twice these amounts).[1]

(ii) Marketing and demand

Marketing was predominantly independent and local, yet there was a large emphasis placed by the NGO on the joint city marketing of premium fresh produce (perhaps up to 10 per cent) with the establishment of village sales agents. Sales agents were linked to several input suppliers, packaging agents, wholesalers and grocery stalls in Kabul and Charikar. In addition, villages were connected to microfinance organisations for agricultural loans to facilitate access to credit for the women farmers. At the time of the research, the women were selling their produce within communities, in the market town of Charikar, and in exhibitions and markets in Kabul. For the local bazaar, the vegetables were sold loose. For the higher-end city sales, basic packaging in baskets had been introduced for vegetables, and locally sourced plastic jars for processed foods. At city exhibitions, common labels and branding were used during the INGO support, although sales profits remained individual.

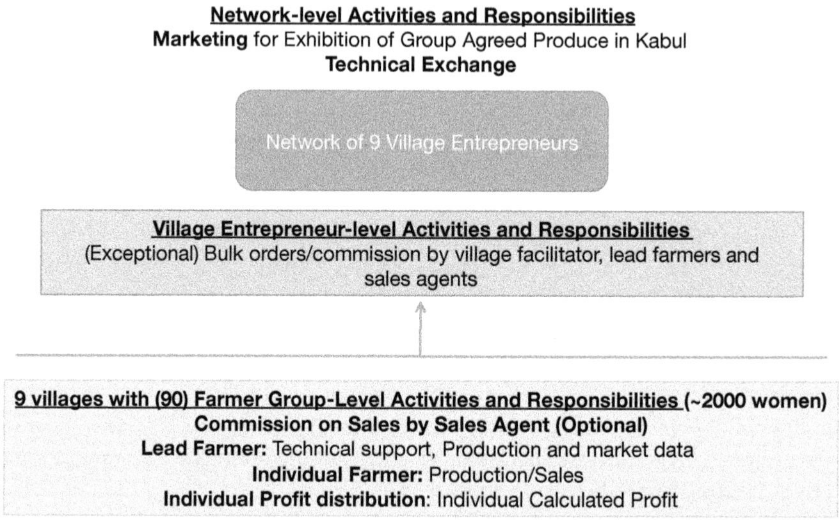

Network-level Activities and Responsibilities
Marketing for Exhibition of Group Agreed Produce in Kabul
Technical Exchange

Network of 9 Village Entrepreneurs

Village Entrepreneur-level Activities and Responsibilities
(Exceptional) Bulk orders/commission by village facilitator, lead farmers and
sales agents

9 villages with (90) Farmer Group-Level Activities and Responsibilities (~2000 women)
Commission on Sales by Sales Agent (Optional)
Lead Farmer: Technical support, Production and market data
Individual Farmer: Production/Sales
Individual Profit distribution: Individual Calculated Profit

Figure A2.3 Women's vegetable business management and operations
Source: Author's own illustration

Towards the end of the research, the village entrepreneurs had begun to receive bulk orders from city offices. They used this new business line to strategically supplement incomes (in the absence of INGO salaries). The entrepreneur was coordinating sourcing with the lead farmers and sales agents. The lead farmers were responsible for sorting and grading produce, and they organised the best produce into a box. In these transactions, approximately 20 per cent commission was added onto the original farmer's vegetable costs, and this was shared out between the entrepreneur (25 per cent), the lead farmers (50 per cent) and sales agents (25 per cent).

(iii) Management/operations

While part of a network of nine villages, management-wise, the enterprise was decentralised to village level with the entrepreneur in charge of the overall village business, and responsible for coordinating activities with the male village council, lead farmers and sales agents. The entrepreneur facilitated troubleshooting in the business, and represented the village business externally at exhibitions and workshops. The lead farmers supported the farmer women in technical assistance (and checked quality of produce), managed the group savings box, recorded all production/marketing data and shared this with the entrepreneur in bimonthly meetings. When exhibitions were held in Kabul, the lead farmers and sales agents assessed the quality before inclusion in village level sales. While marketing was largely individual, the village sales agents supported joint marketing on commission. Profit distribution (after single or group facilitated sales) was arranged at the individual farmer level.

(iv) Technology and assets

Initial group capital expenses were covered by the NGO, and included basic tools and garden equipment. New subsidised (higher-level) technology such as (plastic) greenhouses, drip irrigation, storage facilities and solar driers (individually owned) were later introduced in the research villages. These innovations notably improved yields, aided more flexible market strategies and permitted the development of new marketable dried products. The INGO had successfully encouraged a 'rental' system for these access through owner agreements on commission on end sales. At the time of the research, the two research villages had established two underground vegetable storage facilities, several (plastic) greenhouses, micro-irrigation schemes and four (glass/wooden) solar dryers.

A2.3 Case study 3: women's electronics business

Supported and trained by an international agency, the third case study was a small women's electronics business, situated in the city's women's sanctuary (moving at the end of the research to a compound of another company in the city). Established and registered in 2006, the business initially comprised 13 women workers (from 25 to 30 years of age) from an impoverished community in Kabul City. Yet in the last phases of the study, only four workers remained due to 'limited contracts'. The company was chiefly involved with the manual assemblage of basic electrical appliances. During the research, they were also trained to repair common domestic appliances. Their main customers included international organisations (such as international forces, UN agencies and foreign embassies), and local companies.

(i) Production and supply

Essentially, the group manually produced electrical goods, including solar lamps and panels, circuit boards, and extension cables, on a contract basis. The women worked in a simple and dusty workshop room (8 m²), with a small basic office for the entrepreneur. On receipt of new contracts, the entrepreneur would organise the procurement of basic parts from the market. For example, one typical contract was the production of 10,000 circuit boards for a private company in Kabul City. This took the women workers (eight women at the time) a month to complete. The entrepreneur was responsible for identifying new opportunities, negotiating deals and signing contracts. In addition to electrical products, the women were able to repair common domestic appliances such as refrigerators, washing machines and air conditioner units. Yet contracts for these services were complicated both by poor marketing, and (if domestic) the need for the women workers to enter into people's homes (disallowed by the worker women's husbands).

(ii) Marketing and demand

The business marketed their products and services to customers such as international (military and non-military) agencies, the Afghan government and individual households in Kabul. At the time of the research, however, the marketing was weak, and customer awareness still limited. The business planned to broaden their customer base through local dealers with links to other cities/rural areas. Key potential markets for the business included Kabul-based electronics companies and solar dealers (for assembling products), as well as more regional-based distributors (where solar products were in particular demand),[2] in locations such as Herat, Mazar and Kandahar. Yet these markets were difficult to access since travel was challenging for most of the women (due to family pressures).

In terms of competitors, a few Afghan companies were starting to import and distribute sophisticated solar energy equipment (e.g. solar panels, solar cookers, solar dryers, etc.). One company provided additional installation and repair services selling large panels, and provided training to local villagers on how to install the solar panel systems. Local interest in innovative thermal applications was said to be increasing rapidly, with high local demand, particularly in the Kabul market (e.g. solar cookers, solar dryers). And market players were described to be increasing likewise: the Afghan solar market was already estimated at $2–2.5 million in 2006–2007.[3]

(iii) Management/operations

The entrepreneur was largely responsible for the overall production, marketing, bookkeeping and management. Her family helped with the company administration (husband), as well as managing the accounts (son). Meanwhile, the other worker

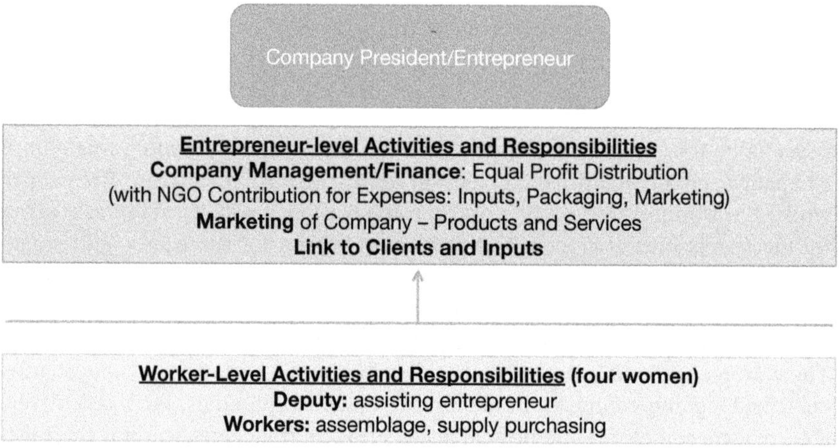

Company President/Entrepreneur

Entrepreneur-level Activities and Responsibilities
Company Management/Finance: Equal Profit Distribution
(with NGO Contribution for Expenses: Inputs, Packaging, Marketing)
Marketing of Company – Products and Services
Link to Clients and Inputs

Worker-Level Activities and Responsibilities (four women)
Deputy: assisting entrepreneur
Workers: assemblage, supply purchasing

Figure A2.4 Women's electronics business management and operations
Source: Author's own illustration

women were mainly only involved in production and on occasions helping with purchasing electrical items. While the entrepreneur worked full-time, the workers were only expected to work according to contracts gained. Towards the end of the research, the NGO was still partly supporting the company through contributing to costs for the workshop, diesel, generator, and worker salaries, as well as providing technical and business support. Overall, even after several years of support, the profits of the company were negligible. In fact, if total expenses were taken into account (i.e. NGO paid salaries), the company had largely been running at a loss of between $3,000 and $6,000 per annum, due to inconsistent contracts and low volumes.

In the final stage of the research, the business established a tentative new business partnership with a medium-sized electronics company that imported large-scale and small-scale solar equipment (home systems, panels, batteries, solar water pumps, etc.). This partnership was envisaged to facilitate access to potential subcontracting and new business opportunities. The company also agreed to pay the rent of the women's workshop ($400 per month) (but within their own office!), and to pay four staff stipends (including the entrepreneur, $150 per month, and three staff, $80–90 per month). While the arrangement provided much opportunity for the women's business (salary contribution, rent, training, potential subcontracting), as a weak small company, there were dangers of simply being absorbed into the larger company with little independent work and autonomy.

(iv) Technology and assets

At the time of the research, the company still only had basic electronics equipment and assets to make circuit boards and solar lanterns, worth in total around US$1,500. These were deemed insufficient for producing items at scale required by the market (e.g. solar lanterns). During the research, a new business plan drafted by an external consultant recommended upgrading machinery and equipment to improve operational facilities in Kabul, and to increase their production capacity and lower costs.

Notes

1 Notably, the village farmer groups were also involved in savings and credit activities. At the end of the research, over $11,000 had been mobilised by these groups.
2 Many businesses and households are still without regular power in Afghanistan. While electricity services have improved in urban areas, approximately 80 per cent of the Afghan population lives in the rural areas with limited access to the national power grid.
3 This was indicated in the independent consultant business plan in 2009.

Appendix 3
Case study business dynamics at end of research

This appendix further elaborates on the evolving business dynamics of each of the research cases (and sub-cases) towards the end of the study.

A3.1 Evolving business dynamics in Case 1

In Case 1, in the last phases of the research, the *women's food processing business* in western Afghanistan appeared to be thriving, with increasing levels of sales (the sales had increased by 75 per cent over the previous 12 months). The NGO had formally registered the network as a business association (with a staff member as the initial head of the business). From initial low trust in the women's business (among both the communities and the buyers), with NGO support and group experience, the groups had gained local confidence in their work and in their products, and boasted growing business networks. Individual groups highlighted with much enthusiasm their various 'business' links, including those for resources and supply (to neighbouring communities, local shops, as well as city-based banks and packaging agents), in addition to links for sales (both near the village, as well in the city with shops, exhibitions and local offices). These networks were greatly attributed to the support of the NGO that brokered the relationship – particularly in the city – and at first guaranteed delivery and quality, and handled initial payments. City-based links were shared between groups, particularly more mature groups. Across groups, there tended to be stronger relations between older, mature centres with strong and charismatic heads (including Cases 1a and 1b). And there was significant frustration of these well established groups with newer groups, and their perceived 'free riding' with sub-quality products, and lack of contribution in city exhibitions. Yet there were mixed emotions tied to the development of these new groups, since mature group heads benefited from being employed as trainers! Meanwhile, at the village level, more mature groups were beginning to register themselves as independent associations, motivated by the prospect of gaining international funds. Mature groups had also begun to specialise in certain foodstuffs, such as dried products or tomato paste, with raw materials that were more readily available. And new village subgroups were being added by the groups themselves. The case study groups reported that business was good, and that they tended to receive immediate payment, or sometimes even credit before goods were sold (i.e. confidence in their business was high)! As indicated, the NGO was still involved in the group centre activities from (new) group establishment, technical assistance, spot-checking on quality, checking of books to monthly cross-group troubleshooting. They also assisted with the procurement of (some) packaging from Pakistan.

Looking closer at the village-level dynamics, in Case 1a, the centre had newly registered as an association, and had begun to receive their own funds. With this, they had started to use the same business methodology to establish further subgroups under their own auspices. While the village elders had blocked the expansion of the village food processing centre within the village (due to 'security'), the quiet but ambitious entrepreneur managed to mobilise four other neighbouring villages and set up off-site centres. According to both the entrepreneur and the NGO, the establishment of these new centres was described to be fairly challenging, but the strong reputations of both the entrepreneur and the NGO were cited to be ultimately persuasive! A further 120 trainees were employed in these new sub-centres (with respective subheads). The entrepreneur was responsible for the overall production of the five centres, group marketing, bookkeeping and coordination, and a senior (female) technical assistant supported her. Further minor assistants included 10 'strong' group members from her village that worked as technical assistants and 'resource' people. Yet during the research, the entrepreneur also brought in her husband and son to assist the business (formally as a 'finance manager' and 'secretary', respectively). Since the village power holders restricted the mobility of the other workers, these family men were in fact deliberately engaged to help with growing external tasks such as logistics and marketing. Despite the apparent business success in Case 1a, there were some disturbing indicators. Reflecting a broader sense of persisting uncertainty in the original group village, some women described feeling anxious about the general nature of the growing business, and the social interaction that this required:

> If we increase our business further, we may face more problems from our families and other community members [as we will need to encounter even more men]
>
> (Women workers, Case 1a)

Meanwhile, in Case 1b, the centre was equally flourishing (and expanded considerably even within the course of the research). The group was heavily involved with processing several different food products, with their speciality lying in dried products. The tough and determined entrepreneur (a widow) had used some of her own land (recently claimed) for the business to support the supply of vegetables. The entrepreneur had also registered the centre as an independent association, motivated by possible external funds. She had further started her own shop in a city women's mall (both for her own group; and other group products, on commission). The entrepreneur was responsible for the overall production, marketing, bookkeeping and group coordination. Her assistants included five 'strong' women within the group, with increasing levels of responsibility. Her son also helped, as required, in finance, logistics and bookkeeping. In contrast to

Case 1a, most of the local village leaders appeared to strongly support this enterprise, and its potential growth.

A3.2 Evolving business dynamics in Case 2

In Case 2, while the NGO had been largely successful in mobilising over 2,000 women farmers in a thriving *women's vegetable business* in central Afghanistan, one female staff underscored the persisting sense of local fragility, and feeling like a *'bubble on the water'*, with local law and order resting in the hands of unpredictable local structures and commanders. At the later stages of the research, the INGO handed over their work to a local NGO. But with their modest funds (and limited interest), the local NGO only provided ad hoc support to exhibitions. Yet despite the end of the original project (and the termination of salaries for entrepreneurs and lead farmers), the village set-ups appeared to be continuing in various forms, with loose links between the villages, particularly among more mature villages (established in the first phase of the project). While entrepreneurs still exchanged ideas and organised exhibitions, they tended to be competitive as opposed to collaborative (particularly Case 2b), and were largely driven by opportunities for securing donor funding. Villages had begun to form their own independent associations or cooperatives, and to receive funds for their own projects. At the village level, the roles of participating women (farmers and lead farmers) continued to evolve, but these were largely controlled by the entrepreneur. Meanwhile, selected saleswomen maintained their direct links with local shopkeepers, city-based farm shops, city markets, and restaurants (for exhibitions), taking commission on sales and procurement.

Examining the village-level dynamics further, the elaborate business set-ups in Case 2 appeared to be highly vulnerable to the entrepreneurs, nature of the power holders and context. In Case 2a, the entrepreneur assumed a flexible and supportive role, and actively encouraged lead farmers and producers in their work and in taking on new tasks. She was also happy to delegate work to capable women, and to empower women in the business. With an open village culture and supportive power holders, the village groups were known to be very enterprising with market links both to Charikar (the regional capital) and Kabul City. They were involved with regular exhibitions in the city, and selling bulk produce in a large city vegetable market. Two farmer women were working as sales agents, purchasing supplies and selling farmer produce on commission. The charismatic entrepreneur described herself as 'more than a boss'. She prided herself on providing social support to the women's farmer groups and troubleshooting. Towards the end of the research, she had a new assistant and cashier to help her record all of the data, continuing the INGO-established routines: 'they are good for the health of our business and we can show potential donors'. The lead farmers also continued to advise their groups, record production and marketing information, and submit biweekly reports to the entrepreneur. With INGO assistance, some lead farmers had purchased their own facilities (greenhouses, solar driers and a storage unit), and were successfully renting these out to other farmers, increasing village productivity and extending the marketing season. The entrepreneur felt very happy with the thriving enterprise structure. And as a newly registered association, they were also now legally recognised by ministries and potential donors. In the last phase of the research, she had submitted a proposal for a new village income generation project to a UN agency for broader community development. With this strong and public-spirited entrepreneur at the enterprise helm, the vilage business set-up in Case 2a had evolved to empower lead women, and to support the generation of equitable new contracts at a village level. The entrepreneur seemed highly motivated to expand the business, to increase opportunities for women's employment in the agricultural sector and to work towards more balanced community development:

> While the media is bringing in new ideas, our own work has changed people's attitudes and practices . . . Even the mullah's ideas have changed through seeing the fruits of our efforts . . . We work like men now . . . In the new system, we have gone from being simple to being active . . .
>
> (Lead farmer, Case 2a)

Meanwhile, in Case 2b, while equally busy with production, the farmer groups were not involved with much external marketing, and were described to either use the produce for their own consumption or sell it in the village. In this case, the entrepreneur was more controlling, distrustful and power-oriented. Cooperation on production and marketing between women farmers was hence limited due to a mixture of their restricted mobility, poor local trust and conservative attitudes. Towards the end of the project, and after much pressure from the INGO, two women were finally appointed as village sales agents. Yet they remained sales agents in name only, and physically inactive. With the project over, the enterprise structure persisted, but it was unclear whether the entrepreneur was still collecting the village production and marketing data. The forceful entrepreneur clearly enjoyed her new position of power, and it appeared that she was using intimidation to coerce people (men and women) into doing things for her. She described still holding lead farmers' meetings as and when required (although it was doubtful that there was 'democratic' decision-making). At the end of the research, as a newly registered cooperative, she had managed to secure a government contract for agricultural technical training in the village with (free) transport vouchers (perhaps indeed the sole motivation for registration). Individually owned village assets (facilitated by the INGO to boost productivity) included two solar driers and a storage facility that were both owned and managed by the entrepreneur, with just one additional solar drier owned by a lead farmer. In contrast to Case 2a, the entrepreneur had a less collective social vision. Whether said in jest, the entrepreneur aspired 'to have a bodyguard and to be powerful'! She relished being at the top of the hierarchy but with little interest to devolve any power. A conservative *shura* (with personal family connections) backed her up. Rumours surrounded her, and she was reported to have aligned herself with local militias, and had further extended her power by heading up women's subcommittees in the cluster, notably against the wishes of the village men and women.

A3.3 Evolving business dynamics in Case 3

In Case 3 over the course of the research, it was evident that the *women's electronics business* in Kabul was struggling to stand on its own feet, manage their own contracts and retain staff. Progress was later further hindered by the entrepreneur being employed as a trainer for new women by the NGO, despite the original business flagging (and fundamental sector-specific challenges). At the end of the research, from a total of 13 initial employees, the company had just four remaining staff due to a mixture of family pressures and constraints within and outside of the business. According to the NGO and the business 'deputy', there was a marked contrast between the head of the business and the rest of the workers, despite their initial similar economic backgrounds (although different ethnicities). With the departure of the original deputy, the new business deputy was assisting in contract management but had surprisingly limited knowledge of the enterprise administrational arrangements and appeared to be 'deputy' in name only. Due to the 'closed' nature of the sector (electronics was perceived to be a man's business) and continued control by the NGO, it had been evidently difficult for the women's business to fully establish itself and make business connections; and with little experience and skills, manage enterprise administration. The business head was described to be a natural leader that had grown in capacity and confidence with increasing experience. Her family was supportive of her work and did not require her to request authorisation for her movement and choice of activities. She remained the main administrator of the business and was in charge of procurement, contract management, marketing, finances and quality control with the basic help of her son and husband. Due to her limited literacy, however, the NGO was still involved with contract negotiation and finance control (approving expenses and balancing the books). The other women workers only really provided support to production (and basic administration). Contrasting with previous cases, in this case, rules were less well articulated. The business had little basic structure and cohesion, and notably lacked the strength of the initial SHG framework.

Towards the end of the research, with informal links going back seven years (including training), the company had finally formulated a formal partnership agreement with an established (all-male) electronics company. While the new possible partner suggested that they were just helping a women's business out, it seems they were motivated by an opportunity to receive donor funds and use the workers for small jobs (assembling of solar lamps). Yet to demonstrate their seriousness, they were already paying the rent of the women for an office within their compound, and were paying four staff stipends (taking over from the NGO salary payments). Further, the partner had pledged to assist with sourcing contracts, and had offered one small job in the eastern city of Jalalabad. The head duly organised for the women workers to stay with relatives, but in the end it was deemed too 'insecure' by their families. Generally, despite this new emerging business arrangement, the NGO was still holding the reins of the organisation through supporting record-keeping and contract management, and through facilitating the new training of prospective employees (employing the entrepreneur as a trainer and distracting her from her own business!). As the research phase came to a close, new hope was presented with this forging of links to a new firm, but there was a sense of fragility in their work, particularly as uncertain political times loomed. Others felt that the prevailing culture was not yet ready to accept women in new trades and industries:

> [While] engaging women in business can be 'useful' so that women can become more independent and can support their households, it is not in our culture to do this type of work! For example, if these women want to start repairing domestic electrical appliances, it will not be acceptable for them to go into people's homes. It would be better and easier for them to work in tailoring or handicrafts.
>
> (Community *wakil*)

A young woman from Kabul working in the media sector summed up the challenge perfectly in the current sociopolitical environment:

> I don't think we have the guts to see a woman working in new fields as well as in traditional jobs.
>
> (Young working woman in Kabul)[1]

Note

1 *Afghan Scene Magazine*, March 2012.

Appendix 4

Evolving routines in cases and nature of enterprise

Evolving internal routines in the cases provide an interesting window on the nature of the evolving business, and local business context. In Case 1, three different sets of enterprise routines were observed (entrepreneur, assistants and workers), but with significant overlap in food processing production tasks. With roots in earlier SHG rules, the decentralised and open nature of decision-making and profit distribution appeared to increase accountability and transparency, enhancing the motivation of members and levels of trust. This seems to have bolstered cooperation and social cohesion as a unit, as members felt that they could participate in the basic enterprise rules, their enforcement and development (particularly productive tasks and profit distribution). In Case 1a, general roles remained relatively fixed with control by power holders (i.e. community leaders), yet the entrepreneur endeavoured to be innovative (going beyond the community). In Case 1b, power holders kept light oversight of more mobile tasks (through the women's *shura,* for example observing which women were engaged in marketing and how often), but more control lay with the enterprise women. In the latter case, free riding surfaced as the business grew, and this has led to the need for a register for attendance.

Meanwhile, in Case 2, the vegetable production business had an elaborate institutional set-up at the village level with three to four tiers of women and respective routines depending on the entrepreneur. Production remained individual on the women's own selected plot of land and within the women's family domain. While this facilitated women's engagement in work, it constrained a more collaborative approach. Weekly farmers' group meetings were held in nearby lead farmer houses. The relatively small nature of these groups (15–20 women) has tended to increase women's motivation, cooperation, levels of trust and decentralised exchange. Higher-level routines included exchange between the lead farmers and the entrepreneur, sharing total volumes, technical issues and other group problems. And the entrepreneur was expected to provide overall management and troubleshoot problems. In Case 2a, meetings were reported to be respectful and productive. Meanwhile, in Case 2b, lead farmers complained of control by the entrepreneur, and of having little voice. But with the entrepreneur's proximity to, and hold over, power holders (her father was previously the village head, and her family were considered powerful), there was little opportunity for

Table A4.1 Layered evolving routines (in production): scope, flexibility and change

Case number	Entrepreneur	Assistants/senior workers	Workers	Who shapes rules	Who monitors/ enforces	Who can propose change/flexibility
1a	The entrepreneur agrees to work in the centre on equal shifts as rest of the women on designated days The entrepreneur provides overall orders, and leads on troubleshooting	The women agree to work in the centre on equal shifts as rest of the women on designated days The senior women provide oversight of production (quality control, labour input)	The women agree to work in the centre on equal shifts as rest of the women on designated days	Entrepreneur/ senior workers	Entrepreneur with senior workers Village authorities	Entrepreneur with senior workers Limited flexibility
1b	The entrepreneur agrees to work in the centre on equal shifts as rest of the women on designated days The entrepreneur provides overall orders, and leads on troubleshooting	The women agree to work in the centre on equal shifts as rest of the women on designated days The senior women provide oversight of production (quality control, labour input)	The women agree to work in the centre on equal shifts as rest of the women on designated days	Entrepreneur/ senior workers	Entrepreneur with senior workers Light oversight by village authorities	Entrepreneur with senior workers Medium flexibility
2a	The entrepreneur provides overall leadership through active management, and troubleshooting and coordinating with lead farmers	The lead farmers agree to work on their plots every day, and provide technical support to their farmer group	The worker farmers agree to work on their plots every day and communicate production	Entrepreneur/ senior workers	Entrepreneur/ senior workers Light oversight by village authorities	Entrepreneur/ senior workers Medium flexibility
2b	The entrepreneur provides basic leadership in production through reports from lead farmers	The lead farmers work on their plots every day, and provide technical support to their farmer group	The worker farmers agree to work on their plots every day and communicate production	Entrepreneur	Entrepreneur Village authorities	Entrepreneur Limited flexibility
3	The entrepreneur provides oversight to assemblage and quality control		The workers agree to work in assembling products as required in agreed location	Entrepreneur	Entrepreneur NGO, Husbands	Entrepreneur Limited flexibility

change. It appeared that with more mobility, and new-found power, the entrepreneur was abusing this to intimidate the other women into remaining in secondary fixed roles.

Finally, in Case 3, the nature of internal routines has led to top-heavy firm responsibilities with the head taking on most of the work beyond of basic assemblage, with little delegation of administrative duties to other members. The business was thus disproportionately reliant on, and controlled by one member. Originally, the company was located in a women's sanctuary/commercial area, partly due to the worker women's *purdah*. And this placed them far outside of the sphere of electronics bazaar and potential customers, and constrained business growth. At the end of the research, the women's enterprise relocated to the compound of another firm, but the families of the workers then complained of their proximity to men, leaving the business vulnerable to collapse.

Appendix 5

Indicators of socio-economic change for enterprise women

Table A5.1 Typical indicators for community women before and after the businesses were initiated

Aspect	Typical behaviour before	Typical behaviour after (three years on)
Mobility	90% women remain in the house	Senior women do not need to ask permission of their husbands to move around the village
	Women are not permitted to go to the bazaar, city or doctor alone, and only in situations of urgent need leave the village with their husbands or fathers	30% women visit other non-family homes (e.g. for business and women's meeting)
	Common threats to women: 'if you go out, you go out forever'	Unmarried women can go out with a *maharam*
	100% women covered their face with a hijab outside of the home	20–50% participating women can take a trip out of the province with their husbands' permission
		50–70% women cover their faces in front of a male stranger
Women's socio-political role	20% girl children can go to high school	50% girl children can go to high school
	Low capacity of women's *shura* (only 2% had some degree of responsibility in the community)	Women can jointly make decisions and convene for problem-solving
	Village women tend to keep quiet	There is more respect for women to be involved in community affairs
	Nobody paid any attention to women's ideas/opinions and there was limited participation in the women's *shura*	Women's *shura* can influence male *shura*
		30% women support community events (e.g. weddings, festivals)
Relations with community/ business	Every woman just knows about 20 family members in a village	20% women know people from outside the family in the village
	No business relations	5–10% women have business relationships
Access to banking	None	Groups have their own bank account
		Senior women have taken micro-loans
		Group women have borrowed from SHG

Access to professional training	Most women are not allowed to attend trainings (exceptions include widows and old women)	Senior women regularly attend trainings and NGO workshops inside and outside of the village Non-group women are keen now to participate in training and families are permitting their attendance with *maharams*
Property rights	Women have no rights	Lead or active women have sought to claim their inheritance from their husband or father
	Women belong to men and could be sold or on becoming a widow, be forced to marry the brother-in-law	The villages are more open to Islamic law, and there is more discussion related to property and the rights of widows

Glossary of local terms

Alim	A man of learning, wise. This may also refer to a person who is a religious inspiration, normally a mullah. It stems from the Arabic for knowledge (CPAU, 2007).
Arbab	A traditional village head.
Burka	A long, loose garment covering the whole body that is worn in public by many Muslim women (from Arabic *burku*).
Chadari	A headscarf worn by Muslim women.
Hadith	Recorded sayings of the Prophet Muhammad. Today, they are used as part of Muslims' understanding of Islam, together with the Koran and the *fiqh* (theory of Islamic Law) (CPAU, 2007).
Hafiz	Old term that literally means 'somebody who cannot see'. This is used to describe people who learn and recite the Koran by heart.
Hijab	A head covering worn in public by some Muslim women. It also describes the religious code that governs the wearing of such clothing.
Jerib	A measurement of land. One *jerib* is approximately ⅕ ha or ½ an acre.
Kaari, karria	A religious person (man or woman) who recites the Koran. *Kaari* can be used interchangeably with the term *hafiz*. This word is said to be a product of the Jihad era (1980s).
Khan	An influential figure, more often a landowner in a village or town, above an *arbab* (CPAU, 2007).
Maharam	A male relative (or a woman's husband) that can accompany a woman outside of the household.
Malik	An influential figure that represents a community and is usually in contact with the government. The term is used interchangeably with *arbab* (CPAU, 2007).
Mullah	A local religious representative (male), often with authority over a local mosque.
Pashtun	The most populous ethnic group in Afghanistan, representing about 50 per cent of all Afghans (CPAU, 2007). Known to be the most conservative with regard to women.

Pashtunwali	The tribal code used to regulate *Pashtun* society.
Purdah	The practice among women in certain Muslim and Hindu societies of living in a separate room or behind a curtain, or of dressing in all-enveloping clothes, in order to stay out of the sight of non-family men or strangers.
Qawn	An Afghan tribe, clan.
Sharia	Islamic law.
Shura	A traditional village council/gathering in Afghanistan, assembled as required, no firm membership.
Tajik	The second most populous ethnic group in Afghanistan, predominantly living in the north of the country, possibly representing 25–30 per cent of the population (CPAU, 2007).
Ulema	This refers to Islamic religious leadership. It can be used to refer to a collective (but not organised) religious group in Afghanistan (i.e. the *ulema*). This term can also be used to describe a specific group such as the *Ulema* Council (CPAU, 2007).
Wakil	This refers to a community coordinator (elected locally but approved by the central government authorities). This term is similar to an *arbab* (or head of the *shura)*, but is used in city communities.

References

CPAU (2007) The Role and Functions of Religious Civil Society in Afghanistan, Kabul, Afghanistan: CPAU.

Index

Acemoglu, D. 176, 203
actors 28–9, 35–6, 38–40, 154–60, 165–6, 211–13, 219–26; interaction 132–3, 229; non-chain 130, 165, 241; strategies 87–8, 110–13, 188–95, 224–5; *see also* entrepreneurs; NGOs; power holders
Afghanistan 52–9, 75–6, 215; religious governance 59–63; women 63–8
agency 34–5, 37–9, 59–61, 132–3, 171–6, 202–4; *see also* actors; structure/agency
Alford, R.R. 28
Amanullah (King) 66–7
Appiah, K.A. 85, 87–8
assets 163, 165
attitudes *see* preferences
authority 60–5, 132–3, 171–2, 218–19; *see also* power
Axelrod, R. 84

Baert, P. 5
Baharoglu, D. 42
banking 163
Baron, R.A. 37, 222
Battilana, J. 37–8, 110, 213
Baumol, W. 4, 7, 37, 42, 69, 173
Becker, G.S. 31
Becker, M.C. 125, 127, 154, 161–2, 174
Beckert, J. 38–40, 109, 219, 230
beliefs 27, 31
Berger, P. 5, 83
Berner, E. 37
Bhaskar, R.A. 4, 35
Bhatia, M. 71
Binks, M. 7, 36
biology *see* evolutionary processes
Bird, B.J. 199

Boettke, P. 33, 42, 171
Bourdieu, P. 26, 33–4, 85
Bowles, S. 217–8
Boyer, R. 2, 7, 25, 28, 33, 39, 41, 127–8
Brodsky, A.E. 64
Brousseau, E. 29
Burt, R.S. 173

Campbell, J.L. 28
Centlivres, P. 63, 66
Centlivres-Demont, M. 63, 66
Chang, H.-J. 25–6, 28–30, 41, 209, 219, 228–9, 239
Charikar 13
Christoplos, I. 69
class 33, 73, 164–5
Coe, N.M. 130
cognition 26–7, 34, 237
Cohendet, P. 126, 166
Coleman, J.S. 173
collective action 61, 131–2, 166, 174–6, 198–200, 215–8; rules 139–41, 146–7, 150–1, 154
Collinson, S. 69
Commons, J. 24–5, 30, 132
Community Development Councils (CDCs) 54, 62–3, 184
CPAU 61–2
Crandall, C. 114
critical realism 4–5, 35
culture *see* purdah; sociocultural institutions

Darwin, C. 29, 125–6
Davern, M. 8, 32, 172
Day, D. 176

De Jong, E. 110
development 29, 40–3, 54, 71, 86–7, 240–2
development studies 4, 239, 242
Dewey, J. 83
diffusion 174–6, 201–2, 228
DiMaggio, P.J. 26, 38, 174, 230
dominant entrepreneurs 7, 197–204, 223, 226–8, 234–6, 239–40, 242
Dosi, G. 37
Doubleday, V. 65
Douglas, M. 26, 28, 131, 231, 237
Duffield, M. 41
Dunlop, J. 24–5
Durkheim, E. 34–5, 83

economic development *see* development
economic institutions 124–9, 131–4, 161–6, 231–2, 236–8; coordination 127–30; electronics business 147–51; food processing 134–41; nested rules 132, 153–9, 210–3; vegetable production 141–7
economic sociology 24, 31–3
economics *see* institutional economics
Eisenstadt, S.N. 38
electronics business 15–17, 103–7, 147–51, 179–80, 183–4, 186, 188
elites 71–2, 164–6, 187–8; *see also* power holders
Elster, J. 83–5, 113, 131
embeddedness 31–3, 39, 43, 173; nested rules 132, 153–9, 210–13; *see also* structure/agency
Emirbayer, M. 34, 133, 173
enterprise institutions: chain rules 136–9, 144–6, 149–50, 154; collective action 139–41, 146–7, 150–1, 154; enterprise routines 134–6, 141–4, 147–9, 154
Entezar, E. 60, 64
entrepreneurs 7–8, 36–8, 42, 153–66, 222–4, 232–3; dominant 7, 197–204, 223, 226–8, 234–6, 239–40, 242; electronics business 16–17, 183–4; food processing 12, 181–2; institutional 38, 110, 171–4, 195–204, 222, 227; strategies 190–5; vegetable production 14–15, 143–4, 146–7
ethnicity 56

Evans, P. 25–6
evolutionary processes 29–31, 125–7

Feldman, M.S. 166
Field, J. 32
Fitzherbert, A. 58
Fligstein, N. 2, 39–40, 113, 133, 153, 159, 166, 173, 219, 227
food processing association 10–12, 91–7, 134–41, 177–8, 181–2, 185, 187
Ford, J.D. 172, 176
Foucault, M. 5–6
free rider problem 216
Friedland, R. 28
Fukuyama, F. 26, 43, 132, 218
Furubotn, E.G. 44

Galbraith, J. 30
Gambetta, D. 43
gatekeeper entrepreneurs 7, 197–200, 202–4, 223, 226, 228, 234–6, 240, 242
Gaventa, J. 6
Geertz, C. 86
gender *see* women
Gereffi, G. 129–30
Giddens, A. 31, 35
Gintis, H. 217–8
Giustozzi, A. 79
Gomez, G. 38, 40, 42, 109–10, 153, 155, 210, 219–20, 222, 226, 229–30, 237, 239
Goodhand, J. 69, 71
Goodwin, J. 133, 173
Gough, I. 73–4
governance *see* politics
Grabowski, R. 33
Grace, J. 65
Graf, H. 174, 200–1
Granovetter, M. 32, 39, 172, 176, 203, 228
Greif, A. 26
Greve, H.R. 173
group cooperation *see* collective action

habit 30–1, 40, 83, 126, 226
habitus 26, 34
Hage, R. 37
Hardin, R. 131
Harriss-White, B. 41, 72
Hayami, Y. 86

Hayek, F. 34–5
Hays, S. 133
Hechter, M. 111, 118
Heckathorn, D.D. 210
Helmsing, B. 130, 200
Herat 10–1
hierarchies 125–8, 231–3; *see also* power
Hirschman, A.O. 86
Hodgson, G. 2, 4–5, 8, 17, 25, 29–31,
   34–5, 39–40, 83, 117, 126–7, 161, 165,
   219, 226, 228, 236, 239
Hofstede, G. 60
Hollingsworth, J.R. 2, 7, 25–6, 28–9, 33,
   36, 39, 41, 127–9, 154
Holm, P. 210
honour 63–8, 85, 104
Horne, C. 84, 117–18, 231
Huber, G.P. 174
Humphrey, J. 43

incentives 198
inclusive development 239–42
informal institutions 41–3, 59, 69–72; *see
   also* social norms
INGO 12, 14, 99, 178–9
innovation 37–40, 174–6, 226–7
institutional arrangements 25–6, 28–9, 96,
   101–2, 106, 127–30, 214–17; chain
   rules 136–9, 144–6, 149–50, 154
institutional change 3–4, 27–33, 44,
   109–17, 210–19; agents 35–40, 219–29;
   outcomes 28–9, 230–8
institutional construction *see* actors;
   structure/agency
institutional economics: (IPE) 25, 27; new
   2, 24–5, 27, 44; old 24–5, 28–30, 33
institutional entrepreneurs 38, 110, 171–4,
   195–204, 222, 227
institutions 1–2, 6–7, 23–4, 40–3; *see also*
   economic institutions; enterprise
   institutions; sociocultural institutions
intentionality 174, 199
interests *see* actors; power
Islam *see purdah*; religion; religious
   messages

Johnson, B. 213
Johnson, C. 56
Jutting, J. 42

Kabul 13, 15–16
Kandori, M. 84, 110
Kaplinsky, R. 165, 241
khans 61–2
Kim, J.Y. 85
Klyver, K. 8, 174, 199, 228
Knight, F. 36
Knight, J. 28, 85, 123
Knorringa, P. 32, 130
knowledge 4–5, 174–5
Knudsen, T. 126, 165
Koene, B.A.S. 3
Koford, K.J. 117
Koran *see* religious messages
Kristiansen, S. 7, 32

Landier, A. 37
language 5–6, 151–3
Lanzara, G.F. 213
Lautze, S. 57
Lawson, T. 5, 28, 34
Lazear, E. 37
Lazonick, W. 37
Leeson, P. 42, 171
Legro, J. 29
Leitmann, J. 42
Leslie, J. 56
Levi-Strauss, C. 35
Levinthal, D.A. 127
Lin, N. 32
Lister, S. 71–2, 74–5
literacy 53–4, 59
Llerena, P. 126, 166
local power structures *see* power holders
Long, N. 34
Luckmann, T. 5, 83
Lyon, F. 43, 216

Maguire, S. 173, 227
Maley, W. 52
March, J.G. 36
markets 40–1, 68–75, 127–30, 213–4
Marx, K. 25, 33–5, 87
Maseland, R. 24, 28
methodological collectivism 35
methodological individualism 34–5
Meyer, J.W. 83
migrations 57–9
Miller, J.B. 117

Mills, M.A. 60, 89
Mische, A. 34
Mitchell, W.C. 24–5
Monsutti, A. 58
Morris, M. 165, 241
Morrisson, C. 42
mullahs 61–2, 185–6

Nam, S.H. 85
National Solidarity Programme (NSP)
    54
Naude, W. 42
Nelson, R.R. 29–30, 125
nested rules 132, 153–9, 210–13
networks *see* social networks
new institutional economics 2, 24–5, 27,
    44
NGOs 153–60, 165–6, 211, 215–16,
    218–28, 232–3, 238–40; electronics
    business 15–16, 103–7, 147–51,
    179–80; and entrepreneurs 195–7,
    199–203; food processing 11–12, 91–7,
    134–41, 177–8; strategies 107–11,
    189–90, 192, 194–5; vegetable
    production 13–14, 97–103, 141–7,
    178–9
non-chain actors 130, 165, 241
Nooteboom, B. 43
Nordstrom, C. 32, 41
norms *see* rules; social norms;
    sociocultural institutions
North, D. 2, 27, 36, 44, 234, 237, 239

old institutional economics 24–5, 28–30,
    33
Olson, J.P. 36
Olson, M. 131
Opp, K. 111, 118
organisational innovation *see*
    innovation
Ostrom, E. 2, 7, 28, 131–2, 153–4, 159,
    165, 210–11, 215, 218–20, 234, 236,
    239

Packard, V. 30
Pain, A. 54, 56–7, 65, 69, 71–5
Pakistan 71–2
Parr, H. 210
Parsons, T. 34–5

Parto, S. 210, 230
Parwan 13
Pashtuns 56, 63, 89, 104
Paterson, A. 72, 74
path dependence 29–30, 35–7, 233–6
Pentland, B. 166
Philo, C. 210
Platteau, J.P. 25–6, 84–7
Polanyi, K. 25, 31
politics 27, 29, 41–2, 52–3, 56–7, 87, 130;
    religious governance 59–63;
    sociopolitical institutions 162–6, 236–7
Porter, G. 43, 216
Porter, M. 129
Portes, A. 26, 33, 44
Powell, W. 26, 174, 230
power 5–6, 27–8, 39, 108, 129–30;
    asymmetries 41–2, 71–2, 155, 201;
    authority 59–65, 132–3, 171–2, 218–19;
    hierarchies 125–8, 231–3
power holders 33, 61–2, 113–14, 155–7,
    184–8, 220–31, 233–9; and
    entrepreneurs 195–203; strategies 191,
    193–5
preferences 114–17, 236–7
proverbs 151–2
purdah 6–7, 88–91, 109–18, 162, 210–12,
    230–2; electronics business 103–7; food
    processing 91–7; vegetable production
    97–103

Raynaud, E. 29
reciprocity 43, 57, 131–2
reconstitutive downward causation 30–1,
    117
Redmond, W.H. 39, 175, 203
religion 59–64, 85–90, 180, 215–16,
    224–5, 241; *see also purdah*
religious messages 92–7, 100, 107–11,
    118, 142–3, 148, 179–80, 192–4
resistance 66, 68
risk 73–4
Rogers, E. 175–6
Roland, G. 26
routines 125–7, 159–61, 166, 174–5, 222;
    enterprise 134–6, 141–4, 147–9, 154
Roy, O. 56, 61
Rubin, B. 61, 63, 65
rule-making 237–8

rules 2, 7, 29–30, 39–40, 42, 198–9,
218–19; nested 132, 153–9, 210–13;
see also enterprise institutions
Rutherford, M. 44

Schmitz, H. 43
Schott, T. 8, 174, 199, 228
Schumpeter, J.A. 7, 25, 36–7, 127
Scott, A. 83
Seabright, P. 82–3
self-help groups (SHGs) 11, 75, 217
Sen, A. 240
shura 62, 92–3, 95–6, 98–105, 135–6,
142–3, 163, 182–6
Smith, A. 23, 44, 124, 198
social capital 32, 34, 57
social change 66–8
social constructivism 5
Social Institutions and Gender Index
(SIGI) 240
social networks 32, 39–40, 56–7, 114,
172–4, 176, 198–204, 226–9
social norms 82–8, 117–18, 161–3, 230–1
social relations 33, 41–2
social skill 132–3, 166
social structure *see* structure/agency
sociocultural institutions 25–7, 41–2,
59–63, 72–3, 85–7, 124, 130, 154–5,
213–14; *see also purdah*
sociopolitical institutions 162–6, 236–7
Soraya (Queen) 66–7
Stigter, E. 58
Streeck, W. 26, 28, 222
structure/agency 3–6, 8, 31, 34–5, 133–4,
173, 197, 199–204, 227–8, 242
Sunstein, C.R. 88

Taliban 67–8
Ter Haar, G. 86, 110, 241
trade-offs 238
trailblazer entrepreneurs 7, 197–8, 200–4,
223, 226, 228, 234–6, 239–40, 242
tribes 56–7; *see also purdah*
trust 43, 74, 124–5, 154, 195, 197,
218–19, 234

Udehn, L. 215
Uzzi, B. 173

Vale, P. 7, 36
value chains 129–30, 165, 241; rules
136–9, 144–6, 149–50, 154
values 63–8, 83, 85, 104, 114–17,
215–16
van Staveren, I. 32
Veblen, T. 24–5, 30
vegetable production business 12–15,
97–103, 141–7, 178–9, 185–8
Vellema, S. 130, 200

Weber, M. 25, 33, 36, 83, 86, 118, 215
Wikan, U. 85
Wincott, D. 133
Winter, S.G. 29–30, 125, 127
women 63–8, 72–5, 151–2, 162–3,
217–18, 236–7, 239–42; *see also
purdah*
Wood, G. 42, 73
World Bank 42
Wright, R. 65

Zelizer, V. 176
Zucker, L. 43, 88

Taylor & Francis eBooks

Helping you to choose the right eBooks for your Library

Add Routledge titles to your library's digital collection today. Taylor and Francis ebooks contains over 50,000 titles in the Humanities, Social Sciences, Behavioural Sciences, Built Environment and Law.

Choose from a range of subject packages or create your own!

Benefits for you

- » Free MARC records
- » COUNTER-compliant usage statistics
- » Flexible purchase and pricing options
- » All titles DRM-free.

REQUEST YOUR FREE INSTITUTIONAL TRIAL TODAY

Free Trials Available
We offer free trials to qualifying academic, corporate and government customers.

Benefits for your user

- » Off-site, anytime access via Athens or referring URL
- » Print or copy pages or chapters
- » Full content search
- » Bookmark, highlight and annotate text
- » Access to thousands of pages of quality research at the click of a button.

eCollections – Choose from over 30 subject eCollections, including:

Archaeology	Language Learning
Architecture	Law
Asian Studies	Literature
Business & Management	Media & Communication
Classical Studies	Middle East Studies
Construction	Music
Creative & Media Arts	Philosophy
Criminology & Criminal Justice	Planning
Economics	Politics
Education	Psychology & Mental Health
Energy	Religion
Engineering	Security
English Language & Linguistics	Social Work
Environment & Sustainability	Sociology
Geography	Sport
Health Studies	Theatre & Performance
History	Tourism, Hospitality & Events

For more information, pricing enquiries or to order a free trial, please contact your local sales team: www.tandfebooks.com/page/sales

Routledge
Taylor & Francis Group

The home of
Routledge books

www.tandfebooks.com

For Product Safety Concerns and Information please contact our EU
representative GPSR@taylorandfrancis.com
Taylor & Francis Verlag GmbH, Kaufingerstraße 24, 80331 München, Germany